I0024668

Missouri
1850 Agricultural Census

Volume 5

Transcribed and Compiled by
Linda L. Green

WILLOW BEND BOOKS
2011

WILLOW BEND BOOKS

AN IMPRINT OF HERITAGE BOOKS, INC.

Books, CDs, and more—Worldwide

For our listing of thousands of titles see our website
at
www.HeritageBooks.com

Published 2011 by
HERITAGE BOOKS, INC.
Publishing Division
100 Railroad Ave. #104
Westminster, Maryland 21157

Copyright © 2011 Linda L. Green

All rights reserved. No part of this book may be reproduced or transmitted in any form or by any means, electronic or mechanical, including photocopying, recording or by any information storage and retrieval system without written permission from the author, except for the inclusion of brief quotations in a review.

International Standard Book Numbers
Paperbound: 978-0-7884-5361-8
Clothbound: 978-0-7884-8905-1

Introduction

This census names only the head of the household. Often times when an individual was missed on the regular U. S. Census, they would appear on this agricultural census. So you might try checking this census for your missing relatives. Unfortunately, many of the Agricultural Census records have not survived. But, they do yield unique information about how people lived. There are 48 columns of information. I chose to transcribe only six of the columns. The six are: Name of the Owner, Improved Acreage, Unimproved Acreage, Cash Value of the Farm, Value of Farm Implements and Machinery, and Value of Livestock. Below is a list of other types of information available on this census.

Linda L. Green
217 Sara Sista Circle
Harvest, AL 35749

Data Columns

Column/Title

1. Name
2. Acres of Land Improved
3. Acres of Land Unimproved
4. Cash Value of Farm
5. Value of Farm Implements and Machinery
6. Horses
7. Asses and Mules
8. Milch Cows
9. Working Oxen
10. Other Cattle
11. Sheep
12. Swine
13. Value of Livestock
14. Wheat, bushels of
15. Rye, bushels of
16. Indian Corn, bushels of
17. Oats, bushels of
18. Rice, lbs of
19. Tobacco, lbs of
20. Ginned cotton, bales of 400 lbs each
21. Wood, lbs of
22. Peas and beans, bushels of
23. Irish potatoes, bushels of
24. Sweet potatoes, bushels of
25. Barley, bushels of
26. Buckwheat, bushels of
27. Value of Orchard products in dollars
28. Wine, gallons of
29. Value of Products of Market Gardens
30. Butter, lbs of
31. Cheese, lbs of
32. Hay, tons of
33. Clover seed, bushels of
34. Other grass seeds, bushels of
35. Hops, lbs of
36. Dew Rotten Hemp, tons of
37. Water Rotted Hemp, tons of
38. Other Prepared Hemp
39. Flax, lbs of
40. Flaxseed, bushels of
41. Silk cocoons, lbs of
42. Maple sugar, lbs of

43. Cane Sugar, hunds of 1,000 lbs
44. Molasses, gallons of
45. Beeswax, lbs of
46. Honey, lbs of
47. Value of Home Made Manufactures
48. Value of Animals Slaughtered

Table of Contents

St. Charles County, Missouri (Continued from V.4)
1850 Agricultural Census

St. Charles County 1850 Agricultural Census was filmed by the Central Microfilm Service Corp of St. Louis, Missouri, for the Missouri State Historical Society. There are 46 columns of information on the 1850 agricultural census. I have chosen to transcribe six of those columns. The columns are:

1. Name
2. Acres of Land Improved
3. Acres of Land Unimproved
4. Cash Value of the Farm
5. Value of Farm Implements and Machinery
13. Value of Livestock

James Naylor, 40, -, 500, 100, 250
Alfred Lucekett(Luckett), 175, 525, 5000, 200, 700
D. B. Wells, 55, 275, 2500, 125, 225
John Gill, 120, 170, 3500, 200, 550
Lewis Howell, 170, 290, 5000, 200, 630
C. A. Boyd, 100, 260, 3000, 300, 850
C. C. Stewart, 50, 200, 2500, 150, 610
Henry Hatcher, 200, 500, 7000, 300, 1250
Alex Spence, 60, 190, 2800, 75, 350
J. B. Mushaney, 70, 230, 3000, 170, 500
James Campbell, 200, 440, 10000, 400, 1000
Robert Bailey, 100, 400, 5000, 250, 600
George S. Johnson, 210, 190, 4000, 300, 850
Hiram Custer, 100, 400, 1500, 250, 640
John Bauldridge, 25, 175, 1000, 150, 160
John Naylor, 150, 500, 8000, 200, 580
Peter Peipenbriar, 26, 54, 400, 100, 75
John W. Nelson, 100, 540, 5000, 100, 875
Benj. R. Pitts, 20, 50, 400, 25, 140
H. B. Ferrill, 100, 240, 2000, 200, 720
Wm. Miller, 40, 160, 1600, 75, 200
John P. Gill, 40, 160, 1600, 75, 215
John Adams, 50, 200, 2000, 100, 350
John S. Moore, 50, 90, 1400, 150, 640

Wm. A. Boyd, 100, 200, 2500, 150, 325
James Byan(Bryan), 40, 130, 1020, 100, 240
George Hoffman, 30, 120, 1200, 150, 260
Adam Sheller, 25, 20, 500, 75, 175
Elizabeth Stephens, 25, 15, 500, 50, 125
John Rousch, 25, 35, 600, 100, 200
George Krichbaum 30, 50, 800, 120, 140
Adam Diggledine, 25, 55 700, 100, 175
Jacob Burgemaster, 30, 70, 700, 100, 160
Sowers & Miller, 75, 85, 1600, 100, 350
Deterich Stomberg, 40, 27, 500, 110, 260
Wm. Miller, 20, -, 100, 50, 100
Herman Landware, 16, 24, 400, 100, 100
Elizabeth Teeters, 30, 95, 800, 100, 215
Charles Cole, 10, 90, 3200, 200, -
Sena Simonds, 15, 5, 800, 50, 100
Katy Philips, 20, 30, 500, 20, 150
S. R. Watts & Co., 60, 240, 3000, 150, 185
Samuel McClure, 180, 320, 1500, 350, 650
Thomas Watson, 30, 270, 2000, 120, 160
Nancey Price, 50, 110, 1000, 150, 650
Robt. B. Frazser, 200, 100, 3000, 300, 850

Thos. C. Batte, 200, 280, 3000, 300, 600
Sucinda (Lucinda) McClenney, 80, 120, 1200, 150, 260
Andrew Owens, 50, -, 400, 85, 300
Sarah Ferrill, 30, 10, 500, 100, 210
Jos. H. Moore, 50, 250, 1500, 150, 600
Zachery Moore, 100, 40, 1400, 100, 375
Moses Kempton, 14, -, 140, 45, 30
Tho. B. Hopkins, 10, -, 140, 40, 160
James Journey, 50, 90, 1400, 150, 255
Harvest Journey, 16, 244, 1250, 100 112
G. J. A. & M. Price, 100, 540, 3000, 150, 800
Bartholamew Smith, 100, 400, 2500, 150, 465
C. F. Woodson, 275, 425, 7000, 300, 1080
Earvin Baldridge, 32, -, 300, 100, 165
Robert Baldridge, 160, 180, 2500, 180, 745
John Montgomery, 10, -, 50, 50, 115
J. H. Karuthers, 30, 770, 3000, 150, 500
R. W. Frezes, 20, 100, 500, 50, 150
O. B. Young, 120, 130, 2000, 200, 530
Samuel Weiley, 23, -, 230, 100, 180
Ferd. Neirhoff, 15, 25, 400, 50, 100
Joseph Morrison, 80, -, 800, 100, 260
Fred. Earley, 35, 45, 400, 100, 300
Jos. M. Edwards, 150, 250, 2250, 250, 470
Sarah M. Edwards, 50, 200, 2250, 150, 265
Rodem F. Keviner, 240, 160, 5000, 300, 1000
Gibson Luckett, 60, 80, 1000, 150, 300
John Luckett, 120, 280, 4000, 200, 650
Henry Abington, 100, 140, 1200, 150, 360
James Webb, 40, 100, 1000, 150, 270
Wm. C. Edwards, 185, 45, 1600, 150, 570
Josiah Harrison, 28, -, 280, 100, 180
Mary Thornhill, 30, 110, 600, 120, 210
Leonard Bearley, 43, 117, 500, 50, 210
Fred. Hiner, 25, 135, 500, 100, 170
R. C. Aistrop, 20, 60, 300, 150, 130

Joseph O. Neal, 5, 35, 150, 40, 60
P. E. Scott, 100, 170, 1500, 110, 400
R. H. Anderson, 100, 170, 2500, 205, 310
John Sorrell, 25, -, 200, 50, 13
Thos. Moore, 50, 70, 600, 150, 360
Lucy D. Johnson, 30, 90, 600, 50, 115
J. W. Simpson, 50, 150, 1600, 150, 250
Genkins Phillips Jr., 50, 70, 850, 100, 210
Genkins Phillips Sr., 50 70, 850, 125, 300
James F. Owens, 20, -, 200, 130, 85
Christopher Johnson, 100, 139, 2000, 150, 460
James Mathews, 50, 190, 600, 90, 200
Benj. F. Walker, 60, 140, 1200, 150, 285
Wadda Thompson, 30, 50, 800, 100, 270
Mary H. Pullium, 50, 64, 800, 50, 223
James N. Shelton, 20, -, 200, 75, 180
Samuel Abington, 60, 600, 1200, 150, 310
Feramiah Sullivan, 20, 20, 200, 50, 260
Anderson Hughes, 40, 80, 360, 150, 220
Francis Logan, 40, 160, 1000, 100, 260
Wm. Pearce, 115, 190, 400, 200, 600
Mary H. Simons, 35, 5, 1000, 45, 190
Joseph F. Abbington, 80, 160, 700, 100, 305
George W. Wray, 30, 110, 1000, 100, 200
Moses Higenbottom, 90, 70, 400, 110, 210
Hiram Higenbottom, 40, -, 400, 30, 185
Thos. H. Bowles, 40, -, 2000, 90, 110
Marshall Bird, 100, 500, 600, 150, 400
Joshua Linthacom, 60, 60, 700, 50, 160
Tandy Collins, 40, 200, 400, 50, 200
Morgan Wright, 10, 110, 640, 50, 50
C. F. Herrald, 50, 110, 1000, 50, 180
Nancey Mason, 40, 140, 250, 50, 71
Richard Scruggs, 25, -, 250, 100, 160
Sarah B. Logan, 200, 300, 800, 150, 370
Charles P. May, 70, 10, 2000, 150, 270
Warren Walker, 150, 300, 250, 200, 600
Archibal Watson, 25, -, 150, 45, 160

Isaac W. Keithly, 80, 220, 2500 100, 300
Lea B. Abbington, 25, 55, 600, 100, 130
Francis Abbington, 75, 325, 2000, 150, 450
Paulina Sharp, 80, 50, 1200, 150, 355
Wm. France, 50 100, 1500, 100, 315
Henry Haislip, 50, 70, 800, 140, 225
Alex. Chambers, 60, 180, 1500, 150, 470
Philip Chambers, 30, -, 300, 50, 120
Pinkney May, 100, 140, 2000, 150, 600
Charles D. May, 40, 80, 800, 100, 220
Noble Ferline, 40, 40, 800, 75, 275
Jonathan Thomas, 250, 230, 3000, 150, 1292
Jas. M. Spain, 50, 90, 1600, 120, 360
Ruben Harris, 70, 130, 2000, 100, 400
Benjamin Pearce, 60, 640, 4000, -, 1100
George Meyers, 120, 880, 7000, 300, 870
John B. Allen, 25, -, 250, 200, 626
A. Breadhead, 150, 261, 2900, 200, 585
Francis Lacey, 20, -, 200, 35, 125
Perry Custer, 35, 105, 700, 150, 190
James Lewis, 30, 110, 900, 40, 320
Thos. J. Travis, 60, 43, 520, 150, 450
James Haines, 40, -, 400, 100, 165
Saml. B. Farmer, 50, 110, 100, 150, 320
Joseph Haines, 20, - 200, 110, 220
E. D. Kezle(Kegle), 80, 400, 2500, 150, 540
Wm. McCoy, 60, 195, 2000, 150, 520
Jonathan Zumwalt, 50 125, 2000, 150, 365
R. A. Woolfolk, 40, 120, 1000, 60, 200
Sarah Cohron, 70, 230, 1500, 100, 290
Wm. R. Keithly, 20, 60, 500, 50, 170
Nancey Magers, 60, 60, 800, 50, 195
E. W. & D. H. Richards, 50, 30, 800, 150, 155
Joel Richards, 60, 20, 500, 55, 250
Shadrach Richards, 15, 35, 200, 100, 105
James Travis, 20, 60, 250, 75, 100
John Hill, 20, 60, 400, 75, 75
Geo. T. Herrold, 30, -, 300, 150, 215
Barnadot Ball, 40, 100, 750, 150, 375

Bush & Ben Ball, 80, 300, 2000, 75, 350
Wm. Keithly, 120, 120, 3000, 200, 830
Wm. Ball, 25, 95, 800, 150, 145
Jos. A. Herndon, 12, 38, 200, 50, 95
Samuel Givens, 80, 160, 1200, 150 1025
Clinton Ingeran, 12, 68, 400, 50 85
Marmadage Kimbough, 40, 160, 1200, 150, 395
C.L. Carter, 50, 350, 2000, 150, 415
Cannon & Reigley, 40, 160, 2000, 150, 650
Henry W. Farris, 100, 227, 2500, 300, 700
Benj. Ball, 60, 220, 2000, 110, 235
John Ball, 150, 125, 2500, 200, 700
Benjamin Jones, 30, 10, 400, 80, 175
Ruth Boyd, 120, 300, 3000, 110, 600
Winefred Hubbert, 40, 330, 2250, 100, 440
Macijah McClenney, 80, 70, 1000, 100, 300
Robt. A. May, 200, 185, 2000, 520, 900
Wm. M. Allen, 80, 160, 1800, 150, 585
Russell Lewis, 40, 60, 1000, 150, 170
Harrison Drummons, 50, 110, 1500, 100, 205
Sheltial Ball, 65, 135, 2000, 150, 370
Daniel Lynch, 10, -, 50, 40, 130
John Turnbaugh, 14, -, 140, 35, 205
Solomon Crow, 10, 65, 400, 40, 150
Lewis Crow, 90, 105, 1500, 65, 165
Elizabeth Deger, 20, 20, 700, 75, 245
Pines H. Shelton, 100, 200, 4000, 150, 700
Thomas Pearce, 125, 125, 1500, 150, 760
Mary Hitch, 100, 140, 1400, 300, 800
John Christmon, 4, -, 40, 20, 80
Henry Muller, 30, 50, 400, 50, 135
Antone Schreor, 40, 40, 500, 100, 96
Littleton Cockeall, 80, -, 1000, 100, 210
E. B. Martin, 250, 410, 5000, 634, 1500
James Carr, 100, 500, 3000, 150, 680
Antone Karsteins, 100, 160, 4000, 150, 400

Elizabeth Hutchison, 40, 160, 1000, 125, 220

John Sapp, 16, -, 80, 40, 100

Jacob Wolf, 30, 70, 400, 55, 130

Marton Locke(Socke), 35, 125, 800, 150, 240

Wm. Hensel, 20, 40, 400, 50, 85

Donagry Soter, 20, 40, 300, 40, 145

Fountain Deyer, 6, -, 60, 40, 120

Casper Amptman, 20, 20, 120, 25, 105

Leonard Banger, 30, 63, 500, 150, 120

Peter Redger, 18, 22, 200, 100, 167

Francis Linhoff, 25, 55, 400, 50, 100

Christopher Brune, 15, 65, 400, 65, 120

John H. Deckhaus, 15, 65, 400, 70, 65

And. Davidson, 30, 130, 1200, 50, 130

Jackson Gilmore, 40, 66, 800, 150, 280

John Gilmore, 40, 166, 1000, 85, 40

Eaphraim Gilmore, 30, 250, 1200, 50, 180

Wm. Scott, 50, - 500, 150, 220

Daniel Baldridge, 40, 280, 2500, 200, 265

John Baldridge, 20, 180, 1000, 100, 200

Wm. Randolph, 500, 700, 6000, 250, 1450

Gabrial Gosney, 19, -, 200, 35, 100

John Randolph, 80, 216, 1000, 150, 415

Joseph Thomas, 30, 200, 500, 150, 170

James McBride, 20, -, 200, 25, 100

Francis Hansel, 65,-, 1400, 200, 650

B. A. Alderson, 250, 390, 10000, 400, 740

Jas. W. Denney, 75, 175, 2500, 150, 470

Daniel Smith, 60, 260, 2500, 140, 490

Jas. L. Hensel, 40, 120, 1500, 110, 390

Nancey Hensel, 40, -, 400, 75, 355

John Kramer, 30, 50, 400, 100, 200

Henry Schnerwind, 43, 90, 1000, 100, 140

Richard Haislip, 25, 75, 500, 65, 235

Dabney Bass, 30, 10, 300, 40, 155

Antone Snyder, 6, 34, 250, 35, 40

Edward S. Eans, 12, 48, 600, 85, 150

Henry Earnst, 25, 50, 600, 100, 245

Henry Summer, 6, 34, 200, 45, 65

Nicholas Pouson, 15, 45, 300, 40, 125

Martin Nord, 20, 20, 300, 45, 140

Fred. Muller, 10, 50, 400, 75, 125

Phillip Poinselott, 30, 50, 600, 85, 210

Joseph Meyer, 15, 35, 300, 100, 80

Thos. J. Williams, 15, 35, 400, 40 85

H. H. Goran, 38, -, 380, 110, 300

Absalom Keithly, 55, 345, 3000, 155, 520

Simon Keithly, 80, 60, 1500, 125, 260

Spencer Weichens, 20, 20, 500, 100, 165

Susanah Riggs, 30, 45, 1000, 85, 180

Christopher Leake, 25, 44, 400, 44, 160

R. & D. Heald, 200, 300, 2500, 150, 1000

Christopher Hutchins, 75, 317, 1500, 1200, 820

Frederick Terrill, 50, 104, 1500, 150, 310

Henry Algermesser, 25, 40, 600, 110, 126

Robert McClenney, 16, 60, 700, 95, 100

John B. Knoust, 20, 100, 1000, 75, 270

Robinson Dugan, 65, 55, 2000, 500, 1300

W. Dugan, 20, 400, 1200, 500, 300

Samuel Gaetor, 20, 140, 1800, 120, 245

John Cunningham, 20, 40, 1000, 65, 150

Isaac Smith, 40, 100, 1000, 100, 150

Henry Sporr, 14, 100, 1000, 65, 105

John Jones, 90, 130, 5000, 120, 370

Thomas Black, 15, 165, 1000, 95, 350

Wm. B. Berkelow, 75, 165, 2400, 300, 775

Adam Kruse, 7, -, 70, 75, 190

Daniel Keithly, 114, 135, 3000, 250, 1150

John Reifer, 20, 30, 1000, 100, 325

James H. Audrain, 20, 150, 2500, 120, 330

Francie House, 25, 275, 3000, 200, 390

Matilda Griffith, 250, 2500, 41250, 450, 1157

Frederick Lobeck, 30, 50, 800, 120, 150

George Hass, 20, 108, 600, 100, 280

Wm. C. Lindsey, 240, 360, 6000, 200, 1800

Jas. M. Shockley, 60, 150, 2480, 100, 390

Wm. B. Hayden, 200, 240, 4000, 150, 710

Nancey Burbanks, 40, 70, 1200, 100, 450

Wm. P. Shockley, 10, -, 160, 75, 120

S. L. Barker, 40, 300, 1200, 135, 230

Antone Brown, 15, -, 150, 75, 160

Tilghmon Mockabee, 60, 270, 2500, 100, 250

Daniel Emmerson, 125, 475, 3000, 150, 275

Mrs. L. Shelton, 40, 250, 2500, 125, 300

Walter Bowles, 140, 250, 4000, 200, 680

Wm. Collins, 15, 105, 1200, 50, 340

Clemont Boyce, 40, -, 400, 150, 500

Jno. & N. Guthrie, 30, 140, 1200, 25, 290

Thomas Lee, 170, 75, 3000, 150, 825

Adam Keithly, 60, 200, 2000, 155, 470

George Greenwald, 30, 30, 600, 200, 180

Susan Bowles, 35, 45, 1000, 75, 180

Stephen F. McAtee, 100, 300, 3000, 400, 875

Samuel Keithly Jr., 41, 160, 2000, 200, 230

Herman Hendricks, 5, 45, 500, 50, 125

Amelia Arnes, 43, 80, 1200, 175, 200

Joseph Flare, 15, 35, 400, 75, 140

Mary E. Fetsch, 50, 146, 1000, 135, 150

Adrew Sawle, 25, 50, 500, 125, 240

Gerhart Grauman, 16, 80, 500, 80, 155

Francis Molitor, 15, 175, 1200, 100, 140

John Schene, 30, 50, 800, 75, 200

Ellmonore Sutee, 60, 60, 500, 60, 200

Adam Beckett, 80, 40, 500, 100, 350

Wm. Hedges, 20, 40, 500, 50, 140

Joseph Floyd, 15, -, 150, 43, 105

Anglebest Hour, 24, 57, 200, 150, 122

Saml. Drummons, 12, -, 120, 30, 70

M. & M. Palladee, 40, 80, 500, 135, 700

Jacob Fetsch, 20, 60, 800, 100, 140

Charles Prinster, 20, 16, 500, 85, 140

Francis Albrecht, 30, 30, 600, 100, 125

Peter Link, 20, 20, 400, 75, 158

Joseph Sawley, 15, 35, 400, 50, 140

Stephen Iler, 60, 89, 800, 85, 600

Wm. Berkelow, 25, 65, 500, 60, 150

Joseph Leafler, 12, 32, 500, 100, 140

Antone Gile, 8, 12, 100, 60, 150

Henry Kirchhoff, 40, 180, 1000, 100, 235

Joseph Kretzberger, 18, 62, 500, 110, 200

R. C. Ray, 20, -, 200, 100, 140

Wm. Peiper, 40, 60, 820, 120, 170

Joseph Lindkagle, 20, 40, 600, 110, 132

David K. Pittman, 540, 940, 20000, 735, 1930

Alonzo Cottle, 100, 400, 4000, 100, 270

John Teeter, 40, 160, 1000, 135, 230

Wm. Bakerhide, 40, 20, 1200, 110, 230

Elizabeth Sandford, 40, -, 400, 80, 300

John A. Talley, 150, 450, 6000, 200, 2000

Wilson L. Overall, 360, 3000, 10000, 500, 4000

Robert H. Parks, 250, 429, 8000, 300, 700

James Gallaher, 150, 350, 10000, 500, 1200

Catharine Grave, 10, 30, 400, 50, 140

Henry Beckman, 20, 37, 500, 100, 245

Caleb Rice, 70, 10, 600, 50, 525

John B. Hilbert, 12, 12, 500, 20, 225

Ludwell E. Powell, 40, 55, 800, 100, 320

Samuel B. Smith, 10, 12, 1500, 20, 90

Henry Melkersman, 20, -, 500, 50, 95

Bazel Pallardee, 15, -, 300, 50, 80

St. Clair County 1850 Agricultural Census was filmed by the Central Microfilm Service Corp of St. Louis, Missouri, for the Missouri State Historical Society. There are 46 columns of information on the 1850 agricultural census. I have chosen to transcribe six of those columns. The columns are:

1. Name
2. Acres of Land Improved
3. Acres of Land Unimproved
4. Cash Value of the Farm
5. Value of Farm Implements and Machinery
13. Value of Livestock

Zack Lilly, 60, 280, 1500, 30, 660
John T. Crenshaw, 80, 165, 800, 20, 284
Jacob A. Browning, 150, 410, 1000, 100, 525
Hugh Barwell, 150, 490, 1500, 150, 1402
Ann Corbin, 60, 300, 1000, 100, 656
Wm. H. McCullock, 70, 600, 1000, 200, 369
Joshua Gates, 18, -, 200, 15, 336
Wm. H. Scoby, 25, 15, 200, 24, 206
M. M. Hansbrough, 50, 270, 700, 154, 250
George W. McFarland, 21, 59, 250, 12, 228
Pleasant M. Cox, 300, 700, 3000, 250, 2205
Joseph Culbertson, 90, 510, 1000, 120, 650
D. W. Keeth, 110 450, 1000, 100, 1215
James Bolds, 70, -, 400, 15, 428
Saml. W. Harris, 300, 1000, 3000, 250, 2883
Joseph Walker, 46, 36, 500, 75, 162
Ebenezer Gask, 75, 445, 1500, 200, 614
Lewis Reese, 30, -, 100, 50, 232
Joel Starkie, 75, 125, 1000, 100, 466
Temperance Cox, 152, 328, 1500, 100, 475

John W. Beckley, 160, 160, 2000, 200, 662
W.L. Sutherland, 140, 300, 2500, 125, 1531
James A. Eads, 40, 120, 500, 20, 270
Wm. C. Douglass, 300, 700, 6000, 250, 4705
Jefferson Cummins, 30, -, 10, 300, 30, 264
Thomas N. Henly, 40, 80, 500, 200, 2393
Simeon Postin, 40, 80, 600, 50, 259
James Cole, 55, 275, 1000, 200, 450
Harry C. Douglass, 150, 260, 2000, 100, 1544
George R. Cowan, 50, 470, 1000, 200, 1097
Obediah Vaughan, 10, -, 100, 10, 374
M. G. Hoover, 25, 78, 500, 10, 185
Ash Peebly, 30, 170, 800, 70, 375
George Mozingo, 80, 200, 1000, 50, 319
John Bunch, 90, 100, 1000, 175, 744
David A. Bunch, 100, 140, 1000, 300, 401
James Addington, 16, 70, 125, 50, 215
Joseph Herndon, 30, 50, 500, 100, 145
Clifton G. Browning, 70, 140, 400, 30, 389
Elisha H. Bell, 160, 470, 2000, 200, 1069

Joshua Stewart, 60, 100, 600, 160, 470
William F. Foster, 15, 40 81/100, 200, 10, 50
James A. Gilliam 15, 65, 100, 10, 50
Mace Tipton, 50, 233, 1400, 40, 900
Thomas Copenhaver, 60, 100, 500, 75, 358
Abraham Miller, 30, 56, 300, 15, 217
James D. Gray, 60, 20, 1000, 75, 674
John Thompson, 50, 70, 500, 100, 509
Jessee Looney, 50, 100, 700, 75, 415
Isam Looney, 93, 125, 1000, 73, 438
James Cannada, 50, 100, 500, 20, 335
John C. Looney, 30, 90, 300, 15, 292
Ephraim Rippertor, 80, 40, 500, 150, 486
Thomas F. Wright, 60, 200, 500, 50, 326
Levi Gover, 80, 120, 1000, 110, 455
James Gardener, 100, 280, 3000, 100, 325
William Brown, 70, 400, 1000, 100, 529
Benj. H. Moore, 60, 375, 1000, 100, 474
John Tally, 70, 1600, 2000, 150, 395
Riley Johnson, 18, 22, 80, 15, 324
Eli Phillips, 20, 140, 200, 15, 342
Merrett Clarkson, 40, 40, 500, 100, 350
James Clarkson, 10, 120, 300, 30, 150
A. Sheldon, 18, 102, 500, 100, 499
Reubin Robinson, 40, 126, 600, 100, 544
Harlan Hays, 35, 165, 600, 20, 258
Hugh Graham, 10, 70, 100, 80, 191
Thomas Guise, 25, 15, 250, 20, 325
John Amblin, 25, 55, 100, 10, 100
David McClain, 30, 130, 600, 80, 233
John Cox, 50, 350, 800, 100, 500
John Clarkson, 20, 200, 200, 100, 334
Sarah Fewell, 10, 40, 75, 20, 272
Andrew J. Nichols, 53, 224, 300, 75, 251
Theoderick Snuper, 50, 100, 400, 80, 607
John Bedell, 42, 130, 200, 50, 447
John F. Thompson, 14, 26, 250, 70, 172
Joseph B. Winston, 18, 180, 1000, 50, 806
Joshua Rickman, 30 170, 500, 100, 289
Thomas Walton, 40, 100, 250, 50, 183

Wily B. Myers, 30, 250, 800, 50, 250
Clement C. Walton, 40, 80, 200, 50, 472
Charles Allen, 35, 5, 100, 10, 160
Danl. Martin, 100, 106, 250, 15, 530
Jacob Coonts, 100, 700, 1200, 600, 1155
Richd. Haynie, 25, 55, 115, 10, 340
Hartwell Pace, 20, 180, 250, 15, 370
Hugh Hall, 100, 100, 400, 100, 675
John Ball, 20, 140, 200, 60, 255
Authur Kirkpatrick, 75, 265, 350, 10, 315
Jesse Hall, 25, 55, 110, 75, 237
Albert Ayres, 30, 150, 200, 35, 866
Jos. Raglen, 50, 190, 350, 75, 520
Wm. Duckworth, 15, 25, 150, 30, 130
Isaac Strickland, 30, 10, 150, 16, 205
J. E. Eads, 70, 140, 350, 50, 450
Matthew Boswell, 60, 640, 1300, 200, 630
A. L. Gash, 40, 160, 420, 15, 180
Alex Ritchey, 20, 20, 60, 10, 94
G. B. Culbertson, 40, 40, 120, 15, 375
Wm. Elkin, 10, 30, 60, 15, 125
Wm. Dudley, 80, 320, 800, 150, 455
E. P. McMinn, 40, 40, 120, 20, 290
A. Prichard, 40, 150, 250, 50, 270
Jas. W. Buck, 40, 30, 300, 100, 436
Edward Delogus, 25, 15, 100, 15, 190
Thos. Piper, 50, 190, 450, 50, 467
Richd. Crenshaw, 50, 160, 450, 10, 112
Enoch Lestor, 35, 485, 400, 50, 403
John C. Wolfe, 20, 20, 60, 15, 221
John D. Simms, 40, 40, 100, 40, 530
Richd. Lenon, 25, 15, 100, 30, 155
Wm. R. Cawthon, 40, 40, 150, 75, 220
Jas. Cawthon, 20, 20, 60, 15, 170
Wm. J. Weir, 7, 33, 150, 20, 160
Wilson Estes, 20, 60, 100, 15, 60
Z. Burrows, 20, 20, 60, 15, 78
Wm. Nance, 20, 20, 60, 10, 50
Jesse Fentress, 25, 15, 75, 15, 115
W. W. Walters, 50, 30, 150, 10, 185
Mary E. Hester, 50, 140, 400, 75, 650
L. R. Ashworth, 30, 670, 1000, 100, 314
Abraham Hile(Hite), 18, 35, 150, 12, 130

Jno. Dawson, 15, 25, 60, 15, 86
Anthony Hester, 16, 18, 100, 20, 185
Jno. W. Ritchey, 60, -, 100, 150, 585
Nancy W. Keaton, 20, 20, 60, 15, 325
Elisha Bridges, 15, 25, 50, 15, 160
Bennett Pitts, 30, 210, 400, 15, 400
Hiram Monnay, 10, 30, 60, 12, 140
P. _. Rudman, 40, -, 75, 10, 55
Wm. Lord, 20, 20, 60, 15, 190
Jeremiah Lord, 10, 30, 60, 16, 75
Jas. Delozier, 45, 35, 200, 25, 190
Jos. Todd, 40, 40, 120, 12, 240
Frederick Smith, 20, 20, 60, 10, 115
Jno. Gash, 20, 60, 100, 10, 145
Joel Redmond, 60, 100, 500, 75, 222
Robert Osborne, 25, 65, 100, 75, 327
Elisha Thomas, 30, 60, 100, 75, 320
A. D. Moore, 22, 18, 250, 100, 660
John Barnett, 30, 130, 350, 30, 362
Saml. Cox, 20, 20, 200, 30, 242
Richmond Smith, 45, 155, 500, 120,
1035
Randolph Whitley, 70, 330, 1200, 100,
1000
Calvin Walds, 130, 499, 2500, 150, 2500
Joseph S. Herndon, 30, 50, 500, 100,
145
Clifton G. Browning, 20, 140, 400, 30,
389
Elisha N. Bell, 160, 470, 2000, 200,
1060
Joshua Stewart, 60, 100, 600, 150, 470
James Faster(Foster), 40, 120, 600, 50,
658
Cornelius Clancy, 30, 10, 100, 20, 310
Reuben Vaughan, 67, 133, 1000, 100,
355
Josiah Vaughan, 12, 80, 300, 20, 110
Evan Lawler, 80, 160, 1000, 100, 416
Wm. B. Lawler, 30, 50, 250, -, 233
Geo. Preston, 60, 300, 1500, 50, 579
Taylor G. Gilliam, 40, -, 500, 100, 363
Wm. Moore, 40, 180, 800, 75, 343
A. J. Husbands, 35, 165, 800, 20, 211
Wm. F. Ferguson, 20, 100, 200, 20, 292
Hiram Short, 50, 72, 350, 30, 167

Henry Ruby, 16, 24, 150, 20, 158
Willis Phillips, 22, 30, 110, 10, 237
Busbee Ricketts, 60, 180, 600, 60, 308
Jas. Strain, 30, 170, 250, 20, 339
Frances Pucket, 30, 250, 600, 15, 152
Jno. Haney, 50 190, 400, 30, 549
Jno. Snell, 50, 70, 200, 15, 422
Samuel Keller, 10, 106, 350, 25, 257
Jas. Burford, 30, 170, 450, 50, 205
Jonathan Moore, 20, 15, 300, 15, 96
Andrew Culbertson, 30, 40, 300, 23, 229
Hutchison Witt, 80, 20, 500, 100, 170
Hez. Thompson, 60, 20, 300, 50, 340
Jacob Holsapple, 65, 255, 425, 60, 303
Geo. W. Fairy(Fairx), 40, 40, 120, 30,
754
Francis Yost, 85, 120, 800, 150, 850
Isaac Rogers, 40, 240, 500, 90, 693
Jas. Burchett, 20, 60, 160, 15, 156
Peyton Bristoe, 30, 10, 200, 30, 250
B. C. Bratcher, 22, 70, 150, 13, 140
Matthew Francis, 40, 280, 600, 60, 344
Lem. R. Oaks, 30, 50, 150, 30, 233
Gilbert Deer, 80, 20, 500, 14, 189
William Allen 80, 280, 500, 50, 874
K. C. Allen, 20, 20, 100, 17, 150
Wm. M. Culbertson, 42, 38, 150, 15, 310
Jno. N. Boyd, 40, 20, 350, 10, 230
C. L. Good, 20, 20, 100, 15, 52
Wm. L. King, 60, 95, 500, 60, 1253
Christian Keller, 40, 20, 200, 15, 60
Samuel V. Keller, 35, 35, 200, 10, 100
Wm. Culbertson, 55, 105, 500, 80, 309
Clem Strickland, 60, 60, 300, 75, 409
Henry Strickland, 20, 50, 100, 17, 125
Susan Carmichael, 35, 205, 400, 50, 325
Jas. Culbertson, 44, 20, 100, 60, 215
Jas. Pace, 40, 40, 200 50, 300
C. Bailey, 35, 5, 100, 40, 130
Jas. Dudley, 55, 33, 200, 50, 155
Isaac Culbertson, 175, 1625, 2000, 150,
1050
Wm. B. C. Weir, 70, 163, 400, 20, 213
Pellman Thompson, 80, 100, 300, 10,
300
Jno. Wright, 20, 20, 150, 5, 110

R. L. Nance, 80, 320, 500, 150, 550
Massie Devin, 30, 50, 190, 10, 165
Wm. Dudley, 60, 20, 200, 100, 518
Henry Dudly, 85, 5, 500, 225, 870
Elizabeth Gash, 60, 60, 160, 10, 135
Saml. Scott, 30, 10, 60, 15, 250
Robt. Gardner, 40, 40, 100, 20, 440
Elizabeth Thompson, 100, 60, 200, 100, 325
T. T. Ernest, 62, 18, 200, 120, 575
Richd. Bradshaw, 65, 215, 500, 120, 527
Aron Bradshaw, 30, 50, 100, 20, 230
F. Delozier, 65, 80, 300, 12, 285
Edward Nance, 85, 230, 500, 110, 514
Eligah Rice, 30, 70, 150, 80, 290
Ira Ledbeter, 100, 110, 310, 100, 704
James Terry, 37, 359, 1500, 30, 500
James M. Herndon, 25, 135, 500, 10, 131
John Jiams, 60, 20, 350, 20, 366
E. B. Bunch, 30, 50, 350, 20, 400
S. C. Bruce, 120, 120, 700, 150, 825
Wm. H. Small, 60, 60, 1000, 100, 681
Oscar Kellar, 70, 50, 600, 50, 448
Henry Reese, 40, 40, 200, 75, 340
Geo. W. Reese, 10, 70, 100, 20, 232
Daniel Cline, 40, 160, 500, 20, 275
Joshua Dallas, 60, 160, 900, 200, 737
Mitchell Gash, 60, 307, 1000, 150, 402
Jas. L. Smith, 105, 135, 1000, 75, 1344
John Roberts, 25, 141, 200, 20, 155
John Smith, 53, 290, 1200, 25, 266
Isaac Hednik, 20, 140, 200, 20, 208
Peter Stevens, 70, 90, 800, 125, 393
Wm. A. C. Hill, 45, 455, 1500, 100, 480
Jacob S. Dale, 30, 130, 500, 50, 385
Daniel Dale, 200, 600, 2000, 200, 209
Pleasant Dale, 40, 120, 200, 20, 915
James Beal, 45, 155, 500, 85, 502
K. Morris, 25, 135, 275, 10, 200
Isaac Copenhaver, 60, 100, 825, 10, 250
Samuel V. Shaylor, 40, 100, 200, 10, 66
Avery B. Howard, 30, 160, 1500, 125, 385
Thomas E. Burns, 30, 130, 200, 25, 349

Michael Copenhaver, 10, 150, 200, 15, 224
Snowden T. Morris, 28, 122, 200, 31, 361
Benj. T. Morris, 45, 75, 360, 31, 194
Moses Preston, 35, 206, 1000, 60, 328
Robert Preston, 20, 148, 200, 10, 61
James Preston, 10, 110, 250, 15, 40
Stephen Hogens, 20, 20, 60, 20, 118
Hannah Burger, 20, 20, 60, 20, 140
Benj. F. Reed, 12, 77, 280, 15, 18
Margaret Reed, 16 66, 200, 35, 150
Alexander M. Williams, 40, 120, 200, 100, 531
Daniel Hoots, 6, 160, 200, 12, 85
John R. Whitley, 40, 260, 900, 80, 382
Ro. G. Crockett, 100, 1000, 3000, 60, 927
Thomas Lessly, 70, 90, 200, 80, 487
David Doak, 40, 160, 200, 15, 90
Francis J. Montgomery, 7, 153, 200, 15, 59
Jos. Brown, 300, 540, 3400, 125, 1264
James Brown, 30, 210, 800, 75, 136
James Vickers, 17, 143, 200, 15, 152
John Cockrum, 35, 125, 200, 35, 154
Alvin Phillips, 10, 150, 200, 10, 186
Sandifer Hurt, 30, 130, 200, 40, 277
Samuel Morgan, 30, 130, 200, 15, 270
Levi Taylor, 10, 150, 200, 20, 105
Coonrad G. Carr, 60, 20, 150, 15, 138
Andrew J. Martin, 50, 30, 100, 20, 136
James Martin, 50, 540, 3000, 160, 224
Rebecca Story, 20, 60, 300, 20, 126
William Hill, 10, 150, 200, 15, 135
James E. Story, 30, 130, 300, 15, 110
Taverner Beal, 10, 150, 200, 20, 190
Marcus Monroe, 20, 80, 100, 20, 85
Danl. D. Foster, 20, 78, 125, 30, 254
Hugh Arbuckle, 45, 712, 1800 35, 267
William Arbuckle, 20, 160, 200, 20 81
James Anderson, 60, 440, 1500, 80, 372
Noah Webb, 20, 140, 200, 20, 217
Benj. F. Snider, 20, 140, 400, 15, 270
Wm. L. Browning, 60, 120, 500, 50, 500
John Whitley, 30, 170, 500, 15, 542

S. B. Stone, 12, 158, 200, 15, 747
Francis Hicks, 18, 148, 200, -, 73
Susanna Revis, 22, 98, 400, -, 129
Joseph Potter, 20, 20, 60, 10, 200
John Fleming, 11, 147, 200, -, 384
Wm. Whitley, 70, 330, 800, 60, 755
Joseph Montgomery, 120, 410, 1500, 250, 963
Randolph Bateman, 12, 148, 600, -, 93
John Burch, 60, 180, 1000, 125, 497
Spencer Estis, 50, 208, 400, 110, 856
Chas. W. D. Birrus, 50, 150, 1200, 1500, 1095
Baldwin Dade, 15, 195, 600, 25, 283
Hugh Allison, 26, 136, 200, 50, 277
Jos. Coulthard, -, 160, 200, 10, 168
Andrew Yonce(Tonce, Tona), 40, 120, 400, 30, 288
Jacob Coulthard, 100, 62, 500, 80, 543
Geo. W. Short, 100, 380, 1500, 200, 501
Marshall A. Staton, 40, 120, 300, -, 68

Elizabeth Patterson, 20, 100, 350, 30, 510
Sarah Allison, 60, 100, 320, 20, 410
John Hagens, 70, 110, 540, 80, 756
Joseph Sloss, 10, 150, 200, 10, 110
Wilson Hodges, 14, 144, 200, -, 117
James Rickey, 40, 193, 1500, 50, 1041
Andrew J. Rickey, 10, 90, 300, 10, 162
John Jones, 20, 40, 100, -, 49
Noah S. Caton, 30, 130, 300, 130, 397
Francis Spronlle, 30, 130, 200, 50, 421
Jesse Ridgway, 120, 540, 2000, 50, 1229
Peter B. Cockerell, 50, 190, 600, 30, 217
James Burke, 45, 115, 600, 60, 345
James Ditty, 20, 140, 600, 30, 620
Benj. Hooper, 36, 130, 480, 25, 307
James Bevins, 22, 138, 300, 10, 91
Thomas Spencer, 44, 146, 200, -, 125
John Hillsman, 15, 145, 200, 15,181
John Dice(Dix), 30, 130, 600, 80, 209
Andrew J. Strain, 30, 190, 600, 20, 150

St. Francois County, Missouri
1850 Agricultural Census

St. Francois County 1850 Agricultural Census was filmed by the Central Microfilm Service Corp of St. Louis, Missouri, for the Missouri State Historical Society. There are 46 columns of information on the 1850 agricultural census. I have chosen to transcribe six of those columns. The columns are:

1. Name
2. Acres of Land Improved
3. Acres of Land Unimproved
4. Cash Value of the Farm
5. Value of Farm Implements and Machinery
13. Value of Livestock

James W. Smith, 160, 267, 2000, 15, 400
Nathaniel Cook, 200, 380, 4000, 50, 500
G. W. Sebastian, 200, 100, 2000, 200, 429
Josephus F. Harris, 160, 200, 6000, 200, 1950
John K. Harris, 80, 140, 2000, 25, 415
Samuel Kinkead, 100, 200, 2000, 100, 224
George Stephens, 10, 30, 60, 15, 108
Marion Blanks, 250, 150, 4000, 300, 787
A. B. Kinkead, 40, 184, 1100, 50, 150
William A. Wallace, 20, 105, 300, 65, 119
James C. Wallace, 11, 66, 150, 10, 121
John Needham, 15, 65, 200, 10, 133
John Porter, 45, 90, 600, 25, 240
Isabella Johnson, 15, 60, 100, 15, 150
Samuel Thompson, 20, 60, 100, 75, 68
Austin Y. Kelly, 40, 80, 150, 75, 237
James Tucker, 10, 30, 100, 50, 110
William Tucker, 15, 40, 125, 5, 110
Jane Sellers, 8, 32, 75, 5, -
William Simpson Sr., 30, 130, 400, 25, 88
Wm. Simpson Jr., 65, 135, 600, 20, 230
Asa McKenzie, 150, 150, 3000, 100, 325
David McKenzie, 65, 35, 600, 10, 175
David Needham, 8, 32, 200, 5, 70

James Moore, 50, 12, 200, 55, 265
Abraham Barron, 12, 25, 80, 6, 105
Robert Brownfield, 15, 65, 120, 15, 115
Ben. F. Laurence, 40, 80, 600, 100, 300
William Shaw, 75, 225, 2000, 50, 320
Washington Smith, 50, 550, 1000, 40, 138
Wesley Moore, 40, 120, 800, 40, 115
Wm. Dunaway, 14, 26, 100, 40, 154
Moses W. Baker, 60, 136, 1000, 60, 220
Jacob McFarland, 50, 115, 1600, 25, 230
Reuben McFarland, 70, 106, 1000, 70, 355
Pleasant Maze, 25, 87, 600, 50, 252
A. J. Smith, 50, 110, 800, 25, 100
Ezekiel Smith, 20, 100, 400, 2, 30
George Marks, 75, 125, 1000, 75, 520
Henry Potts, 60, 280, 1000, 75, 210
Moses Cantrell, -, -, -, -, 50
Nancy Townsend, 30, 90, 500, 10, 130
John Miller, -, -, -, 5, 40
Eli Welker, 18, 102, 350, 5, 140
Thomas M. Harris, 140, 260, 2000, 200, 477
Ben Camden, 25, 55, 150, 25, 75
W. J. Misser, -, -, -, 4, 38
Solomon Duese, 100, 100, 500, 10, 150
Larkin Cofer, 25, 55, 250, 15, 155
Jonathan Carmack, 21, 140, 250, 8, 95
L. D. Stark, 45, 75, 360, 57, 125

Saml. Reynolds, 30, 10, 250, 15, 130
James Brewen, 7, 60, 200, 11, 130
Lewis G. Kidwell, 60, 120, 200, 20, 125
Meeke Griffin, 60, 120, 1500, 60, 233
J. V. Sebastian, 80, 405, 1500, 100, 308
J. Jordan, 25, 255, 500, 35, 195
E. H. Hibbits, 30, 130, 50, 8, 100
W. J. Murray, 10, 70, 150, 30, 122
Sam. C. Vance, 10, 30, 100, 95, 158
Daniel Williams, 45, 80, 500, 40, 298
Thomas Needham, 20, 20, 100, 40, 149
Ellet Mounts, 65, 55, 600, 200, 228
David Williams, -, 80, 300, 12, 280
W. J. Obannon, 40, 110, 800, 60, 457
Wm. Brewen, 90, 80, 1700, 120, 441
John C. Farmer, 35, 130, 80, 15, 130
John W. Hill, 140, 360, 5000, 150, 1005
L. Alexander, 22, 134, 1500, 95, 157
Lewis Murphy, 40, 40, 300, 10, 180
Finis Walker, 10, 178, 600, 40, 180
John McHenry, 35,100, 390, 10, 63
Joseph Reed, 35, 100, 390, 25, 185
W. H. Clay, 80, 160, 1500, 75, 275
W. D. Hamilton, 20, 20, 75, 5, 100
Jesse Yates, 50, 280, 800, 125, 418
D. H. Murphy, 40, 80, 500, 80, 305
Nesbit Orten, 30, 90, 1000, 80, 340
Daniel Sebastian, 15, 26, 450, 10, 220
Jno. W. Cooley, 30, 210, 1000, 80, 208
David Sherill, 100, 300, 1000, 150, 390
Gardner Williams, 40, 100, 550, 70, 435
John Jones, 50, 60, 600, 80, 663
Wilson Williams, 45, 11, 300, 10, 52
Thomas Halstead, 15, 25, 80, 40, 162
Elisha Bennet, -, -, -, 4, 25
Elijah Sebastian, 80, 92, 600, 75, 185
John J. Williams, 30, 50, 400, 130, 496
B. G. Grayson, 60, 100, 500, 80, 110
James White, 20, 50, 150, 12, 242
Wm. Blackwell, 25, 55, 200, 3, 165
Jo. N. P. Russell, 30, 110, 600, 55, 287
Wm. Murray, 20, 20, 150, 30, 170
Harris Rigney, 20, 20, 100, 30, 141
John Jacobs, 25, 15, 250, 40, 151
S. U. Bowland, 20, 20, 150, 12, 65
Jo. D. Bayless, 10, 30, 125, 15, 108

Daniel G. Brewen, -, -, -, 5, 84
G. B. Casteel, 15, 25, 150, 10, 106
Reuben Dalton, 35, 45, 300, 100, 254
Luke B. Crawford, 10, 30, 100, 8, 150
Andrew Wise, 18, 62, 100, 3, 60
J. H. Mason, 19, 63, 300, 75, 186
Thomas M. Landrum, 7, 108, 300, 5, 155
A. H. Williams, 60, 100, 1000, 100, 413
J. Flanary, -, -, -, 35, 95
J. H. McFarland, 30, 50, 400, 100, 414
Britain Bridgers, 50, 110, 700, 100, 150
E. Basye, 30, 110, 650, 50, 1000
S. P. Harris, 150, 350, 4500, 300, 703
Anderson Bane, 45, 105, 1000, 6, 148
Thomas Cole, -, -, -, 50, 120
Alexander Gordon, 50, 70, 500, 60, 267
A. Lichafer, 10, 30, 100, 60, 175
Wm. R. Tucker, 20, 20, 100, 12, 100
Adam Ham, -, -, -, 150, 347
A. J. Ham, -, -, -, 75, 270
Moses Brewen, -, -, -, 5, 60
Isaac Ham, -, -, -, 100, 185
James Duncan, -, -, -, 5, 205
Bazil Zolman, 12, 108, 450, 30, 173
Catharine Peers, 65, 550, 6015, 200, 430
Rachel Murphy, 100, 100, 2000, 150, 604
Wm. H. Bess, 15, 22, 200, 90, 105
Henry W. Crow, -, -, - 100, 220
James McDaniel, 30, 50, 60, 100, 262
Richard Murphy, 40, 50, 850, 150, 474
Henderson Murphy, 100, 200, 2500, -, -
Zebulon Murphy, 20, 140, 800, 20, 170
Elijah Wood, 40, 120, 1000, 18, 415
Anderson Crawford, -, -, -, 3, 98
S. E. Douthit, 30, 130, 600, 75, 520
Jo. F. Hurry, 35, 265, 3500, 40, 185
D. M. Crawford, 5, 35, 100, 5, 27
John Bean, 25, 35, 240, 75, 188
George Santee, 30, 50, 300, 75, 170
John Tabor, 35, 210, 1680, 90, 379
Wiley J. Gunter, 10, 70, 200, 45, 139
Joseph C. Ross, 60, 155, 800, 75, 300
Wm. B. Williams, 6, 17, 700, 70, 120
W. O. Ross, 45, 40, 700, 80, 385

Charles Myers, 60, 140, 6000, 60, 154
Isaac H. Perkins, 10, 30, 120, 10, 72
Frank Violet, 17, 183, 1000, 105, 167
William Shannon, 55, 550, 2000, 100, 95
Hardy Wiggins, 30, 85, 250, 20, 165
Harvey Young, 45, 130, 2000, 60, 216
William Pigg, 70, 330, 2000, 80, 320
John Guitar, 10, 30, 75, 25, 80
Elizabeth Haile, 50, 100, 600, 85, 310
Gilbert Peyton, 22, 12, 75, 12, 252
Louis Carron, 60, 60, 360, 40, 310
Batise Bryer, -, -, -, 5, 50
Antoine Carron, 25, 47, 200, 40, 175
Henry Carron, 15, 25, 100, 25, 120
Louis C. Boyer, 40, 40, 200, 25, 115
Bazile Obuchon, 40, 25, 250, 25, 325
Bazile Obuchon Sr., 20, 42, 200, 30, 220
Joseph Levereau, 80, 80, 300, 25, 344
John Levereau, -, -, -, -, 25
Francis Obuchon, 55, 30, 600, 30, 357
Louis Obuchon, 25, 55, 300, 20, 245
Peter Levereau, -, -, -, 2, 28
Amy Layhe, 50, 13, 500, 35, 210
Antoine Obuchon, 20, 100, 400, 20, 170
Vinsent Layhe, 80, 280, 1200, 35, 300
Lucien Obuchon, 5, 35, 100, 25, 110
George Shumate, 40, 40, 200, 5, 85
David P. Hall, 15, 101, 500, 75, 150
Alexr. Patterson, 35, 255, 2500, 80, 500
Samuel Gibbs, 20, 20, 100, 5, 80
And. Stephenson, -, -, -, 5, 88
R. Haverstick, 20, 100, 1500, 50, 240
William Toner, -, -, -, 115, 35
Francis Harris, 20, 50, 125, 5, 200
Wm. Porter, 10, 30, 50, 10, 140
Thomas Tarpley, 20, 60, 1000, 10, 148
Celestin Guijuet, 30, 130, 300, 35, 130
W. J. Estes, 50, 590, 1000, 25, 195
Ami Wuille, 10, 25, 300, 20, 225
John McKee, 45, 255, 400, 20, 240
Erastus Walker, 12, 87, 125, 25, 200
Martin Horn, 20, 20, 100, 25, 155
A. Richardson, 30, 101, 200, 70, 308
John Oatman, 20, 60, 300, 70, 295
George Mostiller, 60, 260, 600, 60, 375

Wm. M. Cruncleton, 75, 125, 500, 100, 317
Jas. Richardson, 10, 30, 300, 5, 95
Patrick H. Snead, 7, 52, 300, 5, 100
Rhoda Bequette, 30, 10, 100, 6, 285
William Richardson, 20, 20, 75, 10, 107
Jas. D. Richardson, 25, 15, 100, 40, 185
Wm. H. Andrews, 35, 130, 500, 10, 385
John Richardson, 40, 40, 200, 35, 270
Elijah Mason, 30, 50, 400, 50, 180
R. C. Poston, 160, 1800, 5000, 150, 1150
Matthew Dunn, 28, 52, 600, 10, 170
James Cabiness, 40, 225, 600, 75, 280
Jas. Cunningham, 50, 22, 350, 25, 365
Isaac Cunningham, 80, 200, 1000, 35, 320
Ansalem Green, 13, 33, 150, -, 260
A. J. Caughran, 27, 8, 550, 75, 110
Wilson Barry, 100, 200, 1200, 150, 556
George H. Marks, 45, 181, 1200, 65, 295
Charles Hart, 75, 125, 1800, 100, 400
Charles Evins, 28, 126, 1000, 12, 182
Gabriel Thomason, 50, 85, 600, 125, 302
A. J. Griffin, 35, 105, 500, 15, 119
George Carder, 70, 150, 1000, 75, 257
Corbin Alexander, 100, 450, 3000, 200, 689
N. L. Fleming, 60, 60, 1000, 30, 284
F. B. McFarland, 50, 70, 500, 15, 175
P. G. Long, 30, 72, 2000, 125, 314
J. J. Brady, 40, 80, 450, 15, 175
William Hunt, 35, 195, 900, 95, 313
John R. Darrow, 85, 160, 400, 70, 580
Isaac N. Purtle, 27, 13, 300, 15, 130
Evan W. King, 12, 28, 100, 5, 100
Wm. A. McFarland, 30, 90, 500, 20, 220
Davis Marks, 4, 75, 400, 20, 95
W. S. Dobbins, 3, 80, 400, 5, 132
Harvey McAlister, 55, 178, 500, 50, 300
David Evans, 80, 119, 2000, 125, 380
Fountain Conway, 60, 140, 700, 50, 165
Mary J. Sutherland, 75, 360, 1500, 75, 220
Abram T. Smith, 30, 90, 1200, 45, 270
Armstrong Ohara, 30, 50, 500, 15, 320

Joseph Conway, 45, 95, 450, 40, 160
William Hiley, 40, 89, 500, 10, 210
John Wall, 26, 16, 200, 10, 212
Jacob Carlton, 24, 56, 300, 30, 155
Irvin M. Haile, 25, 175, 700, 45, 216
Matthew Logan, 15, 25, 100, 8, 95
Elizabeth Smith, 45, 120, 1000, 75, 295
A. J. Turley, 40, 343, 1800, 70, 375
John Shelly, 12, 61, 200, 20, 175
Leonard Parker, 25, 75, 500, 10, 137
William Dawson, 51, 190, 750, 6, 113
Henry Estes, 13, 527, 1000, 35, 115
Alfred White, -, -, -, 6, 120
Penina Surnngen, 15, 25, 100, 5, 104
Achilles Smith, 50, 210, 1200, 35, 385
M. Berkley, 80, 245, 2500, 75, 370
James Owens, -, -, -, 3, 100
A. Lambeth, 70, 168, 1000, 60, 235
W. C. Ashburn, 30 70, 500, 60, 380
Reuben League, 40, 20, 300, 45, 280
Nancy Poston, 150, 160, 2000, 90, 1387
Isaac Baker, 75, 177, 500, 15, 400
C. O'Leary, 40, 600, 4000, 5, 165
Solomon Hilton, 60, 580, 640, 40, 325
A. J. Dobson, 17, 50, 100, 10, 80
Robert McGahan, -, -, -, 10, 125
George Kelley, -, -, -, 15, 90
John Rowan, 15, 25, 150, 10, 110
John Perry, 100, 620, 25000, 300, 1010
John P. Applebury, 36, 84, 500, 85, 350
Isaac Adams, 10, 30, 150, 5, 100
Victor Craig,-, -, -, 5, 85
Joshua Huerman, 20, 20, 200, 6, 170
D. M. Taylor, 170, 537, 1800, 74, 800
Theodore Bisch, 22, 800, 10000, 50, 235
Alexr. McMustreg, 10, 30, 100, 25, 210
J. M. Roberts, 40, 160, 1000, 55, 355
Wm. S. Roberts, 10, 30, 100, 5, 135
John Bentley, 2, 33, 100, 2, 110
Levi N. Walston, 35, 45, 200, 10, 230
Geo. Hilderbrand, 100, 310, 1800, 125, 600
Rhoda Murphy, 40, 120, 1000, 25, 295
Peter B. Pratte, 50, 430, 1500, 65, 230
Peter Janis, 20, 20, 250, 5, 125
Andrew Jones, 50, 680, 3000, 25, 136

Thomas Baile, 80, 512, 3000, 100, 650
Wm. McDowell, 15, 18, 150, 5, 145
Charles L. Edmunds, 70, 50, 800, 100, 255
Robert Ferguson, 20, 20, 150, 2, 65
Wm. Andrew, 14, 88, 300, 14, 215
Winfield Wright, 8, 32, 100, 50, 145
Jacob Shrum, 25, 55, 250, 7, 145
Samuel Shrum, 15, 25, 150, 5, 132
Orrin Munger, 25, 15, 200, 8, 190
Willis Edmunds, 30, 50, 350, 10, 130
Wm. Thurman, 10, 30, 100, 40, 110
Levi Shrum, 15, 25, 100, 5, 185
J. N. Russell, 40, 25, 20, 14, 178
L. P. Munger, 8, 42, 200, 10, 52
Daniel McNeal, -, -, -, 3, 55
Henry Strickland, 10, 30, 100, 15, 90
Daniel Hurt, 15, 65, 150, 10, 165
Wm. H. Andrew, 15, 65, 200, 10, 290
Joseph Hurt, 10, 30, 125, 5, 140
Elisha Stout, 8, 32, 80, 10, 75
Benj. McNeal, 20, 20, 300, 10, 270
Reuben Johnson, 12, 38, 200, 35, 111
Henry Bell, 50, 110, 500, 100, 215
John Bell, 40, 40, 200, 15, 425
John Harbison, 40, 120, 400, 25, 265
James Dennison, 15, 25, 150, 7, 190
Moses Carty, 30, 50, 400, 6, 170
Mary McClure, 20, 60, 200, 5, 120
David Adams, 35, 45, 300, 75, 165
E. H. Clayton, -, -, -, 50, 170
Nelson Adams, 30, 50, 350, 15, 220
Joseph Hampton, 12, 28, 400, 90, 140
William Huff, -, -, -, 2, 60
John Allevin, -, -, -, 60, 122
Wm. Palmer, 10, 30, 150, 3, 230
Jno. P. Haden, 34, 70, 1000, -, 120
John W. Hancock, 22, 58, 500, 115, 240
William Cantrell, -, -, -, 2, 65
Ann E. Callaway, 30, 50, 500, 60, 290
Wm. H. Thomas, 60, 54, 800, 60, 340
David Wiley, -, -, -, 10, 27
Nathan Trumbull, 20, 10, 300, 15, 56
Lewis Orrick, 20, 20, 150, 75, 130
Francis Clark, 40, 300, 1800, 75, 153
John B. Jones, 30, 70, 200, 15, 270

Fielding Snider, 15, 25, 100, 10, 90
Wm. Levingston, 10, 300, 80, 10, 150
J. H. Hoover, 20, 60, 400, 10, 140
Moses Elvins, 25, 15, 250, 33, 185
Ross. Jelkyl, 15, 25, 250, 15, 125
Abram Zolman, 30, 90, 565, 92, 250
D. Y. Swinney, 35, 125, 500, 90, 160
Susanna Powell, 30, 50, 500, 50, 177
G. W. Smith, 15, 80, 150, 30, 110
Calvin Chapman, 15, 25, 80, 8, 135
Abner Goen, 25, 50, 400, 80, 270
John Reysinger, 10, 30, 100, 35, 217
Rachol Meredith, 13, 67, 250, 10, 155
Mary Glendy, 60, 100, 700, 40, 130
Barnet Fry, 30, 50, 200, 15, 85
Henry Gaines, 15, 25, 125, 10, 110
Joel Zolman, 14, 106, 500, 75, 140
J. B. Perkins, 12, 108, 600, 70, 290
William Perkins, 15, 65, 400, 60, 200
M. M. Doughty, 25, 55, 800, 138, 177
J. G. Hunt, 21, 19, 120, 150, 475
Jas. Cunningham, 80, 70, 1500, 75, 525
Ann Mitchell, 50, 110, 600, 50, 325
B. M. Marshall, 40, 50, 400, 60, 180
Palitha Mitchell, 60, 60, 1000, 90, 310
W. S. Matkin, 10, 30, 150, 50, 295
H. Alexander, 35, 400, 200, 15, 200
James Mitchell, 30, 90, 1000, 100, 285
B. Huddleston, -, -, -, 5, 145
James Howerton, 50, 570, 50, 290
J. L. Taylor, 60, 300, 1500, 70, 265
Wm. Poston Sr., 80, 221, 1500, 55, 395
Sarah McHenry, 50, 80, 500, 65, 340
James Minter, 70, 54, 1200, 70, 302
Wm. Rogers, 100, 300, 1500, 40, 490
George Doggett, 25, 300, 1000, 15, 230
John Alley, 60, 150, 1500, 70, 250
Wm. Bryan, 10, 157, 700, 70, 270
Susan Crump, 50, 50, 250, 4, 280
R. J. Hill, 70, 50, 2000, 80, 350
Israel McGahan, 40, 300, 2000, 15, 77
F. Murphy, 30, 90, 300, 15, 180
F. Moon, 15, 65, 300, 2, 765
Wm. Whitehan, 40, 70, 500, 20, 300
Wm. Doggett, 20, 20, 150, 35, 210
P. A. Wigger, 20, 20, 150, 5, 125

J. B. Pratte, 40, 120, 500, 50, 135
E. Crump, 25, 15, 200, 25, 275
Geo. Crump, 20, 20, 200, 25, 240
John House, 10, 30, 100, 2, 102
Willis Armon, 20, 425, 1200, 10, 190
Thomas Hill, 50, 150, 500, 85, 250
Isaac Baker Sr., 250, 130, 4000, 125, 615
James Ransome, 100, 160, 1000, 75, 340
Wm. Evans, 45, 120, 1500, 80, 242
William Rix, 10, 40, 200, 10, 82
Wm. Spradling, 80, 80, 1000, 90, 640
G. Williams, 40, 40, 250, 50, 215
L. Boardwine, 60, 20, 500, 40, 2100
Joseph Coleman, 30, 60, 150, 50, 159
James Brim, 20, 20, 100, 8, 104
Lewis Sago, 6, 74, 100, 25, 195
George Hathhorn, 20, 60, 220, 100, 230
Z. Obuchon, 20, 60, 200, 10, 108
J. W. Clay, 30, 50, 240, 110, 240
John Williams, 15, 25, 80, 10, 265
John Totten, 10, 30, 100, 25, 187
Sarah Day, 35, 55, 300, 40, 285
R. P. Mitchell, 100, 165, 1000, 55, 160
Abner Bane, 30, 50, 240, 8, 150
J. Cunningham, 40, 40, 150, 70, 125
Luke Davis, 20, 20, 150, 40, 200
Thomas Sparks, 15, 25, 150, 50, 220
Lewis Sims, 80, 280, 2000, 150, 560
W. J. Lane, 20, 20, 100, 12, 145
Peter Denham, 6, 34, 50, 5, 185
Rankin Davis, 5, 79, 225, 40, 114
W. B. Bradshaw, 30, 40, 200, 20, 175
Henry Hodge, 10, 30, 100, 45, 58
John Simmons, 10, 30, 100, 5, 78
James Sims, 23, 97, 800, 100, 180
D. B. Coffman, 15, 25, 150, 7, 185
John Lane, 54, 106, 1000, 70, 425
H. Banister, 25, 15, 100, 25, 105
John Banister, 10, 30, 80, 5, 95
G. B. Gibson, 15, 25, 100, 5, 68
Wm. Banister, 20, 20, 150, 25, 145
Henry Harris, 25, 80, 200, 10, 142
John Wilson, 10, 30, 100, 5, 59
Henry Hampton, 30, 50, 250, 25, 246
Letty Stuart, -, -, -, 25, 210

C. Walton, 25, 84, 800, 75,185
Daniel Coffman, -, -, -, 10, 102
C. B. Cunningham, 115, 82, 1500, 300, 500
B. S. Kenner, 17, 63, 190, 5, 200
Hardy Koen, 100, 2045, 1300, 10, 400
Wm. Nelson, -, -, -, -, 125
Solomon Eaves, 30, 50, 225, 10, 189
Henry Mitchell, 20, 20, 150, 70, 210
Joshua Carter, 30, 50, 300, 12, 230
John Mayo, 40, 40, 200, 45, 185
L. B. Burns, 50, 30, 250, 75, 260
James Henderson, 24, 16, 150, 30, 425
A. J. Nance, -, -, -, -, 109
James Carter, 40, 40, 400, 35, 87
James Crawford, 30, 10, 150, 25, 147
Wm. Crawford, 20, 20, 150, 15, 146
E. G. Clay, 20, 70, 500, 100, 220
Wm. Reed, 80, 120, 1200, 100, 337
Noah Reed, -, -, -, 4, 50
Eleazar Clay, 100, 260, 5400, 200, 600
Alvin Rucker, 20, 70, 500, 100, 180
T. Davidson, 30, 10, 100, 30, 95
Reuben King, 30, 10, 100, 10, 195
George W. Brown, 15, 65, 300, 10, 161
James M. Brown, 35, 45, 500, 20, 405
Jesse Bounds, 40, 120, 1000, 75, 355
Henry L. Tullock, 110, 250, 2000, 200, 760
Absalom Dent, 80, 280, 3600, 280, 455
Nancy Dent, 100, 300, 4000, 150, 540
T. Grider, 95, 190, 2500, 200, 624
Nick Yates, 30, 190, 1000, 45, 228
John Crass, 15, 25, 150, 15, 180
Wm. Garret, 70, 180, 1000, 55, 478
David Gibson, 20, 156, 100, 10, 73
John Carter, 50, 70, 700, 70, 365
John Dent, 50, 220, 2000, 70, 328
James Ritter, 100, 50, 750, 60, 475
James Beard, 40, -, 200, 75, 295
Henry Beard, 30, 50, 150, 40, 156
John Young, 30, 50, 300, 85, 281
John Tullock, 55, 300, 1500, 185, 540
John Drennon, 30, 10, 150, 60, 178
Ann Meloy (McCoy), 40, 40, 400, 60, 160

David J. Meloy (McCoy), 100, 140, 1500, 100, 456
John Reed, 25, 100, 400, 15, 181
Josiah Egbert, 14, 26, 450, 10, 34
Thomas Wellborn, 100, 100, 1000, 65, 320
J. Alexander, 18, 62, 300, 15, 140
Lewis Renick, 24, 56, 300, 75, 222
J. D. Matkin, 20, 36, 200, 45, 203
Wm. Boyd, 11, 104, 500, 2, 75
G. Renick, 30, 130, 600, 60, 235
E. Matkin, 65, 145, 1000, 15, 288
C. T. Welborn, 20, 20, 200, 50, 150
Ben. Matkin, 25, 29, 250, 10, 225
R. H. Marks, 18, 62, 500, 60, 170
E. Robinson, 30, 170, 200, 10, 78
A. Vance, 11, 29, 100, 5, 15
John Reicus, 15, 25, 150, 10, 120
W. R. Vance, 100, 122, 1500, 20, 425
Andrew Beck, 25, 176, 1000, 75, 218
Jarvis Holstead, 20, 60, 300, 8, 173
Mary Burnham, 35, 55, 1500, 150, 476
A. Bennet, -, -, -, 10, 62
Tabitha Murphy, 100, 100, 1500, 55, 320
Elisha Hunt, 30, 50, 300, 8, 65
Robert Clay, 35, 45, 500, 100, 225
Josiah Link, 40, 40, 200, 35, 227
John Bressie, 12, 28, 150, 60, 298
John Davis, 30, 130, 480, 20, 350
Mary Estes, 50, 120, 700, 5, 58
Allen C. Cash, 10, 30, 100, 5, 86
Zeno Westover, 60, 460, 3500, 150, 730
Hiram Davis, 26, -, 100, 40, 348
J. Welborn, 50, 30, 1000, 60, 270
John Renick, 60, 88, 800, 60, 176
M. P. Cayce, 337, 652, 4600, 500, 1025
John Kennedy, 150, 300, 2500, 30, 847
Daniel Miller, 60, 140, 800, 20, 152
Elizabeth Walker, 75, 55, 1000, 20, 140
James Gregory, 16, 24, 200, 15, 205
R. Cleveland, 45, 35, 500, 110, 430
J. Copeland, 18, 62, 250, 10, 190
W. M. Swinny, 20, 60, 310, 15, 110

J. Milligan, 17, 63, 400, 40, 105
Moses Sebastian, 70, 130, 800, 100, 300
Hiram Matkin, 80, 160, 1000, 75, 490
R. Hutchings, 50, 138, 500, 50, 230

E. C. Sebastian, 120, 280, 4000, 300, 825
E. Arnold, 65, 215, 1500, 120, 225

St. Genevieve County, Missouri
1850 Agricultural Census

St. Genevieve County 1850 Agricultural Census was filmed by the Central Microfilm Service Corp of St. Louis, Missouri, for the Missouri State Historical Society. There are 46 columns of information on the 1850 agricultural census. I have chosen to transcribe six of those columns. The columns are:

1. Name
2. Acres of Land Improved
3. Acres of Land Unimproved
4. Cash Value of the Farm
5. Value of Farm Implements and Machinery
13. Value of Livestock

Sebastian Ziegler, 220, 240, 2000, 50, 130
Antoine Lalemundin, 20, 100, 500, 50, 230
Isaac Thomas, 25, 80, 200, 50, 165
Henry Laruse, 20, -, 100, 30, 100
Ant. Thomas, 20, -, 100, 40, 100
Bto. Lalemundine, 10, 50, 125, 20, 120
Joseph Thomas, 20, 60, 160, 30, 130
John Ribauh, 15, -, 150, 30, 170
Benj. Wilson, 18, -, 180, 10, 40
Titus Strickland, 80, 65, 300, 10, 70
Auguste St. Gernne, 80, 600, 900, 100, 400
Jacab Auguste, 20, -, 100, 10, 104
E. J. Govrro, 25, 50, 250, 50, 165
B. C. Amarne, 40, -, 400, 250, 600
Felix Varri (Vaui, Valli), 75, 2000, 6000, 100, 100
Eugene Guiband, 40, -, 150, 50, 210
Jno. Thomas, 26, 40, 150, 30, 180
Peter Morice, 12, -, 50, 15, 125
Lumis(Lomis, Lewis) Andrew, 30, -, 150, 25, 170
Buthal Seebich, 10, -, 50, 50, 200
John Seate(Scott), 15, 550, 650, 50, 475
Gabriel Thomas, 35, 100, 1000, 60, 121
Jno. B. Larass, 14,-, 70, 10, 150
Joseph Bautilit, 10, -, 50, 75, 145
F. B. Valli, 22, 136, 279, 50, 312

John Caupli__, 20, -, 100, 20, 100
Clay LeCompte, 127, 1300, 3250, 200, 940
Mary Bagy, 300,-, 600, 50, 140
__enis Zigler, 15, 150, 500, 41, 550
Joseph Moro, 100, 1500, 7000, 200, 950
Peter Moro, 80, 80, 640, 52, 600
Melanie Valis(Valli), 140, -, 280, 40, 170
John Moran, 22, -, 200, 44, 325
And. Crisnce(Crisace), 23, -, 150, 37, 220
Louis Laraso, 30, -, 100, 22,181
Frais Sumisa(Surnison), 15, 35, 250, 82, 311
Btc. V. Bovuis, 35, 60, 175, 28, 285
Michael Crisace, 105, 295, 800, 72, 281
Mary J. Surmisa, 20, -, 100, 7, 114
Austin Bice, 30, -, 150, 11, 62
John Suicik, 218, 247, 1200, 100, 1146
Gail Fraring, 50, -, 250, 18, 259
Gab Culciah, 16, -, 100, 15, 125
Arch. Carntois, 27, -, 135, 15, 40
Thos. S. McKee, 24, -, 168, 22, 251
William Hunlin, 10, -, 70, 33, 285
John C. Taylor, 50, -, 350, 35, 225
Joseph Dold (Dowl), 27, -, 200, 28, 122
Mengurih Davis, 18,-, 100, 10, 114
Henry Senno, 18, -, 100, 25, 126
Chas. W. Thomas, 22, -, 170, 28, 126

Travis Durand, 25, 60, 600, 73, 290
Joseph Thurmond, 20, -, 100, 30, 108
Evelin(Enubin) Laraso, 16, -, 170, 18, 159
Alexr. Laraso, 18, -, 100, 19, 88
S. E. Raussin, 125, -, 700, 150, 400
William Bice, 18, -, 150, 30, 173
Francis Dald, 18, -, 100, 25, 112
Marie Lakelumdin(Lalemundin), 25, 215, 500, 28, 153
Louis Baguette, 22, 44, 500, 27, 212
Christian Rath, 200, 160, 4000, 49, 200
Joseph Lungelin, 24, -, 100, 32, 170
Michael Hinsh, 30, 240, 500, 12, 119
Robert Blackwell, 35, 52,200, 39, 451
Cal. C. Crane, 60, 170, 1000, 10, 125
H. N. Kelly, 35, 135, 1000, 15, 110
Nab Bridgerand, 35, 165, 1100, 200, 483
Cath. Bauman, 50, 80, 600, 78, 394
Bribe Lakelumdin (Lalemundin), 20, 220, 200, 13, 157
Erkaul Kluie, 50, 150, 500, 5, 55
Mary Rath, 50, 150, 500, 10, 51
John Montgomery, 65, 85, 1500, 92, 332
And. Rath, 25, -, 150, 32, 122
Jervais Johenlab, 60, 121, 1000, 85, 266
Joseph Keifer, 30, 120, 400, 84, 165
Severin Eckunflg, 15, 65, 200, 28, 57
George Saxlinbin, 18, 22, 200, 24, 169
George Kutlaf, 25, 15, 200, 40, 168
Gabriel Borges, 15, 35, 400, 20, 125
Henney Burger, 20, -, 100, 55, 100
Baph Thomas, 20, -, 200, 54, 171
Louis Gerero, 25, -, 125, 30, 116
Peter Thomas, 15, 38, 200, 10, 75
Peter Maser, 25, 100, 500, 60, 114
Berthal Swindle, 30, 90, 600, 45, 165
Thomas Hoag, 40, 800, 1000, 29, 233
And. Jakush, 25, 100, 500, 35, 192
And. Herman, 30, 70, 500, 25, 90
Peter Dorlac, 20, 100, 800, 83, 392
Ang. Labruegue, 35, 365, 100, 65, 173
Simon Gracs (Cracs), 26, 54, 500, 30, 167
Henry Seibush, 30, 90, 300, 100, 191
Fleurnis Huck, 80, 169, 400, 60, 185

Bernard Jakush, 100, 600, 2500, 145, 428
Paul Guithy, 20, 100, 300, 45, 200
Jacob Stuppy, 40, 80, 300, 125, 166
Nick Jakush (Jakust), 80, 45, 500, 82, 135
Mathias Nager, 50, 190 700, 41, 216
John Crider, 28, 92, 600, 34, 183
Michael Fischer, 28, 52, 500, 35, 175
Peter Vaith, 40, 90, 700, 80, 251
John Missic, 40, 40, 500, 200, 325
Philip Stunb, 30, 90, 600, 30, 185
Louis Wilder, 22, 58, 400, 30, 135
Bindh Hulin, 30, 130, 500, 62, 125
Joseph Gaeck, 30, 110, 400, 50, 199
Lorance Jakush(Jakust), 30, 60, 400, 30, 213
Joseph Boyer, 25, 15, 200, 10, 224
Travis (Frois) Thumin, 25, 35, 150, 20, 179
Jacob Bashe, 12, 68, 200, 30, 96
Peter Tronstrum, 13, 20, 125, 15, 130
Frois F. Gerero(Goverd), 15, 35, 200, 40, 200
John Bashe, 55, 70, 500, 45, 185
John Eascasinian, 30, 50, 800, 50, 225
Joseph Hoganison, 30, 107, 150, 32, 246
Jeb Gandu, 30, -, 150, 35, 165
Frank Richend, 35,-, 175, 32, 169
Nick Gushaln, 18, -, 125, 10, 147
Caspar Carl, 30, 43, 500, 35, 132
Chas. D. Nacci, 16, 18, 300, 41, 111
Joseph Biser, 30, 50, 400, 45,188
Isadora Girshater, 40, 100, 400, 50, 150
Thois X. Gaick, 28, 54, 500, 45, 217
Carl Fucen, 40, 40, 500, 48, 388
Thois C. Vacci, 35, 15, 300, 40, 224
And. Schinger, 40, 40, 50, 40, 171
Joseph Swink, 28, 52, 600 70, 305
Joseph Frednand, 30, 50, 700, 40, 150
Thois. Racts, 25, 125, 600, 25, 129
Val Humern, 25, 200, 1000, 30, 246
Olivis Penel, 30, 120, 600, 40, 159
Simon Fitzcom, 45, 65, 600, 200, 251
Henry Greithy, 25, 275, 800, 40, 195
Joseph Rheino, 30, 50, 200, 90, 185

Aush Weiler, 12, 75, 100, 10, 50

Chas. Seebul, 26, 54, 200, 90 161

Peter Mae, 30, 82, 400, 40, 91

John Staikly, 18, -, 100, 28, 111

Frois Hugoe(Hagoe), 18, 130, 400, 49, 118

Elisabeth Kuchen, 20, -, 150, 90, 295

Enus Palmern, 10, 30, 200, 30, 41

William Skeens, 200, 1400, 5000, 250, 624

George Fack, 25, 15, 300, 20, 168

Martin Burk(Bush), 25, 19, 300, 50, 185

August Hugoe, 18, 70, 150, 30, 72

Paul Keltn, 16, 64, 154, 30, 86

Adam Swartz, 30, 73, 200, 20, 298

Joseph Hagoe, 30, 50, 300, 60, 138

Mathias Seveis, 40, 80, 250, 100, 300

Joseph Schilln, 50, 90, 800, 77, 214

Henry Cunnifer(Cunniperd), 30, 50, 400, 20, 85

Ant. Nuyn(Nugro), 20, 47, 300, 23, 83

Fidel Pulum, 30, 60, 500, 30, 183

August Seibuch, 40, 110, 300, 60, 178

Simon Kempfy, 40, 40, 600, 60, 189

George Woerend, 30, 57, 600, 80, 166

Jacob Rock(Rath), 50, 50, 400, 100, 152

Lorance Suches, 40, 160, 600 70, 323

George Grass, 24, 57, 300, 47, 137

John Gaithly, 24, 96, 30, 25, 157

Godfrey Ochlis, 12, 68, 200, 12, 71

Peter Busler, 10, 30, 150, 20, 80

Louis Laraso Jr., 22, -, 150, 25, 107

Amis Laraso, 100, 160, 1000, 93, 654

Henny Banty, 200, 5600, 4000, 100, 350

Alex. Morice, 25, 55, 300, 30, 135

John B. Boyn, 30, 17, 600, 30, 203

Joseph Dill, 80, 70, 1800, 48, 160

Ed. D. Janis, 28, 92, 800, 28, 206

Alex. Bruger, 18, -, 100, 50, 175

Auh Govne, 12, -, 75, 25, 106

Eli Lalumindine, 15,-, 75, 45, 149

Jno. B. Lalumindine, 110, 120, 1500, 140, 618

Auh Farrish, 100, 207, 1500, 100, 434

Frois Janis, 40, 160, 1500, 50, 205

Lewis V. Bogy, 150, -, 5000, 500, 700

Willis Y. Owsly, 40, 60, 800, 50, 640

F. J. Kettinger, 50, 70, 1000, 100, 282

Peter Bequetre, 50, 150, 800, 10, -

Auh. Ulmiston, 24, -, 100, 10, 100

John M. Godin, 25, -, 100, 18, 350

Auh(Anh) Kist, 30, -, 250, 44, 200

William Holmes, 90, 110, 600, 170, 500

John Farleigh, 25, -, 1100, 15, 174

William P. Wade, 35, -, 100, 40, 100

A. H. Tucker, 40, -, 250, 60, 305

Ignatius Boarman, 35, -, 350, 30, 244

Mary A. Valle, 40, 660, 700, 15, 225

J. S. Brown, 75, 418, 2000, 50, 65

Joseph Coffman Jr., 75, 418, 2000, 50, 665

Francis Thomuse, 40, -, 100, 35, 220

Joseph Griffith, 75, 40, 500, 75, 557

Harman Williams, 15, 45, 100, 25, 138

Louis Griffas, 36, 120, 500, 28, 254

James Brown, 40, 120, 700, 20, 120

Absolem Robey, 26, -, 100, 5, 70

Valentine Underwood, 100, 150, 1500, 100, 599

Peter Hernden, 30, 40, 150, 15, 143

Antoine Janis, 250, 800, 5000, 300, 825

William M. Mead, 8, -, 50, 20, 145

Vallentine Bearland, 30, 200, 500, 10, 114

Wesley Farleigh, 80, 185, 600, 50, 548

John Kemper, 20, -, 100, 10, 205

Manuel Smith, 24, 156, 600, 30, 375

William A. Brown, 30, 270, 600, 20, 114

M. A. Gilbert, 50, 1425, 8000, 200, 500

B. S. Pratte, 70, 640, 5000, 100, 275

C. C. Keolegan, 125, 750, 1500, 300, 625

Burwell Johnson, 65, 162, 1200, 70, 10

Eveline Duval, 75, 125, 800, 44, 220

Kavin Byrne, 160, 1540, 4000, 157, 715

John P. Bearland, 20, 60, 200, 25, 199

A. W. Farleigh, 50, 100, 500, 30, 194

George Hurst, 16, -, 100, 32, 142

George Scott, 25, -, 125, 65, 371

Joseph P. Hunt, 12, 72, 300, 51, 175

Abner Baugh, 45, -, 600, 20, 150

James Townsley, 17, -, 80, 8, 160

William Townsley, 14, -, 75, 7, 84
James Hand, 30, -, 200, 75, 327
Robert Holaday, 20, -, 100, 5, 90
John S. Beard, 60, 60, 800, 80, 468
Robert B. Griffith, 60, 140, 1000, 80, 492
Ignatius Boarman, 110, 90, 1000, 90, 521
Philip Barry, 12, -, 100, 10, 123
William James, 150, 350, 3000, 100, 682
George Geesler, 10, 30, 100, 15, 102
D. M. Anderson, 40, 40, 600, 89, 460
William Hancock, 40, -, 200, 40, 157
Absolem Hart, 10, -, 75, 77, 280
Wm. C. Varner, 80, 290, 1400, 187, 852
Housan Kenner, 90, 240, 3000, 30, 340
William Beard, 20, -, 100, 15, 59
Antoine Obuchon, 23, -, 125, 30, 110
Etienne Goore, 45, 125, 700, 35, 247
Pelagis Langelier, 25, 15, 300, 27, 195
Joseph Westell, 18, 42, 500, 20, 308
John H. Berry, 15, -, 75, 11, 137
James Pinkley, 15, 65, 100, 21, 131
George Smootz, 29, 9, 200, 15, 134
John D. Holley, 16, -, 100, 25, 85
John Coffman, 275, 325, 4000, 300, 1355
William Bloom, 30, 10, 200, 15, 160
Peter Bloom, 60, 83, 900, 80, 618
William Bryan, 80, 50, 700, 50, 870
Talton Robinson, 18, -, 150, 15, 125
Francis Obuchon, 70, 180, 1300, 115, 401
James Alexander, 20, -, 150, 15, 146
Thomas Bryan, 80, 260, 2500, 85, 1095
Samuel B. Runnells, 40, -, 150, 12, 175
John Abshire, 18, -, 100, 10, 152
Edmond B. Beard, 40, 80, 500, 55, 232
James Ballard, 20, -, 200, 20, 191
Francis Hauthorn, 70, 210, 800, 177, 583
William S. Boke, 20, -, 200, 45, 291
Aaron Counts, 45, 135, 800, 80, 356
John Boyd, 30, 90, 300, 54, 350
William G. Boyd, 60, 20, 300, 45, 110
Enos Hammers, 40, -, 125, 15, 129
Jobe May Berry, 25, 125, 800, 15, 170

Samuel Hughes, 8, -, 100, 8 199
Louis Griffas, 60, 100, 600, 10, 153
Dudly Horn, 60, 140, 600, 12, 155
A. G. Jones, 60, 140, 900, 78, 330
Nicolas Heberly, 100, 120, 1500, 70, 585
Gilearl Sayphaw, 20, -, 100, 18, 315
B. Pflager, 20, 20, 150, 20, 141
George Leech, 90, 93, 2000, 63, 314
Hiram Blockledge, 85, 595, 2500, 35, 425
Elliott Boyd, 27, 133, 500, 20, 161
James Young, 24, 94, 400, 48, 175
George H. Madison, 25, -, 250, 25, 378
Joel Counts, 35, 107, 600, 20, 173
John Hadock, 16, 24, 250, 8, 91
John W. Church, 35, -, 150, 18, 87
Ellis Counts, 23, -, 250, 12, 170
Martha Counts, 10, -, 150, 10, 141
Aaron Counts, 15, -, 75, -, 147
William Womac, 27, 15, 300, 31, 115
Henry Counts, 24, 96, 600, 20, 170
Uel Jackson, 85, 155, 900, 94, 249
William Couzens, 100, 100, 900, 212, 564
James W. Counts, 22, -, 100, 15, 103
James Holmes, 25, 112, 600, 100, 292
L. B. Paterson, 20, 40, 400, 70, 245
P G. Keith, 30, 89, 450, 25, 157
Charles Maddin, 100, 900, 4500, 60, 511
Ralph Levenworth, 40, -, 400, 75, 228
Anthony Henn, 20, 140, 500, 43, 165
Henry Harter, 20, 20, 200, 40, 108
James Daniels, 40, 80, 600, 29, 251
Robert Miller, 100, 100, 1500, 186, 711
William Evans, 120, 100, 1000, 98, 720
Jeremiah Haney, 35, -, 175, 137, 196
Joseph Coffman, 850, 3150, 16700, 580, 2240
William Townsand, 60, 100, 550, 39, 231
John L. Hanes, 25, -, 200, 15, 126
William Bosler, 40, -, 500, 20, 142
Peter Falk, 20, 60, 250, 40, 75
Simon Leiturt, 30, 50, 300, 30, 100
Augustine Smither, 24, 56, 250, 30, 145

Philip Keifer, 22, -, 250, 30, 180
Joel L. Counts, 15, -, 100, 17, 418
William Swink, 80, 120, 700, 65, 518
Zebe Evans, 12, -, 75, 8, 205
John Cannon, 30, -, 100, 6, 178
Hughes Cannon, 16, -, 100, 5, 92
Jeremiah Robinson, 100, 220, 600, 50, 431
Thomas McCollum, 25, 55, 300, 10, 162
W. F. Donaldson, 80, 192, 1000, 110, 350
Catherine Resinger, 12, 28, 200, 41, 170
Joseph McGlauthlen, 20, -, 175, 10, 116
John F. Rudy, 20, 20, 300, 15, 104
Jonathan Chandler, 35, 205, 1000, 12, 223
W. R. Laws, 38, 42, 300, 12, 119
W. H. Shephard, 20, 60, 300, 112, 205
Wm. Covington, 30, -, 150, 10, 98
Davis Laseter, 25, 135, 500, 79, 80
Hudson Davis, 11, -, 150, 12, 85
Nicolas Conner, 17, 63, 150, 10, 116
Cristopher Aiden, 25, 95, 600, 82, 228
Thomas Elders, 25, -, 200, 125, 368
Jacob Rickard, 35, 85, 300, 40, 174
Jos. Vansickles, 45, 75, 800, 150, 395
James B. Adams, 50, 230, 660, 60, 189
Lucas Bahle, 40, 40, 500, 42, 180
William Hinkle, 20, 20, 150, 28, 117
James H. Edwards, 10,-, 75, 12, 69
William Pinkston, 18, -, 100, 50, 188
Wm. H. Edwards, 22, -, 150, 125, 120
Job T. Poe, 30, 10, 250, 9, 80
Henry Wallace, 28, 27, 200, 85, 285
Martin Lunsford, 50, -, 600, 35, 239
David Pinkston, 35, 105, 700, 100, 400
Julie Lussource, 50, 450, 1200, 35, 266
Wm. Wolridge, 30, 50, 250, 25, 282
John Lachance, 16, 24, 150, 29, 71
Andrew Thurmon, 40, -, 200, 100, 306
A. H. Janis, 22, 10, 100, 30, 121
Abraham Pullem, 25, 60, 1000, 150, 235
Zac. Turley, 55, 40, 400, 94, 469
R. R. Laseter, 40, 213, 600, 45, 243
J. N. Harris, 22, -, 150, 18, 155
R. B. Turley, 45, 130, 600, 65, 355

W. O. Edwards, 75, 85, 800, 83, 444
Lot. W. Turley, 25, -, 200, 50, 230
William Williams, 30, 189, 700, 94, 195
Alex. S. Jennings, 60, 281, 1000, 108, 456
James Parkes, 20, 100, 400, 15, 147
W. P. Doss, 70, 130, 800, 135, 719
John Hunt, 30, -, 150, 15, 105
Robt. P. Gentry, 45, 35, 400, 100, 311
Alfred Doss, 28, 122, 500, 60, 212
William Horn, 38, 130, 325, 58, 203
Charles Burks, 120, 380, 2000, 150, 726
Cordel Horn, 30, 50, 20, 10, 151
Wilson Laws, 30, 50, 400, 65, 225
Jas. F. Hurry, 35, 245, 1400, 75, 233
George Taylor, 195, 1200, 3000, 200, 1027
J. D. P. Freeman, 60, 150, 700, 105, 365
Thos. F. Edwards, 40, 160, 500, 150, 250
John Burkes, 35, 115, 800, 100, 257
J. H. Grady, 78, 310, 1500, 40, 190
Wm. Sebastian, 30, 100, 500, 100, 295
Doswell Wright, 20, -, 75, 35, 92
Jesse J. Edwards, 60, 430, 1500, 100, 1077
J. E. Patterson, 60, 575, 2000, 60, 202
Joseph Herrod, 35, 230, 475, 10, 100
Richard Candif, 25, 115, 300, 35, 161
Mary Blue, 40, 240, 1500, 45, 306
Samuel Herrod, 50, 150, 2000, 50, 170
Z. B. Jennings, 20, 40, 250, 10, 122
William Usky, 40, 320, 1500, 10, 222
Ramsey Watts, 27, -, 100, 9, 90
John Byington, 18, 182, 400, 49, 147
Mrs. E. Byington, 20, 220, 450, 18, 158
J. B. Clardy, 150, 850, 4000, 100, 620
Mary O. Drury, 100, 250, 1500, 84, 235
John Drury, 9, 31, 100, -, 152
Paul Calliot, 12, 68, 200, 30, 145
Henry Cuningham, 30, -, 150, 72, 319
John McClenahan, 25, -, 150, 65, 225
Edward Coats, 25, 50, 300, 150, 422
Woodson Jennings, 22, -, 100, 10, 285
S. C. Hennings, 50, 56, 300, 22, 270
Moise Obuchon, 22, 35, 150, 17, 90

Leon Obuchon, 20, 14, 200, 36, 110
Bazile Boyes, 80, 219, 800, 37, 288
Bte. B. Boyes(Boyer), 15, -, 50, 10, 101
Hiram Smith, 25, -, 125, 5, 63
Toussin Lahaie, 25, 75, 1000, 40, 188
James F. Dutton, 40, -, 200, 45, 280
Isaac Placet, 25, 55, 200, 15, 160
Melanie Calliot, 55, 225, 1200, 32, 322
Francis Carron, 20, -, 100, 36, 153
J. B. Charleville, 50, 70, 800, 43, 77
Louis Roassin, 24, 96, 300, 20, 178
Francis Roussin, 30, 50, 400, 20, 186
Atanase Carron, 20, 60, 300, 15, 257
Felix Dufour, 14, -, 100, 30, 151
M. McClenahan, 73, 167, 1500, 116, 565
William Patton, 13, 67, 100, 10, 105
Mic McClenahan, 23, 9, 200, 19, 210
William Taylor, 28, -, 300, 10, 267
Jane Williams, 16, -, 100, 10, 120
John Lee, 60, 328, 1000, 100, 300

Robt. B. Akens, 20, -, 125, 15, 152
Henry McMullin, 30, 10, 300, 8, 120
Rebecca Wines, 20, -, 100, 10, 167
Louis G. Berry, 20, 60, 300, 38, 232
Felix T. Poston, 23, 57, 500, 70, 317
Nuton O. Edwards, 14, -, 100, 10, 233
James Morris, 30, 250, 900, 45, 370
Peter Primo, 30, 90, 400, 50, 384
James Mordock, 24, 108, 400, 13, 310
Joseph Carron, 60, 140, 600, 92, 405
L. Williamson, 30, 160, 450, 6, 93
Fred Pyatt, 21, 19, 250, 40, 225
Robert J. Bous, 60, 1940, 5000, 200, 415
Fr. Lalamendiex Jr., 12, -, 75, 15, 150
Louis Lalumendiex, 30, 50, 200, 25, 250
Fr. Lalumendiex Sr., 10, 30, 200, 15, 114
Julien David, 20, 100, 400, 15, 152
Elie Janis, 25, -, 125, 40, 151
Benjamin Baldwin, 20, -, 100, 20, 170

St. Louis County, Missouri
1850 Agricultural Census

St. Louis County 1850 Agricultural Census was filmed by the Central Microfilm Service Corp of St. Louis, Missouri, for the Missouri State Historical Society. There are 46 columns of information on the 1850 agricultural census. I have chosen to transcribe six of those columns. The columns are:

1. Name
2. Acres of Land Improved
3. Acres of Land Unimproved
4. Cash Value of the Farm
5. Value of Farm Implements and Machinery
13. Value of Livestock

Henry Stodard, 39, -, 20000, 10, 800
Lesers Bissell, 250, 50, 50000, 250, 600
John Gena Bryan, 160, 40, 40000, 200, 640
John O'Fallon, 1660, 800, 120000, 400, 1800
Michael Shehan, 40, -, -, 50, 10
Francis Galey, 65, -, -, 100, 325
George M. Doggett, 33, -, 4000, 100, 400
Mathias V. Stigers, 110, -, 25000, 200, 2700
John Baker, 130, 8, 6000, 100, 450
Garrett H. Williamson, 18, 34, 1000, 100, 265
Henry Moke, 22, 13, 1000, 100, 120
Robert N. Martin, 203, 28, 9240, 450, 1520
William Terry, 33, 47, 1500, 30, 77
James Reubee, 50, -, -, 75, 265
Rachael Vanleer, 50, 110, 3200, 50, 300
James M. Link, 40, 90, 3900, 100, 224
John G. Cook, 125, -, 1250, 250, 717
George Hall, 147, 71, 230, 200, 575
George M. Moore, 100, 220, 33000, 200, 400
John B. Davis, 100, 32, 6000, 150, 500
Johnson Post, 150, 75, 9000, 75, 750
Erastus Pitt(Patt), 40, 100, 5600, 150, 450

Catharine Marten, 30, 28, 5000, 100, 425
William Palmer, 70, 130, 10000, 150, 300
William H. Eads, 100, -, -, 250, 1530
Elizabeth Avery, 40, 45, 2000, 50, 205
Mary Williams, 50, 22, 2500, 100, 270
John Carter, 46, 50, 3000, 70, 455
George W. March, 75, 90, 4500, 200, 630
Oliver H. Perry, 100, 96, 6000, 200, 900
Lewis Zasti(Yasti), 100, 450, 15000, 150, 740
Silvester Chovan, 40, 37, 1000, 50, 325
Lewis Beaupried, 60, 110, 2000, 75, 130
Olly Williams, 70, 200, 10000, 200, 1140
Nathaniel Covington, 80, 95, 4000, 100, 300
Robert C. Lucky, 35, 65, 2000, 75, 260
John Evans, 25, 210, 2000, 100, 240
William Mahon, 20, 16, 800, 75, 200
Henry Vohlhousen, 25, 30, 1000, 75, 125
Phillip Kerker, 30, 25, 500, 50, 200
George L. Lackland, 125, 100, 10000, 250, 610
James S. Quisenbery, 150, 100, 10000, 200, 800

Walker D. Shumate, 75, 100, 5000, 150, 2275

James Brackenridge, 200, 15, 10000, 150, 515

John L. Furgason, 90, 94, 6500, 200, 778

Joseph G. Lakeman, 45, 85, 5200, 150, 925

Lewellen Brown, 120, 255, 19000, 500, 1025

George L. Davis, 20, 20, 1700, 225, 395

Hampton Looker, 100, 36, 6800, 200, 490

John T. Stinson, 32, 8, 2000, 100, 160

David M. Martin, 200, 100, 12000, 500, 1645

Martin Douglass, 75, 95, 6800, 200, 902

Antoine Gartin, 40, 237, 3000, 100, 400

Joseph Garrett, 100, 150, 9000, 200, 626

Antoine Creely, 45, 48, 2000, 300, 220

James Ball, 186, -, -, 100, 395

S. F. Bonfils, 90, 110, 5000, 150, 250

George W. Sullivan, 160, 150, 12400, 300, 960

John Havener, 60, 40, 4000, 100, 340

James C. Edwards, 300, 156, 25000, 500, 1400

Zehorada J. Musick, 40, 50, 3000, 75, 250

Amable St. Cin, 80, 100, 5000, 150, 355

Richard Lucas, 26, 19, 2000, 80, 120

Prestley Martin, 50, -, 2500, 100, 200

Lewis Martin, 200, -, 6500, 60, 260

John Howdeshell, 100, 177, 10000, 120, 826

Franklin P. Utz, 25, 336, 15000, 200, 1045

Levi Smith, 110, 200, 5000, 200, 700

John Rant, 65, 105, 7000, 250, 746

Francis Creely, 60, 40, 4000, 100, 300

Stanislaus College Farm, 175, 55, 10000, 300, 1100

Joseph Presse, 20, -, 1000, 60, 710

John P. Dawson, 35, -, 1500, 75, 180

Francis Tesson, 25, -, 1500, 100, 150

Frank Obuchon, 40, 30, 2500, 75, 200

Charles Mercier, 70, 30, 4000, 150, 340

Pierre Merishall, 50, 28, 2000, 50, 100

Smith Miner, 100, -, 4000, 120, 235

Sarah E. Graham, 166, 50, 10750, 250, 1360

Richard Graham, 850, 587, 40000, 800, 2220

John B. Payter, 145, 60, 8000, 200, 820

Savara Ruell, 32, 20, 1200, 50, 300

Bernard Hanley, 130, 150, 12000, 300, 820

John Peron, 40, 13, 1000, 75, 205

Bernard Fortin, 45, 5, 1200, 10, 270

Leurs Mantre, 17, 10, 170, 75, 100

Lewis Larlett, 17, 5, 200, 75, 100

Marcus Beller, 25, 7, 1000, 75, 200

Gregory Obuchon, 120, 42, 2000, 110, 200

John B. Chappee, 35, 15, 1000, 70, 150

John Obuchon, 50, 15, 1000, 70, 130

Agustus Alvarez, 69, -, 2000, 75, 250

Bernard McMannamy, 400, 230, 25000, 200, 4730

George Hume, 100, 125, 9000, 200, 971

P. A. Wise, 100, 125, 10000, 200, 400

James Miller, 100, 175, 15000, 250, 650

Henry Duncan, 50, 102, 5000, 100, 422

Carter Moss, 60, 130, 6000, 100, 428

Thomas January, 600, 460, 40000, 1000, 6000

Andrew Harper, 500, 35, 21000, 400, 1715

Charles Chambers, 140, 160, 15000, 200, 1290

John B. Behnar, 40, -, 1000, 100, 150

John B. Bogart, 28, -, 1000, 100, 300

Augustus Fargus, 20, -, 900, 100, 180

Vatter Earnco, 55, 12, 1200, 80, 270

John Eavans, 180, 330, 15600, 450, 1070

Joseph Patterson, 35, 125, 3000, 200, 440

David Patterson, 50, 50, 5000, 200, 525

John Northern, 45, 125, 3000, 100, 200

Mary Patterson, 50, 150, 4000, 50, 200

Alford Hodges, 40, -, 1600, 150, 400

Sarah Blackburn, 70, 200, 6000, 150, 400

William R. Hyatt, 75, 400, 2000, 140, 250

Joseph L. Hyatt, 100, 140, 7000, 250, 200

Lewis F. Hume, 45, 45, 3000, 150, 220

William James, 50, 190, 5000, 100, 340

Clement Brown, 25, 63, 200, 60, 150

James James, 50, 230, 2000, 30, 250

Mariah Douglass, 80, 90, 2500, 150, 460

Elizabeth Blackburn, 25, 127, 2000, 50, 140

Thomas M. Tunstall, 100, 200, 15000, 200, 950

Warrick Tunstall, 300, 450, 20000, 256, 1840

Mary Davis, 100, 1200, 7000, 100, 300

Alexander Davidson, 40, -, 1200, 100, 250

Frederick Hyatt, 150, 250, 12000, 350, 1500

Leurs Hume, 155, 315, 15000, 100, 300

Edward Hall, 90, 110, 6000, 200, 800

Elisha Patterson 160, 300, 12000, 200, 820

William Patterson, 65, 170, 5000, 100, 350

Henry Payne, 40, 130, 6000, 100, 500

Robert Wash, 292, 395, 100000, 500, 1350

John Lay, 130, 60, 35000, 500, 1000

Martin Wash, 125, 100, 10000, 300, 650

Thomas Hoke, 50, 122, 5000, 300, 675

Christian Hienlon, 50, 50, 20000, 150, 265

George Renkel, 4, 5, 8000, 100, 300

Thomas Pagen, 80, 150, 20000, 200, 100

Charles Semple, 65, 200, 25000, 100, 760

Marshal Brotherton, 200, 800, 40000, 600, 3575

Haskel Alexander, 50, 110, 4000, 100, 500

William Gardener, 600, 400, 4000, 300, 925

James Jenings, 320, 2000, 60000, 1000, 920

James Redman, 100, 120, 12000, 800, 1200

Thomas F. Blair, 100, 300, 40000, 500, 1340

John R. Walker, 450, 500, 30000, 800, 1200

Elza H. Rose, 80, 80, 5600, 200, 520

Rolla F. Rose, 28, 32, 2400, 7, 235

Charles Barg, 15, 5, 1000, 150, 280

Phillip Webb, 16, 10, 1000, 156, 250

David Stune, 10, 10, 800, 100, 200

William Frantz, 30, 20, 1500, 150, 150

Christoph Frantz, 20, 20, 1500, 150, 260

French Rayburn, 350, 350, 28000, 400, 850

James B. Walker, 150, 170, 12000, 450, 700

William Wise, 180, 20, 10000, 200, 650

John Long, 15, 12, 1400, 100, 200

Peter Long, 15, 12, 1400, 20, 100

Agustus Brazo, 60, 220, 9000, 150, 350

William L. Dickman, 30, 50, 4000, 100, 220

James R. Bessell, 400, 750, 57000, 350, 1600

James Fry, 90, 130, 10000, 200, 150

John Dyson, 60, 80, 7000, 200, 500

James Adams, 25, 80, 4000, 100, 310

James Carson, 50, 50, 6000, 250, 350

John M. Wilson, 150, 200, 10000, 250, 550

Benjamin G. Watkens, 100, 137, 7000, 200, 490

John S. Wilson, 25, 75, 3000, 100, 400

Powel Sinks, 90, 210, 6000, 100, 300

Domitelle H. Vrain, 40, 110, 2250, 150, 500

James Murphy, 40, 60, 1000, 100, 270

Henry G. Franklin, 18, 32, 500, 100, 150

John Crow, 30, 12, 550, 20, 150

James B. Walker, 40, -, 600, 80, 205

Henry W. Carter, 85, 29, 2000, 100, 540

Thomas R. Musick, 27, -, 300, 100, 205

James A. Husbands, 70, 80, 1500, 100, 225

William Bealeys, 15, -, 200, 10, 50

Walter Carrico, 120, 42, 4000, 200, 600

Burr Fugate, 125, 90, 5000, 200, 700

Jacob Veale, 80, 134, 3500, 130, 530

Thomas Booth, 20, 30, 1000, 75, 150

Joseph D. Reid, 33, 23, 900, 100, 125

William Ruff, 40, 45, 1000, 150, 200

Hugh L. Henshaw, 30, 55, 1000, 150, 270

Susanah James, 25, -, 500, 100, 230

John M. Patterson, 25, -, 500, 150, 150

James Lattamore, 35, 100, 1000, 150, 550

Thomas C. Baker, 80, 80, 4500, 150, 710

David Shepperd, 50, 116, 3500, 150, 185

John B. Chappee, 40, 32, 1500, 100, 350

John B. Hubert, 65, 30, 800, 100, 620

John H. Twillman, 37, 30, 600, 60, 220

William Twillman, 100, 60, 3000, 200, 400

Reuben Musick, 200, 27, 7000, 200, 2500

Patrick Loughin, 34, 67, 3000, 100, 140

Frederick Price, 95, 90, 8000, 150, 500

Alexander Lober, 70, 92, 3510, 150, 254

Harman Rosenhetter, 27, -, 500, 100, 200

Emelia Todd, 45, 90, 3000, 175, 465

John Chardson, 40, 6, 2000, 400, 300

Isaac Murry, 63, 5, 1600, 100, 320

Wilson L. Larimore, 550, 450, 4000, 600, 2240

H. H. Wardlaw, 70, 75, 6000, 200, 400

William Evans, 65, 52, 3000, 150, 765

Michael Thebeau, 60, 5, 1500, 150, 450

Joseph Thebeau, 70, 28, 2000, 150, 200

Joseph Langueven, 80, -, 3000, 120, 300

Christian Schmacks, 14, 16, 1000, 100, 150

Henry N. Shreve, 300, 43, 60000, 1000, 2591

B. S. Garland, 200, 100, 60000, 500, 1100

William C. Taylor, 50, 111, 16000, 500, 5000

James H. Lucas, 1000, -, 40000, 1000, 2835

James Hardman, 45, 20, 13000, 100, 250

Frank Schetal, 80, -, 14000, 1500, 200

Richard F. Barrett, 21, -, 10000, 100, 500

Martin Lepere, 300, 300, 60000, 2000, 1080

Solomon P. Sublett, 120, 205, 40000, 500, 1000

David W. Graham, 50, 250, 30000, 400, 1000

James C. Sutton, 150, 350, 30000, 250, 1780

Thomas A. Hensley, 60, 20, 4000, 100, 200

William McCutchen, 170, 85, 25000, 200, 750

Ralph Clayton, 180, 522, 45000, 250, 1000

James G. Brown, 90, 35, 8000, 200, 230

John Kennedy, 75, 75, 15000, 150, 400

James McCausland, 95, 65, 16000, 30, 380

Aaron Bullard, 60, 23, 2400, 100, 150

William P. Penn, 170, -, 29000, 700, 3950

N. G. Woods, 75, -, 15000, 200, 600

Robert Farsythe, 200, 600, 100000, 200, 1300

John Sutter, 300, -, 60000, 1000, 4000

Thomas Skinder, 125, 151, 20700, 200, 1100

Theadore Prouhit, 45, 5, 2000, 200, 180

R. D. Watson, 180, 297, 60000, 1500, 950

George Klein, 30, 30, 6000, 100, 180

Theobold Renkel, 25, 55, 4000, 100, 250

Emanuel Hodsamont, 70, 100, 20000, 100, 220

Giles Bradford, 50, 70, 6000, 150, 170

John Monder, 40, 40, 3000, 100, 130

James Walton, 100, 40, 10000, 200, 720

William C. Woodson, 75, 100, 8000, 300, 585
John Meld, 16, 64, 2000, 150, 140
Henry Grobe, 22, 38, 1500, 100, 200
Thomas Buck, 45, 113, 3000, 50, 100
Ernst Greler, 30, 89, 1500, 50, 100
Jacob S. Brown, 75, 70, 3000, 100, 600
Joseph Brown, 100, 155, 8000, 300, 600
John Roswago, 30, 10, 600, 50, 124
Frederick Hildebrand, 20, 20, 500, 50, 120
John Voll, 25, 30, 1000, 100, 175,
Henry Grotpeter, 28, 80, 1500, 50, 150
John Ohlhausen, 75, 32, 4000, 150, 400
George Kudir, 25, 37, 1000, 50, 150
James W. Hawkins, 100, 155, 6000, 100, 200
Magdalen Link, 160, 743, 13545, 200, 640
Dennis Lackland, 52, 118, 4000, 150, 300
William Spurr, 15, 48, 1000, 7, 320
George Apple, 45, 53, 2000, 100, 250
Thomas Isvernson, 100, 60, 5000, 150, 300
Thomas Hempstead, 40, 65, 4000, 1000, 220
Joseph S. Ritnour, -, 50, 4400, 150, 350
Walter H. Boswell, 40, 60, 5000, 100, 390
Charles Renard, 160, 40, 8000, 200, 600
James A. McDonald, 165, 65, 7150, 200, 640
Charles H. Ashby, 30, 320, 10500, 200, 300
Lewis Adei, 75, 95, 4000, 250, 520
Benjamin W. Hawkins, 70, 80, 4000, 150, 380
John F. Quisinbury, 40, 64, 3000, 200, 675
Siemon Bruster, 50, 75, 3500, 150, 500
Andrew Link, 90, 79, 5000, 150, 415
George Bruster, 40, 51, 3000, 1200, 430
Sarah Boothe, 20, 53, 1500, 40, 195
Martha Harris, 20, -, 300, 40, 150
Jesse Craig, 40, 60, 3000, 100, 230

John Neihaus, 30, 38, 1500, 100, 160
James Craig, 40, 47, 1100, 100, 230
Thomas Murphy, 60, 77, 3500, 75, 450
William Bonham, 90, 450, 12000, 200, 450
Walter H. Dawset, 380, 335, 18700, 400, 1540
Frederick Watts, 60, 40, 1600, 100, 250
James McMusick, 30, -, 600, 50, 300
Wm. Musick, 100, 200, 6000, 150, 620
John H. Schultz, 95, 65, 1600, 75, 150
William Emelong, 20, -, 300, 75, 100
Amos Jenkins, 25, 65, 1800, 120, 700
Macky M. Wherry, 60, 147, 4000, 100, 350
William McCabry, 50, 150, 4000, 100, 570
Samuel S. Hibler, 60, 68, 2000, 100, 300
Merrick Shearer, 50, 350, 4000, 100, 300
Walter C. Kinkead, 90, 110, 3500, 200, 400
Power Link, 55, 100, 2500, 50, 200
John H. Dawning, 30, 20, 1000, 100, 170
Harris Downing, 55, 175, 2000, 100, 550
Hiram Cordwell, 100, 100, 4000, 150, 450
Richard H. Stephens, 90, 205, 6000, 150, 700
Harrison Cardwell, 65, 131, 4000, 100, 400
John L. Davenport, 100, 150, 5000, 100, 270
Alexander Kinkead, 80, 184, 6000, 100, 585
Robert A. Walton, 100, 233, 5000, 200, 775
Lucus L. Bates, 69, 413, 8000, 150, 550
Joseph Conway, 100, 100, 4000, 400, 420
Samuel Conway, 150, 430, 6000, 500, 600
Isaac Woods, 70, 44, 2000, 100, 240
George White, 65, 55, 1500, 100, 250
Thomas West, 30, 30, 1200, 50, 150

John Eoff, 25, 35, 1200, 100, 180
Phillip Morris, 50, 110, 2500, 150, 250
Samuel Chambers, 35, -, 600, 60, 350
Thomas K. Humphries, 80, 180, 3000, 300, 300
Alvin West, 65, 50, 2000, 150, 480
James Long, 100, 155, 4000, 150, 750
Thomas L. Long, 60, 195, 3000, 100, 360
Nicholas Long, 35, 220, 2000, 50, 260
George Eoff, 40, 138, 2000, 80, 320
Joseph Hardy, 30, 690, 7000, 100, 330
John Baxter, 35, 125, 3000, 120, 310
Fleming G. Woody, 16, 100, 1000, 50, 75
Henry Ebenvien, 90, 335, 5000, 150, 280
Thomas H. Barnett, 70, 61, 1900, 170, 475
William L. Jackson, 55, 75, 1200, 100, 350
Jacob Lash, 15, 65, 800, 75, 90
James O. Defoe, 40, -, 800, 50, 100
Richard Chesley, 70, 330, 4000, 150, 400
Kenneth Shotwell, 120, 200, 6000, 200, 500
Samuel Killgore, 40, 102, 1200, 100, 230
Volentine P. Carney, 40, -, 800, 50, 300
Alexander Eoff, 50, 89, 3000, 100, 200
Henry H. Duvall, 100, 200, 6000, 100, 525
Mastrom Lewis, 45, 38, 2000, 100, 275
William Nicholds, 90, 110, 3000, 150, 500
Joseph Harrison, 90, 154, 3000, 150, 325
John Jones, 50, 59, 2000, 100, 320
Cornelius Carman, 40, 120, 1500, 100, 300
William Hogg, 80, 80, 2000, 100, 350
Joshua Ball, 20, 13, 500, 100, 135
William Marmion, 25, 90, 2000, 50, 100
George Smith, 85, 200, 4500, 50, 350
Levi Defoe, 70, 40, 2700, 100, 500

William Triplett, 80, 320, 8000, 150, 300
Benjamin Lacy, 70, 90, 5000, 100, 330
Martin Manding, 40, 41, 1500, 100, 215
Mary Mason, 100, 350, 6000, 100, 300
Nathan Jones, 100, 133, 7000, 75, 250
James Dunlap, 100, 370, 7000, 100, 340
Phillip Mertz, 22, 18, 500, 60, 100
Nelson Tindall, 60, 20, 1600, 200, 300
William H. Harwood, 70, 93, 5000, 200, 350
Harman H. Roseman, 55, 65, 2000, 100, 130
William Walton, 30, 51, 2000, 50, 100
Henry Walter, 20, 60, 2000, 50, 100
Bryan Cross, 50, -, 2000, 60, 155
Francis A. Pfeiffer, 90, 520, 6000, 200, 375
Ann H. Glanville, 40, 40, 1600, 100, 275
John Bass, 35, 85, 1200, 100, 230
Thomas Gibson, 35, 50, 2500, 25, 175
William Phillips, 35, 56, 2300, 60, 200
John Gesler, 20, 20, 1000, 60, 150
John Ledluff, 50, 160, 4800, 100, 150
Margaret Wyatt, 100, 100, 6000, 100, 160
Gerhart Sprede, 60, 20, 1500, 100, 200
John F. Wilson, 30, 50, 1200, 100, 135
John Bray, 80, 370, 8000, 100, 300
Isaac Q. Price, 60, 90, 4000, 200, 300
John Rinkle, 25, 55, 1000, 100, 150
John Moseley, 200, 650, 10000, 100, 254
Harman H. Hackman, 15, 55, 1000, 50, 130
James Reynolds, 40, 62, 1500, 100, 260
Alexander Craig, 25, 32, 1200, 100, 125
Thomas Emerson, 80, 100, 3500, 200, 360
Andrew Ross, 65, 189, 5000, 300, 300
Washington Ross, 32, 198, 4000, 100, 600
Rob. Pollock, 50, 160, 3000, 100, 25
John Hempstead, 130, 718, 15000, 200, 375
John Wenting, 25, 37, 1000, 100, 190

Elizabeth Kelly, 18, -, 500, 30, 150
Joseph Fitzgerald, 40, 40, 1500, 50, 270
Alton Hibler, 80, 100, 6000, 200, 520
William J. Hibler, 40, 120, 5000, 200, 335
Alexander McGlhary, 30, 130, 3500, 100, 210
William Hogg Jr., 110, 257, 7000, 250, 550
Joshua Barton, 25, 25, 1000, 100, 280
Amanda Wiseman, 50, 143, 3000, 100, 240
George Power, 25, 25, 1000, 100, 170
Samuel Smith, 50, 150, 4000, 120, 600
Jeremiah Smith, 50, 143, 2300, 100, 225
Daniel Russ, 30, 50, 1000, 75, 100
Joseph Brooks, 60, 117, 2000, 100, 400
John Burford, 100, 200, 2500, 100, 520
Thomas E. Huckstep, 24, 73, 1500, 100, 150
Robert P. Huckstep, 60, 140, 2000, 100, 300
William H. Huckstep, 50, 72, 2000, 100, 350
Thomas _. Mason, 95, 333, 5000, 100, 400
William P. Smoth, 30, 75, 1000, 75, 180
David Barton (Baston), 20, 92, 1200, 75, 300
John Alt, 30, 28, 800, 40, 201
Peter Zeigenhein, 32, 10, 500, 60, 200
Johnson Shultz, 50 62, 2000, 100, 330
Michael Hock, 40, 38, 1000, 100, 200
James McKenney, 70, 170, 3300, 100, 250
Michael Zurlling, 30, 50, 1500, 150, 250
Washington Fitzgerald, 120, 390, 10200, 300, 375
George Bellas, 120, 160, 7000, 200, 385
Daniel Miller, 25, 11, 500, 50, 100
Frederick Kuster, 30, -, 600, 30, 130
George Ashbrand, 30, 500, 1200, 75, 150
Catharine Stonn, 65, 55, 1500, 75, 140
Phillip Rhinehart, 20, 28, 1000, 75, 150
Henry Bower, 12, 29, 500, 75, 140

John Sundy(Lundy), 35, 125, 2000, 75, 100
George Lastman, 18, 22, 600, 75, 100
John Henderson, 165, 235, 10000, 300, 515
Adam Zeenmer, 15, 35, 1000, 75, 100
Nicholas Ruhl, 30, 130, 4000, 100, 300
Alfred Smith, 74, 99, 4325, 200, 765
Schonot Klein, 50, 90, 2500, 150, 360
Aandrew J. Hebler, 50, 110, 4000, 150, 300
James W. Fitzgerald, 40, 120, 3500, 150, 375
Mason Fitzgerald, 35, 85, 2000, 150, 500
John T. Smith, 40, 88, 2000, 100, 240
Samuel Smith, 40, 40, 1200, 100, 225
Samuel Honeyman, 60, 20, 2000, 100, 220
Michael Hardspeer, 90, 70, 2500, 200, 500
Frederick J. Douglass, 130, 140, 6000, 200, 325
William Berry, 80, 80, 4000, 100, 200
James T. Small, 130, 30, 7000, 400, 520
David Small's Estate, 200, 240, 17000, 100, 250
William Ennis, 50, 50, 3000, 150, 400
William T. F. Densey, 85, 165, 7200, 200, 450
Frederick Descomb, 40, 28, 2000, 150, 325
David Fink, 63, 36, 2000, 100, 350
George Price, 85, 160, 4000, 200, 300
Joseph Harding, 120, 165, 10000, 300, 800
Samuel Mount, 300, 200, 15000, 500, 1070
Lewis Descomb, 40, 30, 2000, 100, 175
Elizabeth Barbee, 100, 150, 6000, 150, 550
Francis Genell, 45, 45, 2000, 150, 200
Michael Everhard, 50, 30, 1600, 100, 180
Peter Miller, 16, 24, 600, 75, 75
Henry S. Turner, -, 113, 1000, 100, 1200

B. Guion, 30, -, 1000, 100, 200
Auguste Gamache, 40, -, 1600, 60, 60
Julien Gamache, 6, -, 500, 30, 160
Henry Curling, 20, -, 1500, 60, 250
Bartholomew Guion, 35, -, 3500, 100, 125
Joseph Marechal, 20, -, 2000, -, 125
Peter Detore, 27, -, 2000, 100, 350
Arnable(Amable) Chartran, 40, 78, 5000, 50, 150
Thomas Kellerman, 28, -, 1500, -, 1100
Benoist Marechal, 40, -, 8000, 150, 350
Antoine Vien, 60, -, 6000, 100, 250
Constant Dauphin, 30, -, 3000, 70, 200
John Threarah, 30, -, 3000, 50, 200
Conrad Whitmore, 20, -, 2000, 50, 150
Emily Stine, 30, 40, 10000, -, 170
Benoist J. Marechal Jr., 8, -, 1000, 50, 200
John Purcelli, 60, -, 500, -, 250
Joseph Usey, 20, -, 1000, 80, 150
John Usey, 9, -, 2000, 150, 150
Alzia Kemmerly, 60, 121, 20000, 100, 350
Charles Stephani, 2, -, 1000, 20, 25
Dr. Allen C. Tindall, 35, 90, 2000, 15, 100
John Higgins, 15, 65, 800, 10, 160
John P. Clarke, 18, 125, 800, 15, 150
James Gentry, 28, -, 500, 5, 175
Thos. Williams, 70, 192, 2000, 65, 480
Saml. Vandoever, 80, 160, 1000, 125, 400
Benj. Corvin, 12, 200, 2000, 75, 510
John Vandoever, 100, 237, 3370, 55, 680
John Griffin, 27, -, 300, 10, 50
Lee Wilson, 16, 75, 150, 15, 105
George Lemphiras, 12, -, 400, 10, 110
Thos. Price, 40, 83, 400, 75, 300
Marshall Price, 30, 90, 600, 50, 250
J. G. Hale, 40, 40, 500, 75, 300
Mason Hale, 50, 110, 500, 75, 430
Charles Rust, 20, 202, 800, 80, 120
Starks S. Cockrill, 100, 140, 2000, 300, 1510

Isaac Williamson, 40, 165, 1000, 80, 325
Jane Williamson, 45, 135, 900, 10, 250
George Smiser, 130, 300, 6000, 250, 620
John Gesting, 30, 178, 2000, 40, 310
George Kofer, 18, 62, 800, 18, 158
Isaac Hockurn, 21, 19, 200, 30, 150
Humphrey Donivan, 50, 850, 3000, 185, 670
James Longrill, 60, 200, 1800, 75, 265
Robert McDonnell, 50, -, 400, 75, 250
Ellen Link, 12, 51, 315, 50, 285
Wm. B. Donivan, 75, 87, 1600, 80, 430
Saml. Rutters, 100, 200, 3000, 200, 615
Thos. Rutters, 30 7, 300, 70, 365
Elisabeth Sepp, 30, 100, 1000, 15, 195
Benj. Williams, 42, 12, 470, 25, 160
Henderson Dobbins, 8, -, 125, 10, 65
Frederich Herddel, 33, 67, 800, 90, 270
Larkin Williams, 100, 256, 3500, 200, 650
David H. Sailor, 40, 20, 900, 200, 850
John Hill, 30, 100, 1500, 35, 120
Elisabeth Farris, 100, 120, 4600, 10, 375
John D. Hall, 30, -, 400, 10, 70
John Evans, 9, 631, 3000, 10, 100
Mary Patterson, 5, 25, 200, -, 80
Edmund Caher, 12, 68, 300, 15, 50
Henry Langhebel, 20, 44, 400, 70, 160
Wm. H. Heters, 20, 55, 1200, 50, 145
Michael Whiteman, 31, 250, 6000, 40, 110
Alexd. Donaton, 12, 40, 500, 15, 80
Edward Lancaster, 30, 10, 800, 70, 230
James Spencer, -, -, -, -, -
Cathrine Hill, 12, 8, 200, 40, 170
Charles Gray, 14, 36, 1000, 100, 140
James M. Berry, 12, 38, 400, 10, 60
Walter Taylor, 18, 24, 800, 40, 85
Helena Rewey, 45, 42, 1740, 45, 645
Henry Rewey, 14, 36, 600, 40, 125
Thornton Armstrong, 55, 45, 2000, 100, 310
Bernhart Finneman, 20, 60, 1000, 40, 200
Harvey Ersie(Erne), 26, 14, 800, 60, 140
Anthony Rhine, 60, 100, 1500, 30, 80

Owen Collins, 80, 40, 2000, 150, 265
Dennis C. Higgens, 50, 70, 2000, 100, 180
Theodore Wellis, 18, 62, 800, 30, 60
John McLaughlin, 50, 190, 2500, 100, 135
James Lawless, 55, 111, 5000, 20, 450
Saml. Purdy, 30, 50, 2500, 30, 145
Preston Jordon, 150, 350, 10000, 300, 1264
Joseph S. Berry, 15, 65, 1500, 80, 120
Granville V. Edes, 100, 65, 4125, 150, 735
Thos. Sappington, 60, 120, 4500, 150, 175
March Sappington 80, 80, 4325, 150, 615
John Sapington Sr., 150, 720, 20000, 600, 650
To. Sappington, 60, 300, 7000, 200, 450
John Parke, 70, 51, 3000, 100, 175
Zeno Mackay, 75, 300, 1000, 300, 300
Enos Pipkin, 50, 32, 2000, 100, 800
Thos. Eddy, 80, 380, 4600, 150, 380
Richard Wells, 60, 177, 5000, 150, 325
Thos. S. Long, 100, 75, 45000, 150, 350
Harrison Long, 65, 85, 2500, 100, 300
Joseph Wells, 15, 186, 7000, 300, 1110
Nancy McKameck, 80, 79, 4000, 150, 350
Thos. Yates, 100, 80, 5460, 123, 460
Thomas Fahlbusch, 20, 80, 1200, 25, 60
William Triplett, 100, 300, 6000, 125, 400
Diederich Renecke, 12, 28, 400, 50, 85
E. Basey, 200, 392, 23720, 100, 500
L. Gillan, 12, -, 1500, 360, 40
John Filmar, 17, 30, 375, 60, 125
F. Filmar, 11, 15, 208, 55, 40
Thos. Nichols, 20, 20, 400, 75, 80
John Baal, 70, 138, 3000, 60, 150
G. Herschbach, 20, 60, 500, 80, 100
L. Kesler, 45, 45, 2500, 75, 200
Silus Duvall, 60, 214, 5500, 100, 360
Dr. B. F. Wilson, 400, 560, 20000, 200, 1200

Samuel Price, 13, 120, 3800, 125, 150
George W. Higgins, 350, 510, 12000, 350, 950
Mary Tomblety, 38, 262, 4500, 25, 150
Richard Tomblety, 100, 200, 6000, 75, 150
Robert King, 75, 135, 3600, 50, 180
Thos. Koff, 6, -, 100, 50, 95
Robert Kansh, 110, 415, 8875, 200, 550
Christopher Weidener, 18, 42, 500, 35, 60
Lorenz Hofmeister, 15, 45, 500, 30, 75
Henry Usinger, 17, -, 200, 70, 125
Martens & Schniedemeyer, 30, 187, 1400, 40, 125
John Kesler, 25, 35, 200, 15, 60
William Hansels, 45, 100 700, 100, 250
Frederick Holte, 3, 37, 100, 15, 50
Henry Niere, 20, 60, 400, 20, 75
Frederick Kleinsorge, 45, 65, 600, 40, 125
Osborn Pruet, 25, 42, 600, 30, 300
Daniel Andrac Sr., 60, 90, 1500, 150, 250
Meyers Loflin, 15, -, 100, 75, 75
Adam Doring, 15, 25, 600, 70, 300
James Davidson, 50, 107, 3355, 225, 200
Wm. E. Doeschler, 20, 20, 700, 50, 320
Henry Kochnemann, 6, 34, 100, 25, 50
John Schmidt, 9, 31, 300, 30, 60
Christian Berkemeyer, 12, 8, 200, 15, 45
Peter Engels, 12, 28, 150, 50, 100
Henry Lambach, 5, 75, 150, 25, 50
Urban Schneider, 10, 70, 200, 25, 100
Nancy N. Lewis, 80, 150, 2000, 100, 400
Zacharias Schuste, 40, 232, 1600, 50, 200
James Votaw, 40, 240, 3000, 300, 400
George King, 108, -, 1500, 150, 175
John King, 100, -, 1500, 50, 75
Andrew W. Darby, 50, 150, 2000, 60, 30
Robert W. King, 60, 60, 1600, 50, 200
Joshua Ball, 20, 10, 300, 50, 125
F. Wallenstein, 20, 60, 500, 60, 125

Adolph Hausmann, 20, 60, 1000, 75, 100

John Dougherty, 50, 110, 1600, 30, 127

Christian Fr. Koch, 16, 34, 360, 100, 65

Adam Tiener, 15, 65, 800, 10, 50

Johannes Hoffman, 60, 240, 4000, 75, 150

As. Sturdy, 50, 110, 2000, 80, 220

Michael Willing, 25, 65, 500, 40, 120

Michael Wock, 8, 10, 160, 15, 85

Martin Roth, 15, 35, 700, 75, 140

James Jones, 25, 15, 250, 40, 100

Frederick Grosherr, 14, 116, 1100, 25, 135

Balshasar Roth, 36, 34, 700, 70, 100

James Murphey, 30, 50, 100, 40, 75

George Green, 50, 75, 2500, 50, 190

Martin Oilker, 9, 31, 150, 40, 55

Richard Anderson, -, 60, 600, 30, 25

Robert Haukstep, 20, 80, 1400, 10, 110

Jeremiah Straub, 20, 5, 400, 25, 60

Frederick Obemeyer, 30, 10, 550, 30, 80

Henry Straub, 10, 5, 200, -, 80

Arther Marquerd, 40, 65, 910, 40, 50

John Urig Engel, 50, 116, 2000, 55, 125

William Kemper, 22, -, 200, 30, 60

Alfred Borden, 45, -, 450, 60, 1000

Henry Grab, 21, -, 200, 15, 35

John Miller, 12, -, 150, 15, 35

George Grab, 40, 120, 2000, 50, 80

Caspar Werlher, 25, 15, 500, 30, 94

Jacob Werlher, 9, 24, 300, 25, 80

George H. Rauchen, 10, 25, 450, 60, 90

Johannes Muhl, 12, -, -, 40, 40

George Miller, 35, 40, 700, 50, 90

George Wiener, 15, 25, 300, 50, 70

Erhard Egger, 9, 31, 300, 80, 65

Kuniguide Schneith, 15, 25, 400, 40, 140

Gottlieb Lindemann, 25, 15, 20, 60, 100

John Lockhaus, 10, 30, 400, 50, 125

Johs. Low, 30, 180, 2000, 80, 130

Balthaser Lockhaus, 10, 30, 500, 180, 100

Johs. Koch, 40, 40, 800, 75, 65

Sebastian Bobb, 18, 32, 500, 50, 87

Claus Mild, 80, 40, 500, 50, 85

Gerhard Hanreth, 40, 50, 1500, 150, 145

Charles Hohns, 15, 52, 600, 40, 110

Conrad Berglar, 20, 40, 300, -, 20

Frederick Stowje, 30, 60, 1000, 15, 40

Frederick Clamor 25, 66, 800, 40, 85

John Manis, 25, -, 250, 60, 70

Henry Lindomann, 20, 20, 400, 40, 60

Gottfried Marz, 25, 15, 600, 50, 50

Susanna Calbert, 1, 119, 1000, 10, 23

Joseph Weihard, 20, 80, 600, 50, 30

John Stowje, 40, 200, 1100, 75, 300

William Stowje, 8, 84, 400, 5, 60

John Bohrer, 20, 40, 500, 100, 80

Green C. Niesewonder, 30, 210, 2510, 5, 50

Henry Lochhaus, 30, 153, 1000, 200, 120

Franz Pohlmann, 30, 130, 1000, 70, 155

Martin Kraus, 16, 24, 300, 50, 80

George Berthole, 8, 32, 300, 20, 40

Henry Usinger, 50, 340, 3000, 60, 200

William S. Wheeler, 50, 340, 3000, 60, 200

Zephanie Sappington, 100, 203, 4500, 150, 725

John F. Long, 30, 20, 1500, 80, 170

Madame Detelier, 35, 45, 1600, 30, 105

Asa Tiron, 45, 95, 2000, 100, 300

John Sappington Jr., 75, 185, 3900, 200, 1000

Matthew Combs, 20, 44, 600, 50, 60

Steffen Golden, 53, -, -, 75, 395

David Hahl, 30, -, -, 75, 200

Samuel Anderson, 60, 310, 3500, 100, 280

John G. Hauch, 30, 25, 1000, 50, 100

Michael Schlessen, 16, 84, 800, 50, 250

John Klund, 20, 65, 500, 50, 85

Perris Pipkins, 75, 57, 2400, 70, 200

James Sappington, 100, 60, 4000, 125, 700

Frederick Sodgreen, 120, 280, 11000, 300, 650

Andrew Fox, 25, 26, 1000, 60, 200

Joseph Sale, 200, 140, 6000, 200, 1000

Elisabeth Sappington, 75, 135, 6000, 200, 850

Margareth Notr, 35, 10, 1500, 100, 160

Poser (Toser) Brees, 100, 150, 3010, 100, 350

Matthew Brees, 20, 20 650, 30, 80

Joseph Ridamann, 25, 75, 700, 35, 150

Christian Klump, 20, 90, 700, 50, 155

Patrick Janety, 15, 85, 400, 15, 140

Charles Paffroth, 25, 133, 1600, 50, 335

Frederick Mismeyer, 20, 70, 400, 10, 85

Frederick Langenhider, 10, 30, 200, 25, 80

Charles Schueler, 12, 28, 200, 10, 92

William Rahm, 6, 34, 150, 10, 80

Lorenz Henzle, 60, 30, 900, 70, 150

Michael Maick, 20, 60, 300, 10, 45

William Farmer, 80, 40, 2000, 150, 240

Heisman Steines, 60, 220, 2000, 200, 350

Frederick Assenford, 15, 95, 800, 80, 200

Samuel Harris, 70, 210, 4000, 75, 250

William Bartold, 20, 70, 800, 70, 120

Henry Sewing, 20, 60, 600, 10, 90

William Niesen, 16, 144, 300, 8, 50

Martin Henken, 40, 80, 500, 60, 280

Ephraim Burkte, 11, 39, 150, 40, 80

William Heidorn, 40, 80, 1000, 10, 150

Daniel Warfield, 30, 70, 1000, 50, 220

Jackson Sublett, 45, 35, 1200, 30, 175

Marc. Stevenson, 48, 72, 1200, 50, 245

Peregrene Tippett, 50, 70, 2000, 150, 300

Adam Warrenburg, 36, 42, 3000, 10, 137

George W. Smith, 20, 20, 800, 30, 90

William Edertom, 75, 285, 4300, 90, 290

William Cox, 15, 35, 300, 50, 120

William Morris, 30, 90, 1000, 75, 120

John Brach, 20, 15, 400, 50, 225

Gerhard Sonn, 34, 86, 1500, 85, 230

Gustar Hausman, 11, 24, 500, 40, 100

John Neele, 15, 35, 200, 15, 45

Jacob Hadspat, 30 ½, 40, 250, 10, 47

John Whiteside, 60, 490, 5000, 100, 453

Sarah Hamilton, 50, 550, 3500, 60, 255

Henry McColough, 35, 205, 2000, 60, 275

Alexander Miller, 15, 35, 300, 40, 55

Martha Hamilton, 23, 78, 500, 50, 330

John P. Taffrey, 23, 227, 800, 20, 70

James Richardson, 15, 25, 350, 15, 100

John Heidel, 1 86/100, -, 1500, -, 10

John Toode, 3 1/3, -, 3500, 80, 35

William Kennedy, 10, -, 15000, 40, 60

Bernhard Griese, 10, -, 10000, 45, 91

Caspar Keittsmimer, 3, -, 4000, 50, 100

H. Meier, 3, -, 3000, 35, 51

Mongomery Blair, 7, -, 21000, 45, 150

James Page, 8, -, 20000, 61, 61

J. F. Weldprecht, 3, -, 6000, 45, 60

William B. Barber, 3, -, 6000, 50, 50

Louisa Hofner, 3, -, 6000, 45, 70

G. Chapmann, 8 70/100, -, 6800, 60, 90

J. B. Moulton 19 70/100, -, 1000, 200, 270

Mathias Nagel, 10, -, 8000, 35, 95

Henry April, 10, -, 8000, 45, 100

John Withorell, 30, -, 9000, 100, 250

Lucy Russell, 250, 186, 25000, 150, 1000

Henry Luicking, 10, -, 2100, 50, 110

John Bingham, 100, 60, 12000, 500, 650

James Aines, 14, -, 2800, 40, 75

John Callahan, 30, -, 3000, 60, 90

John Rughel, 20, -, 2000, 50, 50

G. Schneider, 10, -, 15000, 20, 25

Englehardt & Epstein, 5, -, 5000, 40, 80

Philip Zepp, 10, -, 8000, 300, 450

Daniel Lievenecker, 4, -, 3000, 50, 100

Henry Irke, 10,-, 15000, 40, 60

Small Poor Hospital of City of St. Louis, 10, -, 12000, 50, 15

C. F. Hoffmann, 4 7/8, -, 1600, 75, 95

Henry Willow, 6 ½, -, 1500, 25, 75

August Ahrens, 6, -, 1800, 60, 90

Henry Drehaman, 26, -, 1500, 40, 110

Bernhard Koeck, 6, -, 1500, 40, 60

Clemens Wesfall(Wessel), 13, -, 2600, 50, 91

Ferdinand Hoffmann, 33 30/100, -, 10000, 100, 150

Sebastian Betz, 10, -, 3000, 50, 50

M. Woechle, 5, -, 1500, 60, 90

Henry Klincke, 5, -, 1500, 75, 110

Milehe Ernest, 4, -, 1200, 50, 50

Michael Sutter, 10, -, 5000, 150, 200

Michael Holocher, 5, -, 1500, 100, 225

Peter Weitzonecker, 10, -, 7500, 50, 60

George Anderdonk, 20, -, 11000, 50, 95

John Atting, 5, -, 2500, 25, 90

John H. Albers, 5, -, 2500, 35, 80

Wm. Kockeritz, 10, -, 5000, 25, 40

Henry Meyer, 9 75/100, -, 3500, 50, 95

Bernhard Dickman, 15, -, 6500, 40, 72

Isaac Martin, 11, -, 5000, 25, 40

Conrad Eggert, 18, -, 9000, 40, 90

William Reiley, 10, -, 5000, 50, 110

Diobold Uhl, 5, -, 2500, 40, 40

Adam Schelinger, 4 35/100, -, 2500, 35, 55

L. A. Benoist, 10, -, 800, 500, 130

F. Ridgley, 70, -, 70000, 300, 91

James B. Reiley, 10, -, 5000, 50, 110

Ernest Hoffmann, 23, -, 15000, 150, 40

Henry Rupp, 10, -, 8000, 25, 40

Bernhard Osleke, 12, -, 10000, 40, 80

Wm. Wible, 15, -, 15000, 350, 350

J. McDonald, 60, -, 50000, 60, 110

John Kruechter, 13 50/100, -, 7500, 35, 60

Bryan Burns, 35, -, 2100, 40, 120

Emil Bohn, 3, -, 2000, 90, 450

Tobias Blom, 35, -, 15000, 75, 425

John Black, 60, -, 30000, 45, 40

Joab Toney, 48, -, 48000, 150, 225

Robert Gunnury, 3, -, 2400, 25, 40

Patrick M. Tolly, 4, -, 2000, 30, 75

Frederick Miltelberg, 6, -, 3000, 100, 150

William Miller, 90, 160, 12000, 150, 250

Wm. Nedderhuth, 1 ¾, -, 2000, 40, 50

David Tatum, 5, -, 20000, 100, 200

Henry Ellmuceller, 2, -, 8000, 50, 60

Tamms & Meyer, 6, -, 8000, 200, 650

George Mincke, 13, -, 17000, 60, 50

Bernhard Martin, 5 18/100, -, 5700, 50, 60

James R. Lahe, 5, -, 6000, 225, 1600

Philip Feg, 5, -, 5000, 30, 30

H. Becherer, 5, -, 5000, 45, 40

John Foeke, 3, -, 3000, 35, 35

John Riegler, 4, -, 4000, 35, 30

Nicholas Bacon, 35, 115, 700, 50, 135

George Tyler, 60, 45, 1200, 30, 175

Benjamin Libcum, 130, 70, 1200, 50, 250

James Stuard, 35, 152, 1600, 50, 250

Samuel Spelherd, 70, 550, 2000, 150, 620

William Rett, 12, 118, 600, 25, 160

Caspar Kroenung, 20, 60, 500, 15, 110

George Herz, 35, 105, 800, 50 270

Thomas Bacon, 80, 48, 1000, 60, 405

William Kroner, 50, 150, 1000, 100, 160

Diederich Kleibecher, 15, 75, 200, 15, 90

Frederick Geble, 25, 55, 600, 60, 120

George Farris, 40, 88, 1200, 100, 185

Otto Von Grueben, 25, 100, 1250, 50, 175

Ludwig Poellmann, 39, 120, 1200, 150, 200

Christian Weber, 12, 32, 400, 5, 105

Minard Farris, 80, 50, 1100, 100, 255

Philip Smith, 11, 81, 400, 25, 140

George H. Lahman, 17, 23, 200, 30, 80

George Bates, 20, 60, 400, 20, 150

Williamson Bacon, 15, 48, 300, 40, 125

Thomas Johnson, 30, 73, 450, 20, 160

Andrew Miller, 40, 140, 800, 10, 55

Conrad Jung, 50, 110, 800, 100, 240

Charles Von Gruben, 15, 40, 400, 10, 75

Charles Oelbeck, 30, 45, 500, 40, 70

John W. Steffens, 14, 8, 200, 10, 95

Henry Wendel, 16, 24, 200, 10, 65

Oby. Harien, 50, 70, 600, 40, 150

William J. T. Seal, 21, 69, 400, 50, 100

David Neele, 20, 60, 800, 120, 125

Charles Boenning, 11, 20, 400, 15, 100

John F. Decinhoener, 70, 130, 2000, 60, 130

August Von Gruben 20, 40, 800, 15, 130

William McCannon, 14, 24, 200, 6, 140

Liddy Bacon, 16, 64, 1000, 15, 47

Frederick Liemann, 27, 53, 400, 60, 214

Baldwin Locher, 15, 45, 500, 10, 115

William J. Hale, 30, 5, 150, 90, 325

John G. Schrolder, 25, 160, 1000, 45, 150

Thos. Harberson, 50, 30, 1500, 120, 400

Ludwig W. Halloway, 30, 57, 1000, 40, 230

Daniel Andrews, 14, 70, 1000, 50, 160

John McCollough, 45, 35, 1500, 100, 250

Louis Bertram, 21, 139, 1800, 15, 133

William Morris, 30, 90, 600, 40, 165

Grandville Farris, 40, 157, 3000, 120, 450

Reinhardt Strecker, 34, 46, 600, 100, 160

Freda Gerling, 25, 55, 500, 100, 160

Martin Sontag, 40, 80, 800, 100, 295

Charles Kehn, 95, 605, 5000, 100, 220

August Witreck, 30, 10, 600, 140, 281

Michael Roiteux, 10, 70, 320, 50, 90

Sarah Miller, 18, 24, 400, 40, 165

Sarah Clarke, 10, 30, 220, 200, 100

Ruben Long, 40, 260, 250, 150, 260

Wm. Dayley, 29, 86, 1200, 50, 100

Pauline Lutkin, 50, 100, 1500, 40, 200

Edward Becker, 30, 30, 1000, 60, 355

Michael Mosbucker, 11, 154, 200, 60, 200

Hartman Steffan, 40, 40, 1000, 100, 200

William Boxley, 400, 700, 11000, 500, 1150

Louis Stevans, 400, 300, 11000, 500, 3000

Judy Stevans, 100, 340, 4000, 20, 100

Elisabeth C. Ferguson, 100, 190, 2500, 80, 475

Amoron Howel, 125, 100, 2000, 10, 645

William Tylor, 150, 370, 5000, 450, 1050

Martin Bates, 25, 100, 600, 100, 100

Johannes Tonges, 60, 78, 500, 50, 100

Henry Tylor, 190, 663, 10000, 300, 3000

William Coleman, 150, 250, 6000, 400, 1300

Robert J. Coleman, 270, 180, 6000, 200, 1200

Martin McCurtney, 40, 150, 1000, 20, 150

Maria Coleman, 250, 350, 3000, 100, 210

Henry Schilly, 30, 12, 200, 10, 130

Langton Bacon, 75, 95, 600, 60, 170

Henry Sandford, 30, 610, 1500, 20, -

Joachim Sandford, 20, 30, 600, 25, 75

William Bacon, 25, 135, 500, 65, 260

James Wright, 60, 225, 500, 100, 400

Margaret Bacon, 60, 140, 1000, 25, 150

Herman Wilmer, 51, 110, 1100, 75, 200

August Berghorn, 35, 45, 500, 30, 125

Samuel Stuard, 50, 110, 1500, 100, 285

Hiram Griffin, 20, 20, 150, 15, 80

Valentine Kroening, 52, 55, 900, 100, 475

Sebastian Galley, 28, 52, 1000, 70, 260

Robert Lewis, 30, 110, 1600, 150, 400

Anna Bacon, 40, 130, 2000, 50, 400

Barbara Boeme, 50, 150, 3000, 100, 250

Christian Fey, 55, 140, 2500, 125, 200

Nicholas Rigert, 50, 110, 2000, 50, 400

John F. Rapp(Rupp), 50, 70, 1200, 80, 750

Thos. John Kroening, 60, 100, 2000, 100, 400

John Marks, 35, 41, 1000, 60, 300

Spencer C. Tylor, 50, 135, 3000, 75, 800

Edward Bacon, 35, 125, 2000, 6, 80

Abner Bly, 45, 240, 1200, 120, 400

Conrad Kroening, 40, 40, 1500, 100, 400

Thos. Beyer, 10, -, 300, 10, 100

Edward Rosselier, 50, 30, 1300, 150, 300

John G. Sterling, 20, 40, 200, 60, 60

A. Sterling, 20, 40, 180, 10, 50

George Miller, 6, 1050, 2000, 10, 40

James F. Gorden, 18, 250, 3000, 45, 100

Abraham Fisher, 90, 70, 1500, 150, 660
Robert Orr, 35, 180, 2500, 150, 440
Margaret Burdlong, 50, 35, 1200, 100, 400
Gottlieb Ludwig, 35, 55, 1000, 50, 670
Susanna Dachroden, 50, 170, 2500, 25, 220
Peter Stephans, 80, 300, 4500, 50, 400
John Orr, 100, 150, 2500, 70, 300
Hypolite Tiron, 130, 210, 3400, 300, 700
Henry Kihre, 17, 104, 450, 50, 128
William Griffin, 20, 40, 100, 20, 115
Jacob Weithammer, 32, 192, 1200, 150, 338
William Stuard, 30, 81, 1000, 30, 28
Edward A. Locus, 12, 28, 400, 15, 30
Elisabeth Ficke, 30, 65, 800, 75, 150
Stephan Bolton, 16, 44, 400, 25, 100
Isaac Markane, 16, 175, 1000, 5, 85
James Sappington, 40, 80, 1200, 100, 200
John P. Lawlas, 30, 50, 500, 5, 175
Jackson Holloway, 20, 60, 500, 10, 320
Ruben Lawlas, 40, 67, 1200, 100, 305
William Sublet, 12, 31, 200, 20, 200
Robert B. Christy, 30, 130, 500, 25, 150
William Harris, 70, 350, 4000, 200, 800
Andreas McClore, 30, 120, 900, 15, 290
Aron Francis, 10, 30, 200, 60, 155
Benjamin G. Braun, 50, 220, 2000, 100, 145
John Braun, 18, 72, 500, -, 112
Wilson Sled, 25, 90, 800, 60, 337
Henry Keaton, 12, 145, 750, 8, 105
Larshe F. Ink, 60, 110, 1800, 10, 200
William C. Ink, 65, 108, 2000, 100, 1400
John Piot, 25, 18, 402, 15, 135
James Harrison, 15, 65, 300, 20, 150
Elisha Beat, 20, 60, 500, 35, 68
Anthon Rolfs, 18, 80, 200, 15, 85
Benj. Boyd, 70, 330, 1000, 20, 200
Isaac Potterfield, 105, 100, 700, 100, 680
Andreas Cawen, 15, 65, 400, 15, 120
Dennis Sawer, 20, 85, 600, 15, 110

Nancy Fray, 50, 95, 1000, 18, 75
Silus Vothaw, 50, 180, 1200, 25, 235
Sebastian Sontag, 12, 150, 500, 60, 129
Dennis Sawer, 21, -, 300, 15, 170
John W. Watson, 25, 135, 600, 60, 190
Egidus Rosenzweig, 14, 26, 500, 20, 55
Gerard Urion, 13, 67, 150, 50, 500
Jacob Lawlas, 25, 189, 1500, 85, 330
Edward Bacon, 22, 53, 550, 30, 175
Joseph Harris, 45, 67, 1500, 100, 559
Isaiah Brown, 75, 280, 3000, 300, 670
William Hale, 50, 190, 1000, 50, 280
Robert Patton, 20, 60, 500, 15, 165
Lawrason May, 12, 50, 400, 10, 75
Rebecca Hooper, 20, 95, 700, 55, 200
William Pirot, 14, 142, 370, 15, 120
Martha S. Liming, 8, 28, 175, 12, 190
Samuel Green, 25, 55, 500, 60, 150
William F. Harris, 30, 130, 600, 50, 75
James Bell, 14, 140, 800, 50, 190
John O'Keef, 30, 50, 1500, 30, 150
Robert B. Hamilton, 15, 65, 500, 10, 70
Ruben Bacon, 20, 60, 500, 10, 110
Ann Roberts, 15, 25, 200, 10, 100
Peter Off, 50, 110, 1500, 100, 340
John Gran, 30, 66, 800, 34, 150
Alfred Sled, 60, 135, 2000, 100, 655
Marshal Sled, 30, 130, 800, 75, 375
Jacob Hamilton, 13, 147, 800, 15, 15
John W. Cockrill, 50, 30, 700, 20, 257
Burt Chesser, 21, 39, 100, 10, 45
William Keller, 16, 21, 1500, 10, 245
John Keller, 10, -, -, 10, 132
David Keller, 15, -, -, 50, 208
John Guttermuth, 40, 115, 800, 30, 220
George Guttermuth, 10, 30, 400, 20, 52
Charles Ridel, 20, 60, 500, 10, 30
Johannes Warncer, 12, 25, 160, 5, 25
David Horn, 25, 135, 1000, 30, 200
Frederick Kaiser, 15, -, 3000, 150, 550
William Nisbet, 4, -, 1300, 100, 200
Joseph Miller, 3 50/100, -, 1400, 50, 500
George Scheibel, 5, -, 1600, 60, 110
George Manning, 8, -, 2500, 150, 500
William McDonald, 50, 50, 25000, 250, 850

D. G. Morton, 50, 50, 25000, 200, 500
H. W. Hunt, 87, -, 43500, 150, 80
Martin Haushalter, 35, 45, 1100, 115, 90
George Haushalter, 35, 15, 800, 25, 80
Frederick Naw, 26, 54, 450, 50, 85
Henry Koch, 20, 60, 450, 25, 100
Galt Koester, 30, -, 250, 65, 120
Chas. Lovercheck, 26, 49, 2300, 40, 150
Benjamin Enman, 40, 140, 4500, 200, 320
Robert & John Enman, 60, -, 1000, -, -
Thos. Wash, 150, 170, 6500, 150, 450
Rebecca Harrison, 100, 152, 6250, 75, 200
James Walcher, 12, -, 300, -, -
Saphir Erne, 23, 18, 900, 75, 125
Frederick Wagner, 40, 14, 1000, 30, 100
Wm. H. Ledford, 15, 25, 550, 75, 125
Daniel Harper, 30, 70, 2000, 65, 175
Wm. Walton, 30, 51, 2000, 25, 100
Eliza Calbert, 2 50/100, -, 800, 50, 150
Louis Monnier, 65, 125, 4700, 150, 250
Lorenz B. Brian, 8, -, 300, 50, 70
B. Bonpas, 60, 220, 9000, 100, 400
Charles Rotterman, 44, -, 1800, 50, 45
John C. Marshall, 200, 400, 24000, 300, 500
James C. Marshall, 100, 200, 15000, 1500, 600
St. Louis County Farm-Poor House, 160, -, 30000, 200, 1200
James Bailey, 40, -, 3500, 75, 170
Michael Humes, 8, -, 700, 75, 240
William Williams, 8 ½, -, 750, 65, 275
John Kindall, 8 ½, -, 800, 85, 185
John Wilson, 20, -, 2000, 75, 300
David Hilderbrandt, 80, -, 6000, 125, 300
McHose & English, 7, -, 7500, 150, 80
B. F. Baldwin, 9 75/100, -, 3000, 35, 65
Moses Forbes, 22, 11, 9000, 55, 95
Michael Eppstein, 11, -, 3500, 60, 170
William Milburn 19 17/100, -, 15000, 100, 260
Thadeus Lovejoy, 18, 75, 3255, 60, 310
Wesley Watson, 22, 20, 2100, 75, 225

Joseph Kanklin, 12, 8, 500, 60, 150
Francis Mess, 18, Dent's, Land, 40, 130
Johannes Hock, 17, -, -, 40, 80
Peter Hahn, 100, 100, 3000, 75, 200
H. M. Bernes, 100, 100, 6000, 150, 325
Eliza Willes, 12, 28, 800, 40, 150
Nancy Wright, 30, 70, 3000, 150, 250
Sylvester Meyer, 24, 15, 400, 60, 125
John Fey, 16, 30, 550, 25, 25
John Jr. Edecker, 10, 30, 400, 40, 65
Bernh. Burgel, 20, 75, 800, 100, 185
Zacharias Kraugh, 16, 24, 400, 40, 100
George Hahn, 35, 160, 3000, 70, 70
Valentine Sulls, 20, 62, 2000, 80, 150
Philip Rotherbucher, 20, 54, 1200, 100, 150
Harbenson Herbert(Herbel), 40, 55, 2000, 150, 200
John D. Wolf, 12, 42, 1000, 100, 150
Hermann W. Menkens, 22, 22, 3000, 160, 200
Marcas Zuchs, 22, 30, 600, 50, 60
August Tiekirpe, 5, -, 1000, -, 60
H. W. Nox, 50, -, 35000, -, -
Conrad Hoffmann, 30, 10, 350, 60, 200
James Eddy, 65, 85, 2500, 100, 300
John P. Louis, 25, 15, 700, 60, 150
Nicholai Miller, 30, -, 300, 45, 250
J. D. Coleman, 70, -, 1400, 50, 170
D. Johnson, 86, 84, 7000, 50, 200
Mary Kennerly, 180, 20, 4000, 100, 350
Author Bauer, 20, 75, 1600, 40, 120
John A. Kehr, 20, 35, 1400, 40, 175
Thos. Tritsch, 68, -, 1600, 35, 90
J. F. Schneider, 20, 78, 1600, 45, 95
Gustav Becker, 20, 22, 1300, 35, 80
Valentine Heines, 37, -, 1200, 30, 75
M. Koch, 12, 12, 1400, 25, 85
M. Guion, 80, 150, 2500, 65, 250
John Ziegler, 80, -, 1600, 55, 400
John Diehl, 10, 62, 1100, 45, 95
Gregor Mueller, 20, 20, 1400, 50, 105
Michael Fuchs, 50, 75, 2400, 80, 175
George Scheuer, 40, -, 1400, 100, 170
John Hauck, 20, 35, 900, 60, 300
H. VanTalge, 20, -, 500, 65, 125

Andreas Meier, 20, -, 500, 55, 110
J. C. Crecilius, 45, 83, 2600, 50, 225
Philip Crecilius, 48 75/100, 50, 1600, 100, 250
J. H. Mueller, 45, 39, 1800, 150, 200
J. H. Muller, 40, 40, 1300, 80, 300
James Kennerly, 20, 54, 1500, -, -
George Mehl, 45, 25, 1100, 70, 225
Johannes Schuetz, 30, 34, 1000, 70, 125
Jacob Crecilius, 20, 20, 700, 50, 175
Wm. E. Werner, 30, 40, 1100, 70, 250
H. Hubel, 20, 20, 700, 40, 75
H. Theisz, 18, 12, 500, 25, 125
Jacob Theisz, 20, -, 400, 40, 135
John Theisz, 30, 34, 1100, 100, 150
Josiah Gehring, 10, 10, 450, 35, 60
Christian Stephan & Bros, 150, 200, 45000, 150, 325
Diederich Wilche, 20, 37, 750, 45, 175
H. Wilmington, 10, -, 1000, 70, 60
E. Turner, 30, 32, 1200, 55, 175
Jacob W. Michel, 12, 3, 2250, 55, 80
Herman Haslack, 19, -, 2500, 75, 90
Arnold H. Mueller, 150, -, 10500, 150, 150
Rudolph Moehlenhoff, 26, 25, 4200, 100, 250
Friedr. W. Heidorn, 113, -, 14124, 200, 600
Philip Watkins, 65, 10, 4000, 85, 225
J. A. Griffin, 100, -, 5500, 55, 125
Thos. M. Brennan, 125, 100, 9000, 75, 210
John A. Friechle, 4, 30, 2500, 75, 110
Charles Weber, 52, -, 3000, 65, 125
Jacob John Sr., 25, 15, 2750, 50, 125
Daniel Joung, 30, 50, 1500, 70 190
John Stein, 40, -, 1500, 35, 65
David McMeans, 8, 50, 1800, 40, 50
Francis Kirk, 18, 62, 2200, 30, 40
Author Lefort, 40, -, 700, 55, 10
Conrad Stein, 27, -, 675, 65, 60
Anthon Schultz, 40, -, 900, 50, 85
Wm. Sleah, 40, -, 850, 65, 120
Daniel Roninger, 27, -, 600, 15, 55
Henry Mund, 34, -, 75, 45, 80

Authorinette Calvin, 40, -, 900, 75, 110
Michael Tanzberger, 40, 80, 1400, 200, 300
G. Wainreich, 40, 120, 1750, 75, 275
Christ. Cresicilius, 40, 40, 1000, 75, 135
Andrews Eile, 20, 20, 600, 65, 275
John Early, 30, 50, 900, 55, 200
George Early, 30, 60, 1200, 65, 250
James H. Bailey, 120, 180, 4000, 25, 550
Wm. Fruechle, 70, 330, 4500, 75, 125
Wm. A. Grate, 100, 172, 3000, 125, 400
John A. Merlein, 40, -, 600, 35, 60
Chas. Becker, 35, 25, 750, 50, 225
Matthias Lepp, 40, 60, 1800, 100, 150
Joseph Olean, 18, 42, 700, 65, 145
Thos. Ritchie, 40, 50, 1100, 50, 235
Eliza Horn, 18, 182, 1700, 35, 125
N. Robinson, 40, 120, 2200, 50, 250
Wm. Sost, 20, 40, 800, 45, 150
Chas. Steinhauer, 14, 26, 500, 50, 95
Jacob Casper, 25, 55, 900, 50, 145
John Gebhardt, 30, 40, 1200, 75, 160
Chas. Forman, 60, 185, 14000, 100, 150
Thos. W. Hornsby, 100, 100, 10000, 150, 500
Nicholas Riehl, 25, 40, 3250, 125, 175
Chas. Hoffmann, 30, 35, 4875, 80, 350
R. C. Jones, 130, 110, 12000, 100, 400
Delphis Curlin, 20, 50, 8000, 250, 300
Frederick Fuchs, 25, 45, 800, 80, 120
Michael Kampf, 4, 13, 231, 30, 30
Joseph E. Sale, 30, 30, 720, 50, 250
Philip Sype(Lype), 20, 17, 500, 50, 70
William Gerke, 25, 38, 800, 50, 140
John Kroeninger, 7, 18, 300, 30, 100
Christian Grim, 10, 3, 200, 100, 50
Franciska Hanebruck, 10, 40, 500, 30, 100
John Wells, 15, 15, 200, 30, 80
John Runnels, 30, 130, 2000, 40, 100
Delia Wickersham, 100, 223, 3000, 100, 250
John Reheis, 30, 130, 1500, 80, 250
Philip Hame, 18, 17, 400, 40, 50
John Walker, 20, 21, 350, 18, 250

Enest Bertram, 20, 20, 500, 30, 60
John Burkhardt, 12, 28, 500, 25, 100
Robert Burele, 27, 57, 3000, 100, 200
William Toole, 15, 35, 800, 50, 125
Joseph Worms, 16, 10, 200, 50, 60
Frederick Dent, 250, 640, 40000, 400, 600
William A. Darby, 30, 120, 2000, 100, 300
Bernhard Steinkamper, 20, 20, 600, 80, 80
George Grabe, 90, 210, 3200, 100, 150
John Shottville, 60, 144, 2000, 100, 300
David Huckstep, 30, 46, 2000, 120, 75
Charles Hauser, 30, 50, 3000, 75, 215
J. N. Gilbreth, 75, 135, 7200, 75, 250
Philip Fins, 60, 68, 2000, 100, 150
Jasper Toney, 45, 52, 1500, 60, 100
William Mehl, 15, 65, 500, 50, 120
Johannes Happel, 30, 35, 1500, 50, 105
Louis Beckler, 9, 31, 400, 15, 10
Chas. Meyer, 10, 30, 400, 25, 50
Francis L. Given, 8, 150, 1050, 21, 60
Herman Boche, 5, -, 1700, 55, 50
John Steffenauer, 20, 122, 6050, 40, 150
A. Stoner, 20, -, 3000, 25, 125
Christian Hofmeister, 40, 40, 7000, 60, 140
Johannes Stecke, 10, 50, 3000, 20, 100
John B. Kalan, 40, 10, 5500, 50, 80
Henry Hilbrecht, 5, -, 1700, 45, 50
A. C. Nore, 50, -, 5000, 60, 150
Gregory Delore, 30, 70, 5000, 65, 160
Wm. Forder, 60, 90, 6500, 75, 150
Diederich Schulenburg, 25, -, 2000, 30, 65
John Schneider, 40, -, 3500, 45, 150
Philip Waldorf, 40, -, 1000, 200, 160
George Kert, 50, 233, 2000, 100, 190
Theodore Hoffmann, 25, -, 500, 100, 160
Wm. Horstmeier, 25, -, 450, 60, 175
John Schuehrmann, 100, -, 5000, 100, 180
Francis Zimmermann, 80, -, 1200, 50, 95
Joseph Schmidt, 15, -, 350, 34, 106

John A. Kleinschmidt, 20, 40, 1400, 35, 60
George Luther, 24, 56, 1000, 50, 110
Wm. Musick, 25, 13, 1000, 15, 300
Nancy Musick, 70, 100, 3000, 150, 300
Christ. Prissel, 30, 25, 950, 60, 80
Thos. Kelly, 10, -, 250, 50, 80
J. A. Reiker, 38 81/100, -, 750, 45, 70
Christian Becker, 38 81/100, 800, 35, 85
Louis Rapp, 40, -, 900, -, -
Henry Erbe, 40, 28, 1100, 40, 150
Chas. Runkal, 20, 20, 750, 35, 100
Chas. Mehl, 30, 10, 850, 150, 200
H. P. Kraemer, 25, 15, 900, 65, 180
A. Feuerbach, 20, 47, 1200, 45, 110
Chas. Zufall, 7, 33, 600, 35, 80
Henry Schmidt, 20, 55, 1125, 30, 100
F. Wohlschlaeger, 20, 40, 1000, 55, 95
Ad. Heinz, 15, -, 300, 35, 95
Henry Mueller, 30, 45, 1150, 150, 150
Adam Mueller, 45, 35, 2500, 60, 125
G. Burg, 51 ½, -, 650, 35, 90
J. Burget, 25, 55, 700, 55, 145
James W. Sigerson, 1000, 600, 150000, 600, 1500
Francis Poupeney, 15, -, 1700, 50, 100
John E. Ruffien, 8, -, 20000, 150, 30
Gottfried Schoenthaler, 13, -, 7000, 100, 65
David Arneis, 4 85/100, -, 1600, 50, 75
D. Buchshort, 5, -, 1700, 50, 50
W. S. Allen, 50, -, 1500, 150, 210
Wm. Templeton, 40, -, 4000, 45, 100
Henry Quensing(Duensing), 25, -, 2500, 50, 70
Herman Moehlenhamp, 27, -, 2800, 45, 100
Herm. Bullmaner, 40, -, 4000, 45, 93
Adeline Constine, 27 ½, -, 3000, 55, 30
Fredr. Ketler, 27 ½, -, 3000, 50, 140
Rudolph Huebold, 27 ½, -, 3000, 85, 165
Joseph Poupeney, 33, -, 4500, 75, 100
Francis Corier, 14, -, 1500, 45, 95
Christ. Brandt, 30, -, 3500, 60, 55
Christ. Vanzandt, 52 ½, -, 5500, 45, 75
Henry Claas, 8, 4, 1500, 55, 62

Fr. Stuenkel, 45, 4800, 45, 155
Henry Bartler, 10, -, 1200, 40, 110
Herm. Rode, 21, -, 2400, 45, 90
Henry Koehn, 4, -, 200, 40, 40
Stephan Becker, 4, -, 400, 40, 110
F. Luether, 4, -, 450, 35, 50
_. Marsot, 10, -, 1500, 40, 45
Wm. Schnuhr, 15, -, 4000, 45, 85
Martha Johnson, 18, -, 1950, 20, 15
Wm. Behr, 10, 10, 1000, 50, 100
J. H. Hortebeck, 10, -, 1700, 60, 100
John Lorenz, 10, -, 1500, 30, 150
B. Warnbrodt, 14, -, 2000, 45, 100
H. H. Henche, 14, -, 2000, 30, 50
Louis Brown, 5, 5, 1000, 35, 45
T. Revau, 3, -, 600, 45, 45
M. Carroll, 3, -, 600, 35, 55
J. Joseph Kueper, 3, -, 600, 25, 50
Peter E. Meyer, 5, -, 1700, 65, 50
H. Pignaud, 3, -, 350, 35, 55
Henry Riecke, 48 3/100, -, 1600, 55, 50
J. B. Trenaux, 20, -, 2500, 65, 65
Jacob Schwuab, 25, 15, 500, 50, 125
William Crecelius, 20, 21, 600, 50, 150
John Erb, 18, 62, 1000, 45, 160
Henry Null, 18, 22, 400, 50, 125
John Gelbach, 15, 25, 450, 35, 75
Daniel Brauch, 20, 20, 600, 45, 150
J.P. Gebhardt, 30, 45, 800, 50, 110
Henry Denius, 16, 64, 900, 55, 150
John Jaegar, 6, 74, 750, 20, 60
Fr. Heimost, 25,-, 250, 55, 165
Adam Cross, 25, 15, 400, 45, 85
Wendel Kraft, 10, 70, 500, 25, 70
G. M. Baumgertner, 35, 25, 450, 45, 125
John Meyer, 5, 30, 260, 50, 100
Jacob Gregert, 25, 13, 500, 30, 100
Thos. Kelly, 30, 50, 650, 45, 150
Gerh. Weigers, 25, 15, 500, 25, 100

Louisa Anderson, 100, -, 2500, 150, 500
Caspar Lang, 25, 15, 600, 65, 95
Henry Neal, 30, -, 650, 75, 105
Henry Bosick, 40, 40, 1300, 65, 160
Valentine Darst, 35, 45, 1200, 55, 140
Ferdinand Kauna, 4, 32, 550, 40, 150
Philip Arnold, 30, 10, 650, 50, 180
Cathrine Berker, 20, 80, 1000, 45, 95
Peter Horst, 15, 25, 460, 55, 150
Wm. Schuler, 25, 15, 550, 65, 160
Adolph Neimeier, 30, 15, 750, 55, 120
Henry Tanzberger, 20, 40, 2000, 200, 100
Henry Braun, 40, 40, 2500, 150, 125
Christoph Hubert, 22, 18, 750, 150, 125
John Volz, 20, 100, 1000, 75, 125
Philip Clippel, 40, 40, 1200, 85, 140
Christoph Bernard, 25, 15, 750, 65, 120
Lawrence Tanzberger, 30, 10, 800, 150, 125
Peter Fardor, 60, 100, 2000, 100, 200
William Hoeckor, 20, 60, 800, 75, 225
Mary Davis, 35, 188, 1600, 150, 200
William Wermeier, 30, 50, 800, 75, 175
William Tremmeier, 15, 25, 700, 45, 75
Herman Nichof, 40, 60, 1100, 35, 60
Carl Bullenbacher, 5 ½, -, 1500, 90, 120
Adam Schwuab, 14, -, 1000, 50, 60
Franz Kunz, 14, -, 1200, 42, 35
Rurah Martin, 52, -, 4500, 65, 95
Hugh Daly, 5, -, 3500, 125, 450
Gashar Edhart, 1/3, -, 600, 12, -
George Feder, 5, -, 1500, -, 80
H. & N. Oberbeck, 10, -, 10000, -, 75
Wilse Barth & John F. Suchwisah, 3, -, 4000, 15, -
Gerh. Gebel, 2, -, 8000, 250, -
John Thomas, 3 ½, -, 5000, 55, 70
Aug. Fr. Schneider, 4 ½, -, 55000, 60, 55

Saline County 1850 Agricultural Census was filmed by the Central Microfilm Service Corp of St. Louis, Missouri, for the Missouri State Historical Society. There are 46 columns of information on the 1850 agricultural census. I have chosen to transcribe six of those columns. The columns are:

1. Name
2. Acres of Land Improved
3. Acres of Land Unimproved
4. Cash Value of the Farm
5. Value of Farm Implements and Machinery
13. Value of Livestock

William W. Field, 160, 400, 450, 400, 1200
Mordecai Hall, 16, -, 80, 10, 60
Richard J. Hall, 60, 270, 2400, 75, 459
William Horner, 16, -, -, -, 90
Francis Hampton, 40, 80, 1000, 40, 300
Robert Jackson, 7, 33, 160, 20, 100
John Jackson, 60, 340, 2000, 50, 305
George Jackson, 20, -, 80, 10, 35
Joshua Jackson, 20, -, 80, 5, 20
John Epperson, 20, -, 100, 10, 20
Jesse Epperson, 15, -, 155, 15, 125
Laban Garrett, 100, 400, 3500, 225, 1520
George Rhoades, 100, 532, 3000, 200, 915
Samuel Freet, 20, 100, 500, 90, 210
Peter S. Huff, 15, 105, 500, 40, 205
Abel Hampton, 40, 140, 720, 30, 236
Clairbone Hill, 40, 140, 6540, 70, 280
John Copeland, 25, 55, 100, 15, 430
Philip Hill, 16, 264, 800, 70, 425
William T. Gilliam, 300, 1100, 8400, 225, 1830
Andrew Thrailkill, 60, -, 250, 50, 675
Jesse Hanks, 30, -, 100, 30, 200
James Thrailkill, 16, 285, 2000, 100, 360
Jacob Pea, 25, 135, 480, 30, 260
Edmund Whittle, 10, -, 100, 10, 165
John T. Williams, 18, 38, 100, 25, 125

John T. Hughs, 20, -, 100, 15, 190
McBride Hays, 35, 40, 375, 150, 415
James Hays, 28, 372, 700, 175, 340
John J. Dille, 40, -, 250, 25, 215
Louis Thixton, 75, 245, 2000, 120, 800
James Wilhite, 80, 420, 2500, 200, 675
Elizabeth Haley, 30, 200, 2000, 70, 230
Garner C. Haley, 10, -, 50, 10, 115
James Croslin, 110, 370, 1600, 100, 1100
John Croslin, 20, 200, 800, 20, 330
Elijah Jackson, 33 1/3, -, 125, 10, 60
Thos. L. D. Mead, 40, 160, 800, 105, 280
Adam Ham, 150, 290, 2500, 80, 550
Thompson J. Whitson, 55, 185, 1600, 15, 210
Robert Y. Thompson, 300, 1500, 10800, 620, 1190
Margaret W. Wilson, 50, 254, 1520, 50, 265
John A. Reid, 35, 160, 975, 12, 145
George Quisenberry, 40, 160, 1000, 75, 260
E. L. Beeding, 30, 50, 400, 80, 200
A. R. Goodman, 4, -, 20, 10, 160
Littleberry Goodman, 25, 100, 500, 15, 100
C. P. Beeding, 45, 255, 1550, 100, 150
Edward Goodman, 20, -, 80, 15, 240

Wm. J. Wolfskill, 130, 410, 3200, 150, 600

Joseph Wolfskill, 40, -, 300, 70, 235

Henry M. Johnson, 15, 225, 720, 110, 40

Samuel Wheeler, 50, 150, 1600, 75, 825

Mathias Ayres, 120, 440, 2500, 65, 375

Walter Ayres, 30, -, 150, 20, 100

Addison Botts, 25, 101, 500, 5, 140

Edward Wirining, 120, 125, 1715, 200, 940

Eaton Emerson, 60, 340, 1750, 65, 300

Jonathan Millsaps, 40, 160, 800, 55, 270

Bartholomew Huff, 20, -, 100, 15, 130

William Campbell, 12, 138, 350, 20, 160

Allen McLean, 25, 50, 350, 30, 100

Nicholas Hawkins, 120, 380, 2000, 75, 815

Weston Wollard, 45, 175, 1100, 70, 385

Anderson Kirbey, 30, 130, 1000, 125, 210

Henry Neff, 14, 316, 1500, 80, 150

James Harring, 50, 110, 600, 60, 190

Pike M. Thompson, 100, 95, 780, 125, 525

Garrett W. Piper, 55, 185, 720, 50, 350

John Neff, 35, 125, 640, 20, 335

Betty Butt, 30, 50, 200, 60, 285

William Hunten, 10, -, 50, 10, 50

David Hizer, 11, 79, 400, 15, 70

Squire Dille, 40, 160, 800, 15, 600

Nehemiah Dille, 20, 100, 480, 25, 275

Stephen H. Dille, 15, 72, 348, 10, 110

Solomon Cat, 24, 20, 75, 10, 270

William Hays, 45,255, 1200, 100, 365

Mildred Page, 9, 31, 160, 30, 180

Henry Johnson, 18, 22, 120, 30, 135

Joseph Warson, 25, 200, 500, 35, 600

Ephraim McLean, 40, 129, 250, 35, 200

John Murphy, 10, 30, 120, 15, 70

William Wilhite, 30, 280, 1000, 105, 265

William Smith, 120, 480, 5000, 200, 1165

Harrison Harris, 15, 485, 1000, 60, 450

Thos. W. Powell, 20, 200, 1200, 80, 430

William W. Goode, 55, 115, 1360, 100, 310

Robert C. Land, 30, 140, 850, 30, 450

Joseph Grove, 100, 600, 4800, 85, 215

Daniel K. Rule, 41, 160, 600, 75, 470

Edward Clemms, 70, 430, 1600, 40, 175

John Fulton, 30, 100, 650, 40, 320

Jonathan Ferril, 20, 75, 250, 45, 225

Randall Latimer, 160, 500, 2000, 125, 500

Daniel Ham, 25, 175, 700, 25, 170

Eliza Shackelford, 300, 160, 5000, 160, 1200

James Reid, 60, 340, 3000, 81, 250

John C. Pulliam, 40, 160, 2000, 100, 700

Mary Dennis, 35, 75, 400, 50, 225

Caleb Hogshead, 30, 50, 240, 25, 130

Simon Dennis, 20, -, 80, 15, 70

Pembroke S. Epperson, 25, -, 100, 25, 105

Martin McMahan, 35, 50, 500, 60, 245

Wesly McMahan, 20, 30, 250, 35, 130

Polly McMahan, 35, 40, 350, 25, 190

Levi Crane, 30, 125, 1000, 100, 150

Cuthbert Hickman, 75, 395, 3000, 100, 575

James R. Johnson, 55, 345, 2000, 100, 300

David Ford, 30, 95, 1000, 80, 290

Joseph Smith, 4, 86, 600, 65, 105

Jane Fletchall, 15, 205, 800, 50, 100

Matthew C. Gwinn, 50, 320, 1480, 200, 450

Elias Wilhite, 50, 250, 1500, 75, 315

William Barnes, 25, 180, 1000, 100, 160

William E. Thompson, 150, 650, 2400, 300, 355

Carville Nickell, 9, 34, 200, 30, 85

James Norvell, 60, 140, 1500, 70, 315

Houston Blakely, 12, 154, 640, 10, 220

Fayette H. Gilliam, 12, 108, 800, 55, 275

Benjamin F. Duncan, 40, 60, 300, 35, 465

Fred. A. Brightwell, 65, 70, 1200, 50, 190

John G. Fletcher, 115, 256, 900, 150, 325
Charles C. Copeland, 60, 20, 200, 20, 205
Isaih Huff, 70, 95, 500, 50, 295
Permelia McMahan, 10, -, 50, 15, 135
George S. Hawkins, 80, 200, 1800, 125, 375
William A. Gwinn, 80, 50, 1000, 100, 575
Bartholomire Huff, 30, 210, 1200, 10, 95
Allmon Huff, 10, 50, 200, 35, 155
Peter Huff, 60, 220, 1400, 100 730
William Huff, 20, 120, 700, 70, 210
Mary S. Quisenberry, 25, 65, 400, 75, 205
Abner Gwinn, 40, 160, 800, 75, 585
Mathew Mullins, 20, 140, 500, 85, 155
Washington Lucas, 60, 540, 2500, 75, 565
Francis Tymony, 65, 148, 1200, 95, 205
Baxter D. Hartison, 80, 320, 3200, 120, 380
Dennis Thorp, 18, 107, 300, 5, 165
Jacob Rue, 66, 250, 60, 3, 170
William Wheeler, 60, 154, 1400, 75, 370
Richard C. Vaughan, 200, 300, 5000, 100, 735
Edward Garnett, 85, 220, 3000, 100, 295
William H. Graves, 70, 100, 1360, 150, 520
Sarah Graves, 160, 140, 1500, 75, 300
Thomas Hickman, 20, -, 160, 40, 115
Velones M. Woodworth, 80, 110, 1900, 35, 85
James Jones, 70, 220, 2000, 150, 500
Daniel Hickenson, 90, 230, 2500, 150, 425
John A. Watson, 60, 100, 1000, 150, 690
James Watson, 80, 100, 1400, 10, 170
Joseph H. Payne, 80, 206, 1430, 200, 500
Thomas Duggins, 90, 760, 4000, 200, 365
John Hyland, 10, 110, 600, 10, 55

Thomas Jackson, 70, 250, 2000, 150, 420
John P. Jackson, 40, 200, 1600, 75, 240
Louis Duggins, 27, 373, -, 25, 215
Tillman H. Cameron, 70, 530, 2000, 125, 320
Timothy Harris, 70, 175, 1500, 100, 310
Moses Harris, 16, -, 100, 20, 1056
John C. Johnson, 60, 140, 1000, 100, 240
Samuel Sullivan, 30, 170, 750, 50, 335
Tobias Cooper, 40, 160, 750, 65, 300
Garrett Yates, 80, 160, 1000, 200, 290
Joseph Auderley, 50, 85, 670, 50, 300
Ferdinand Tillman, 40, 80, 480, 40, 125
Ira Tillman, 60, 16, 265, -, 75
George Ryder, 125, 325, 2500, 160, 1200
Samuel Hughes, 70, 230, 2000, 100, 250
John Scott, 20, 80, 400, 20, 200
David Harris, 20, 30, 250, 15, 175
Wilkinson Teeton, 15, 65, 250, 40, 155
Richard Cunsen, 60, 580, 2500, 45, 490
Steven Wheeler, 120, 480, 3000, 100, 1800
Tempest Sulivan, 35, 85, 600, 45, 345
James Steel, 24, 68, 368, 20, 335
Matthew Smith, 16, 25, 50, 65, 245
William Clark, 18, -, 25, 10, 220
Abner Gwinn, 7, 8, 25, 5, 245
Morris Martin, 100, 100, 2500, 300, 440
George Casebott, 35, 70, 250, 60, 210
John Davis, 28, 172, 600, 50, 305
Nathan Perry, 13, -, 50, 15, 165
George Kile, 120, 380, 1000, 35, 680
Absolum Corn, 20, 65, 150, 50, 250
William C. Hill, 125, 400, 2000, 45, 280
William Mullin, 200, 130, 2000, 100, 1725
Abner Mullin, 25, 55, 350, 20, 140
Thomas Clemmons, 70, 250, 2500, 75, 250
Patrick Maupin, 13, -, 130, 15, 150
William McMahan, 25, 275, 2400, 150, 900
John T. Davis, 65, 115, 1000, 100, 335

Isaac Parsons, 200, 200, 3000, 160, 745
Judith Haynie, 50, 50, 1000, 95, 240
Singleton Vaughn, 100, 200, 3500, 190, 540
Alfred Wheeler, 60, 140, 1200, 75, 550
Samuel Keiffer, 20, 140, 1000, 50, 145
Ann Galbrath, 55, 105, 1100, 50, 320
Isaac Kyle, 60, 340, 1250, 150, 480
John Williams, 20, 20, 200, 75, 160
Joseph Keiffer, 35, 85, 600, 10, 185
George Keiffer, 60, 540, 3500, 100, 475
Joseph Miles, 48, 112, 800, 32, 155
Archibald Burnsides, 20, 60, 500, 30, 145
Jonathan Burnsides, 35, 55, 540, 50, 220
William Casebott, 30, 70, 250, 35, 375
Samuel Sullivan, 20, 75, 500, 10, 250
Davidson Ervin, 100, 340, 2300, 55, 440
John S. Gaulding, 20, -, 200, 70, 175
Benjamin M. Gaulding, 30, 470, 2500, 75, 385
Josiah Gaulding, 200 250, 4000, 200, 800
Henry Brown, 300, 200, 4000, 100, 740
Jacob Boatright, 60, 320, 2200, 50, 275
William Brown, 150, 180, 2000, 200, 600
Thomas Caffey, 40, -, 300, 70, 115
Philander Y. Twine, 100, 390, 3000, 200, 540
Edmond Brown, 60, 120, 1400, 150, 440
Three Swellass Minos, 75, 155, 1500, 125, 400
C. & S. Ross, 100, 500, 3000, 175, 500
Thomas H. Harvey, 700, 1300, 10000, 500, 1590
John Hisey, 40, -, 1500, 75, 385
Charles Stevenson, 25, 115, 1000, 25, 65
James Stevenson, 80, 90, 1700, 50, 190
Alfred Towles, 140, 360, 3000, 150, 780
Amos A. Brice, 40, 210, 1800, 70, 312
Joseph Wolfskill, 40, 120, 800, 45, 75
Reuben E. McDaniel, 280, 920, 12000, 300, 1750
Lawrence B. Lewis, 100, 90, 1600, 55, 385

Lewis A. Smith, 60, 160, 1500, 200, 490
William O. Smith, 45, 175, 1500, 150, 385
George W. Gant, 150, 215, 3600, 250, 670
Charles P. Bondurant, 200, 900, 10000, 400, 1050
Pink _. Booker, 380, 624, 12000, 500, 1950
Archibalt Paxton, 200, 150, 2000, 75, 825
Michael Rice, 23, 8, 200, 15, 90
John C. Scott, 130, 219, 2500, 150, 330
Thomas Rogers, 200, 200, 3500, 200, 3150
Samuel H. Coleman, 40, 40, 300, 40, 35
William Gwinn, 40, 30, 250, 20, 225
John H. Eustace, 300, 200, 5000, 150, 720
James M. Dinkel, 115, 177, 2500, 60, 440
Richard E. Snelling, 160, 280, 4000, 200, 1250
Thomas Cheatham, 100, 60, 1600, 100, 620
Benjamin Pulliam, 300, 200, 4000, 200, 1500
Charles M. Kavenaugh, 50, 300, 2100, 220, 465
George H. Vaughn, 25, 150, 1000, 50, 190
William W. Akres, 60, 30, 700, 55, 300
William Surbaugh, 300, 260, 3500, 100, 525
N. & T. Robertson, 400, 436, 6000, 600, 1480
Winson Rice, 30, -, 200, 35, 290
Auscrae(Huscrae) Haynie, 10, 90, 300, 15, 100
Nathan Holloway, 200, 200, 3500, 120, 1500
Addison Carthie, 52, 60, 1500, 75, 335
Phillip Reynolds, 40, 75, 1200, 50, 365
Edwin Haynie, 35, 100, 1000, 50, 285
Joseph G. Prosser, 45, 140, 2500, 100, 450

Sylvester Welsh, 20, 20, 400, 20, 130
John Brown, 250, 1135, 15000, 445, 740
Abraham VanMeter, 500, 500, 500, 200, 1600
William Parsons, 150, 350, 7500, 200, 1180
Barnett Huff, 35, 20, 400, 50, 175
Robert Huff, 30, 15, 250, 40, 280
Thomas T. Edwards, 50, 120, 1000, 80, 270
Thomas Bird, 25, 135, 1000, 60, 315
William Hunter, 15, 145, 800, 25, 350
John W. Sandige, 100, 260, 2100, 200, 625
Charles Hunden, 40, 200, 1500, 20, 440
William Prior, 80, 240, 1000, 75, 565
Mathew King, 35, 275, 1000, 80, 450
Jesse Davis (Segns), 125, 555, 3500, 100, 370
Harvey H. McDowell, 275, 700, 7000, 300, 750
William S. Renick, 50, 110, 6000, 60, 900
John & T. Reeves, 60, 1000, 6000, 120, 425
Elizabeth Little, 20, 25, 150, 55, 185
William C. Sharp, 19, -, 100, 70, 140
William Decker, 40, 40, 550, 45, 335
Andrew Armstrong, 20, 20, 200, 100, 275
William Wallace, 20, 20, 200, 5, 165
George C. Davis, 70, -, 700, 15, 195
Jacob VanMeter, 30, 400, 2800, 75, 750
John C. DeMoss, 120, 820, 9400, 120, 560
John Garner, 20, 600, 6000, 100, 80
George W. Lewis, 160, 400, 6720, 200, 600
James H. McMillan, 300, 320, 3500, 150, 725
Michael Hoke, 10, 5, 75, 20, 160
John Frizzell, 40, 60, 580, 100, 290
John White & G. Tiven(Twen), 25, 30, 200, 300, 240
Jacob Fackler, 250, 400, 5000, 150, 1750

Allison Frizzell, 15, -, 150, 10, 180
James Osland, 45, 37, 250, 60, 240
Milton Gilbraith, 80, 200, 200, 120, 540
William Horner, 15, 25, 200, 40, 125
William Fifer, 20, 20, 200, 60, 165
Miles Meadows, 80, 120, 1000, 65, 535
George W. Hereford, 75, 125, 3000, 175, 775
Baltimore Thomas, 120, 470, 7000, 250, 870
Oscar F. Thomas, 140, 260, 4500, 150, 700
David McReynolds, 100, 300, 1000, 100, 450
John M. Lewis, 275, 495, 10000, 400, 890
Edward F. Webb, 20, 115, 1000, 50, 160
George Krutsinger, 65, 140, 2500, 150, 460
Allen McReynolds, 100, 160, 3500, 100, 420
John DeMoss, 300, 200, 7000, 300, 1440
William H. Lewis, 200, 200, 4800, 200, 1100
John B. Ervin, 80, 140, 2500, 100, 520
Nancy T. Major, 40, 180, 2500, 75, 340
Thomas A. Gunnell, 160, 120, 3000, 150, 560
Samuel Webb, 70, 260, 2300, 75, 195
John Major, 60, 180, 2000, 85, 490
John McReynolds, 80, 320, 3000, 100, 410
Isaac Meadows, 90, 235, 2500, 100, 480
Samuel Meadows, 50, 110, 1400, 60, 330
John H. Taylor, 140, 360, 4000, 180, 750
William O'dell, 25, 15, 75, 10, 250
Jeremiah O'dell, 120, 160, 2000, 150, 430
James C. Russell, 55, 145, 1000, 350, 624
Richard C. Head, 30, 170, 1000, 100, 140
Richard W. Bowen, 100, 150, 1250, 150, 550

David C. Malone, 50, 65, 500, 100, 170

Phillip Sidenstricker, 150, 270, 5000, 250, 800

Thomas H. Pemberton, 50, 450, 2500, 50, 170

Jacob H. Smith, 80, 170, 3000, 100, 520

Catlett Orear, 40, 120, 800, 25, 450

Henry T. Weeden, 80, 320, 2000, 125, 390

Jacob Kester, 70, 350, 1900, 100, 680

Jeremiah Miller, 100, 100, 1200, 90, 600

James H. McCallister, 18, 182, 800, 20, 200

Milton Wood, 200, 440, 3000, 150, 650

Benjamin Weller, 150, 420, 2500, 100, 340

William Lisle, 40, 160, 1200, 50, 20

Daniel Rummons, 50, 160, 1400, 50, 170

Stephen Smith, 200, 300, 5000, 150, 800

Daniel Kiser, 120, 600, 7200, 400, 875

James Kiser, 20, -, 200, -, 150

Martin Gauldin, 20, 70, 500, -, 130

William C. Davis, 100, 320, 3000, 125, 490

James Howard, 50, 70, 400, 50, 300

Howel Oneal, 180, 240, 7200, 250, 1150

Andrew Beaty, 80, 254, 1500, 50, 630

Russell Romines, 140, 460, 2500, 250, 1350

William S. Dueritt, 200, 330, 7000, 250, 1200

George T. Crisman, 200, 770, 9000, 150, 430

William Jackman, 30, 90, 300, 25, 100

David N. Jones, 70, 330, 2000, 125, 350

Thomas Finley, 90, 440, 3000, 80, 400

William Hansbrough, 100, 200, 1000, 100, 400

James H. Irvine, 150, 380, 5000, 350, 920

Mortimore D. Gaines, 70, 480, 2000, 100, 540

John Gilmer, 110, 440, 2000, 70, 560

Joseph Field, 325, 200, 5000, 500, 1150

David B. Wood, 100, 300, 1500, 150, 820

Peter Duffey, 16, 185, 600, 70, 185

James Mitchell, 35, 660, 1500, 7, 320

Obidiah B. Pearson, 250, 330, 5000, 265, 1250

Isaac Hays, 10, -, 100, 10, 170

Silas E. Combs, 75, 375, 2000, 100, 300

Robert Field, 100, 400, 4000, 250, 900

Fountain Roberts, 100, 380, 4000, 150, 460

Benjamin F. Down, 40, 80, 700, 100, 390

William H. Moore, 60, 270, 1000, 65, 280

Richard D. Richardson, 100, 700, 3000, 60, 425

Nathaniel W. Noel, 17, 43, 250, 60, 75

William O. Maupin, 100, 400, 2500, 150, 490

James Brown, 300, 1000, 7000, 200, 1175

Elisha Erwin, 65, 265, 2000, 100, 425

James F. Fegram, 80, 270, 1750, 100, 565

William Pemberton, 65, 175, 1000, 150, 390

David Durrett, 80, 410, 2500, 100, 450

Marshall Allen, 20, 160, 800, 45, 245

John Sheridan, 130, 230, 2800, 200, 300

Luther Dickerson, 10, 30, 200, 20, 60

William McClanaham, 160, 730, 6000, 35, 450

Martin Langan, 30, 330, 1500, -, 145

Joseph Gilchrist, 80, 320, 1800, 150, 335

Fielding Calmes, 250, 410, 3000, 200, 385

Samuel Steel, 50, 58 ½, 400, 30, 200

Hugh Murphy, 87, 450, 3000, 55, 420

William Price, 240, 420, 9000, 600, 1250

George Francisco, 80, 270, 3000, 150, 400

Caleb Witcher, 160, 60, 1400, 150, 650

William Babbit, 40, 810, 1500, 250, 100

Jesse E. Crew, 40, 110, 1000, 25, 250

David Spotts, 75, 85, 900, 15, 200
Brutus W. Finley, 65, 375, 1760, 100, 600
John W. Gallagher, 105, 395, 3000, 200, 500
Abner Trigg, 90, 280, 2000, 100, 720
James W. Finley, 90, 236, 2000, 100, 1800
Porus Q. Finley, 50, 420, 1800, 10, 325
William Burke, 45, 275, 2000, 125, 280
Joseph Barnes, 20, 50, 300, 15, 115
James Lockney, 60, 110, 800, 10, 300
John Babbit, 80, 525, 4000, 300, 640
Jno. C. Hansbrough, 20, 300, 1800, 85, 165
James R. Davis, 45, 95, 800, 80, 240
John Townsend, 50, 430, 2000, 60, 400
Adam France, 30, 58, 450, 10, 140
William Adkisson, 30, 50, 500, 50, 110
Ann Adkisson, 60, 380, 2500, 250, 375
Paris M. Walker, 300, 240, 3000, 200, 1400
Thos. M. Harrison, 20, 360, 1000, 50, 70
William Miller, 450, 1450, 15000, 210, 1500
John Hawkins, 20, 140, 700, 40, 135
John McMillan, 48, 36, 500, 15, 135
Benjamin Lawless, 70, 309, 800, 100, 600
Moses Woodfin, 30, 235, 2500, 80, 165
William Hays, 120, 383, 5000, 150, 1300
Samuel Wall, 100, 100, 1600, 65, 725
Michael Langan, 80, 375, 3000, 100, 650
Hiram Weedon, 20, 220, 800, 125, 150
Thomas Johnson, 30, 50, 250, 100, 110
Warren Compton, 50, 70, 800, 75, 280
Jane Compton, 35, 85, 1000, 20, 355
James Higgins, 65, 100, 9000, 100, 280
Andrew Stevenson, 35, 205, 1250, 200, 260
Jane Trigg, 35, 115, 850, 1115, 215
William Ervin, 100, 220, 1600, 100, 245
Mary Bingham, 100, 200, 3000, 100, 425

Cunrod A. Claycomb, 40, 600, 3000, 120, 700
Elisha Chappell, 30, 50, 500, 25, 340
Thomas W. Chappell, 30, 50, 500, 100, 225
George W. Rockwell, 75, 173, 2000, 140, 200
William Piper, 60, 180, 1000, 40, 240
Richard Durrett, 200, 600, 2800, 200, 580
Willis W. Piper, 200, 390, 7000, 275, 1700
Nathan W. Keaton, 35, 205, 1000, 50, 180
George W. Hall, 20, 20, 250, 40, 100
William Beaty, 65, 95, 1000, 50, 400
W. M. Rett, 200, 263, 740, 200, 825
Jefferson James, 40, 100, 500, 35, 195
Thomas Gagan, 20, 120, 600, 30, 45
James H. Dudley, 30, 20, 250, 20, 110
Joseph Wheeler, 20, 20, 200, 15, 75
Jeremiah Wiley, 25, 40, 250, 35, 200
James O'Dell, 10, 30, 400, 15, 75
Joel Moore, 9, 31, 400, 75, 340
Ossemus Hurt, 200, 500, 3000, 300, 1600
George Tucker, 50, 80, 500, 30, 340
Albert McCallister, 25, 55, 500, 50, 225
Lewis C. Hiley, 6, 34, 60, 25, 150
John Buck, 10, -, 50, 70, 60
Andrew Brownlee, 100, 370, 2350, 65, 525
Charles Beasley, 75, 245, 1800, 125, 400
Frederick Lockney, 25, 40, 300, 20, 50
Burr Harris, 200, 900, 5000, 100, 300
Henry Johnson, 50, 30, 320, 60, 300
Job Parker, 20, 20, 150, 35, 150
Thomas Miller, 100, 300, 1200, 45, 330
John D. Bailey, 40, 120, 800, 150, 470
John Buford, 40, 120, 800, 70, 275
James L. Bailey, 130, 270, 2800, 70, 740
Isaac Hays, 50, 300, 1800, 55, 175
Andrew M. Francisco, 125, 175, 1800, 100, 550
Levi J. Aulgur, 40, 80, 800, 65 475
Mary Pennington, 60, 180, 900, 70, 150

Acy Pennington, 30, 170, 1200, 60, 160
Martin Dutten, 35, 105, 1000, 20, 260
Charles Taliaferro, 80, 120, 1400, 80, 400
Archibald McPhail, 20, 260, 1200, 75, 210
James B. Beatty, 90, 230, 1600, 100, 425
John Jackman, 20, 20, 250, 20, 90
Christopher Faber, 160, 120, 3700, 200, 550
Andrew Francisco, 40, 160, 1800, 50, 300
William Harris, 30, 90, 450, 40, 225
John K. Owens, 25 95, 700, 60, 325
John S. Owens, 20, 140, 1000, 55, 550
Thomas Hunter, 80, 240, 1800, 50, 670
John F. Harris, 28, 52, 1000, 50, 830
Robert Owens, 50, 250, 1800, 75, 900
John H. Owens, 25, 55, 750, 45, 285
William D. Harris, 20, 30, 400, 40, 115
Mary E. Etter, 25, 135, 700, 25, 75
William Hunter, 30, 90, 350, 40, 275
Joseph W. Hall, 28, 272, 2000, 15, 400
John Lynch, 40, 20, 300, 25, 275
Gilmore Hays, 150, 470, 3000, 100, 590
George Haynes, 10, -, 70, -, 160
Samuel Williams, 35, 85, 500, 40, 150
Jonathon Knight, 30, 810, 3000, 40, 400
Joel Lee, 15, 25, 200, 15, 150
Lewis Marshall, 20, 40, 200, 25, 85
James Owens, 25, 55, 300, 20, 165
Margaret Anderson, 20, 140, 700, 30, 170
Edward Parsons, 55, 185, 1000, 50, 350
Isaac Parsons, 300, 700, 5000, 150, 950
Beverly Carey, 30, 50, 600, 40, 470
Joseph Carmack, 60, 100, 800, 50, 375
William Browning, 20, 20, 200, 25, 155
William Cooper, 25, 55, 350, 40, 240
George R. Cooper, 30, 50, 300, 45, 175
John L. Tucker, 20, 80, 500, 25, 195
John Campbell, 15, 25, 150, 10, 50
John Bright, 20, 80, 450, 30, 150
John L. Yantes, 16, 304, 7500, 100, 430
James Fuguson, 80, 160, 1000, 100, 460
Thomas Cox, 40, 210, 1200, 30, 195

John S. Dederick, 500, 1000, 6500, 500, 1550
Thomas W. Gaines, 350, 210, 3300, 200, 1100
Aaron B. Lawten, 90, 330, 2500, 125, 470
Thomas King, 10, 30, 200, 35, 195
Johnson Hunt, 70, 130, 1000, 50, 290
Alexander Hamilton, 25, 135, 700, 35, 275
Charles _. Clark, 36, 85, 600, 40, 225
Johnathan T. Gresham, 80, 320, 1500, 100, 2000
Isaac Buck, 20, 100, 450, 25, 200
James Cuningham, 160, 80, 1200, 100, 900
John Hunt, 40, 120, 550, 40, 350
James Witaker, 80, 320, 1500, 75, 550
Steven S. Sutherland, 40, 240, 1000, 50, 180
Walker H. Finley, 130, 470, 2400, 185, 1800
Stephen Dial, 100, 220, 1900, 60, 925
Watson Dial, 20, 40, 300, 25, 150
William Simons, 20, 20, 200, 20, 140
Mathew Weeden, 10, 40, 275, 15, 60
Aaron Stone, 25, 55, 300, 40, 210
William Rucker, 50 70, 800, 50, 575
Joseph R. Gray, 35, 35, 500, 60, 200
Joseph T. Gray, 25, 15, 150, 20, 185
Richard Howard, 60, 140, 800, 73, 390
Barnett Wease, 40, 80, 450, 45, 315
Robert Crockett, 30, 50, 350, 40, 250
Higginbothan Ramky, 30, 170, 700, 25, 250
James O. Howell, 10, 30, 250, 30, 265
Richard Marshall, 300, 1000, 5000, 250, 3750
William B. Marshall, 30, 130, 650, 40, 265
James Staples, 70, 850, 6000, 175, 530
William Townsend, 45, 250, 1800, 75, 375
Thomas Dickerson, 15, 60, 300, 40, 100
Almire Kester, 60, 380, 1400, 65, 275
James Hood, 30, 50, 320, 15, 75

Jesse Langford, 20, 140, 700, 45, 315
William Brown, 30, 360, 1200, 50, 105
James F. Jeffrie, 40, 180, 1200, 65, 160
John R. Hancock, 100, 500, 3000, 200, 625
James W. Smith, 1000, 6800, 39000, 600, 3800
Rebecca Bingham, 150, 640, 4000, 160, 1060
Peter Thornton, 240, 80, 2500, 150, 750
Elizabeth Fizer, 23, 67, 500, 40, 150
Virginia F. Howard, 200, 300, 2500, 150, 525
William Davidson, 20, 60, 600, 50, 190
Danial Eclbeck(Edbeck), 28, 222, 1500, 65, 215
Jane Thompson, 80, 80, 1000, 50, 335
James Dennis, 125, 175, 1800, 65, 450
Joseph Liggett, 30, 470, 2000, 60, 415
Thomas Jackson, 40, 120, 700, 85, 1175
John Piper, 100, 100, 1200, 125, 600
Nancy Sappington, 35, 30, 500, 100, 630
John C. Thompson, 35, 315, 700, 50, 440
Georg W. Burnett, 35, 55, 300, 25, 55
Edmond Burnett, 15, 40, 250, 15, 40
Richard Burnett, 15, 25, 150, 10, 25
John C. Johnson, 14, 25, 100, 15, 115
Andrew F. Lacey, 15, 40, 150, 50, 140
Benjamin Cooper, 10, 110, 450, 45, 155
James Hubbard, 24, 140, 400, 35, 200
John Grove, 30, 50, 400, 25, 150
Jessee Romine, 40, 220, 1300, 100, 520
Charles W. Wood, 150, 450, 300, 250, 850
Daniel Thornton, 140, 760, 8000, 225, 950
John Jones Sr., 100, 450, 5000, 200, 425
Robert Dysart, 150, 370, 5000, 225, 780
Philip W. Thompson, 300, 900, 9000, 300, 1400
Rudolph Hawpe, 60, 220, 1800, 100, 400
George Fall, 20, 139, 1500, 40, 150
Samuel Green, 35, 45, 700, 40, 350

Benjamin Huston, 75, 475, 4000, 170, 470
John Dyreby, 20, 270, 1500, 40, 220
James Knox, 60, 140, 1500, 50, 520
Prunett(Burnett) Thompson, 80, 250, 2400, 120, 650
Sidney Petitt, 18, 390, 2400, 50, 200
William G. Sappington, 350, 250, 14000, 300, 1750
Erasmus D. Sappington, 300, 500, 15000, 300, 1000
John Sappington, 300, 1500, 10000, 300, 2500
Lewis D. Harwood, 200, 320, 5300, 300, 700
Meredith M. Marmaduke, 400, 1100, 7500, 300, 3900
Henry Neff, 100, 400, 3000, 175, 1900
Emsley Cravens, 30, 50, 320, 35, 275
Isaac Neff, 160, 724, 4500, 200, 1675
Charles W. Carthrae, 100, 160, 2600, 100, 360
James B. Brown, 100, 800, 4500, 120, 500
Isaac Neff Jr., 25, 15, 350, 55, 165
Marshall Piper, 45, 97, 420, 75, 200
Bernis Brown, 250, 1050, 10000, 175, 820
Augustus Stevenson, 30, 270, 3000, 70, 290
John L. Hardeman, 600, 900, 13000, 400, 1675
Ezekiel Scott, 300, 900, 7500, 250, 2800
Aaron F. Bruce, 300 700, 7500, 150, 624
Samuel M. McDowell, 65, 265, 2200, 45, 390
John D. Kinkead, 55, 545, 1800, 125, 425
Minor W. O'Bannon, 300, 130, 3500, 300, 624
William Harrelson, 200, 800, 4500, 150, 825
Presley Shroyer, 350, 500, 5000, 200, 1500

Schuyler County, Missouri
1850 Agricultural Census

Schuyler County 1850 Agricultural Census was filmed by the Central Microfilm Service Corp of St. Louis, Missouri, for the Missouri State Historical Society. There are 46 columns of information on the 1850 agricultural census. I have chosen to transcribe six of those columns. The columns are:

1. Name
2. Acres of Land Improved
3. Acres of Land Unimproved
4. Cash Value of the Farm
5. Value of Farm Implements and Machinery
13. Value of Livestock

James F. White, 50, 50, 300, 40, 30
Eliza B. Fletcher, 20, 60, 230, 100, 15
Reuben Wright, 40, 160, 400, 100, 440
Samuel Mineas, 60, -, 250, 100, 339
Wm. H. Collins, -, -, -, 50, 190
John W. Collins, 15, 25, 100, 50, -
Allen Reed, 60, 100, 700, 100, 232
Henry Powell, 60, 62, 600, 175, 385
Samuel Webster, 30, 146, 1000, 30, 96
B. J. Tompkins, 30, 40, 150, 40, 238
Thomas Butts, 40, 100 700, 100, 310
Edward Butts, 30, 90, 300, 75, 205
Newton Whitaker, 25, 15, 150, 15, 172
Benj. Brown, 50, 30, 300, 30, 265
George Naylor, 40, 80, 300, 75, 205
John Bradburn, 22, -, 140, 10, 47
Reuben Whitwell, 20, -, 100, 10, 105
John Tusk, 60, 180, 1000, 20, 179
Christian Miller, 12, 28, 100, 10, 144
Samuel Ow, 100, 140, 2500, 75, 494
Robert S. Neeley, 94, 404, 1000, 100, 301
Jackson Bloid, 15, 25, 200, 10, 85
Wm. Parton, 50, 110, 500, 50, 230
Z. Nichols, 6, -, 50, 5, 70
Eliza Nichols, 5, -, 30, 5, 50
Edward Hughes, 25, 40, 200, 40, 262
James Hall, 35, 45, 400, 65, 310
Elias Fletcher, 15, 5, 100, 10, 102
A. D. Farris, 35, 65, 500, 25, 215

Isaac Foster, 8, 152, 300, 15, 100
George Alfrey, 15, 145, 550, 20, 60
Joseph Leedom, 25, 35, 300, 100, 195
Thomas McGoldrich, 15, -, 35, 60, 150
Jesse Gray, 36, 285, 100, 25, 245
John M. Brown, 30, 50, 200, 80, 132
Moses Hughes, 12, 148, 250, 20, 135
Andrew Miller, 40, 220, 600, 15, 173
George F. Palmer, 80, 30, 300, 25, 842
Wm. Beasley, 100, 350, 2000, 125, 436
Edwin Firinch(Fornich), 100, -, 2000, 100, 885
Howell Brewer, 30, 70, 400, 50, 152
M. J. Back, 10, -, 30, 5, 40
John C. Gray, 6, 74, 100, 6, 80
Peter Sloas, 15, 65, 130, 40, 180
Thomas Martin, 60, 60, 200, 15, 321
S. H. Shumate, 30, 30, 300, 10, 128
James Wells, 70, 210, 800, 100, 360
Alex. Wells, -, -, -, -, 120
John Wells, -, -, -, -, 105
Jonathan Hilton, 10, 130, 200, 15, 137
Alexander Claus, -, -, -, -, 40
E. W. Myers, 23, 57, 300, 10, 87
James Myers, 100, 160, 1000, 60, 398
G. B. Bradley, 40, 160, 800, 75, 247
Green Robbins, 20, 20, 100, 8, 90
L. T. Bradley, 20, 60, 300, 65, 113
John W. Burns, 40, 10, 300, 100, 207
L. Waugh, 400, 100, 300, -, 50

Freeman Elliott, 30, 45, 200, 15, 80
J. M. Fish, 160, 230, 3500, 400, 1263
Noah Beeler, -, -, -, -, 70
G. N. Clevenger, 12, -, 75, -, 131
John J. White, 12, 80, 200, 50, 100
Isaac Burgin, 20, 80, 200, 40, 147
Dennis Burgin, 16, 40, 130, 15, 160
George Mitchell, 15, 65, 200, 10, 140
George Nichols, 60, 60, 500, 75, 400
Susan Lindsay, -, 35, 50, -, 125
James Davis, 16, -, 40, 10, 95
John Mikel, 50, -, 100, 20, 278
E__ Richardson, 25, -, 75, 10, 157
Martha Ayers, 10, 30, 100, 5, 190
Wesley Barks, 25, 135, 500, 50, 100
Enoch Cleaton, 15, -, 30, 10, 60
Thomas Leedom(Teedom), 40, 100, 400, 100, 180
Z. Croson, 25, 15, 200, 50, 310
Hiram Knight, 45, 115, 700, 75, 316
Peter Varner, 60, 123, 1000, 75, 272
Henry Smith, 25, 100, 550, 50, 450
Hiram Reevis, 80, 40, 500, 75, 367
C. G. Hill, 45, 115, 400, 20, 80
Wm. Bledsoe, 50, 70, 800, 75, 332
Wm. Forbes (Torbes), 16, 144, 500, 5, 70
Isaac H. Farris, 15, 65, 200, 4, 75
R. D. Lee, 25, 135, 300, 15, 203
Robert Majors, 10, 40, 65, 5, 150
Wm. R. Sears, 12, -, 40, 10, 130
Alexander Pagr, 25, -, 150, 75, 215
Douglass Bowen, 85, 82, 1000, 100, 274
Martin Johnson, 8, 32, 75, 10, 108
Garton Pitty, 60, 310, 1500, 20, 265
E. M. Harlan, 11, 149, 350, 8, 133
W. H. Roberts, 30, 90, 350, 10, 80
D. A. Roberts, 18, 40, 125, 20, 100
John S. Johnson, 45, 115, 300, 50, 135
George Payton, 6, -, 30, 35, 75
Patton Martin, 75, 45, 600, 100, 530
Nicholas Shobe, 1, -, 10, -, 30
Cath. Newman, 23, 27, 100, 15, 100
J. W. Powell, 65, 155, 300, 60, 120
George Holloway, 80, 200, 1000, 100, 160

Daniel Lile, 15, 65, 100, 15, 144
H. W. Burks, 20, -, 100, 20, 145
Joseph Bradl__, 35, 45, 500, 75, 304
Thomas Mills, 25, 15, 200, 10, 168
Richard Riff(Kiff), 20, -, 100, 12, 133
John Powell, 9, - , 30, 10, 64
Wm. Hoskins, 10, -, 60, 5, 75
G. W. Johnson, 10, 30, 150, 7, 195
Henry Snead, 25, 135, 200, 10, 150
Harnett Davis, 12, 188, 300, 30, 147
John Farris, 16, -, 50, 50, 132
Wm. Hulin, 30, 10, 200, 20, 130
Dudley Barnes, 20, -, 75, 10, 100
J. F. Ragsdale, 23, -, 100, 100, 300
Isaac McNeeley, -, -, -, 60, 125
Henry McAtee, 50, 110, 800, 25, 200
Henry Whitlow, 40, 40, 400, 15, 216
Sam. Lockett, 18, -, 50, 5, 148
F. T. Foster, 5, 35, 125, 10, 180
T. Threldkeld, 30, 130, 600, 25, 215
R. Caywood, 32, 90, 500, 30, 154
M. Fairbanks, 40, 120, 500, 100, 353
Daniel D. Smith, 24, -, 100, 50, 225
James Hepbern, 30, 130, 600, 165, 172
M. Richardson, 75, 30, 1200, 150, 430
Elkanah Keane, -, -, -, -, 40
Nicholas Roberts, 15, 105, 200, 10, 115
Jacob Dodge, 25, -, 200, 25, 180
Thomas E. Fulton, 17, 143, 400, 50, 151
Wm. Caspar, 30, 141, 600, 75, 160
Cal. Dunnington, 25, 60, 300, 20, 170
Caswell Dennis, 30, 130, 400, 75, 227
James Ornburn, 30, 110, 200, 100, 173
Theophileus Ryals, 60, 20, 325, 50, 395
Robert Towles, 20, 20, 150, 15, 200
Squire Thompson, 12, 30, 100, 65, 163
Richard Morton, 25, -, 100, 4, 83
John Wamick, 14, -, 100, 5, 100
Daniel Minick, 6, -, 20, 10, 100
D. M. T. Brassfield, 40, 200, 400, 200, 425
Hansford Wilcher, 50, 110, 500, 60, 110
Alfred Adams, 40, -, 200, 100, 276
A. Adams, -, -, -, 10, 50
H. P. Buford, 30, -, 150, 25, 155
Wm. Rowland, 75, 80, 1150, 100, 180

S. B. Knox, 150, 250, 3000, 130, 1232
Henry Capps, 25, -, 200, 25, 137
Joel Taylor, 9, 40, 130, 7, 80
John S. Mikel, 22, -, 100, 10, 35
Peter Kline, 60, 100, 800, 150, 392
Thomas Arnold, 30, 131, 300, 60, 265
Asa Cook, 30, -, 130, 10, 136
T. W. Donnell, 40, -, 100, -, 106
F. C. Hulin, 50, 70, 600, 15, 150
James J. Burks, 25, -, 100, 6, 113
M. W. Lockett, 40, 30, 500, 50, 156
John Seamster, 24, -, 100, 100, 160
Fields Tramell, -, -, -, -, -
Perrin Bryant, -, -, -, -, 20
Jackson Bryant, -, -, -, -, 20
David Bozarth, 30, 40, 300, 75, 176
Cantley W. Stewart, 50, 210, 1200, 100, 261
S. D. Ruddle, 100, 100, 1000, 83, 634
Joseph Wilson, 20, 100, 400, 50, 195
Patton Nichols, 20, 165, 600, 10, 270
Thompson Bucey, 45, -, 150, 8, 100
Wm. L. Robinson, 80, 80, 600, 75, 290
Wm. E. Hite, 40, 80, 400, 50, 175
A. J. Towles, 40, 60, 500, 40, 287
Wm. Batton, 16, 144, 400, 60, 154
Isaac Mitchell, 30, 130, 1200, 60, 208
Hiram Cooksey, 34, 133, 1000, 20, 195
John C. Lane, 8, 72, 200, 10, 95
George W. Lane, 12, 68, 250, 10, 80
Job Wright, 18, -, 65, 3, 60
Wm. Ingram, 35, 75, 500, 60, 235
Murray Tipton, 10, -, 50, 25, 222
L. H. Conklin, 75, 85, 500, 100, 536
Mancel Garnett, 150, 210, 2000, 500, 773
Martin S. Garrett, 50, 30, 400, 15, 60
David Powell, 90, 110, 1000, 100, 355
Elizabeth Rice, 85, 115, 1000, 60, 180
S. C. Davidson, 30, 130, 600, 10, 256
Thomas Poor, 16, 24, 200, 5, 38
Henry Lile, 16, 144, 250, 10, 186
John Brower, 15, -, 100, 10, 131
James H. Goodman, 16, -, 50, 10, 220
A. Meadows, 18, 142, 400, 5, 60
J. Fulcher, 180, 400, 4000, 50, 660

Edwin Snyder, 50, 70, 600, 75, 430
Mark Philips, 28, 95, 100, 20, 350
Samuel Bradley, 50, 80, 400, 150, 372
David Watson, 20, 60, 700, 25, 323
Peter Basinger, -, 160, 300, 50, 90
Thomas Nichols, 15, 85, 300, 75, 122
J. Grossclose, 60, 70, 500, 75, 163
John Standford, 30, 50, 400, 40, 210
David Watkins, 40, 120, 800, 50, 160
Richard Griggs, 22, 20, 250, 100, 230
Levin Tucker, 8, 72, 100, 50, 130
James Kincaid, 60, 20, 100, 25, 170
Laona Johnson, 10, -, 40, 4, 60
John Jones, 150, 700, 5000, 850, 480
Wm. Buford, 50, 230, 980, 300, 105
James Johnson, 14, -, 50, 60, 80
_. Hawkins, 100, 183, 1000, 150, 297
Wm. Hulin, 20, 20, 150, 15, 105
David Z. Wright, 11, -, 30, 15, 140
Robert S. Brame, 25, 95, 600, 10, 106
John D. Hott, 10, 93, 40, 25, 105
G. A. Beeler, 50, 190, 900, 100, 280
Jacob Beeler, 30, -, 100, 25, 207
G. C. Rippey, 20, -, 100, 6, 494
Wm. V. Rippey, 130, 150, 1500, 125, 930
Sandy Rice, 130, 110, 1500, 200, 430
E. H. Lake, 40, 50, 300, 20, 85
M. Goldsberry, 100, 260, 2000, 100, 397
Samuel Arnold, 10, -, 100, 10, 125
M. Jamison, 65, 55, 500, 40, 235
David Barnett, 22, 58, 200, 15, 165
Richard Hopchurch, 18, 22, 100, 8, 107
Mark Arnold, 10, 30, 125, 8, 110
George Winn, 15, 25, 80, 10, 125
Price Arnold, 20, -, 150, 20, 210
R. W. Hacker, 30, 130, 450, 15, 115
John A. Whitesides, 17, -, 50, 10, 40
Wm. A. Coffee, 16, -, 50, 70, 420
Wm. Jones, 25, 15, 150, 15, 172
N. Williams, 25, 135, 400, 35, 180
George Hocker, 30, 130, 300, 10, 62
Lance Newcomb, 25, -, 100, 10, 135
J. Glendening, 12, -, 30, 60, 105
John Pipes, 15, 65, 250, 100, 85
David J. Saunders, 7, 135, 300, 35, 65

Leonard Griggs, 20, 300, 600, 25, 216
E. Fletcher, 12, 28, 150, 5, 82
S. Crowder, 30, 170, 1000, 75, 320
J. W. Legrande, 7, 152, 500, 10, 56
John Slightom, 50, 110, 800, 125, 284
Henry Legrande, 20, -, 100, 75, 100
John Lile, 15, -, 100, 12, 290
Jahiel Parks, 25, 115, 500, 90, 280
John Arnold, 35, 125, 600, 30, 95
Henry Hinsey, 15, 65, 200, 50, 145
Henry Whitzel, 20, 140, 300, 15, 200
Herman Figgy, 10, 30, 100, 5, 114
Wesley Jackson, 50, 340, 1500, 200, 475
Thomas Jackson, 80, 80, 1000, 200, 505
W. Seamster, 40, 25, 400, 100, 238
John Seamster, 9, 72, 150, 10, 90
J. R. Meek, 40, 120, 800, 75, 180
Hamilton Neil, 40, 31, 200, 15, 186
Wm. Bailey, 37, 3, 150, 100, 345
R. Speers, 17, 115, 200, 15, 55
Daniel E. Savage, 15, 65, 150, 19, 75
L. M. Alverson, 12, 120, 200, 40, 180
John S. Fulcher, 70, 15, 800, 60, 399
John Rhodes, 30, 50, 150, 50, 315
James C. Capps, 20, 60, 200, 10, 128
David Capps, -, -, -, -, 50
Wm. Yadon, 15, 25, 100, 10, 188
Thomas Lay, 50, 30, 200, 30, 321
Wm. Brower, 10, 70, 150, 10, 255
Martha Eason, 60, 340, 2000, 6, 155
Sam. G. Eason, 100, 220, 1000, 50, 310
George Minick, 20, 60, 150, 10, 333
Mary Galasper, 20, 60, 200, 10, 183
Daniel Coy, 68, 125, 1000, 75, 453
Wm. Johnson, 10, 70, 140, 3, 80
Wm. Young, 50, 110, 300, 15, 193
Hiram P. Capps, 40, 120, 300, 5, 95
Nancy Lay, 30, 170, 600, 5, 167
Wm. A. Hamilton, 35, 45, 200, 10, 190
Sherrod Baker, 30, 50, 200, 20, 210
R. Boulware, 20, 140, 250, 20, 120
Lydia Bennett, 15, 65, 175, 5, 159
Samuel Morton, 20, 60, 150, 5, 55
Robert B. Fugate, 75, 5, 600, 60, 652
Lawyer Brower, 20, 60, 200, 15, 180
James H. Fugate, 20, 140, 300, 100, 304

R. M. Pierce, 50, 110, 350, 75, 428
E. McClenaham, 15, 65, 150, 50, 139
James Wood, 20, 60, 175, 50, 228
Wm. Barlow, 100, 60, 800, 100, 796
J. C. Hartman, 12, 128, 230, 50, 160
Mathias Speer, 15, -, 150, 5, 110
George Crump, 20, -, 50, 10, 65
Joseph Johnson, 10, -, 40, 60, 71
John R. Beeler, 12, -, 40, 10, 90
Lewis Lay, 10, -, 25, 10, 138
Nicholas Sloop, 50, 110, 500, 110, 453
M. L. Sallee, 50, 30, 100, 25, 126
Wm. Hewlett, 12, 40, 100, 5, 99
Benj. Tompkins, 20, 60, 300, 125, 227
P. Duckworth, 30, 20, 150, 520, 100
James Yates, 60, 100, 500, 75, 358
F. Warner, 12, 68, 150, 80, 101
J. J. Snowbarger, 24, 25, 150, 100, 250
Jerome Bridges, 30, 10, 100, 12, 175
Stephen Hewlett, 30, 10, 200, 20, 190
John Chatton, 28, 230, 500, 30, 143
Anderson Jay, -, -, -, 5, -
Wm. Blomett, 9, 31, 150, 10, 85
John Ragen, 80, 220, 1000, 15, 260
Wm. Searcy, 16, 64, 200, 10, 69
Joseph Grosseclose, 70, 170, 2000, 40, 410
Wm. D. Jeffries, 20, -, 150, 12, 170
Daniel Griggs, 14, 66, 300, 20, 155
Samuel Parker, 100, 30, 700, 100, 447
Henry Winkler, 31, -, 100, 20, 145
Math. D. Oliver, 18, 62, 300, 80, 109
Charles Cook, 40, 120, 600, 75, 251
Ewing Kerby, 16, - ,130, 10, 180
Wm. Olds, 16, 24, 200, 60, 85
John Hawkins, -, -, -, -, 60
John G. Davis, 40, 80, 500, 85, 272
T. Adams, 35, -, 100, 25, 152
S. B. Fulcher, 80, -, 500, 30, 103
F. D. Loyd, 30, 50, 350, 50, 285
Daniel Cook, 10, -, 50, 20, 85
J. Brower, 40, 80, 400, 15, 98
A. J. Norman, 14, -, 70, 12, 70
J. W. Hall, 40, 40, 500, 100, 195
John Fugate, 160, 60, 2000, 100, 662
Henry Newcome, 30, 50, 300, 50, 165

J. H. Hathaway, 25, -, 200, 100, 350
Thomas Morehead, 65, 85, 800, 75, 235
David Floyd, 40, 220, 800, 20, 115
R. Fulcher, -, -, -, -, 17
C. M. H. London, 45, -, 500, 40, 278
Wm. B. London, 37, -, 300, 30, 199
Henry Keetes(Keeter), 60, 148, 1000, 100, 250
Wm. Biswell, 40, -, 200, 35, 90
John B. Baker, 12, 68, 350, 12, 100
Elisha Baldwin, 16, 40, 150, 60, 160
George Moreland, 34, 24, 200, 30, 200
Garrett N. Stewart, 20, 140, 1000, 35, 150
Wm. G. Boyce, 20, -, 150, 100, 367
B. McAtee, 40, 104, 300, 40, 150
Charles Burks, 21, -, 100, 10, 95
Charles Gray, 15, 145, 200, 70, 125
Isaac Dunn, 50, 13, 200, 8, 165
J. G. Montgomery, 30, 33, 200, 12, 140
John Sawyer, 125, 195, 2000, 110, 356
Nelson Laslie, 40, 40, 200, 200, 335
J. M. Weatherford, 30, 50, 300, 50, 140
John Homes, 9, 151, 250, 10, 103
Stephen Combs, 22, 138, 300, 20, 202
Samuel Wright, 35, 131, 300, 15, 60
L. W. Ross, 20, 140, 300, 20, 130
Abel Friend, 80, 150, 1150, 85, 800
M. J. Norman, 19, 141, 200, 10, 104
Wm. H. Standiford, 12, 148, 300, 8, 35
Lewis B. Piper, 35, 45, 400, 70, 308
Jacob Capps, 36, 125, 300, 35, 229
Meekley Spray, 20, -, 100, 15, 125
Madison Kelly, 24, 146, 500, 75, 335
Robert Stull, 15, 65, 100, 4, 180
Wm. C. Warriner, 40, 200, 1200, 60, 160
Phebe Ash, 5, 75, 300, 4, 132
J. R. Webster, 50, 70, 600, 10, 139
Jesse Hott(Holt), 30, 130, 500, 10, 492
John Kernitte(Kemittle), 40, 40, 400, 10, 70
John Kemittle, 20, 40, 200, 40, 401
Henry Moll(Mott), 9, 231, 400, 5, 63
Henry Davis, 120, 120, 1000, 25, 744
James Wells, 20, 60, 150, 30, 100
John Brown, 50, 30, 200, 50, 300

Henry Winkle, 12, 28, 100, 5, 170
Ir__s Collette, 10, 30, 125, 5, 100
Oliver Towles, 175, 265, 1000, 30, 665
D. H. Welbourn, 40, 40, 200, 10, 158
Asa W. Barnes, 20, 20, 200, 50, 156
Wm. Hendron, 30, 10, 600, 75, 175
Woodson Hulin, 40, 40, 300, 30, 137
Wm. Webster, 20, 60, 200, 40, 190
G. Emmurman, 20, 30, 200, -, 42
David B. Dixon, -, -, -, -, 120
M. Crawford, 40, 40, 400, 20, 166
H. Downing, 25, 136, 600, 30, 220
James Piper, 17, 40, 150, 50, 130
Henry Varner, 12, 68, 400, 8, 113
C. Foglesong, 125, 35, 700, 125, 343
P. Foglesong, 30, 30, 500, 40, 150
Ephraim Maize, 10, 80, 200, 10, 100
George Bridwell, 46, 74, 1000, 75, 195
Wm. Maize, 28, 52, 225, 60, 220
Isaac Morris, 12, 38, 200, 20, 61
D. B. Rice, 75, 235, 1854, 100, 240
George Tobin, 100, 140, 1000, 100, 1102
Thomas Bradley, 80, 160, 1000, 100, 160
Mahala Baker, -, -, -, 10, 60
Andy Trible, 37, 43, 300, 12, 245
Eleanor Bryant, 30, 90, 500, 20, 156
Elijah Mock, 40, 100, 700, 75, 252
John Dewitt, 30, 10, 100, 5, 65
Mary Harrison, 50, 30, 400, 300, 260
Richard Collins, 20, 20, 100, 110, 120
Wm. Hendron, 12, 28, 100, 70, 170
L. Montgomery, 20, 20, 100, -, -
Morris James, 22, 58, 200, 10, 150
Isaac Veatch, 35, 45, 250, 50, 164
Allen Locker, 80, 500, 2000, 100, 510
Wm. Oglesby, 50, 70, 700, 20, 147
C. G. Button, 9, 31, 100, 5, 70
Samuel Nelson, 25, 54, 200, 85, 155
George Homes, 30, 50, 200, 30, 165
Emilerson Barnes, -, -, -, 40, 100
Henry Piercy, 54, 106, 300, 10, 213
Ruth Taylor, 20, 40, 150, 10, 116
Eliza Smith, 36, 124, 700, -, 110
James W. Wright, 75, 25, 130, 10, 140

Wm. Myers, 20, 40, 130, 30, 146
Wm. Ogg, 20, 20, 200, 20, 192
Joseph Marrin, 23, 17, 100, 10, 70
Peter Blancett, 20, 50, 100, 10, 120
Lewis Hewlett, 20, 140, 500, 20, 157
Joel Tipton, 20, 50, 50, 80, 325
Francis Newsom, 12, 28, 100, 10, 65
Wm. Roden, 60, 180, 600, 100, 733
Charles Hail, 30, 210, 1000, 30, 109
George Whorton, 14, 146, 270, 10, 137
John Sicining, 40, 80, 600, 42, 280
B. McNulty, 22, 58, 200, 10, 175
Wm. E. Malone, 15, 65, 200, 5, 86
John Goosey, 50, 110, 600, 100, 295
C. Foglesong, 10, 130, 300, 12, 55
Henry Prince, 40, 240, 800, 50, 260
M. Anderson, 15, 145, 350, 10, 118
Henry Rhodes, 100, 60, 1000, 15, 233
John G. Slavin, 100, 220, 1000, 160, 321
Wm. Pell, 30, 10, 200, 10, 208
Wm. Hicks, 20, 140, 500, 5, 66
Charles Cooper, 40, 40, 300, 20, 180
Kendnell Morris, 20, 50, 200, 30, 7
Wm. Morris, 25, 55, 200, 55, 90
Reuben Abbot, 12, 80, 400, 50, 145

Henry Terrill, 50, 90, 1000, 60, 260
Jesse M. Hunt, 25, 30, 150, 100, 170
George Tompkins, 30, 90, 900, 10, 155
John Tompkins, 30, 40, 500, 10, 161
James Hall, 20, 20, 200, 2, 11
Hezekiah Mudd, 30, 50, 600, 20, 105
J. A. Westoph, 80, 80, 320, 12, 217
Jeremiah Buford, 50, 370, 1500, 100, 290
Joseph Rambolt, 10, 40, 100, 85, 200
Henry Batton, 30, 50, 200, 55, 90
Ellis Pickering, 15, 65, 200, 10, 75
Jacob Titus, 40, 80, 300, 80, 210
Wm. Whittome, 100, 60, 1500, 300, 250
F. G. Williams, 6, 75, 130, 1, 88
Thomas Parrias, 8, 72, 180, 5, 62
G. W. Johnson, 10, 80, -, -, 50
Thomas J. Bennett, -, -, -, -, 10
Y. W. Payton, 10, 200, 2000, 100, 262
Daniel Roberts, 160, 160, 1000, 100, 670
Hugh Mikel, 70, 90, 300, 50, 255
E. D. Hensley, 20, 60, 300, 20, 160
Peter Grosse, -, -, 30, -, 40
B. G. Fleming, 10, 30, 150, 10, 180

Scotland County, Missouri
1850 Agricultural Census

Scotland County 1850 Agricultural Census was filmed by the Central Microfilm Service Corp of St. Louis, Missouri, for the Missouri State Historical Society. There are 46 columns of information on the 1850 agricultural census. I have chosen to transcribe six of those columns. The columns are:

1. Name
2. Acres of Land Improved
3. Acres of Land Unimproved
4. Cash Value of the Farm
5. Value of Farm Implements and Machinery
13. Value of Livestock

Thomas Darniel, 12, 28, 150, 60, 125
Thomas S. Richardson, 5, 1055, 2500, -, 100
William Bourne, 25, 55, 300, 20, 167
John Owens, -, -, -, 15, 80
John Townsend, -, -, -, 15, 211
John M. T. Smith, 40, 130, 800, 75, 195
Harrison Baker, -, -, -, 90, 176
Moses Hudnell, -, -, -, -, 195
Austin Quisenberry, 420, 260, 3300, 125, 1505
William Calloway, 70, 410, 1000, 150, 520
Tubman Ralph, 15, 25, 200, 50, 156
Andrew Lovell, 35, -, 300, 120, 320
Daniel Smith, 35, 45, 800, -, 210
Abraham W. Love, -, -, -, -, 190
William G. Downing, -, -, -, -, 220
Preston T. Huff, -, -, -, -, 225
William L. Felix, 80, 80, 2000, 200, 2530
Isaac Butler, 60, 180, 800, 150, 302
John O. Conner, -, 40, 150, -, 245
James L. Jones, 150, 250, 3000, 150, 1620
William Foreman, 30, 50, 400, 100, 263
Richmond Saling, 20, 20, 150, -, -
William Saling, 40, -, 500, 60, 520
Jackson Baker, -, -, -, -, 175
Alfred Lovell, -, -, -, -, 90

Robert Childers, 60, 20, 500, -, 310
Alexander Tate, 60, 60, 500, 150, 465
William Childers, 130, 222, 1200, 100, 654
Thomas Gunn, -, -, -, 100, 290
John L. Reser, 18, 62, 500, 100, 263
Jacob Clapper, -, -, -, -, 285
Charles Metz(Mety), 140, 200, 3000, 300, 2033
Harriet Storer, 60, 240, 1500, -, -
Samuel Cecil, 100, 215, 2000, 50, 300
Isaac Sowers, 55, 150, 600, 50, 212
William D. Smith, 30, 130, 800, 130, 340
Samuel Lewis, 8, 72, 200, -, 85
Gibson Palmer, 12, 32, 200, 10, 114
Miller Harben, 18, 62, 1000, 100, 432
Solomon Thrust, 23, 38, 250, 75, 165
James D. Dunn, 55, 89, 700, 100, 581
William Neal, 40, 120, 500, 5, 90
Frederick Eshelman, 27, 75, 400, 25, 190
Isaac B. Hon, 11, 29, 100, 10, 100
Aaron Dunn, 50, 30, 700, 50, 135
Stephen McPherson, 75, 215, 1500, 50, 650
Jefferson Collins, 29, 109, 800, 25, 175
Joseph Justice, 16, 144, 700, 100, 431
Richard Allen, 60, 140, 1500, 100, 400
William Smith, 35, 165, 1000, 100, 486

Presley T. Harris, 30, 80, 800, 100, 370
George Booll, -, -, -, -, 180
Abraham Patterson, 175, 165, 2500, 150, 520
Solomon Justice, 80, 80, 600, 100, 676
O. T. Ellis, 50, 110, 1000, 80, 240
James Fairbanks, 30, 50, 300, 15, 271
Aaron Pearce, 50, 150, 1200, 120, 350
Aaron Chambers, 80, 40, 500, 100, 325
John Lewis, 40, 40, 500, 70, 289
David Wilson, 40, 40, 300, -, 140
Daniel Saling, -, -, -, -, 148
George Fields, 20, 60, 400, 50, 179
John Smoot, 80, 80, 800, 100, 350
Hiram Inman, 75, 5, 1000, 125, 350
Matthew Buchanan, -, -, -, -, 110
Riley Gale, -, -, -, -, 250
John Clarkson, 20, 140, 500, 8, 186
Amos Darniel, 5, 35, 150, 75, 95
P. H. Herod, 30, 210, 1000, 50, 210
James McManamer, 4, 40, 200, 20, 82
Edmund Saling, 20, 120, 1000, -, 386
Thomas Fawver, 80, 160, 1800, 10, 45
Jesse Allen, 20, 20, 200, -, 148
Wilson Hudnall, 28, 92, 1000, 40, 220
Joseph Foreman, 150, 190, 1500, 45, 230
John Baker, 90, 390, 2500, 150, 550
Peter Tolbert, -, -, -, -, 150
Hawsey Daniels, 50, 190, 600, 60, 235
James Davis, 60, 50, 1500, 25, 230
Harvey Montgomery, 43, 397, 2000, 100, 530
Andrew G. Darby, 100, 467, 2000, 100, 494
Pemberton Watson, -, -, -, -, 100
John Snodgrass, 36, 44, 500, 65, 266
Jeremiah Ballard, -, -, -, -, 490
Jacob Crow, 130, 300, 1500, 150, 800
William Talbott, -, -, -, -, 170
David Cline, 100, 100, 1000, 100, 280
Isaac Lemons, -, -, -, -, 127
Calvin Weber, 11, 69, 300, -, 170
Daniel Foulk, 45, 115, 300, 60, 315
Isham Bagby, 50, 30, 1000, 25, 179

Samuel Davidson, 40, 280, 1200, 130, 325
George W. Conoway, 100, 240, 800, 50, 435
Thomas T. McIntyre, 40, 120, 200, 10, 205
Joseph Bish, -, 160, 300, -, 70
John Martin, 30, 50, 300, 25, 95
John D. Bourne, 102, 920, 6000, 150, 685
Joseph Bourne, 40, 100, 500, 8, 100
William Bilups, 25, 295, 1000, 125, 336
Robert Bilups, 10, 230, 600, 100, 414
Jehiel Smith, 30, 200, 500, 20, 285
Nancy Weyer, 40, 100, 600, 50, 150
Solomon Fifer, 80, 80, 1000, 100, 240
Barward Tadlock, 30, 140, 500, 75, 250
Nathaniel Wilson, 30, 140, 400, 20, 165
Hezekiah Cline, 34, 166, 500, 125, 485
George Knisely, 40, 115, 600, 15, 365
Benjamin Mudd, 60, 180, 1000, 125, 570
Hawley Talbott, -, -, -, -, 180
Edward Snow, 100, 80, 500, 150, 507
Simeon Wiley, 20, 60, 150, 85, 225
Nancy Kimble, 40, 120, 200, 10, 142
John Wiley, 40, 140, 420, 100, 212
Benjamin F. Wiley, 15, 45, 200, -, 150
Felix Williams, 35, 135, 500, 80, 180
David Brown, 70, 66, 800, 100, 389
Henry Crutcher, 100, 100, 1000, -, 170
Alfred Sandford, 120, 120, 800, 100, 217
Andrew Arnett, 15, 65, 250, 15, 80
Jefferson Bucklin, -, -, -, -, 148
Jefferson Allen, 50, 150, 1000, 75, 342
Charles Fryrean(Frysean), 100, 100, 1000, 100, 710
William Slavin, 20, 20, 200, 15, 155
Peter Cline, 40, 160, 800, 75, 205
Thomas Marlow, 15, 25, 250, 20, 245
Jeremiah Fryrean(Frysean), -, -, -, -, 106
John Paris, 40, 5, 300, -, 110
R. M. Mudd, 45, 155, 1000, 60, 370
James Brackenridge, 40, 40, 400, 60, 170

George Bish, 60, 100, 600, 75, 430
William Durham, 25, 55, 200, 15, 60
Thomas O'Brien, 35, 45, 300, 15, 150
Simeon Gristy, 35, 45, 300, 40, 140
Stephen Gristy, 11, 109, 150, 80, 190
Littleton Baily, 1, 160, 500, 15, 105
Branch Miller, 50, 70, 1000, 50, 195
Patrick Neil, -, -, -, -, 520
Richard Finch, 25, 25, 150, -, 148
Elias Barbee, 50, 70, 600, 60, 227
Benjamin Vanarsdel, -, -, -, -, 190
Dana Philips, -, -, -, -, 150
Seth Finney, 10, 30, 200, 10, 140
Alfred Hays, 75, 16, 500, 80, 290
Hamilton Crawford, 30, 90, 1000, 100, 295
Ephraim McGlaughlin, -, -, -, -, 178
Moses Shanks, 70, 50, 800, 100, 550
Endingen Hall, 105, 215, 1500, 140, 593
Lewis Hall, -, -, -, -, 103
John Cradick, 50, 30, 400, 100, 277
Nathaniel Jones, -, -, -, -, 144
Minerva Kincheloe, 40, 40, 400, 10, 127
William Hall, 40, 40, 400, 100, 210
Washington Smith, 30, 130, 400, 25, 125
Hercules Smith, 30, 130, 500, 35, 130
Hiram Colvin, 45, 35, 400, 15, 105
William Colvin, 26, 54, 600, 10, 267
David Smith, 24, 340, 800, 10, 112
Henry C. Carter, 30, 130, 500, 100, 183
Addison Fifer, 100, 100, 1000, 10, 232
John Fifer, 40, 40, 800, 20, 100
Alexander Hays, 140, 160, 1000, 35, 305
Joseph Kite, 40, 40, 300, 35, 191
John Kite, 70, 90, 400, 125, 330
Robert P. Wayland, 300, 1040, 5000, 200, 992
Robert Hendricks, 42, 38, 250, 25, 229
John B. Gains, -, -, -, -, 695
James Crawford, 60, 100, 800, 100, 377
S. J. Williams, 40, 120, 200, 10, 105
William Moore, 15, 65, 150, -, 67
Joshua Cox, 50, 110, 600, 50, 397
Jacob G__by, 40, 120, 200, 100, 281
Robert Colvin, -, -, -, -, 90
Thomas Heard, 21, 59, 200, 10, 162

Samuel Crafton, 14, 66, 200, 30, 68
Jacob Maggard, 10, 238, 700, 100, 368
Aquilla Barnes, 80, 120, 1500, 120, 200
Jesse S. Steel(Stice), 70, 160, 1000, 75, 349
John C. Collins, 80, 200, 2000, 100, 125
Abraham Stice, 22, 58, 500, 20, 166
Charles Burrus, 112, 1012, 4000, 117, 239
Alexander Williams, 130, 390, 1600, 150, 432
Joseph Johnson, 35, 85, 800, 25, 243
Casper Fetters, 120, 440, 1500, 200, 615
John Philips, -, -, -, -, 200
James Hereford, 5, 75, 200 80, 100
Thomas Donaldson, 100, 220, 1500, 100, 585
Moses Stice, 100, 220, 2200, 100, 265
John Hendricks, 60, 260, 1500, 120, 457
Richard Gale, 320, 400, 2500, 200, 2100
John Crowley, 25, 95, 600, 100, 405
Caleb Crandall, 70, 95, 600, 100, 405
Irwin Johnson, 125, 35, 1200, 100, 300
Charles Cole, 35, 125, 800, 100, 615
Elijah Whitten, 80, 160, 1000, 100, 540
James T. Foster, 20, 60, 300, 15, 78
Samuel Wilfley, 50, -, 1000, 100, 352
Adam Smith, 25, 135, 350, 100, 400
Jacob Conrad, 30, 130, 500, 30, 270
Henry Maggard, 50, 110, 600, 130, 289
Presley F. Hendricks, -, -, -, -, 195
Joel Bradley, 25, 55, 250, 60, 202
Addison Maret, 14, 66, 100, 20, 179
Samuel Jaynes, 40, 120, 1000, 15, 128
Thomas A. Chaney, 100, 500, 1500, 100, 852
John West, 36, 4, 300, 100, 182
William Barr, 45, 75, 600, 10, 135
James Hicks, 75, 205, 1000, 80, 553
Willis Hicks, 80, 157, 2000, 200, 323
Stephen Bryant, 200, 120, 2500, 50, 467
John Edwards, 21, -, 100, -, 149
Richard Blane, 30, 210, 1500, 30, 308
Alexander Trimble, 40, 180, 1000, 80, 258
Robert Trimble, 35, 25, 300, 75, 260

Henry Highbarger, 18, 62, 300, 15, 145
Robert T. Smith, 150, 170, 1400, 150, 665
John Locks, -, -, -, -, 145
George Stevenson, -, -, -, -, 180
James Hickman, -, -, -, -, 175
Michael E. Spilman, 33, 2222, 1500, 100, 295
Joseph Cole, 20, 60, 200, 30, 105
Martin Cole, -, -, -, -, 140
Henry Ferryman, 30, 90, 500, 75, 210
Josiah Matlock, 50, 110, 600, 100, 218
Josiah Matlock, 80, 120, 800, 75, 217
William R. Steele, 60, 20, 500, 15, 163
Elizabeth Chany, 60, 260, 800, -, 114
Samuel Sullivan, 50, 280, 3000, 65, 252
George Forester, 80, 160, 2400, 100, 418
Joseph Hicks, 40, 120, 700, 10, 252
Thomas Myers, -, -, -, - 455
Michael Myers, 120, 680, 3000, 100, 450
John Hillbrant, -, -, -, -, 190
Frederick Fields, -, -, -, -, 230
Paul Hereford, 80, 160, 1500, 100, 205
William Myers, 40, 117, 800, 10, 230
John Pettitt, -, -, -, -, 205
Henry Myers, 40, 120, 500, 125, 325
Martin Loe, 40, 120, 1000, 20, 180
Jeremiah Standley, 40, 120, 800, 75, 375
Jonothan Stone, 40, 40, 500, 30, 255
Lorenzo D. Gale, -, -, -, -, 450
William Christian, 30, 50, 200, 65, 385
Gasper Pope, 80, 40, 400, 150, 320
John Standard, 35, 45, 200, -, 125
Thomas Standard, -, -, -, -, 143
Peter Fordney, 60, 60, 800, 100, 494
Aaron K. Chambers, 26, 94, 600, -, 125
James Chambers, 40, 200, 600, 80, 202
Joseph Petty, 50, 30, 500, 100, 730
Levi Rhodes, 80, 160, 1000, 100, 650
William Myers, -, 100, 400, 75, 275
John Rounsaville, 75, 105, 800, 100,782
Joseph Price, 70, 250, 800, 50, 180
Andrew Kincaid, -, -, -, -, 130
John Walters, -, -, -, -, 195

William McIntyre, 60, 160, 1600, 60, 290
Martin D. Stone, 125, 263, 2000, 100, 519
Nathaniel Theobalds, 48, 320, 2700, 75, 300
Cornelius Holliday, 55, 105, 1000, 60, 300
John McPherson, 30, 87, 500, 20, 514
Stephen McPherson, 50, 190, 800, -, -
James Walker, 1, 40, 75, 100, 233
John H. Lane, -, -, -, -, 120
Thomas Allen, 60, 220, 2000, 115, 483
Tyre March, 23, 113, 400, 100, 197
Elias Swope, 28, 62, 300, 60, 154
Thomas Felps, 25, 25, 150, 40, 185
John Wayland, 14, 56, 150, 12, 203
James Hearn, 25, 200, 600, 15, 200
Alfred Myers, 40, 160, 1000, 60, 240
Luke Fetters, 30, 33, 250, 14, 200
George W. Booker, 8, 143, 200, 20, 150
Charles Kincaid, 40, -, 100, -, 227
Andrew Kincaid, -, -, -, -, 110
Jacob Chambers, 30, -, 100, 15, 202
William Chambers, -, -, -, -, 158
William Booker, 125, 135, 500, 100, 190
Abington Stice, 14, -, 150, 5, 130
John J. March, 20, 20, 500, 20, 145
Daniel Morris, 40, -, 200, 70, 586
John Prewitt, 25, 175, 500, 60, 200
John M. Richardson, 50, 110, 1000, 100, 206
Joseph Johnson, 20, 140, 400, 35, 185
Philip Pervis, 50, 250, 1000, 30, 266
George Blaine, 20, 100, 500, -, -
David Allen, 50, 70, 700, 60, 212
Jonathan March, 35, 85, 600, 30, 35
Micajah Southard, -, -, -, -, 180
David William, 30, 50, 250, 15, 180
Rudolph March, -, -, -, -, 60
Rudolph March, 50, 175, 1000, 100, 212
William Huston, 50, 190, 1200, 125, 275
Austin Foreman, 45, 115, 600, 100, 113
Abraham Baker, 45, 35, 650, 100, 192
William Herman, 40, 280, 500, 60, 230
Henry H. Fowler, 40, 100, 500, 15, 185

John Bryant, 70, 130, 1000, 200, 384
William Step, 140, 60, 2000, 125, 6650
Ely Yeager, -, -, -, -, 209
Sarah Palmer, 50, 110, 1000, 25, 182
Thomas Palmer, 40, 140, 1000, 80, 462
Moses Roberts, 50, 80, 300, 100, 303
Ludwell Musgrove, 100, 60, 1000, 75, 632
Charles Crocker, 40, 120, 1000, -, 90
Catharine Bear, 7, 70, 200, -, 158
Madison Palmer, 40, -, 150, 10, 158
Carman Dunn, 18, 22, 50, 50, 246
George Buskirk, 35, 125, 800, 20, 125
Curtis Codey, 2, -, 240, 800, 50, 216
William Dawson, 60, 140, 1200, 50, 300
James Amerman, -, -, -, 60, 263
Charles Owens, 13, 67, 200, 10, 140
Handy Smack, 60, 100, 500, 175, 266
Jacob Gray, 100, 300, 2400, -, 100
John B. Maupin, -, -, -, -, 905
Thomas Hope, 100, 120, 1200, 100, 560
Thomas M. Stroude, 60, 50, 600, -, 26
John Johnson, 50, 230, 1500, 100, 760
James A. Felps, -, -, -, -, 100
Samuel Barnett, 30, 50, 500, 25, 155
Samuel Rippey, -, -, -, -, 178
William Clarkson, 40, 120, 600, 20, 148
Thomas W. Green, 48, 40, 1000, 90, 295
William Sloan, 25, 135, 400, 50, 117
Edward Smoot, 75, 165, 2000, 125, 616
James A. Hendricks, 35, 160, 250, 75, 390
James B. Prior, 25, 20, 200, 60, 185
Thomas Rhodes, 70, 130, 1000, 125, 328
Freman Farmsworth, 30, 10, 350, 40, 198
George Slavin, 36, 166, 500, 85, 449
Robert Walker, 16, 68, 100, 5, 85
Samuel Rhodes, -, -, -, -, 155
Jesse Givins, 30, 50, 200, 10, 60
John F. Holcomb, 75, 145, 800, 15, 332
William G. Rice, 75, 165, 2000, 100, 257
David McDowell, 200, 180, 2800, 150, 842
A. M. Hope, 55, 105, 1000, 60, 275

George W. Rhodes, 50, 105, 1000, 20, 118
Richard Myers, 36, 166, 800, 45, 331
Charles Carter, 35, 85, 500, 10, 165
David K. Arnold, 80, 219, 2000, 125, 688
John Barnett, 30, 123, 200, 100, 247
Martha North, -, -, -, -, 139
Tol. Loe, 32, 128, 600, 40, 398
Alexander Givins, 60, 100, 1000, 65, 429
William Records, -, -, -, -, 130
Henry Downing, 170, 430, 3000, 100, 2295
Jesse Alexander, 35, 85, 600, 10, 70
Washington Jones, 30, 90, 300, 100, 390
John Rhodes, 70, 210, 800, 100, 340
Flower Mullins, 60, 100, 500, 75, 255
George H. Stubblefield, -, -, -, -, 200
Samuel Briggs, 50, 110, 1000, 95, 257
James Lewis, 30, 10, 300, 100, 416
Charles Owens, 12, 28, 50, 12, 145
Sarah Owens, -, -, -, -, 360
William Fields, -, -, -, -, 120
Philip Bealer, 15, 65, 200, 30, 114
William Cathel, 30, 130, 300, 116, 200
William Asberry, -, -, -, -, 372
Martin Finney, 40, 120, 800, 60, 330
John A. Walker, 20, 60, 200, 15, 172
Anna Asberry, 15, 65, 200, 20, 207
Hosea Collins, 60, 100, 800, 50, 442
George W. Covey, -, -, -, -, 150
Bland Ballard, -, -, -, -, 119
John Runyon, 200, 200, 1600, 300, 930
Mark Walters, 80, 160, 1000, 80, 454
John Woodsmall, 40, 50, 270, 75, 115
Abraham Hunter, 46, 104, 700, 40, 202
William Forsha, 250, 790, 7000, 150, 681
William T. Newcomb, 80, 160, 1000, 80, 300
Joseph Raine, -, -, -, -, 147
Samuel Cox, 125, 675, 4000, 150, 1815
James F. Suter, 100, 200, 1500, 200, 316
Nicholas Corbin, 50, 101, 500, 100, 391
Thomas Hicks, 30, 50, 400, 100, 290

Charles Parish, 40, 40, 350, 75, 120
Milton Price, 80, 370, 2000, 100, 255
George Price, 60, 500, 2800, 100, 302
Nancy Spear, 50, 110, 600, 50, 330
Walter P. Ellis, 150, 190, 1680, 150, 860
Price Starks, 175, 575, 5000, 1000, 899
Orin Jones, 30, 170, 600, 20, 401
Jane Miller, 50, 350, 1600, 100, 238
William Woodsmall, 100, 60, 800, 100, 226
Hopkins Watkins, 60, 140, 1500, 100, 200
John Turtle, 30, 130, 200, 25, 196
James McVey, 12, 68, 300, 6, 139
Thomas M. Milburn, -, 800, 1000, - ,140
Benjamin Dye, 40, 360, 1200, 30, 248
John Dye, 130, 270, 1500, 100, 717
Alexander Turner, 30, 32, 350, 60, 207
William Turner, 40, 80, 400, 50, 122
Turner Smith, 15, 54, 300, 100, 177
Thomas Haryman, 35, 90, 400, 60, 240
James Fenton, 80, 196, 1600, 100, 322
Michael Miller, 40, 120, 1000, 100, 622
John Fry, 60, 145, 700, 80, 200
Joseph V. Hayden, 15, 225, 1600, 20, 151
Mary A. Dickson, -, -, -, -, 105
Milo Haryman, 30, 360, 1200, -, 438
Nathan Bounds, 78, 242, 1600, 75, 115
Charles Jones, 28, 132, 1000, -, -
Alexander Smith, 30, 50, 500, 50, 434
Herfield Lewis, -, -, -, -, 219
Simson McFarlane, 31, 69, 400, 12, 102
E. M. Beckwith, 170, 30, 2500, 120, 1208
Charles Runkle, 80, 360, 1500, 140, 511
William Clemens, 40, 110, 1000, 75, 164
James H. Clemens, -, -, -, -, 130
Benjamin Powers, 70, 230, 750, 75, 225
Thomas Dickson, 40, 40, 240, 50, 90
Robert Padget, 45, 137, 1000, 65, 238
Edwin B. Toombs, 90, 610, 7000, 100, 500
Charles Laswell, 40, 135, 1000, 100, 225
William Ewing, 60, 135, 1000, 100, 375

William Short, 5, 195, 500, 60, 520
Reubin Cornelius, 34, 116, 500, 60, 387
Jacob McClure, 100, 140, 2000, 150, 369
Michael Spate, 40, 120, 1500, 20, 329
Stephen Darby, 22, 98, 600, 50, 75
Henry Sprague, 30, 50, 400, 50, 210
William Kirkpatrick, 60, 100, 1000, 100, 252
Joseph K. Morgan, 50, 30, 300, 100, 190
William Trouth, 200, 200, 1600, 100, 437
John Noble, 25, 375, 800, 100, 541
William H. Coombs, 75, 150, 1800, 50, 636
Sandford Penn, 45, 95, 420, 10, 195
Hamilton H. Bryant, -, -, -, -, 68
Joseph Graves, 25, 71, 550, 10, 151
Richard Powers, 150, 450, 3000, 100, 883
George Shaw, 70, 90, 800, 275, 442
Andrew J. Daggs, 110, 170, 1000, 100, 1265
Samuel Cariston, 225, 135, 1500, 145, 375
William Barbridge, 30, 90, 350, 90, 528
Harwood Penn, 40, 160, 600, 20, 118
William Penn, 30, 50, 100, -, -
Hiram Daggs, 40, 151, 550, 75, 192
Stephen Maddox, 140, 100, 1000, -, 100
Thomas H. Ridgely, 50, 110, 500, 100, 273
John Brookhart, -, -, -, -, 125
Joseph Stevenson, 200, 1000, 4000, 100, 763
Joseph Miller, 114, 366, 1400, 75, 1187
Jefferson Lockhart, 20, 60, 100, -, 260
James Cornley, 30, 130, 400, 70, 338
James Coombs, 30, 130, 800, 90, 415
William Morris, 60, 140, 1000, 50, 100
David Bibb, 80, -, 1000, 125, 760
Adam Case, 60, -, 450, 20, 476
James Smith, 34, -, 350, 75, 306
Charles Leper, 40, -, 200, 50, 196
Thomas Smith, 50, -, 600, 25, 477
Noble Butler, 5, -, 50, -, -

William Park, 50, -, 300, -, -
Samson Moore, 40, -, 400, 100, 230
Salmon Park, 90, -, 600, -, -
William Heald, 50, -, 250, 50, 450
Ephraim Heald, 58, -, 300, 10, 150
Samuel Powers, 32, -, 300, 60, 220
Thomas Childers, 80, -, 800, 25, 200
Susan Burner, -, -, -, -, 125
Charles Case, 30, -, 250, 50, 249
Joseph Leper, 30, -, 250, 15, 225
Joseph Carberry, 33, -, 300, 60, 150
William Farris, 35, -, 150, -, 160
John Circles, 128, -, 1000, 65, 335
William Circles, 60, -, 450, 20, 320
Charles Carter, 60, -, 460, 20, 320
Charles Lewis, 60, 20, 600, -, 349
William Penwell, -, -, -, -, 106
Lemuel Needham, 70, 102, 1000, 100, 366
George Daggs, 60, 180, 1000, 100, 375
James Bilups, 60, 100, 800, 100, 217

John Vinsent, 55, 55, 600, 60, 579
John McHenry, 50, 110, 600, 75, 208
Harrison Daggs, 60, 220, 2000, 125, 787
James Martin, 20, 60, 150, 15, 200
Matthew Hickson, 60, 20, 300, 150, 452
Thomas W. Whitten, -, -, -, -, 157
John Ailward, 30, 210, 600, 75, 100
A. Small, 50, 60, 1000, 100, 265
David Brewer, 80, 120, 800, 100, 280
James P. McGee, 100, 60, 1200, 15, 300
Asa Brewer, 30, -, 250, 75, 169
William Covey(Corey), 36, -, 180, 70, 245
Pinckney Bilups, 40, 40, 200, -, 293
Joseph Bilups, 120, 120, 2000, 125, 755
Henry Powell, 10, -, 300, 50, 240
James Briggs, 30, -, 200, -, 20
Nicholas Jones, 30, 130, 1000, 50, 158
Elisha Wade, 12, 68, 100, 50, 140
Robert Webb, 30, 110, 500, 20, 150
Luther Stephens, 80, 80, 500, 110, 380

Scott County 1850 Agricultural Census was filmed by the Central Microfilm Service Corp of St. Louis, Missouri, for the Missouri State Historical Society. There are 46 columns of information on the 1850 agricultural census. I have chosen to transcribe six of those columns. The columns are:

1. Name
2. Acres of Land Improved
3. Acres of Land Unimproved
4. Cash Value of the Farm
5. Value of Farm Implements and Machinery
13. Value of Livestock

Thomas M. Shaw, 250, 1650, 10000, 200, 1000
Felix G. Allin, 157, 797, 5000, 150, 1500
Albion Crow, 230, 800, 1500, 200, 387
William Hutson, 150, 350, 2000, 200, 1400
John D. Ancell, 60, 220, 500, 125 275
Jacob Finley, 65, 83, 600, 75, 320
Dennis T. Mills, 40, 60, 400, 40, 100
Richard Finley, 50, 110, 400, 50, 260
Ann Bertholomey, 30, 50, 500, 100, 200
Balzer Etter, 50, 120, 500, 100, 220
William Manning, 95, 323, 4000, 100, 375
William Mulricks, 35, 139, 500, 75, 200
William Nunn, 35, 96, 600, 100, 190
Daniel Bohart, 50 70, 800, 150, 175
Charles P. Wilburn, 105, 215, 1200, 150, 300
Thornton Ancell, 50, 190, 1000, 225, 275
Augustus Hillman, 20, 60, 400, 100, 100
Henry Toule, 20, 79, 400, 50, 150
William Fonpelt, 16, 24, 200, 50, 100
Paschall Ancell, 60, 400, 3000, 100, 385
Joseph G. Mansfield, 120, 380, 3000, 100, 150
George T. Taylor, 50, 150, 900, 75, 435
Casper Iceley, 20, 40, 200, 60, 150

Louis Miller, 15, 45, 200, 60, 60
Augustus Harmon, 15, 45, 200, 75, 60
Milton Fowler, 60, 100, 800, 125, 680
William M. Prince, 70, 150, 2200, 100, 430
William Gracey, 55, 55, 1000, 225, 590
Charles Moore, 150, 400, 1600, 200, 420
John W. Price, 50, 100, 450, 125, 200
William Daugherty, 75, 150, 2000, 150, 280
William Mansfield, 50, 150, 1000, 150, 150
William Foster, 25, 55, 200, 50, 150
Jehu Montgomery, 60, 100, 1000, 150, 275
Asa Foster, 30, 200, 500, 40, 170
Alexander Waugh, 135, 70, 1500, 140, 300
Isaiah Carico, 10, 30, 150, 25, 58
Columbus McFerrin, 65, 257, 1200, 100, 390
Epominandes McFerrin, 15, 87, 600, 50, 80
Milford Wiley, 85, 67, 600, 60, 275
William H. Howell, 25, 125, 600, 40, 200
David Trotter, 20, 100, 800, 30, 260
Daniel D. Adams, 15, 55, 300, 20, 100
Ithamux Williams, 50, 110, 600, 30, 120
Sarah Williams, 100, 130, 800, 50, 180

Mary Holder, 20, 60, 400, 50, 150
John Glouce, 40, 40, 400, 50, 175
Lewis Tauner, 40, 40, 600, 40, 190
John Martin, 20, 20, 300, 30, 100
Mary Coxe, 100, 650, 1500, 50, 600
Redick Jones, 30, 90, 500, 60, 175
Henry Ancell, 30, 90, 550, 75, 200
James Ancell, 60, 220, 1000, 150, 350
George Rasberry, 25, 55, 200, 175, 150
William Cassels, 50, 100, 800, 100, 200
Asa Hawkins, 35, 67, 800, 100, 320
Preston Moore, 20, 140, 500, 50, 150
Stephen Myres, 65, 578, 1600, 150, 380
Mariah Harberson, 50, 110, 600, 100, 200
Rolly E. Evans, 40, 200, 1000, 100, 226
Adam Berger, 35, 165, 400, 60, 150
Michael Hazier, 30, 130, 500, 75, 125
Benjamin Moore, 100, 70, 2000, 150, 385
Frances Metz, 40, 80, 450, 60, 240
Oscar H. Watts, 20, 20, 150, 50, 90
William Myres, 100, 900, 3000, 200, 900
Daniel Payne, 38, 15, 500, 50, 130
James Payne, 25, 50, 400, 20, 125
John Hall, 100, 900, 2500, 100, 710
Edward B. Kelsoe, 80, 500, 3000, 100, 660
Robert Racinkroft, 80, 330, 1000, 30, 340
Washington C. Ancell, 60, 100, 500, 150, 280
Pressley M. Kinnerson, 25, 135, 800, 100, 180
Joseph Stupee, 30, 60, 500, 20, 100
David Owens, 80, 160, 1000, 80, 485
Thomas J. Calhouin, 30, 130, 500, 50, 280
Thomas A. Matthews, 60, 222, 1000, 50, 250
Morgan Byrnes, 40, 121, 500, 30, 240
Charles Norman, 40, 100, 500, 75, 300
Samuel Patterson, 50, 110, 500, 75, 300
John Patterson, 15, 25, 100, 20, 200
John B. Stringer, 40, 120, 500, 20, 390

William Allin, 40, 80, 500, 50, 310
John Allin, 10, 30, 100, 20, 120
James Hollingshead, 80, 200, 1000, 80, 280
John Friend, 50, 70, 800, 80, 300
John A. McClain, 40, 160, 2000, 50, 390
Ally Norman, 30, 10, 200, 20, 140
John Norman, 30, 130, 400, 100, 330
Uriah Montgomery, 40, 90, 1000, 60, 570
Lorenzo D. Montgomery, 30, 10, 300, 50, 250
Alexander Montgomery, 80, 120, 2000, 150, 420
George Metz, 15, 65, 350, 10, 100
Elisha D. Barnes, 60, 100, 1200, 130, 230
Fereby Harrison, 20, 80, 800, 20, 100
Edward Ellis, 60, 60, 300, 50, 260
Elisha Lewis, 50, 70, 500, 50, 250
Ephraim Lemly, 40, 40, 400, 14, 580
Alsa Riggs, 80, -, 500, 25, 150
Jesse Friend, 70, 170, 1000, 150, 330
Charles Friend, 50, 190, 1000, 50, 260
Thomas McMullin Sr., 50, 30, 500, 50, 300
George Black, 20, 60, 200, 30, 150
Theopoles Black, 30, 50, 200, 81, 150
John Hale, 75, 125, 900, 100, 540
Sylvester Young, 70, 100, 500, 75, 570
Berry Greer, 60, 490, 1000, 100, 578
Thomas McMullin Jr., 40, 130, 750, 100, 395
Mary Matthews, 30, 36, 200, 15, 200
David Andrews, 35, 135, 600, 40, 380
William Martin, 20, 96, 600, 120, 340
Hannah Stalcup, 40, 860, 1600, 175, 650
James Trotter, 100, 50, 1000, 200, 460
John Sikes, 80, 175, 1000, 175, 400
Albert Hughs, 30, 10, 100, 100, 570
Bennett Carpenter, 25, 55, 300, 60, 280
Levi Chaney, 40, 80, 400, 100, 400
Mark Maner, 40, 40, 500, 100, 100
Lamlee Hatcher, 40, 40, 400, 50, 250
Peter Marshall, 15, 25, 300, 100, 400

William Winchester, 25, 55, 300, 25, 325

Benjamin B. Bennefield, 90, 440, 1500, 100, 820

Mark Retherford, 23, 97, 400, 20, 390

Edward G. Archer, 20, 60, 300, 75, 200

James Marshall, 30, 50, 300, 100, 250

John Ellis, 35, 165, 450, 20, 235

Charnat Glascock, 25, 25, 100, 30, 320

Abraham Hunter, 300, 2000, 10000, 1000, 2575

Isaac Hinkle, 100, 130, 800, 200, 1115

Washington Jones, 250, 50, 1000, 100, 780

Henderson Winchester, 70, 36, 500, 100, 300

Nancy Smith, 50, 150, 1000, 100, 220

Daniel Houk, 25, 55, 250, 20, 220

James F. Ross, 250, 2000, 8000, 250, 1400

Braxton Peck, 30, 50, 500, 100, 335

William Waller, 40, 100, 600, 50, 280

Woodson Parrott, 100, 100, 1500, 200, 520

Hayden M. Coxe, 58, 117, 850, 100, 325

Edward Hood, 60, 180, 4000, 75, 340

George Hireing, 20, 220, 400, 100, 120

Wendal Bohart, 25, 100, 500, 120, 120

Matthias Holder, 25, 135, 500, 75, 200

Louis Peppercorn, 30, 130, 700, 50, 175

Hugh Dobbins, 40, 160, 1500, 40, 780

Sebastian Iceman, 25, 55, 300, 40, 150

Howsen Hood, 20, 120, 480, 50, 108

John Stone, 25, 75, 500, 20, 150

John Barnes, 60, 270, 1200, 100, 355

Frances Retter, 60, 140, 1200, 100, 150

Dennis Debolt, 40, 40, 600, 70, 175

Michael Nichols, 25, 55, 500, 20, 120

Mary J. Evans, 60, 220, 1500, 50, 150

Jefferson Adams, 40, 80, 500, 50, 125

John Russell, 20, 30, 100, 20, 100

James Worley, 20, 30, 200, 20, 75

Robert Walker, 40, 70, 500, 150, 200

John Moore, 60, 300, 1500, 175, 450

John Dobbins, 20, 20, 200, 40, 125

James Friend, 35, 125, 500, 30, 20

Redman Anderson, 15, 25, 100, 20, 175

William G. Bowman, 60, 140, 2000, 125, 415

Susan Gibbs, 30, 90, 500, 25, 200

John Lewis, 40, 80, 500, 100, 300

Job Woreley, 46, 6, 500, 100, 225

Samuel W. Scofield, 40, 230, 1000, 60, 125

Edward Kew Sr., 40, 160, 1500, 150, 250

Robert T. Lane, 100, 160 1000, 250, 725

Philip J. McMahon, 70, 90, 1000, 100, 400

William T. Russell, 30, 50, 400, 50, 250

John P. Hunt, 30, 110, 2000, 100, 550

William M. Lusk, 30, 130, 1500, 80, 320

Gabriel G. Foulks, 50, 77, 1000, 100, 435

Cowen Barnes, 30, 130, 800, 100, 390

John Glascock, 80, 140, 2000, 100, 525

David Sweden, 20, 100, 700, 75, 350

B. L. Johns, 40, 40, 250, 40, 150

William Benion, 30, 10, 100, 25, 200

Henry C. Gist, 103, 200, 1200, 200, 3750

John Northcut, 140, 400, 1200, 150, 1000

Francis Kirkpatrick, 130, 60, 500, 100, 480

Newell Randall, 60 400, 1200, 100, 250

Elizabeth Boteman, 30, 47, 500, 40, 200

Archibald A. Price, 215, 1285, 5000, 300, 1020

William Griffith, 145, 225, 3000, 150, 900

David Griffith, 100, 415, 3000, 25, 500

Louis Willis, 80, -, 300, 100, 550

James H. Bryant, 25, -, 100, 25, 200

Benjamin Penn, 50, -, 300, 50, 375

Elbert Bryant, 30, -, 200, 30, 350

Margaret Bryant, 30, -, 200, 25, 225

John Dunlap, 20, -, 100, 15, 250

Andrew J. Hughs, 20, 20, 150, 20, 154

Nathan Hughs, 20, 20, 150, 25, 250

Nancy Hamilton, 20, -, 50, 50, 450

John Hayden, 30, -, 150, 50, 250

Morris Moore, 50, -, 200, 50, 150

John Neeley, 25, -, 100, 20, 150

Milton Kinnerson, 50, -, 200, 100, 450

Richmond Cobb, 20, -, 120, 60, 360

Ire Moore, 20, -, 100, 25, 150

Elijah Denton, 30, -, 250, 50, 250

Bartlet R. Conyers, 25, -, 150, 50, 250

James Northcut, 20, -, 100, 20, 150

John Frish, 30, 50, 250, 20, 165

John Turner, 30, -, 200, 25, 250

William Hale, 35, -, 150, 50, 275

Seburn Hughs, 45, -, 150, 25, 275

John Fisk, 25, -, 100, 25, 300

Shannon County, Missouri
1850 Agricultural Census

Shannon County 1850 Agricultural Census was filmed by the Central Microfilm Service Corp of St. Louis, Missouri, for the Missouri State Historical Society. There are 46 columns of information on the 1850 agricultural census. I have chosen to transcribe six of those columns. The columns are:

1. Name
2. Acres of Land Improved
3. Acres of Land Unimproved
4. Cash Value of the Farm
5. Value of Farm Implements and Machinery
13. Value of Livestock

Joseph Stevenson, 5, -, 100, 30, 75
John Cox, 8, -, 100, 30, 180
Thomas Smith, 8, 4, 30, 3, 40
Porter Isaac, 10, -, 75, 3, 34
David Dotson, 24, -, 100, 15, 150
John Nash, 11,-, 125, 15, 210
Ninian Bay, 25, -, 100, 20, 225
William Patterson, 24, -, 150, 55, 298
Matthew Patterson, 13, -, 50, 10, 150
Adam Meade, 12, -, 150, 8, 125
John Goforth, 8, -, 50, 3, 100
Joseph McLane, 10, -, 75, 148, 500
Jackson Counts, 10, -, 50, 8, 400
William Whitworth, 15, -, 300, 10, 88
Mark Durry, 8, -, 50, 3, 25
Thomas Chitton, 50, -, 1500, 60, 600
Joseph Asher, 30, -, 500, 40, 80
Thomas Reed, 46, 1000, 150, 600
Clinton Reed, 24, -, 300, -, 224
David Slusher, 20, -, 150, 3, 123
William Slusher, 18, -, 150, 3, 100
Ellis Campbell, 20, -, 150, 5, 125
Emer Stallcup, 12, -, 100, 10, 150
Mary Barker, 10, -, 100, 8, 75
Wesley Fancher, 40, -, 200, 50, 300
Thomas Quigly, 20, -, 200, 5, 75
Marston Stegall, 25, -, 200, 8, 90
John Mears, 5, -, 40, 8, 40
Nathaniel Baker, 11, -, 100, 75, 200
John Smith, 16, -, 200, 5, 150

Sarah West, 16, -, 200, 30, 150
Andrew McElmurry, 40, -, 200, 50, 320
Timothy Moore, 40, -, 200, 45, 193
William Dawson, 21, -, 150, 13, 370
Owen Hawkins, 30, 15, 500, 5, 236
Samuel Douglass, 45, -, 170, 7, 60
Andrew J. Holland, 5, -, 100, 8, 150
James Williams, 9, -, 50, 1, 100
Pleasant Holland, 10, -, 100, 12, 112
John Williams, 7, 4, 50, 5, 127
Jesse Thomas, 40, 40, 100, 15, 125
C. J. Pruitt, -, -, -, -, 100
Larkin Storey, 5, -, 50, 10, 100
Henry Mahan, 24, -, 100, 20, 170
Jesse Storey, 12, -, 50, 5, 80
Samuel Mahan, 30, -, 300, 10, 155
Richard Jones, 16, -, 100, 7, 200
William Chitton, -, -, -, -, 100
Matthew Harrison, 25, -, 37, 10, 100
George Smith, 26, -, 200, 10, 200
Shadrach Chitton, 40, -, 500, 60, 400
James Coil, 25, -, 100, 40, 250
Jackson Suggs, 40, -, 100, 5, 100
Dorias Rogers, 30, -, 150, 60, 200
James Thomas, 12, -, 100, 3, 61
Willoughby Suggs, 20, -, 200, 20, 200
Thomas T. Chitton(Chilton), 15, -, 200, 5, 228
John Chitton, 20, -, 50, -, 70
James Thompson, 20, -, 200, 20, 150

Thos. T. Chitton, 40, -, 500, 40, 235
Thomas Conway, 5, -, 50, 7, 75
Charles Conway, 25, -, 60, -, 95
Jesse Conway, 15, -, 25, 75, 615
Phoenix Cox, 20, -, 75, 5, 70
Alfred Deathurage, 30, 3, 200, 80, 200
John George, 30, -, 200, 45, 300
Thos. T. Chitton, 45, -, 220, 20, 400
Andrew J. Summers, 20, -, 150, 20, 200
Samuel Shumate, 12, 3, 100, 30, 100
Benj. B. Turpin, 18, -, 150, 7, 93
George W. Paulding, 25, -, 125, 10, 120
Mary Boyd, 20, -, 100, 5, 150
George Boyd, 20, -, 100, -, 100
Rubin Windham, 16, -, 100, 2, 68
Michael Harrison, 13, -, 100, 3, 150
John Harrison, 18, -, 150, 5, 150
Andrew Thomas, 19, -, 100, 75, 500
William Crowder, 25, -, 150, 50, 227
William Short, 20, -, 150, 5, 125
Michael Crowder, 12, -, 100, 8, 100
Thomas Wells, 16, 19, 100, 58, 200
John Marcus, 16, -, 70, 4, 135
William Mahan, 35, -, 300, 52, 362
John Mahan, 12, -, 150, 10, 150
Wallace Mahan, 15, -, 200, 20, 250
William C. Shedd, 50, -, 400, 150, 500
Wm. McCormack, 26, 4, 400, 25, 360
James McCormack, 60, 3, 600, 125, 300
Saml. Sinclear, 55, 5, 500, 70, 320
Stephen Perkins, 15, -, 100, 5, 90
William Wyatt, 20, -, 400, -, 100
John Smith, 18, -, 100, 100, 200
William Thomas, 10, -, 100, 1, 200
Thos. Capps, 15, -, 100, 5, 100
Alexr. Deathurage, 15, -, 100, 5, 100
John Brooks, 70, -, 600, 100, 2000
Page Roark, 12, -, 100, 3, 40
Stephen J. K. Bartisvale, 90, -, 1500, 100, 360
Mary Mitchell, 35, -, 150, 25, 250
Wm. Holman, 35, -, 400, 30, 250
James Williams, 40, -, 200, 50, 200
David Williams, 20, -, 150, 50, 150
Susan Groves, 65, -, 1000, 50, 125
Harmon Clinton, 12, -, 600, 30, 100

Lucinda Shirley, 40, -, 400, 60, 400
Andrew Clinton, 40, -, 200, 160, 250
John Orchard, 18, 3, 150, 75, 366
Campbell Stuart, 30, -, 200, 35, 350
Geo. Norris, 10, 5, 150, 75, 486
J. Newsom, 9, 5, 60, 12, 150
Jno. McGee, 15, -, 200, 10, 350
William McGee, 25, -, 300, 10, 215
Arthur Hobson, 16, -, 250, 30, 80
William Berry, 14, -, 150, 5, 75
J. B. Parker, 12, -, 250, 20, 250
C. Howell, 30, -, 200, 100, 568
John Mooney, 11,-, 100, 10, 100
Jn. Crabtree, 25, -, 100, 40, 100
Daniel Dugan, 20, -, 60, 10, 100
James Cole, 7, -, 60, 2, 200
Hiram Green, 12, -, 100, 8, 150
Gabriel Green, 15, 5, 70, 10, 110
T. Hodges, 12, -, 50, 2, 40
G. Rozier, 40, -, 400, 40, 60
H. Cole, 17, -, 150, 5, 127
James Mooney, 15, -, 140, 25, 160
Stanmore Nobles, 18, -, 200, 50, 200
Samuel Hodges, 45, -, 700, 70, 100
Nicholas McDonald, 12, -, 150, 10, 100
Wm. McDonald, 10, -, 40, 3, 70
Job Crabtree, 12, -, 150, 5, 63
S. Crabtree, 30, -, 150, 200, 250
J. Lewis, 14, -, 150, 5, 200
Jno. A. Summers, 70, 10, 500, 100, 400
Amos Summers, 8, -, 150, 5, 100
Danl. Summers, 20, -, 200, 5, 200
Geo. Roberts, 16, -, 100, 5, 160
William McDonald, 10, -, 75, 75, 180
William Lewis, 12, -, 100, 10, 100
James Boyce, 30, -, 250, 50, 250
John Hodges, 15, -, 250, 50, 250
L. McDonald, 16, -, 100, 75, 194
M. Craddock, 16, -, 150, 30, 200
Wm. Clark, 30, -, 200, 25, 400
Simeon Howell, 13, -, 150, 15, 128
H. McDonald, 25, -, 500, 80, 400
J. Levalley, 19, -, 60, 2, 75
A. Cox, 23, -, 100, 8, 150
T. Purcell, 25, -, 300, 40, 250
Thos. Summers, 8, -, 50, 2, 62

James R. Hill, 25, -, 300, 5, 130
Simeon Summers, 40, 30, 400, 100, 492
William Baskitt, 15, -, 200, 5, 109
D. C. Patton, 1, 5, 25, 5, 90
James F. Morris, 22, -, 200, 8, 44

Joshua Chitton(Chilton), 35, 4, 1000, 15, 577
Thos. J. Chitton, 57, -, 1100, 20, 702
David Alley, 60, -, 350, 75, 936

Shelby County 1850 Agricultural Census was filmed by the Central Microfilm Service Corp of St. Louis, Missouri, for the Missouri State Historical Society. There are 46 columns of information on the 1850 agricultural census. I have chosen to transcribe six of those columns. The columns are:

1. Name
2. Acres of Land Improved
3. Acres of Land Unimproved
4. Cash Value of the Farm
5. Value of Farm Implements and Machinery
13. Value of Livestock

Martin Stahl, -, -, -, -, 8
George Schnauffer, -, -, -, -, 25
Philip Chrisman, -, -, -, -, 13
J. King, -, -, -, -, 15
Henry Will, -, -, -, -, 24
John Will, -, -, -, -, 8
John Bower, -, -, -, -, 25
John D. Hottsman, -, -, -, -, 8
Henry Fink, -, -, -, -, 8
Charles Weaver, -, -, -, -, 8
Adam Fahner, -, -, -, -, 8
Joseph Derfler, -, -, -, -, 16
Joseph Knight, -, -, -, -, 32
John Staufffer, -, -, -, -, 25
Rudolph Marks, -, -, -, -, 8
G. Ceigler, -, -, -, -, 16
Michael Shafer, -, -, -, -, 60
William Fagar, -, -, -, -, 16
Reuben Bear, -, -, -, -, 16
C. Behring, -, -, -, -, 16
H. Girkin, -, -, -, -, 8
Jacob Krail, -, -, -, - 16
Adam Steinbach, -, -, -, -, 16
Frederick Luty, -, -, -, -, 16
Casper Bier, -, -, -, -, 16
Michael Forstner, -, -, -, -, 16
George Forstner, -, -, -, -, 16
Henry Kelfenbein, -, -, -, -, 16
Frederick Miley(Wiley), -, -, -, -, 16
John D. Ehleu, -, -, -, -, 16

Frederick Cook, -, -, -, -, 16
Philip Steinbach, -, -, -, -, 8
Coonrad Cookes(Cooker), -, -, -, -, 25
Henry Schneider, -, -, -, -, 8
Andrew Geisey, -, -, -, -, 25
Samuel Mohler, -, -, -, -, 16
Michael Crouse, -, -, -, -, 25
Samuel Miller, -, -, -, -, 40
Elizabeth Grosman, -, -, -, -, 8
Catherine Bacher, -, -, -, -, 8
David Waggoner, 35, 40, 750, 100, 100
Thomas S. Priest, 175, 325, 3000, 200, 1400
Josiah Bethards, 145, 305, 2500, 100, 400
Barnard Vanderen, 20, 150, 300, 50, 270
Phebe Earnest, 40, 55, 250, 40, 240
William S. Chinn, 90, 610, 4000, 130, 500
Minor W. Singleton, -, -, -, -, 350
Peyton Harding, -, -, -, 10, 60
Albert McAfee, 40, 600, 2000, 30, 230
Robt. Hall, 50, 50, 1000, 70, 170
George W. Leonard, 27, 333, 1500, 20, 240
James W. Gunby, 15, -, 500, 75, 90
Samuel O. Vanvacter, 90, 190, 1200, 100, 400
Jesse D. Grey, 80, 80, 800, 100, 400
Jonathan W. Barker, -, -, -, -, 115

Lewis Jacobs, 45, 75, 1000, 130, 390
William McMurry, 160, 200, 2000, 150, 1280
Tyrey Ford, -, -, -, - 125
Hill Shaw, 60, 225, 1500, 140, 360
William B. Magruder, -, -, -, -, 26
Jesse Brown, -, -, -, -, 25
William T. Yost, 42, 158, 1200, 10, 180
Sampson Melson (Nelson), 12, 68, 400, 12, 120
Joseph Griffith, 60, 220, 1500, 300, 565
Ellen Anderson, 120, 140, 1500 30, 320
William Gooch, 95, 65, 1500, 100, 436
Isaac Loar, -, -, -, 50, 80
Henry Brawner, 47, 193, 850, 110, 225
James M. Suggle(Tuggle), 15, 225, 400, 25, 103
John Garner, 80, 120, 1500, 60, 470
Joseph Chick, 15, 145, 500, 75, 200
Mathew Patton, 30, 50, 400, 110, 400
Thomas Jackson, 60, 500, 3000, 100, 360
Jeremiah Rust, -, -, -, -, 25
William B. Victor, -, -, - 30, 90
John T. Victor,-, -, -, 30, 60
Joseph Watson, 40, 130, 500, 200, 720
Major H. Jones, 30, 50, 300, 50, 100
Jacob Earnest, 35, 115, 600, 40, 420
Charles W. Gay, 38, 362, 2000, 15, 120
Charles Christian, 60, 60, 450, 60, 395
Samuel F. Dunn, 40, 110, 500, 25, 350
Fleming Turner, -, -, -, -, 130
William Minor, -, -, -, -, 14
James Russell, 7, 73, 160, 20, 55
Stephen R. Gunby, 100, 300, 2000, 15, 310
Levin Duncan, 28, 52, 400, 100, 360
Martin Baker, 100, 156, 2000, 100, 410
Elbert J. King, 80, 148, 1500, 150, 300
Robert C. Snyder, 33, 47, 400, 50, 260
Robert McAfee, 120, 540, 4000, 25, 340
Thomas Atchison, 45, 196, 1000, 20, 125
John W. Vandiver, 100, 300, 2500, 200, 580
James M. Eaton, 40, 200, 1000, 80, 285

John Hardin, 150, 430, 2500, 100, 340
James Caruthers, 75, 85, 800, 120, 250
John H. Caruthers, -, -, -, -, 100
James Bell, -, -, -, -, 85
Nathan McBride, 30, 104, 1000, 30, 170
Richard Perry, 75, 85, 1000, 175, 440
Griffith D. Shelton, 30, 50, 500, 20, 130
Robert Graham, 60, 180, 1000, 70, 650
James Clark, 25, 55, 500, -, 160
Joel Wolverton, -, -, -, -, 60
William Baker, 80, 240, 1500, -, 100
Patrick Coates, 45, 195, 1200, 55, 500
William Griffith, -, -, -, 270, 135
Littleton Victor, -, -, -, -, 70
William Kemper, 50, 70, 1000, 70, 200
Meshack Hale, -, -, -, 5, 50
John A. Clark, -, -, -, -, 70
John R. Clavert, 70, 90, 800, 100, 1300
Joseph Hilton, 80, 240, 2000, 100, 950
John C. Caruthers, 40, 160, 1000, 20, 240
Thomas Waltham, 55, 185, 800, 75, 250
John Selsor, -, -, -, -, 35
Peter Roff, 75, 130, 1500, 75, 520
Frances Coard, 35, 85, 600, 50, 260
David Wood, 32, 88, 600, 70, 250
Rebecca Thomas, -, -, -, -, 60
Nicholas Watkins, 12, 28, 2000, 45, 160
Spencer Vaughn, 75, 645, 3500, 15, 160
William Carnaham, -, -, -, 10, 85
Hawkins D. Smith, 36, 64, 500, 25, 340
Madison J. Priest, 100, 400, 2500, 155, 620
James Y. Anderson, 80, 160, 1200, 100, 480
William Wood, 35, 25, 300, 100, 310
Abner Mundle, 30, 210, 1000, 50, 240
Jane Eaton, 25, 55, 200, 15, 170
Elizabeth Smith, 60, 180, 1000, 75, 250
Charles Smith, 70, 360, 2200, 300, 530
William Conner, 38, 122, 800, 135, 360
Samuel Greenfield, 40, 120, 600, 100, 420
Louisa T. McAfee, 50, 150, 1600, 200, 400
Joseph J. West, 30, 130, 600, 60, 230

Elijah G. S. Chinn, -, -, -, -, 125
Samuel M. Victor, -, -, -, 125, 170
John Peoples, 130, 430, 2800, 300, 1320
Keen Phillips, -, -, -, 6, 90
John Hagar, 40, 260, 1500, 80, 340
John Hughes, 125, 315, 2000, 100, 670
James W. Miller, -, -, -, 15, 140
Benjamin Vanvacter, 55, 145, 1000, 100, 350
Nathan Peoples, 80, 200, 1500, 100, 890
Alexander Clark, 20, 100, 600, 50, 115
Edy Arnett, 55, 135, 500, 20, 320
Preston Manuel, 36, 134, 800, 75, 215
William McCoy, -, -, -, 40, 180
Elizabeth F. Pollard, 40, 240, 1500, 25, 300
John Dunn, 250, 160, 2400, 200, 2820
Peter B. Greer, 3, 37, 100, 10, 150
Joshua Smith, 20, 60, 400, 60, 260
John Hayden, 30, 290, 800, 40, 100
Benjamin L. Elsey, 23, 57, 300, 100, 305
William Sharp, 40, 40, 500, 50, 340
Ralph Arthur, 16, 24, 150, 10, 180
Elizabeth Miller, 40, 40, 400, 20, 70
William Forman, 30, 170, 1000, 10, 80
Lilburn W. Hale, 70, 570, 3500, 75, 300
Alexander Holton, 40, 120, 800, 10, 100
James S. Picket, 65, 90, 800, 110, 350
Stephen E. Lay, 120, 160, 2000, 200, 1000
Thomas Bakhouse, -, -, -, -, 45
Hiram Rookwood, 30, 90, 1000, 100, 490
Samuel G. Wadkins, 75, 200, 1400, 100, 310
William Adams, 26, 66, 300, 40, 240
Gilbert F. Edmonds, 60, 140, 1000, 100, 490
John Short, 55, 30, 450, 15, 250
Jacob Vandiver, 60, 100, 800, 100, 280
Abraham Vandiver, -, -, -, -, 100
John Sykes, 65, 206, 1500, 100, 280
John Adams, 18, 102, 300, 10, 100
William D. B. Hill, 47, 153, 800, 115, 250
John Laws, 30, 90, 600, 100, 220

Sarah Vanlandingham, 16, 24, 200, 10, 170
James Shaw, 40, 160, 800, 5, 150
Daniel J. Lake, 23, 137, 800, 25, 140
Wilhelmina Fisher, -, -, -, -, 20
Jacob Findling, -, -, -, -, 20
Barbara Kurlhaus, -, -, -, -, 10
William Keil, -, -, -, -, 200
George Ginger,-, -, -, -, 15
Anna Ginger, -, -, -, -, 10
George Vacher, -, -, -, -, 20
John Miller, -, -, -, -, 20
Margarett Smith, -, -, -, -, 10
George Reutz,-, -, -, -, 20
William Miller, -, -, -, -, 10
Maria Stauffer, -, -, -, -, 20
David Zimmerman, -, -, -, -, 10
Lewis Swarder, -, -, -, -, 20
Jessee Jentry, 120, 280, 5000, 250, 770
Elizabeth Pickett, 180, 220, 3000, 100, 620
Jacob Culler,-, -, -, -, 25
Lewis Miller, 50, 50, 600, 12, 100
Orson Oaks, 25, 175, 1000, 50, 130
John Oaks, 97, 153, 1000, 10, 60
William Miller, 60, 100, 1400, 100, 300
Thomas G. McCullough, 28, 132, 800, 12, 100
David Miller, 30, 170, 1000, 15, 150
William Powell, 54, 106, 800, 130, 230
Edward R. Naylor, 15, 145, 800, 14, 60
William Glossner, 24, 101, 600, 20, 250
Alexander W. Knipper, -, -, -, 20, 100
Thomas L. Comedy, 4, 118, 200, 20, 175
Sarah Hall, 30, 130, 600, -, 10
Avary G. Hall, -, -, -, 10, 90
Hamilton Shouse, 70, 90, 1200, 130, 550
Thomas O. Eskridge, 30, 50, 600, 10, 325
Franklin Brawner, 5, 75, 400, 20, 120
Henry Keil, 20, 100, 800, -, 60
Thomas Parish, 50, 190, 1000, 20, 120
William Straehn, 12,148,400, 40, 180
Henry Simbrook(Timbrook), -, -, -, -, 75, 75
John Mills, 30, 220, 1200, 100, 160

Lacy Morris, 30, 130, 800, 100, 400
Daniel Maupin, 30, 158, 400, 50, 160
John English, 40, 120, 800, 10, 100
Charles O. Shoemaker, 45, 195,800, 70, 380
John Kyle, 65, 34, 300, 75, 430
Alfred Vannort, -, -, -, -, 350
James R. Barr, 40, 120, 800, 100, 190
William Webb, 30, 110, 500, 30, 250
Prettyman Blizzard, 22, 58, 300, 150, 140
John S. Duncan, 50, 110, 800, 50, 370
George Parker, -, -, -, -, 10
Armstrong Caruthers, 78, 82, 800, 150, 580
Major Taylor, 100, 330, 2000, 100, 400
Isaac Tobin, 30, 130, 800, 60, 375
George W. Hall, 12, 108, 500, 5, 100
John W. Wailes, 10 70, 400, 50, 150
Stanford Drane, 20, 60, 250, 5, 80
Malcolm Wood, 46, 114, 800, 25, 150
Rufus Moore, 32, 128, 400, 75,180
Reuben Taylor, 35, 125, 800, 40, 350
Margarett Moore, -, -, -, -, 30
Isaac A. Wales, 24, 56, 300, 15, 125
James Carroll, 35, 125, 800, 75, 320
Christopher J.T. Maupin, 50, 110, 800, 40, 500
James Parker, -, -, -, -, 25
Bartlett Carrol, 40, 60, 400, 10, 125
Levi Bishop, 25, 55, 500, 10, 500
Margarett Forsythe, -, -, -, -, 36
Perry B. Moore, 50, 270, 1500, 50, 150
Daniel Thrasher, 40, 80, 400, 20, 280
Henry Kidwell, 40, 160, 1000, 60, 590
Henry Clutter, -, -, -, 5, 40
James B. Ryland, 21, 200, 1000, 780, 390
Fleming Lee, -, -, -, 100, 230
Benjamin N. Wilson, 40, 160, 800, 35, 170
Thomas C. Dawson, 22, 18, 250, 20, 310
Alexander Clark, 35, 125, 400, 8, 110
Commodore McFarland, 40, 260, 600, 100, 340
John H. Byrne, 20, 140, 350, 5, 115

Joseph Moss, 60, 180, 1500, 75, 450
Joseph Forman, 60, 100, 1600, 150, 770
George W. Gore, -, -, -, -, 30
Robert A. Moffett, 50, 170, 1200, 120, 650
Robert Joiner, 100, 76, 1000, 75, 720
Pleasant W. Stowe, -, -, -, 15, 150
William Looney, 35, 55, 500, 60, 130
Robert Lair, 75, 165, 1500, 200, 605
Charles Hollyman, 40, 120, 1000, 100, 380
John Nesbit, 150, 410, 2500, 100, 410
William Payne Sr., 50, 110, 600, 100, 340
James Riggs, 110, 490, 2000, 175, 510
Daniel Taylor, 50, 150, 1500, 60, 360
Solomon W. Miller, 40, 80, 600, 100, 170
Charles Moffett, 60, 140, 1200, 50, 250
Joshua T. Roper, 40, 160, 800, 150, 200
Caleb Aduddle, 30, 130, 600, 100, 160
James G. Glenn, 50, 110, 1200, 150, 300
Austin J. Smith, 45, 235, 1500, 25, 150
Edward F. Wilson, -, -, -, 150, 180
H. Vanshoike, 30, 100, 500, 20, 100
Edward Wilson, 50, 169, 1000, 700, 300
James D. Parsons, 320, 300, 3000, 300, 1470
Alexander Buford, 100, 360, 2600, 50, 550
Caroline Looney, 35, 55, 500, 50, 260
Matilda Sage, 50, 150, 1200, -, 150
Frances Cockran, 70, 170, 1500, 80, 450
William H. Payne, 40, 80, 500, 75, 360
William B. Moore, 80, 400, 2500, 200, 2025
Jessee Farris, 45, 75, 600, 50, 180
James Z. Graves, 22, 178, 800, 25, 280
Sarah McKethan, 20, 20, 300, 150, 500
Henry Louthan, 240, 320, 6000, 380, 2150
John Hines, -, -, -, -, 60
Anthony Minter, 150, 390, 3000, 100, 605
Jonathan Parsons, 200, 440, 3000, 300, 1400

David Parsons, 300, 473, 5400, 100, 2000
Robert P. Forsythe, 50, 110, 600, -, 40
Addison Lair, 100, 63, 1600, 125, 380
Alfred Vanshoike, 60, 80, 450, 15, 140
Perry Waters, 20, 60, 300, 45, 180
Andrew Browning, 9, 71, 300, 10, 180
John J. Rutter, 75, 245, 1600, 80, 450
John Allen, -, -, -, -, 425
Sylvanus J. Bragg, 200, 240, 2000, 150, 900
Robert B. Morgan, -, -, -, -, 125
Thomas C. Lear, 40, 40, 400, 100, 340
William White, -, -, -, -, 50
Kemp M. Glascock, 90, 190, 2000, 140, 340
Francis Lefflett, 60, 150, 1000, 100, 390
Bedford Brown, 62, 138, 1000, 50, 200
John Wilson, 23, 137, 100, 100, 150
Daniel Woolf, 70, 230, 1200, 40, 120
French Flewrer, 150, 90, 1200, 200, 700
Jacob Whoberry, 18, 62, 200, 10, 170
Thomas P. Lair, 90, 190, 1400, 150, 600
Richard B. Settle, 35, 135, 1000, 50, 250
Thomas G. Turner, 48, 122, 600, 36, 260
Abel Turner, 60, 180, 1200, 85, 450
William A. Rawlings, 120, 160, 1400, 175, 760
Thomas W. Glascock, 75, 85, 1200, 130, 400
Benjamin P. Glascock, 38, 122, 600, 10, 225
Benjamin T. Talbott, 30, 90, 400, 100, 290
John K. Stone, 50, 630, 3500, 100, 440
Peter C. Rust(Rast), 45, 115, 800, 15, 400
Mandley Elgin, 30, 110, 800, 100, 450
Robert Vanshoike, 60, 80, 450, 10, 100
Edmund Rutter, 90, 400, 1500, 100, 300
Elias Winchell, 100, 260, 2000, 100, 430
William G. Bragg, -, -, -, 50, 100
John Cadle, 30, 10, 100, 40, 190
Margarett J. Moore, -, -, -, -, 60
Henry C. White, 30, 120, 750, 30, 220
Ann M. Anderson, 40, 120, 800, 50, 275

John Kaylor, 50, 380, 2000, 75, 250
George M. Kaylor, -, -, -, -, 30
William T. Whitelock, 15, 65, 300, 10, 140
Robert Poore, 50, 230, 1000, 75, 400
Thomas M. Poore, -, -, -, -, 100
Eliza Anderson, 100, 177, 1500, -, 140
Mary S. Anderson, -, -, -, -, 10
John D. Couch, 40, 180, 1000, 10, 260
Saml. Cutbertson, 30, 10, 250, 30, 200
Thomas F. Tucker, -, -, -, -, 70
John Franklin, 38, 42, 300, 50, 85
Thomas J. Claggett, 140, 137, 1500, 100, 600
Benjamin Jones, 23, 57, 300, 100, 250
John Jones, 20, 60, 150, 20, 180
William J. Mays, 40, 80, 600, 150, 460
James H. Mays, 20, 60, 300, 70, 90
Calep N. Gallaher, 100, 300, 2000, 50, 470
Elisha Moore, 100, 220, 1800, 50, 750
Daniel C. Bird, 60, 90, 600, 200, 240
John White, 30, 110, 600, 20, 190
Robert Allen, -, -, -, 10, 160
George L. Elgin, 40, 160, 900, 50, 240
William Vanshoike, 50, 190, 1200, 100, 325
Jesse Vanshoike, 5, 75, 250, 50, 300
David Brown, -, -, -, 50, 120
John J. Neal, 85, 95, 1000, 100, 550
Samuel M. Hewitt, 85, 55, 900, 20, 210
William Todd, 50, 110, 1000, 50, 300
Levin Brown, 110, 50, 1200, 100, 610
James T. Crenshaw, 40, 80, 500, 25, 260
Joseph Steward, 35, 86, 600, 100, 280
John W. Ray, 55, 145, 1000, 200, 170
Larkin Garnett, 50, 110, 800, 50, 330
Lewis Baldwin, 50, 230, 1000, 100, 40
Joseph T. Garnett, 50, 135, 900, 50, 500
Cyrus A. Sanders, 43, 157, 1000, 50, 250
John C. Garnett, 50, 230, 1400, 50, 290
James Garnett, 40, 120, 900, 100, 400
Henry Sheets, 100, 500, 2500, 75, 1325
Ambrose B. Perry, 75, 325, 1500, 110, 600

William Fagan, 60, 140, 1000, 50, 240
Lewis Matthews, 35, 125, 400, 20, 170
James L. Vandiver, 50, 270, 1000, 130, 450
Benjamin Forman Sr., 60, 60, 800, 400, 390
Samuel Singleton, 28, 132, 500, 50, 220
Lewis Gillaspy, 73, 224, 1600, 300, 350
Thomas G. Magruder, 70, 330, 2000, 90, 200
Robert Gillaspy, 30, 50, 400, 15, 240
Samuel P. Gaines, -, -, -, -, 120
Alexander Gillaspy, 10, -, -, -, 130
Woolry Hooper, 30, 50, 400, 25, 180
James Harrington, 43, 157, 1000, 40, 220
Pleasant Wilburn, 30, 50, 400, 20, 240
Edwin Brinchley(Bunchley), 40, 80, 500, 35, 140
Milton Parish,-, -, -, -, 155
Samuel Vandiver, 120, 400, 2500, 150, 580
James Springer, -, -, -, 100, 255
William Montgomery, 85, 100, 800, 10, 90
John McWilliams, 80, 160, 1200, 75, 350
Henry Dill, 17, 463, 1200, 30, 150
Elijah R. Moore, 55, 225, 1000, 50, 430
Samuel B. Hardy, 65, 95, 500, 75, 260
Alexander Anderson, 45, 75, 500, 120, 580
George Eaton, 81, 79, 1000, 175, 780
Charles G. Gilerson, 120, 280, 2000, 80, 460
George M. Dickerson, 35, 125, 500, 10, 120
Elam Evans, 40, 120, 800, 20, 90
John Turner, 60, 140, 800, 170, 280
James Gooch, 100, 215, 2500, 100, 125
Samuel J. Smith, 10, 110, 400, 85, 390
William J. Holliday, 45, 115, 2000, 500, 360
James Swast, 50, 110, 800, 200, 380
Andrew Finney, 50, 250, 1000, 20, 150
John W. Moore, -, -, -, -, 30

John Howe, 35, 5, 200, 40, 115
William Morris, 20, 60, 200, 10, 160
Fountain Howe, 10, 30, 100, -, 60
Hughy Moore, 33, 127, 600, 20, 110
James Graham, 140, 260, 1500, 100, 1600
Frances Lowen, -, -, -, -, 130
George E. Bell, 40, 80, 800, 20, 150
John Biggs, 60, 380, 2000, 200, 260
John Smith, 21, 99, 400, 70, 140
John B. Robb, -, -, -, -, 260
John Maddox, 65, 62, 800, 25, 390
William H. Eakle, 15, 66, 500, 80, 150
William K. Broughton, 58, 310, 2000, 100, 290
Thornton Parker, 90, 130, 900, 100, 310
George Parker, 30, 130, 800, 150, 530
Elijah Pepper, 60, 220, 1500, 200, 300
Robert Duncan, 22, 178, 800, 20, 200
Ann M. Holliday, 35, 205, 1000, 15, 165
Robert Bell, 43, 119, 750, 70, 420
Lewis Maddox, 18, 23, 150, 200, 335
Nathan Berry, 50, 150, 800, 20, 220
John Thomas, 40, 80, 400, 15, 180
Joseph M. Roby, 50, 110, 800, 60, 270
Fleming Hester, 18, 142, 400, 10, 180
Nancy Davis, 10, 110, 200, 5, 100
John G. Myers, 40, 280, 1000, -, 140
William Blackburn, -, -, -, -, 160
Frederick Panter, 90, 310, 2000, 100, 320
Daniel Givans, 80, 320, 1600, 20, 520
George Coleman, -, -, -, -, 20
James Blackford, 70, 150, 1000, 100, 290
Hardin Blackford, 55, 485, 3000, 150, 2570
James Bell, 70, 250, 1500, 25, 165
James A. Sherry, 40, 120, 1000, 20, 3125
James B. Howe, 20, 60, 450, 20, 200
Samuel R. Howe, 50, 110, 800, 60, 270
R. L. Kinchloe, 140, 160, 1500, 100, 990
James M. Holliday, 65, 95, 1000, 100, 415
Lewis Sanders, 80, 120, 1200, 100, 1235

William C. Mitchell, 90, 230, 1600, 75, 375

Samuel Blackburn, 70, 290, 2000, 150, 780

Robert Givans, -, -, -, -, 430

Mrs. Willie Smith, 50, 110, 800, 10, 95

Franklin Pepper, 25, 135, 600, 25, 150

John Dye, 30, 145, 500, 15, 180

George Hardy, 14, 46, 450, 30, 150

Faning Bell, 50, 110, 800, 10, 160

George Gaines Jr., 10, 70, 400, 25, 240

George Gaines Sr., 120, 100, 1600, 260, 670

Nancy Gullett, 20, 60, 300, -, 75

Solomon Evans, 25, 60, 400, 25, 100

Lemuel Franklin, 50, 150, 1500, 80, 160

William J. Gosh, 80, 120, 1200, 75, 200

Mathias Neff, -, -, -, 10, 25

Barbay Maddox, 160, 90, 1600, 125, 225

Isabella Cochran, 70, 570, 2500, 80, 160

Joseph Musgrove, 60, 140, 1600, 100, 360

Harvey Eidson, 35, 125, 800, 25, 175

John H. Snider, -, -, -, -, 205

James E. Utz, -, -, -, 55, 120

Rosannah Utz, -, -, -, -, 30

William G. Lee(See), 17, 23, 300, 55, 170

John W. Moore, 12, 38, 150, 10, 160

Fautleroy Dye, 70, 210, 1400, 140, 470

Kendall W. Hay, 70, 230, 1500, 60, 750

James Sanders, 100, 236, 2000, 150, 625

John Worland, 60, 100, 800, 100, 250

George W. Smith, -, -, -, 15, 140

Robert Combs, 75, 165, 1200, 50, 470

William Hightower, -, -, -, -, 20

Adrian A. Robbins, 50, 110, 900, 100, 630

Russell W. Moss, 166, 374, 3000, 100, 700

Thomas Davison, 75, 145, 1000, 30, 230

John C. Utz, 20, 68, 400, 5, 50

William A. Deer, 50, 150, 800, 85, 330

Alexander Fowler, 75, 225, 1500, 40, 150

William H. Cook, -, -, -, 75, 10

Jeremiah Fudge, 125, 175, 1500, 200, 450

Baptiste Hardy, 140, 227, 2000, 125, 800

William H. Sary(Lary), 40, 40, 400, 10, 310

John V. Cox, 70, 210, 1400, 115, 280

George P. Mays, 30, 50, 500, 35, 250

James F. Murray, 12, 58, 300, 5, 150

Sinah Hickman, 60, 100, 800, 50, 225

Gabriel Davis, 80, 120, 1000, 150, 290

Robert K. Mays, 35, 45, 600, 5, 175

Johnathan Rogers, 50, 70, 600, 175, 270

William Howes, 30, 90, 600, 10, 130

Ann. G. Finney, 36, 84, 300, 10, 70

John B. Mitchell, 20, 20, 200, -, 100

Henry H. Goodwin, 130, 200, 2000, 200, 740

Thomas F. Barker(Parker), 30, 610, 2500, 20, 290

Anthony Gooch, 70, 130, 1500, 100, 250

Adolpheus E. Wood, -, -, -, -, 170

William O. Huston, 40, 400, 1600, 100, 280

Elijah Barnes, 30, 130, 400, 10, 150

Isaac Stalcup, 40, 191, 1000, 20, 170

Joseph Totten, 12, 148, 500, 20, 100

Thomas Estridge, 25, 135, 600, 25, 150

William Bush, 4, 396, 1000, -, 60

William Stalcup, 50, 110, 800, 150, 340

Upton Webb, -, -, -, -, 1180

William Lowrey, 30, 290, 500, 10, 100

James M. Donalson, -, -, -, 20, 50

James M. Hagan, 65, 55, 600, 20, 180

Sampson Waddle, -, -, -, -, 35

George Reynolds, 70, 130, 450, 50, 615

George M. Reynolds, 20, 20, 250, 6, 1145

Shelton Lowrey, 25, 55, 400, 20, 340

Perry Whiles, 13, 67, 400, 60, 120

Linsey (Sinsey) Whiles, 14, 66, 400, -, 112

Samuel Whiles, -, -, -, -, 20

Henry Spires, 100, 60, 800,175, 500

John Wailes, 35, 79, 400, 40, 160

Irwin Million, 25, 55, 400, 20, 160

Joel Million, 90, 140, 1200, 200, 950
William P. Hord, 25, 75, 400, 10, 150
Stephen Mullins, 30, 170, 800, 10, 140
Enoch R. Miller, -, -, -, 5, 220
Elijah T. Gore(Gose), -, -, -, -, 40
Hannah Dungan, -, -, -, -, 115
Stephen R. Thrasher, -, -, -, -, 12
Simeon McCoy, 5, 35, 150, 60, 150
William S. Sheet, 30, 50, 350, -, 160
Martha Bynum, 30, 130, 800, 5, 170

James Turner, 20, 20, 200, 15, 250
Bethel Company Farm, 150, 370, 5200, -, -
Bethel Company Farm, 200, 470, 8500, -, -
Bethel Company Farm, 150, 140, 3500, -, -
Bethel Company Farm, 120, 680, 5000, 1000, 3700

Stoddard County 1850 Agricultural Census was filmed by the Central Microfilm Service Corp of St. Louis, Missouri, for the Missouri State Historical Society. There are 46 columns of information on the 1850 agricultural census. I have chosen to transcribe six of those columns. The columns are:

1. Name
2. Acres of Land Improved
3. Acres of Land Unimproved
4. Cash Value of the Farm
5. Value of Farm Implements and Machinery
13. Value of Livestock

Jacob Wilfong, 12, -, 50, 15, 107
James C. Smith, 10, -, 50, 10, 80
William H. Norman, 40, 20, 300, 75, 300
Peter Sifford, 18, -, 100, 10, 72
Henry Sifford, 8, -, 50, 20, 75
Hesekiah Sifford, 15, -, 50, 20, 61
David Scott, 18, 40, 100, 10, 44
Robert Stewart, 25, -, 100, 12, 40
Martin Rogers, 15, -, 150, 20, 100
Lewis Sifford, 30, -, 300, 50, 250
Henry Sifford Jr., 20, -, 300, 10, 138
James Goodin, 20, -, 200, 15, 75
Elisabeth Walker, 25, -, 150, 10, 73
Terry Poe, 40, -, 300, 35, 160
John Story, 30, -, 250, 125, 208
John Taylor, 17, -, 125, 15, 86
William Randol, 32, -, 250, 250, 184
Nancy Gilly, 20, -, 200, 20, 125
Gushen Allen, 20, -, 250, 65, 220
Seth G. Hollis, 30, -, 300, 40 278
William A. Hollis, 17, -, 200, 12, 87
Stephen Hollis, 12, -, 100, 20, 104
Thomas B. Warren, 15, -, 100, 6, 140
Little B. Harvy, 30, -, 150, 70, 242
John Hartz, 90, 100, 800, 150, 937
Daniel Hartz, Jr., 35, -, 200, 20, 250
Willson Caldwell, 18, -, 200, 10, 397
Rhoda Caldwell, 20, -, 200, 10, 150
John W. Horbush, 45, -, 300, 50, 1965

James Caldwell, 11, -, 70, 10, 170
Robert Ramey, 50, -, 200, 75, 230
Granville Caldwell, 22, -, 100, 8, 258
Isaac Rogers, 12, -, 50, 6, 88
Alexander Findley, 25, -, 75, 10, 203
Thomas Black, 90, 49, 600, 250, 565
Sarah Claze, 19, -, 200, 16, 158
Martin Asher, 136, 40, 560, 50, 483
Abram Rogers, 85, 9, 200, 20, 956
John Black, 25, -, 200, 35, 187
James Williams, 70, 36, 500, 70, 366
Montgomery Williams, 16, -, 100, 40, 150
Isaac Gaily, 20, -, 100, 8, 95
Benjamin Taylor, 35, 55, 150, 8, 145
Samuel Dodson, 30, 55, 200, 15, 100
George Macon, 35,-, 250, 15, 275
Phillip Bright, 30, -, 100, 20, 178
Eli Williams, 30, 5, 150, 30, 152
William Williams, 20, -, 100, 15, 136
James Lacewell, 12, -, 150 10, 101
Joseph Johnson, 22, -, 100, 10, 180
Johnathan Johnson, 23, 57, 125, 4, 170
Isaac Cook, 22, -, 150, 40, 109
Nicholas Cook, 25, -, 150, 5, 26
Miles Johnson, 25, -, 150, 35, 79
William Macon, 35, -, 300, 25, 600
Robert Duglas, 60 -, 400, 150, 376
Wilson Johnson, 12, -, 100, 20, 202
John Stewart, 20, -, 100, 25, 190

Sarah Spivy, 20, -, 100, 25, 98
Archabald Spivy, 12, -, 50, 12, 115
Pleasant Spivy, 35,-, 200, 20, 160
David Johnson, 14, -, 50, 40, 155
Robert Stewart, 16, -, 150, 80, 323
Washington Johnson, 15, -, 100, 25, 175
Alfred Chronister, 12, -, 100, 25, 163
Joseph Lacewell, 16, -, 100, 10, 81
James Strong, 9, -, 60, 20, 85
William Macon Jr., 16, -, 120, 20, 137
Lemuel Stewart, 16, -, 125, 12, 146
William Cummins, 33, -, 250, 25, 123
Riley Short, 8, -, 50, 11, 124
Wilson Gray, 16, -, 60, 20, 120
George W. Oder, 25, -, 100, 10, 40
Nancy Gray, 19, -, 250, 75, 283
William W. Campbell, 90, -, 600, 26, 303
William McClain, 60, -, 570, 80, 366
David Sifford, 43, -, 500, 90, 307
Francis Foster, 25, -, 350, 12, 140
Hannah Knee, 40, -, 300, 25, 168
Jacob Clingensmith, 12, -, 160, 25, 75
Milton Wilson, 20, -, 400, 57, 433
Greenfield Brideshaw, 30, -, 350, 10, 145
Isham Strong, 40, 50, 300, 300, 640
Monroe Sitz, 23, -, 350, 12, 126
Joel Like, 14, -, 275, 4, 50
George W. Rhodes, 70, 170, 500, 300, 1100
Joshua Maberry, 100, 340, 2000, 100, 592
David Bolinger, 35, 85, 500, 30, 86
Henry Masters, 14, -, 300, 60, 142
Davis Revell, 12, -, 300, 20, 265
Denton Revell, 45, 35, 500, 110, 400
John Bowlin, 30, 110, 500, 15, 366
Elisabeth Bowlin, 40, 40, 200, 10, 347
David Adams, 20, 24, 325, 10, 95
Turner Brown, 30, 50, 300, 10, 239
William Welch, 35, -, 350, 200, 310
Jacob Shrum, 70, 90, 1000, 200, 412
James Kinnion, 30, 50, 600, 80, 185
Benjamine Hitt, 40, 80, 500, 70, 345

Orvel Behorst, 18, 22, 160, 10, 197
Roberson Brideshaw, 15, 35, 250, 20, 215
Beverly B. Foster, 50, 70, 350, 60, 642
Gerin McFerron, 16, 114, 4000, 15, 110
Perry Brideshaw, 20 60, 300, 20 95
George Cox, 50, 70, 300, 50, 485
Green Hitt, 20, 20, 300, 30, 269
John M. Milton, 25, 15, 300, 10, 360
Peter Slinkard, 20, 100, 200, 100, 232
Joseph Shrum, 26, 95, 700, 60, 184
John Shrum, 15, -, 250, 15, 105
William Vangilder, 20, -, 200, 25, 206
Frederick Shrum, 60, 5, 250, 200, 108
Daniel Ryan, 26, -, 200, 50, 221
Nancy Adams, 50, 30, 500, 25, 146
William W. Hicks, 60, 50, 400, 75, 1173
James Doyle, 36, 44, 250, 20, 269
Alfred Bolinger, 9, -, 75, 5, 50
Jacob Miller, 30, -, 237, 10, 265
John Bolinger, 17, -, 175, 10, 77
Joseph Bolinger, 22, 53, 300, 20, 197
Isaac U. Armstrong, 37, 43, 250, 190, 310
Sarah Bolinger, 35, 125, 500, 30, 162
Nathan Welch, 42, 38, 250, 25, 214
Solomon Wilson, 26, -, 275, 10, 368
William Gunnels, 60, -, 500, 80, 297
Calvin Aust, 17, -, 225, 8, 172
Aaron Helderman, 35, 89, 300, 151, 218
Wilson Bridshaw, 22, -, 222, 20, 162
Robert Bridshaw, 40, 40, 400, 30, 155
Hiram A. Shook, 15, -, 120, 15, 133
Alfred Wilson, 35, 5, 350, 25, 187
Susan Jinkins, 50, -, 297, 25, 223
Elijah Jinkins, 32, 48, 300, 40, 337
Solomon Perkins, 36, -, 300, 25, 385
Isaac S. Ford, 17, -, 175, 20, 155
John Holn, 12, 75, 200, 100, 195
Christenor Bolinger, 16, -, 150, 20, 63
William Stephens, 18, 72, 500, 500, 271
Rachael Lane, 25, 54, 300, 75, 133
Gabrel Little, 50, -, 312, 25, 486
John Ashabran, 15, -, 125, 15, 88
John Rhodes, 25, -, 175, 25, 132
Martin Hefner, 60, -, 325, 100, 120

Abram Hefner, 25, -, 225, 20, 177
Christopher Hains, 20, 100, 250, 20, 188
Joseph Greenlee, 26, 32, 250, 20, 152
Christopher Stewart, 25, 15, 150, 15, 56
William Hale, 30, 90, 500, 70, 180
John B. Hale(Hall), 35, -, 250, 25, 116
William M. Galaspie, 25, -, 180, 50, 233
Joseph Lavender, 30, -, 241, 30, 427
Marcus Sitz, 50, 2, 300, 40, 260
Ruphus Sitz, 25, 40, 250, 25, 50
John Proffer, 40, 40, 300, 25, 185
Jonas Sitz, 27, 65, 400 40, 165
Emanuel Cross, 58, 62, 600, 100, 115
William G. Palmer, 40, 80, 500, 25, 251
Jonas Oaks, 70, 80, 1000, 100, 340
George Adams, 16, -, 200, 80, 280
Noah W. Sitz, 60, 180, 1200, 75, 795
Joel Brantley, 44, 96, 500, 70, 381
George Miller, 40, -, 200, 50, 442
Samuel Moore, 65, 135, 500, 50, 414
Joshua Poplin, 20, 32, 300, 20, 188
Nathaniel Purtell, 16, -, 170, 12, 158
Peter Proffer, 60, 30, 500, 150, 435
John Whitford, 16, -, 60, 12, 110
Phillip Holn, 15, -, 125, 20, 65
Japhat Bolinger, 18, 22, 200, 10, 127
Jacob Like, 50, 113, 500, 60, 256
George Nations, 65, 28, 500, 150, 483
Clinton P. Conyers, 37, 44, 325, 20, 103
William Strop, 30, 10, 400, 25, 178
Thomas Revell, 13, -, 250, 25, 135
George Harris, 80, -, 400, 95, 490
Henry Gosey, 46, -, 600, 80, 228
Benjamine Gains, 16, -, 150, 30, 212
Henry Sitz, 17, -, 150, 10, 93
James F. Henderson, 35, -, 300, 50, 160
Nelson W. Comdre, 16, -, 125, 25, 60
James Rhodes, 75, 48, 800, 350, 1270
Jessee Purtell, 22, -, 20, 35, 154
Levi Cook, 40, -, 250, 100, 180
Andrew Hollock, 60, -, 300, 100, 278
James Purtell, 17, -, 175, 75, 140
William M. Gunn, 23, 137, 500, 20, 75
William Morgan, 16, 77, 350, 5, 210
Jessee Wilson, 44, -, 350, 150, 460
John Lovesey, 16, -, 175, 12, 86

Daniel B. Miller, 20, 17, 500, 100, 800
Jonas Keaker, 50, -, 800, 80, 278
Henry Harper, 40, 40, 600, 20, 160
Henry Miller, 120, 237, 2500 150, 1635
Loranso D. Frederick, 30, -, 150, 15, 115
William Bailey, 12, -, 40, 60, 94
Charles Kitchen, 40, 14, 400, 27, 120
Alfred Griggs, 50, 20, 318, 12, 156
James Sitton, 45, 35, 500, 50, 260
Joseph Culberson Jr., 10, -, 100, 5, 80
James Culberson, 10, -, 50, 5, 52
Eli Culberson, 15, -, 75, 15, 91
Joseph Culberson, 25, -, 300, 15, 179
Willis R. Webb, 18, 80, 300, 80, 248
Andrew Thomison, 8, 32, 100, 50, 178
James W. Hardin, 27, -, 150, 15, 95
Joseph B. Davis, 26, 94, 1000, 20, 470
James R. Bowlin, 9, -, 50, 8, 60
Michael Kinder, 50, -, 300, 100, 352
Zegnel J. Smith, 18, -, 100, 25, 185
William Ramsey, 15, -, 100, 125, 175
Wesley F. Suttles, 20, -, 100, 20, 157
John Johnson, 23, -, 150, 15, 76
James D. Denny, 25, -, 150, 10, 148
Jessee Vaughn, 15, -, 100, 14, 91
Allen Dowdy, 60, -, 500, 25, 617
Anderson Parsley, 26, -, 300, 20, 226
William Puckett, 15, -, 50, 60, 100
Wiley Johnakin, 12, -, 60, 10, 82
Wiley Johnakin Sr., 16, -, 100, 7, 77
John Whitehead, 40, -, 200, 20, 164
George Askue, 20, -, 200, 70, 283
John Taylor, 20, -, 150, 20, 194
Stephen Taylor, 8, -, 50, 8, 113
Daniel J. Warren, 10, -, 50, 10, 242
Sterling Smith, 25, -, 100, 5, 169
William Arterbery, 10, -, 40, 6, 138
John Dickerson, 13, -, 100, 7, 128
Jessee Henson, 25, -, 150, 12, 428
John Ramsey, 13, -, 70, 6, 168
Dunklin Lunsford, 30, -, 500, 100, 382
William H. Tatum, 20, -, 200, 8 265
William Singleton, 25, -, 250, 9, 152
Maria Hill, 15, -, 150, 15, 68
John C. Beason, 20, -, 150, 70, 60
Anderson Lewis, 40, -, 250, 15, 124

Sidney K. Pharis, 60, 100, 500, 15, 125
Levi Lewis, 20, -, 150, 20, 282
Nathan Fulenger, 60, 50, 300, 20, 108
Charles Newton, 25, -, 200, 20, 207
William Kitchen, 25, 15, 150, 12, 106
Lemuel Harvy, 20, 33, 300, 50, 140
John Denington, 24, -, 150, 15, 95
William Culberson, 35, -, 400, 20, 255
Hiram Culberson, 24, -, 300, 50, 159
James Sprinkle, 20, 6, 100, 15, 150
Brooks Bryan, 18, -, 150, 80, 148
Thomas Lincoln, 13, -, 100, 10, 76
Stephen P. Babb, 50, -, 350, 50, 164
David Garner, 40, -, 200, 25, 308
Adrian Owen, 30, -, 250, 30, 900
Joseph Rea, 38, 160, 600, 50, 184
James Kelly, 32, -, 150, 60, 235
David Lewis, 40, -, 250, 20, 192
Isaac Taylor, 60, 220, 1000, 120, 808
Sanders Walker, 30, 50, 500, 25, 207
John Kitchen, 60, 120, 1000, 120, 250
John Walker, 18, -, 100, 15, 97
John M. Denny, 18, -, 100, 20, 290
James Denny, 18, -, 50, 10, 226
John Waggoner, 32, -, 250, 25, 810
Daniel Sanford, 150, 68, 500, 25, 385
William E. Horty, 45, 155, 600, 100, 298
Isaac Hobbs, 20, 65, 500, 10, 130
William Owen, 23, 17, 200, 20, 85
John C. Walker, 14, 26, 250, 10, 58
Thomas T. Walker, 25, 55, 400, 25, 98
John Myers, 40, 40, 400, 25, 173
Robert Hambrick, 30, 15, 150, 6, 35
John Williamson, 30, -, 200, 10, 50
Squire T. Harper, 40, 80, 500, 200, 235
William D. Taylor, 18, 102, 750, 18, 190
Josiah Alsup, 20, 25, 200, 20, 165
Benjamine Snider, 60, 60, 400, 100, 339
Christopher Bess, 60, 100, 1000, 150, 844
George Bess, 40, -, 300, 40, 310
John Tankesly, 30, -, 200, 25, 150
Phillip Babb, 30, -, 300, 15, 265
Benjamine Cline, 150, 50, 600, 370, 1428
Thomas Sulenger, 30, 10, 200, 10, 40

William A. Whitehead, 50, 30, 400, 25, 444
Silvester Hyden, 23, 22, 125, 25, 75
Absalom Lincoln, 40, -, 400, 25, 118
Riley Walker, 24, -, 150, 10, 58
Jessee Walker, 30, 70, 500, 10, 160
James Stafford, 20, 20, 200, 30, 71
Jefferson K. Stafford, 20, -, 100, 50, 56
William K. Lewis, 15, -, 125, 15, 45
Daniel Long, 30, -, 200, 25, 302
James P. Roberson, 50, 40, 200, 40, 165
James Eaker, 25, -, 150, 20, 144
Abram Taylor, 50, 5, 400, 25, 707
James Taylor, 28, 14, 250, 20, 94
Benjamine Taylor, 40, 20, 300, 15, 204
Oliver Creath, 90, 13, 600, 120, 200
Thomas Neel, 35, 20, 300, 15, 81
Anderson Harper, 17, -, 125, 10, 82
John Lee, 45, -, 300, 60, 162
Lawson Strop, 17, -, 100, 15, 98
William P. Harper, 12, -, 150, 20, 58
Arosia Lorance, 30, 65, 200, 80, 355
Thomas Thrower, 18, -, 100, 40, 104
George Siffon, 30, -, 300, 25, 101
David Hopkins, 28, -, 400, 15, 356
William Anderson, 15, -, 250, 15, 155
Peter Proffer, 35, -, 250, 12, 150
Charles Zederick, 25, 55, 400, 15, 175
Samuel Roby, 25, -, 300, 20, 169
Thomas H. Back, 15, 145, 500, 100, 168
John Linck, 70, 150, 500, 100, 413
William Reynolds, 20, -, 100, 15, 160
John H. Wall, 27, -, 100, 20, 143
William Vaughn, 50, -, 300, 80, 893
Elijah Hibbs, 30, 15, 200, 45, 140
Overton L. Parish, 35, 125, 600, 50, 170
William Shipman, 30, -, 200, 70, 1536
Thomas Dowdy, 50, 20, 500, 100, 400
Martin Hagy, 30, 60, 500, 300, 325
Alexander Cunningham, 40, 40, 300, 150, 265
William Jinkins, 60, 110, 400, 100, 252
James Dowdy, 50, 30, 500, 150, 422
John Dowdy, 15, -, 150, 20, 270
John Fields, 40, -, 300, 30, 208
Jordan Garner, 50, 12, 500, 50, 206

Elias Fields, 16, -, 150, 30, 157
Jessee Riddle, 30, -, 150, 100, 181
Elisha G. Riddle, 24, -, 125, 25, 147
Wiley Fields, 10, -, 125, 15, 71
Aaron Elsworth, 40, 40, 250, 300, 426
Mathew Dowdy, 44, -, 300, 125, 246
Armsted Dowdy, 23, -, 200, 15, 423
Peter Singleton, 11, -, 100, 100, 212
Charles Riddle, 30, -, 300, 60, 551
James Singleton, 16, -, 100, 8, 130
William Singleton, 20, -, 200, 30, 143
Alvis B. Riddle, 30, -, 150, 50, 136
William Vandergrif, 40, -, 200, 30, 265
Ransom Ladd, 50, 1, 500, 300, 363
Fanny Norman, 40, 20, 150, 100, 228
Samuel Tempels, 35, -, 150, 10, 110
Elijah Hill, 50, 10, 1000, 200, 370
John Butcher, 18, -, 150, 100, 235
Absalom Guess, 13, -, 150, 25, 263
Jane Smith, 40, -, 200, 20, 102
William Dowdy, 18, -, 200, 30, 142
John Sisco, 40, -, 200, 28, 95
James Horton, 40, -, 150, 15, 339
Thomas Allen, 20, -, 200, 25, 227
Edward Allen, 40, -, 200, 20, 210
John T. Davis, 26, -, 200, 5, 65
Elison M. Davis, 20, -, 150, 10, 196
James Givens, 20, -, 150, 8, 60
Owen Smith, 30, -, 150, 15, 105
Alfred Edwards, 14, -, 100, 6, 111
Alfred Alaxander, 80, 50, 700, 10, 185
Thomas Davis, 14, -, 50, 10, 45
Larkin Davis, 4, -, 25, 9, 20
George Davis, 20, -, 150, 13, 30
James Cooper, 35, -, 250, 25, 304
Andrew Nell, 25, -, 225, 40, 210
Henry Terrel, 11, -, 100, 50, 190
John Terrel, 15, -, 150, 30, 196
Pincking Terrel, 8, -, 80, 15, 130
Morgan Terrel, 40, 5, 200, 100, 353
Henry Saddler, 50, -, 300, 50, 330
John J. Jackson, 40, -, 200, 75, 205
William Neel, 23, -, 200, 12, 238
Sarah H. Knight, 18, -, 100, 30, 130
Reuben Owen, 20, -, 200, 8, 31
Joseph Gains, 18, -, 100, 15, 96

Thomas White, 8, -, 50, 21, 67
Andrew Hoover, 12, -, 150, 60, 185
Ibby Morris, 24, -, 150, 15, 146
Austin Hatley, 50, 80, 500, 100, 226
Robert Miller, 50, 110, 500, 100, 306
Moses Proffer, 30, 20, 200, 30, 228
Jackson Hartz, 30, 90, 300, 40, 201
Archabald Gipson, 42, 20, 200, 75, 200
James Cruse, 16, -, 15, 5, 93
Margarett Shipman, 20, -, 150, 35, 280
David Crytes, 15, 30, 200, 250, 89
Daniel Layton, 34, -, 250, 20, 130
John Beasley, 70, 50, 500, 350, 390
Daniel Hartz, 110, 100, 700, 125, 307
William Scism, 20, 127, 300, 100, 260
James Hodges, 40, -, 400, 10, 226
Andrew Neel, 100, 25, 500, 150, 1172
John C. Miller, 30, 80, 400, 200, 298
James Norman, 40, 80, 300, 80, 540
Godfrey Andrews, 80, -, 400, 100, 1095
Joseph Masters, 25, -, 400, 25, 175
William Harris, 25, -, 230, 5, 106
Moses Hains, 30, -, 300, 5, 132
Thomas W. Pearciful, 100, 50, 500, 50, 818
Berry Harris, 35, 28, 300, 100, 365
Leander Battoe, 35, -, 350, 20, 95
William Moore, 16, 30, 150, 10, 125
John Oxford, 25, -, 300, 20, 165
William W. Moore, 40, -, 300, 15, 128
Johnathan Bozarth, 40, -, 300, 12, 255
James Warren, 24, -, 300, 50, 206
Gethero Johnson, 20, -, 230, 6, 33
William Johnson, 40, -, 350, 60, 160
James McCrory, 10, -, 295, 8, 275
John Gunnels, 15, -, 400, 75, 281
Amey Rice, 17, -, 350, 40, 431
Martin Hodges, 25, -, 400, 30, 411
James Martin, 16, -, 300, 30, 217
Given Owen, 25, -, 350, 25, 455
Jacob Snider, 16, -, 325, 100, 225
Charles Vinson, 35, -, 350, 100, 1550
James Loven, 18, -, 300, 5, 100
Middleton Brashiers, 14, -, 250, 40, 277
William Cross, 18, -, 350, 25, 316
George Ruddle, 21, -, 350, 60, 195

Aaron McIntosh, 17, -, 350, 75, 280
Thomas Williams, 13, -, 225, 5, 88
John Williams, 25, -, 275, 80, 85

Washington Middleton, 15, -, 250, 12, 20

Sullivan County, Missouri
1850 Agricultural Census

Sullivan County 1850 Agricultural Census was filmed by the Central Microfilm Service Corp of St. Louis, Missouri, for the Missouri State Historical Society. There are 46 columns of information on the 1850 agricultural census. I have chosen to transcribe six of those columns. The columns are:

1. Name
2. Acres of Land Improved
3. Acres of Land Unimproved
4. Cash Value of the Farm
5. Value of Farm Implements and Machinery
13. Value of Livestock

H. H. Hozall, 20, 140, 275, 20, 100
Philip Runnels, 30, 50, 150, 15, 200
Salomon Grism, 25, 15, 100, 60, 20
Elijah M. Parker, -, -, -, 20, 10
John L. Wood, 50, 70, 500, 100, 300
George W. Trojast, -, -, -, -, 75
A. S. Porter, 25, 55, 300, 75 250
James R. Sands, -, -, 300, -, 131
A. B. Midley, -, -, -, - 10
David Gerkin, 25, 15, 100, 20, 200
Levi V. Daton, -, -, -, 20, 150
E. K. Eaten, 70, 90, 1000, 100, 450
Nancy Cuol, 15, 40, 200, 5, 100
Thomas Allen, 20, 38, 150, 15, 210
Dinwidee Haller, 100, 24, 500, 120, 900
Geo. Haller, -, -, -, -, 300
James Wood, 14 68, 170, 15, 250
John Arrosmith, 60, 20, 200, 100, 320
John Brackett, 24, 96, 210, 15, 100
William Sandford, 8, 72, 150, 10, 200
Wm. Allen, 40, 160, 500, 100, 253
A. J. Williford, 18, 62, 150, 265
Thomas Harrison, -, -, -, 15, 285
Martin Bennett, 25, 55, 300, 25, 206
Wm. J. Gibbins, 50, 70, 500, 75, 200
John F. Thomas, 46, 114, 600, 40, 473
James C. Triplet, 40, 120, 500, 20, 770
Andrew J. Busick, 38, 122, 700, 800, 615

Peter B. Thomas, 100, 212, 1500, 200, 1460
Joseph T. Bradley, -, -, -, 7, 20
Thos. Wood, 50, 190, 1000, 120, 300
Saml. Lewis, 45, 133, 600, 105, 473
M. B. Wittie, 12, 148, 300, 20, 140
Gabriel Jones, 60, 340, 1500, 125, 402
Thos. Spencer, 35, 165, 500, 100, 337
Tarlton Jones, 40, 120, 500, 50, 250
Andrew J. Triplet, 35, 45, 500, 50, 246
Wm. J. Stone, 100, 60, 500, 50, 520
Meltin Taylor, 13, 37, 150, 75, 424
Martin Stone, 30, 210, 500, 75, 504
James Ross, 23, 137, 400, 40, 220
William Daily, -, -, -, 20, 80
Wm. Sterling, 50, 190, 600, 50, 300
Wm. Pierce, 46, 194, 700, 55, 450
John Montgomery, 70, 530, 500, 80, 450
Mancy(Nancy) Totson, -, -, -, 65, 250
John H. Gose, 30, 50, 150, 10, 170
Robert Murphy, 25, 55, 300, 40, 475
John Jones, 40, 75, 350, 10, 103
Joel Sturgill, 30, 130, 300, 32, 157
John Hollan, 18, 62, 750, 48, 225
Bennet Masey, 28, 62, 350, 50, 160
John Mize, 50, 75, 800, 30, 100
Alexander Woodland, 35, 5, 200, 80, 413
Joseph Bragg, 10, 150, 200, 5, 240
David Nowlin, -, -, -, -, 325

J. D. Stevens, 20, 60, 150, 32, 450
Thos. J. Stevens, 30, 130, 300, 40, 497
Joseph Harris, 40, -, 300, 40, 202
Elias Hudnel, 35, 5, 150, 20, 200
George McKirson, 20, 141, 360, 10, 70
Frances H. Sturgel, 16, 64, 350, 25, 234
Thos. S. Jarbo, 15, 75, 280, 8, 102
James H. Jackson, -, -, -, 2, 17
Rebecca Wolker, -, -, -, 4, 55
E. M. C. Morelock, -, 40, 200, 170, 407
B. E. Dearing, 17, 23, 200, 10, 197
Joseph A. Birel, 60, 45, 825, 25, 100
Wm. J. Tally, 45, 75, 450, 50, 206
S. G. Watkins, 5, 35, 450, 250
Joseph Cough, 35, 125, 325, 25, 244
S. J. Baskett, 40, 40, 260, 25, 370
Robert Baldridge, 40, 120, 500, 200, 578
A. S. Doke, 20, 140, 500, 10, 214
Sinsion Hoover, 23, 57, 225, 6, 155
Geo. Yardley, 28, 160, 370, 6, 249
Levi Thornton, -, -, -, 10, 140
Francis F. Wagers, -, -, -, 9, 60
John Baldridge, 182, 939, 3565, 75, 450
Danl. Baldridge, 50, 110, 1000, 177, 725
Branson Jackson, 20, 100, 300, 30, 160
Wm. Jackson, 6, 75, 700, 5, 70
Richard Wagers, 80, 80, 1500, 70, 839
Ambrose D. Wagers, -, -, -, 5, 50
Joseph Arthur, 30, 130, 300, 5, 102
Saml. Bingham, 40, 360, 1000, 70, 397
David Boid, 50, 30, 500, 50, 400
John Baldridge, 20, 62, 200, 10, 323
Thos. K. Lesure, 25, 15, 200, 75, 361
John W. Leach, -, -, -, 10, 40
John J. Swigurt, -, -, -, 40, 96
John Thurlow, 40, 40, 300, 30, 365
John Hatcher, 100, 100, 1000, 75, 534
Jackson Morgan, -, -, -, 10, 90
Wm. Hatcher, -, -, -, 10, 87
Wm Garnet, 15, 65, 200, 10, 80
John Paine, 25, 55, 300, 10, 150
John F. Jones, 50, 110, 800, 30, 103
Perez Shrock, 130, 319, 1500, 250, 691
John Couch,-, -, -, 10, 141
Alfred Jacobs, 75, 188, 1000, 70,900

Christopher Hoover, 50, 125, 600, 30, 375
John W. Jacobs, -, -, -, 10, 195
James Gillaspie, -, -, -, 100, 814
Leroy Creason, 45, 75, 500, 25, 530
Susan Cornett, 30, 90, 500, 20, 90
Sampson Johnson, 80, 320, 1000, 150, 495
Piercon Tyre, 25, 135, 600, 200, 130
John M. Street, 12, 68, 300, 15, 190
Wm. W. Minis, 15, 35, 300, 20, 175
Lewis Fise(Tire), 80, 260, 6000, 50, 397
John Calihan, 50, 160, 700, 20, 241
David Gilmore, 15, 85, 700, 10, 100
Oliver Mires, 15, 25, 100, 10, 50
Edwin Goodwin, -, 40, 100, 10, 180
Hugh Fraley, 45, 115, 500, 140, 305
James M. Ogle, 20, 80, 300, 10, 171
David Tally, 95, 225, 1500, 130, 401
Wm. N. Holbrook, 20, 60, 350, 15, 150
Volentine S. Mires, 15, 31, 150, 50, 90
Stephen J. Stone, 60, 60, 500, 25, 190
John Smith, 12, 68, 300, 20, 126
James Tunnell, 31, 9, 250, 79, 279
Robert M. Sharp, 30, 10, 200, 50, 251
James Shipley, 94, 506, 1500, 150, 475
Richard Williams, -, -, -, 10, 70
Conrad W. Glaze, 40, 120, 500, 40, 120
Robert M. Glaze, 22, 178, 300, 50, 277
Daniel Shipley, 10, 30, 100, 10, 50
John J. Shipley, -, -, -, 10, 30
Robert Tate, -, -, -, 15, 100
Enoch Clem, 15, 25, 150, 10, 188
Wm. H. Glaze, 60, 64, 800, 100, 617
John Franklin, 15, 145, 600, 30, 120
H.P. Hurlson, -, -, -, 15, 20
Nile B. Creason, -, -, -, -, 61, 180
C. W. Leslie, -, -, -, 60, 205
A. L. Gilstrap, 50, 200, 2000, 150, 200
John Pettigrew, -, -, -, 2, 150
John McClaskey, 40, 40, 350, 40, 392
James McClaskey, 4, 126, 500, 6, 90
Charles Withro, 15, 25, 200, 100, 300
John McClaskey, -, -, -, 2, 60
Wm. Withro, 7, 33, 100, 1, 50
Katharine Shotto, 45, 155, 800, 30, 434

Israel Shotto, -, 130, 300, -, -
Joseph C. Pierce, 30 80, 300, 10, 130
Zachariah Shotto, 25, 75, 500, 10, 166
Danl. Witthighte, 80, 80, 1000, 200, 529
Solomon Wittihighte, 25, 95, 300, 25, 255
Robert Ross, 40, 320, 500, 70, 381
Ann Prother, -, 160, 850, -, 50
M. P. Numan, -, -, -, 3, 20
Connar Glaze, 150, 1370, 4000, 300, 662
Edward Kerns, -, -, -, -, -
Emanuel Clem, 29, 169, 500, 75, 207
Reubin Wilhite, 150, 250, 1000, 100, 842
Geo. B. Henry, -, -, -, 20, 500
Wiley Bennett, -, -, -, 3, 55
Robert Donoho, 3, 37, 100, 4, 214
Jacob Dewit, 45, 155, 700, 98, 550
Wm. H. Elmore, 185, 336, 2000, 185, 604
Thos. Donoho, 30, 180, 450, 20, 149
John C. Sturgil, -, -, -, 10, 100
Saml. Magert, 60, 120, 1800, 227, 680
Spencer H. Hudnel, 20, 20, 150, 10, 160
Lydia Dusky, -, 40, 200, 200, 216
Jonathan Tipton, 40, 40, 350, 70, 205
Nathan Tipton, 15, 25, 150, -, 30
Robert Black, 15, 65, 200, 15, 202
John J. Knifong, 50, 30, 300, 62, 300
Wm. M. Z. Merton, -, -, -, 500, 430
David Malick, -, -, -, 30, 80
Edward S. Rogers, -, -, -, 30, 40
Robt. Barnes, 40, 183, 800, 145, 725
John Shepard, 40, 120, 800, 100, 577
Hugh C. Warren, 80, 160, 1000, 125, 610
Wm. Posey, -, -, -, 5, 80
Isaac Shrock, 50, 94, 700, 173, 519
Mary Watson, 15, 35, 200, 10, 119
Saml. Shrock, 35, 55, 200, -, 343
Wm. Watson, 30, 130, 600, 113, 449
Saml. Merriman, 15, 65, 250, 30, 230
Jefferson Williams, 30, 90, 200, 35, 155
Wm. H. Read, -, -, -, 10, 120
John W. Fields, 30, 130, 300, 10, 90

John W. Stanley, 5, 75, 200, 10, 72
Saml. R. Fields, 100, 260, 2500, 40, 75
John Maloney, 40, 40, 200, 50, 100
Philip Johnson, -, -, -, 20, 60
John Johnson, -, -, -, 5, 50
James M. Swigert, 40, 148, 400, 10, 60
David Swigart, -, -, -, 10 130
John Garrett, -, -, -, 100, 78
Gana Bagwell, -, -, -, 5, 80
Charles Stanley, 20, 60, 200, 10, 58
Henry Mires, -, -, -, 2, 30
Abraham Waters, -, -, -, 50, 221
M. H. Williams, 40, 120, 1000, -, 170
Wm. R. Smith, 30, 130, 400, 40, 40
Henry Dill, 100, 180, 1500, 75, 228
Jacob Numan, -, -, -, 80, 75
Geo. K. Shipley, -, -, -, 2, 127
Margaret Mullins, 25, 95, 500, 15, 150
Alexander Hamm, 30, 50, 350, 50, 175
Jeremiah Smith, 400, 400, 6000, 225, 216
Caleb Knifong, 65, 135, 1000, 89, 654
John Oneal, -, -, -, 60, 184
Jacob Spencer, 50, 190, 1200, 25, 222
James A. Lesure, -, -, -, 25, 145
Lynthia Overman, -, -, -, 6, 85
James Hollan, 15, 16, 200, 100, 132
Isaiah Curtis, -, -, -, 6, 210
Wm. Brookshire, 50, 30, 400, 25, 200
R. W. Dourghty, 40, 160, 1200, 25, 528
Andrew Burdis, 40, 41, 500, 50, 146
Wm. G. Bingham, 78, 162, 1000, 40, 483
Susan Weaver, -, -, -, 5, 70
Jacob Taylor, 70, 90, 600, 10, 105
Anderson Winn, -, -, -, 5, 65
Robinson Jones, -, -, -, 5, 60
Joseph W. Knifong, 60, 100, 500, 70, 515
Charles Read, 40, 40, 300, 20, 170
Robinson Morris, 60, 631, 4000, 75, 685
Hardin Dilinder, -, -, -, 20, 140
Reubin R. Faning, 40, 140, 300, 100, 379
Tignal Owins, -, -, -, 10, 180
Caleb Colier, 40, 40, 200, 30, 165

D. W. Nantz, 40, 40, 300, 40, 140
Rufus Carpenter, -, -, -, 10, 100
Wm. Thomas, -, -, -, 8, 65
Wm. Pinson, -, -, -, 50, 80
Saml. T. Haynes, 40, 120, 300, 15, 115
Josephus Jones, -, -, -, 2, 36
Stokely Bunch, 50, 30, 700, 60, 657
John Bunch, 15, 15, 150, 10, 104
James Bunch, 40, 40, 200, 3, 200
Levi More, -, 40, 150, 4, 220
J. D. Farris, 36, 44, 250, 50, 152
George Paige, 20, 60, 500, 100, 398
John Munsey, 138, 247, 2000, 60, 192
G. P. Taylor, 20, 180, 500, 80, 192
Jeremiah Tharp, 20, 133, 700, 100, 327
Wm. Harris, 23, 137, 500, 20, 100
Thos. J. Hannon, 3, 437, 250, 10, 30
Abraham Spencer, 16, 149, 600, 160, 220
Thos. Hoskins, 8, 32, 150, 10, 120
Ephraim Hollan, 10, 150, 600, 20, 160
Patrick McQuown, 75, 85, 700, 100, 895
John A. Browning, -, -, -, 20, 120
James H. Sturgill, -, -, -, 2, 65
Aaron Spencer, 50, 70, 400, 50, 167
Grist Crist, 21, 129, 800, 10, 57
Uriah Harris, 5, 35, 300, 10, 537
John Spencer, 35, 85, 500, 20, 210
Pudemel Hudson, 40, 140, 600, 100, 335
Hazewell Hurlson, -, -, -, 5, 100
Hugh G. Warren, 40, 140, 300, 7, 339
Wm. Warnum, -, -, -, 85, 225
Henry Warren, -, -, -, 10, 240
Andrew Warren, -, -, -, 100, 70
James Warren, 12, 148, 300, 150, 525
John Q. Reynolds, 12, 28, 250, 2, 82
Susan McLin, -, -, -, 5, 30
Christopher Kidd, 10, 150, 250, 30, 143
Matthew Kidd, 60, 60, 400, 20, 125
Wm. Reynolds, -, -, -, -, 60
Saml. Rogers, 40, 170, 500, 60, 295
Mathew Hunsaker, 70, 170, 1000, 160, 654
Saml. Rouse, 40, 40, 200, 100, 334
Wm. R. Alison, -, -, -, 5, 90
Nicholas Kinny, 22, 165 1000, 100, 350

Saml. P. Cason, 25, 55, 300, 8, 78
Joseph Taylor, -, -, -, 70, 125
Jeremiah Adkins, -, -, -, 30, 32
Joseph Shaw, 40, 120, 250, 2, 135
Wm. Wood, 40, 120, 300, 5, 190
Joseph Wood, -, -, -, 5, 211
John Willson,-, -, -, 5, 220
Isaac Willson, 40, 120, 300, 5, 94
Charles Overstreet, 50, 70, 1000, 120, 188
James Bookout, 30, 130, 250, 15, 238
James Overstreet, 20, 140, 300, 30, 235
Preston Overstreet, 20, 140, 300, 5, 150
Wm. B. Broden, 26, 54, 400, 40, 160
Jefferson Hunsaker, 60, 20, 600, 40, 435
Avery Wood, 40, 40, 300, 75, 262
Wm. N. Cason, -, -, -, 3, 56
Joel C. Hill, 40, 80, 500, 70, 568
Wm. B. Jones, 14, 26, 150, 20, 215
Wm. Carpenter, -, -, -, 10, 110
Andrew J. Hargus, -, -, -, 5, 85
Thos. T. Allred, 20, 60, 200, 5, 120
Frederick Coghill, 25, 145, 300, 25, 145
James Carpenter, 20, 60, 300, 10, 162
Harbert C. Ringo, 45, 35, 200, 10, 185
John T. Miller, 22, 298, 600, 65, 192
Abraham Lafevers, 60, 60, 500, 65, 380
Danl. Lavefers, -, -, -, 20, 60
John L. Oliver, -, -, -, 3, 120
Charles Thompson, 50, 30, 500, 115, 748
Paton Easles (Earles), 30, 130, 300, 200, 165
Benj. Frazure, 50, 175, 600, 300, 640
Wm. J. Tolly, 25,135, 300, 12, 900
Henry Grindstaff, 6, 154, 225, 7, 30
R. L. Williams, 2, 78, 150, 60, 50
Susan Morelock, 30, 50, 150, 20, 127
R. D. Morrison, 20, 60, 500, 20, 180
Alex. Sanderfer, 80, 80, 700, 140, 550
Stephen M. Gose, 15, 66, 250, 5, 150
Joseph Hobfer, 40, 150, 500, 50, 226
Hampton Bennett, -, -, -, 5, 65
Wm. Hurst, 40, 40, 700, 84, 242
Elihue E. Frazure, -, -, -, 4, 53
Wm. Quigler, 20, 140, 270, 10, 121

Jacob Quigler, 15, 65, 400, 5, 244
Washington Webb, 10, 30, 200, 15, 70
Peter Benham, -, -, -, 3, 50
Wm. Benham, -, -, -, 2, 45
Aac Grindstaff, -, -, -, 6, 75
Thos. W. Frazure, 10, 150, 250, 5, 75
Jesse C. Gumm, 20, 140, 275, 25, 70
Aaron Richardson, 20, 140, 350, 60, 239
Nancy Beacham, -, -, -, -, 67
Jacob Conkin, 45, 115, 400, 10, 100
David Dunlap, 30, 130, 400, 12, 70
John McKee, -, -, -, 10, 60
James Dunlap, 10, 150, 300, 15, 130
Wm. Crumpacker, 15, 145, 300, 60, 640
Joseph McKee, 40, 120, 300, 12, 207
Robt. Hines, -, -, -, 30, 98
Benj. Johnson, -, -, -, 5, 65
Amisa G. Pearce, -, -, -, 15, 60
John J. Deeds, 100, 60, 300, 50, 204
L. N. B. Deeds, -, -, -, 70, 57
Willson Baldridge, 21, 59, 300, 60, 175
Thomas Henry, 500, 1900, 50000, 400, 5090
Susan Strong, -, -, -, 3, 80
Wm. Halbert, 60, 20, 300, 50, 213
Elijah Casteel, 40, 120, 350, 70, 300
Meredith Blalock, 30, 130, 350, 50, 339
Wm. Casteel, -, -, -, 10, 100
Albert Wooton, 40, 120, 300, 20, 185
Isaac Montgomery, -, -, -, 50, 100
Wm. Gose, 65, 55, 500, 30, 507
Danl. Doyle, 35, 205, 700, 85, 170
Andrew Kelly, -, -, -, 12, 50
James Harris, 10, 150, 250, 50, 82
John Weaver, 13, 17, 200, 10, 160
J. W. Paige, -, -, -, 5, 139
John Kelly, -, -, -, 3, 30
Jacob Weaver, 25, 55, 150, 5, 130
Mary Couch, -, -, -, 5, 80
Lewis Pilcher, 10, 150, 300, 12, 135
John Huffman, -, -, -, 20, 70
Saml. Read, 40, 40, 200, 35, 150
Saml. Harris, -, -, -, 9, 170
Charles Harrison, -, -, -, 5, 56
Charles Harris, 25, 135, 350, 15, 119
Conrad Franklin, 15, 145, 400, 10, 110

John Harris, 15, 145, 300, 10, 184
Edward Franklin, -, -, -, 5, 131
Patrick Maxie, -, -, -, 2, 20
Anderson Pipes, -, -, -, 4, 197
Solomon Bundridge, -, -, -, 20, 162
John Harmon, -, -, -, 10, 158
Jacob Harmon, -, -, -, 10, 158
Jacob Harmon, 40, 100, 700, 125, 268
Geo. W. Pipes, 70, 111, 1000, 150, 710
James H. Morris, 10, 70, 225, 10, 118
John Kenley, 30, 130, 200, 10, 352
John Dodson, -, -, -, 5, 25
John McCollough, 90, 130, 1500, 20, 1311
Thos. L. Tolson, -, -, -, 12, 100
Joseph Lord, 43, 117, 400, 50, 308
Benj. Stout, 23, 57, 250, 60, 168
James Stout, 45, 115, 225, 40, 259
James M. Clay, 20, 140, 300, 100, 282
Hiram Richardson, -, -, -, 10, 133
Nimrod M. Hamrick, 30, 130, 500, 15, 190
Robert Stout, 80, 80, 400, 14, 243
Wm. Murphey, 35, 365, 1000, 250, 323
Lewis Pigg, -, -, -, 100, 200
Anderson Harris, 60, 140, 600, 150, 325
A. J. McClanahan, 25, 95, 400, 150, 272
Noah Hardwick, -, -, -, 5, 45
Rolla Bundurant, 26, 54, 500, 100, 269
Benj. Gorden, -, -, -, 5, 200
Thomas Harris, 20, 60, 300, 5, 113
John W. Perkins, -, 80, 125, 10, 65
Lewis G. Todd, 65, 175, 1000, 100, 377
Wm. H. Todd, 9, 21, 200, -, -
Ichabod Crofoot, 14, 66, 200, 17, 162
Enoch W. Smith, 18, 22, 150, 50, 80
Philip W. Martin, 100, 200, 1000, 100, 540
Wm. Richardson, 40, -, 700, 100, 321
Saml. C. Smith, 15, 25, 200, 75, 160
James Ford, 40, 120, 350, 25, 300
John Pettit, 20, 20, 150, 25, 220
John Umphries, 40, 40, 250, 50, 165
Thos. Thomas, 20, 60, 200, 25, 80
John Martin, 14, 146, 600, 50, 170
G. B. Gupton, 12, 168, 275, 70, 80

Lewis Martin, 30, 150, 500, 50, 291
Andrew Thompson, 23, 17, 250, 20, 229
Andrew England, 4, 156, 500, 125, 155
William Prevet, 15, 65, 200, 15, 75
Jacob McGee, 8, 132, 300, 225, 329
John McGee, -, -, -, 5, 171
Wm. Kent, 53, 107, 700, 150, 386
Joseph Bomon, 105, 228, 3100, 300, 782
Jacob Bowman, 10, 150, 450, 5, 11
Joseph Bowman, -, -, -, 10, 93
Jesse Tunnell, -, -, -, 10, 110
Wm. Maulley, 30, 130, 500, 100, 343
Barsheba England, 60, 180, 1000, 50, 250
John Tunnell, 220, 260, 1000, 100, 549
Charles Haley, 400, 4740, 10240, 300, 1784
W. H. Haley, -, 80, 300, -, 240
Edward Tate, -, -, -, 4, 75
John M. Millon, -, -, -, 2, 105
Silas Peters, 35, 245, 600, 10, 196
Jacob Watembarger, 39, 201, 500, 125 175
James Mecans, 25, 135, 600, 200, 170
Richard Mecans, -, 120, 300, -, 100
James Lee, 100, 180, 1000, 100, 340
Eben Hellims, -, -, -, 10, 60
Henry Clem, 60, 260, 1500, 100, 363
Pe_ez D. Shrock, 14, 26, 150, 20, 178
Hugh S. Maloney, -, -, -, 5, 100
James Murphy, -, -, -, 3, 30
Matthew Mose(More), 30, 50, 250, 15, 100
John Johnson, 50, 40, 400, 160, 1295
Anderson More, 40, 120, 400, 60, 410
Amstead C. Hill, 60, 60, 500, 30, 270

Saml. Watemberger, 50, 165, 500, 100, 325
Adam Watembarger, 45, 147, 400, 25, 237
Abijah Woods, 150, 490, 1500, 160, 452
Elisha Cowhick, 10, 220, 600, 30, 125
Wm. J. Haydon, 80, 88, 800, 50, 390
Luther Jerman, 12, 68, 100, 8, 105
James G. Greer, 90, 60, 300, 5, 225
Thos. Dobbins, 70, 180, 1100, 100, 400
Robert M. Kirkpatrick, 50, 30, 200, 50, 120
Elisha Kilburn, 80, 40, 350, 100, 400
Geo. Duffield, 80, 80, 700, 100, 303
Booker Dickinson, -, -, -, 15, 100
Richard Young, 10, 180, 300, 300, 100
S. D. Edwards, 25, 80, 200, 10, 350
Martha Scott, 10, 7, 200, 3, 190
Nathan Winters, 20, 140, 300, 10, 90
Henry Mace, 15, 145, 300, 20, 85
Creed Webster, 22, 18, 400, 20, 100
Thomas Norvell, 40, 120, 600, 50, 125
Sarah Brown, 10, 150, 300, 20, 80
Thos. Williams, 8, 40, 150, 103, 40
Thos. Shipley, 10, 70, 200, 50, 80
Wm. Hatcher, 13, 65, 200, 10, 35
Garnet Humfreys, 8, 32, 150, 125, 300
John Dennis, 60, 115, 1100, 125, 295
Elizabeth Foster, -, -, -, 5, 75
William T. Clark, 30, 130, 400, 75, 225
Thomas Iam(Sam), -, -, -, -, 300
David H. Morelock, -, -, -, 5, 100
J. Simman, 30, 270 100, 100, 265
Ira Sears, 5, 70, 470, 150, 363

Taney County, Missouri
1850 Agricultural Census

Taney County 1850 Agricultural Census was filmed by the Central Microfilm Service
Corp of St. Louis, Missouri, for the Missouri State Historical Society. There are 46
columns of information on the 1850 agricultural census. I have chosen to transcribe six
of those columns. The columns are:

1. Name
2. Acres of Land Improved
3. Acres of Land Unimproved
4. Cash Value of the Farm
5. Value of Farm Implements and Machinery
13. Value of Livestock

J. W. Danforth, 70, 300 1000, 35, 310
J. D. Caldwell, 15, 25, 500, -, 238
S. P. Ayres, -, -, -, -, 151
R. S. McKiny, 30, 50, 400, 15, 316
J. Haggard, 14, 26, 300, 10, 200
W. C. Berry, -, -, -, -, 107
A. S. Layton, -, -, -, -, 1110
D. P. Wood, 25, 15, 500, 10, 173
H. Ratcliffe, 18, 22, 601, 15, 279
G. W. Millikin, 15, 25, 450, 11, 150
J. Hall, 40, 40, 400, 10, 276
J. Robertes, 25, 15, 300, 25, 288
J. Adams, 30, 25, 200, 50, 137
A. C. Brown, 30, 30, 500, 75, 182
W. L. Cuningham, 30, 10, 300, 60, 387
R. Scribner, 20, 60, 300, 10, 150
G. W. Jackon(Jackson), 10, 30, 200, 5,
144
J. Mosley, 14, 26, 250, 10, 35
F. Moore, 20, 20, 200, 5, 49
J. M. Richmond, 9, 31, 200, 50, 77
D. Potter, 13, 37, 300, 15, 89
P. Haggard, 20, 100, 450, 15, 279
W. Pearce, 65, 87, 830, 75, 607
P. McShane, 18, 22, 400, 10, 140
A. Botts, 30, 10, 131, 75, 287
L. Boswell, 5, 35, 400, 5, 118
P. S. Franklin, 40, 40, 500, 10, 159
A. Wheler, 100,285, 3000, 70, 215
D. Johnson, 75, 85, 1500, 100, 435

J. Cleanyer, 10, 30, 200, 10, 48
L. H. Gurnings, 15, 25, 200, 12, 131
W. Morgan, 30, 100, 500, 75, 416
W. Yandle, 70, 90, 1000, 100, 318
J. B. Wood, 35, 30, 500, 20, 442
J. Aleaer, 16, 24, 250, 40, 427
J. Chenowerth, 35, 53, 700, 75, 349
H. Laughflin, 45, 80, 700, 100, 336
A. Burke, 40, 15, 400, 10, 206
C. Davis, 12, 28, 200, 10, 166
A. Majors, 20, 60, 300, 50, 204
J. Campbell, 21, 20, 200, 35, 191
P. Hefner, 16, 20, 200, 10, 186
J. Jones, 17, 23, 200, 8, 58
D. Jentery, 18, 21, 250, 10, 282
A. Jentery, 45, 35, 300, 75, 384
J. Jinnings, 60, 137, 1000, 100, 497
J. C. Turnbough, 35, 45, 400, 10, 355
J. Williamson, 60, 20, 800, 30, 284
C. Gibson, 15, 85, 1100, 35, 75
J. Falls, 40, 121, 800, 10, 356
A. G. Hutchens, 15, 25, 150, 5, 159
J. Pfumny, 24, 16, 275, 10, 500
J. Kirkpatrick, 18, 22, 250, 15, 304
A. Hayworth, 20, 20, 300, 60, 270
B. Phiffs, 20, 20, 400, 10, 50
J. W. Wheeler, 24, 16, 200, 10, 166
N. Haggard, 30, 31, 600, 100, 422
J. C. Cook, 40, 40, 450, 75, 665
J. Barker, 20, 20, 250, 75, 251

F. Bowles, 16, 24, 2000, 15, 131
J. Bales, 37, 59, 600, 10, 366
S. D. Nelson, 155, 65, 3000, 100, 860
W. Oliver, 25, 230, 700, 140, 995
J. E. Stalings, -, -, 100, -, 55
J. Wetherman, 16, 24, 150, 10, 95
P. Stallcup, 26, 20, 300, 15, 70
R. H. Parks, 28, 152, 400, 30, 168
J. Natchell, 18, 22, 400, 10, 551
N. Haggard, 30, 31, 600, 100, 422
M. Oliver, 15, 25, 200, 10, 197
G. W. Andrews, 100, 100, 1500, 75, 3112
J. Hedrick, 40,-, 400, 100, 365
R. Thurman, 10, 30, 200, 15, 59
J. Elison, 80, 32, 1000,125, 864
O. Humphrey, 25, 15, 300, 5, 124
J. S. Baker, 30, 50, 800, 50, 297
J. H. Gideon, 70, 170, 900, 62, 600
R. W. Dean, 35, 45, 400, 75, 600
J. Dean, 30, 130, 150, 5, 266
J. Oliver, 35, 205, 600, 100, 568
J. Crowford, 15, 25, 150, 5, 101
T. Y. Scott, 70, 82, 1600, 50, 234
R. Murrel, -, -, -, -, 100
P. Hall, -, -, -, -, 30
T. Morris, 20, 60, 200, 5, 87
L. Sallee, -, -, -, -, 111
J. Mucheler, 20, 20, 150, 5, 98
H. Ginlen, 30, 10, 400, 35, 370
W. Cratbree, 30, 20, 300, 20, 271
J. Smith, 15, 25, 200, 10, 275
J. Richeson, 24, 56, 200, 10, 135
B. Freeman, 20, 20, 150, 5, 143
W. Morris, 17, 30, 100, 75, 437
J. Berry, 15, 65, 1000, 100, 467
J. Cass, 40, 40, 500, 10, 320
H. Jones, 16, 60, 200, 10, 75
J. Wheler, 16, 64, 200, 5, 110
W. H. Rosel, 8, 32, 150, 5, 136
R. Morgan, 30, 50, 500, 20, 485
J. Wammack, 70, 42, 1500, 170, 1450
A. R. Howard, -, -, -, -, 29
J. F. Simmons, -, -, -, -, 43
J. Herst, 17, 23, 150, 5, 259
J. Foster, -, -, -, -, 75

H. Henry, 4, 36, 100, 5, 30
A. Keithley, 16, 64, 150, 20, 50
W. Owen, 16, 64, 230, 25, 144
J. Cunningham, 12, 28, 100, 15, 160
P. Hammonds, 18, 22, 300, 15, 411
S. Hedrick, 25, 15, 300, 15, 259
F. Redford, 25, 23, 230, 10, 180
S. Cheser, 20, 20, 250, 20, 286
S. Morrow, 20, 20, 150, 30, 230
J. Cook, 65, 55, 400, 200, 1276
W. Hamilton, 15, 25, 150, 10, 66
A. Cook, 30, 10, 400, 100, 547
C. Litteral, 30, 10, 300, 100, 256
J. Rosel, 15, 25, 200, 30, 299
M. Henry, 20, 20, 150, 75, 250
J. McNary, 16, 24, 150, 10, 75
T. Laggs, 20, 20, 200, 15, 300
J. Cook, 55, 25, 1000, 250, 1131
J. Keithley, 18, 22, 200, 150, 400
B. S. Chamberlain, -, -, -, -, 100
S. Willard, 35, 5, 400, 35, 180
T. W. Rozell, -, -, -, -, 85
W. Adams, 50, 20, 200, 10, 119
W. S. Pain, 35, 5, 300, 10, 316
D. Lay, 16, 24, 150, 15, 160
J. Parman, 22, 22, 150, 10, 75
M. Adams, 40, 40, 500, 75, 172
J. Clayton, 20, 60, 400, 100, 208
A. White, 15, 25, 250, 15, 95
W. Cliggans, -, -, -, -, 91
J. Tindal, 18, 62, 200, 5, 115
B. Dye, -, -, -, 5, 65
R. Pain, 30, 10, 400, 100, 324
J. White, -, -, -, 15, 60
M. Cutberth, 18, 22, 200, 5, 95
J. Cutberth, 16, 24, 150, 10, 50
A. Kasee, 30, 10, 400, 75, 250
W. Roberts, 30, 130, 400, 15, 485
J. Bledsow, 25, 55, 200, 5, 260
C. Roberts, 17, 23, 300, 10, 232
H. Burkhart, 30, 10, 300, 10, 112
H. Butterton, 36, 44, 300, 75, 268
W. Stacy, 20, 20, 200, 5, 187
J. Williams, -, -, -, 3, 153
M. Adams, 40, 80, 600, 10, 80
M. Cochran, 30, 10, 250, 40, 224

G. W. Pierce, 30, 30, 600, 60, 374
W. Cook, 25, 55, 150, 15, 200
J. Beasley, 70, 90, 2000, 100, 479
J. Rutherford, 20, 20, 200, 10, 74
R. C. Williams, 20, 20, 200, 7, 114
B. Railey, 30, 27, 400, 100, 616
J. M. Cox, 16, 31, 150, 20, 225
D. Jackson, 30, 70, 1000, 100, 569
J. M. Cam (Carn), 30, 130, 450, 100, 998
T. E. Duke, 30, 130, 450, 100, 262
J. Barls, 30, 50, 3000, 10, 222
J. Baker, 20, 20, 250, 30, 96
S. Blevins, -, -, 440, 100, 360
J. M. Archey, 14, 66, 300, 15, 232
J. Costellow, 20, 84, 400, 10, 172
B. Hedrick, 50, 50, 600, 100, 606
J. Maberry, 20, 20, 250, 15, 76
R. Buckner, 18, 22, 150, 30, 97
N. White, 25, 15, 230, 5,122
J. Haggate, 14, 26, 150, 7, 75
C. Pinkney, 28, 18, 200, 5, 103
J. Kerbow, 30, 50, 250, 12, 236
R. Hembre, -, -, -, -, 39
J. Hembre, 30, 50, 300, 10, 96
O. Hurley(Henley), 22, 18, 200, 10, 200
J. Maberry, 20, 20, 200, 10, 362
Z. Tucker, -, -, -, -, 27
B. Gooden, -, -, -, -, 19
W. Hurst, 15, 25, 200, 15, 237
S. Sage, 14, 26, 150, 5, 205
P. Henson, 16, 24, 150, 8, 73
R. Kerkwood, 14, 26, 175, 5, 78
D. Falkner, 22, 68, 250, 10, 561
J. Barber, -, -, -, 5, 163
J. Taber, -, -, -, -, 57
J. Cannefax, -, -, -, -, 38
B. Pinkney, -, -, -, -, 52
J. Grage, -, -, -, -, 48
J. G. Bowman, 30, 50, 500, 15, 376
F. D. Merit, 22, 20, 300, 25, 288
W. Kermikle, 30, 50, 300, 10, 251
A. Cannefax, -, -, -, -, 35
J. Dobs, 14, 26, 100, 5, 148
A. Pinkley, 17, 62, 200, 10, 180
J. C. Bowman, 25, 55, 400, 100, 323

J. Bowman, 15, 25, 200, 10, 58
H. Bowen, 14, 26, 150, 5, 35
D. Myers, 30, 10, 200, 10, 116
J. Bowman, 15, 25, 150, 5, 214
J. Pitts, 72, 88, 800, 55, 890
M. Yokaham, 20, 20, 150, 5, 215
W. Summers, 40, 40, 300, 45, 237
J. Alexander, 21, 19, 250, 10, 127
W. Cannefax, -, -, -, -, 32
J. Crenshaw, 25, 15, 200, 10, 178
W. Crenshaw, -, -, -, -, 63
J. Yong, -, -, -, -, 116
J. Asbern, 15, 25, 150, 100, 87
R. Beasley, 30, 50, 500, 15, 528
S. W. Stevens, 18, 52, 300, 15, 235
M. Edward, 40, 80, 310, 15, 293
R. P. Frost, 18, 80, 310, 5, 74
W. Yoachum, 10, 30, 150, 5, 56
S. Jackson, 15, 25, 150, 5, 37
J. G. McClelland, 40, 120, 600, 10, 104
W. Frost, -, -, -, -, 59
I. Bellew, 30, 10, 300, 40, 309
M. A. Moore, 15, 25, 250, 10, 165
H. Scates, 18, 22, 300, 10, 171
B. A. Day, 2, -, -, 20, 147
J. W. Bellew, 40, 40, 500, 125, 1300
J. H. Bellew, -, -, -, -, 124
I. Bellew, -, -, -, -, 173
J. Bellew, 15, 25, 200, 5, 97
R. Williams, 30, 10, 300, 70, 320
J. M. Barber, 25, 15, 300, 10, 155
N. Brown, 16, 24, 250, 30, 144
D. Lenard, 40, 40, 600, 75, 424
P. Sanders, 30, 10, 200, 100, 247
H. Harbert, 35, 45, 400, 10, 123
J. Speak, 18, 22, 300, 15, 138
R. King, 20, 20, 300, 75, 395
G. W. Malcum, -, -, -, 10, 16
E. Crewnshaw, 17, 23, 150, 5, 65
P. H. Smith, 15, 25, 150, 40, 140
A. G. Smith, -, -, -, 40, 212
P. Hubanks, 15, 35, 175, 100, 172
G. A. Baker, 10, 30, 100, 30, 107
W. Plumly, 17, 23, 200, 10, 297
C. S. Yates, 16, 144, 400, 65, 512
J. Philabert, 50, 30, 1000, 75, 1025

M. Yoachum, 25, 55, 300, 5, -
W. Carr, 16, 24, 350, 10, 97
C. Carr, 20, 20, 350, 10, 192
W. Dunnet, 50, 30, 600, 10, 439
R. Kiper, 15, 25, 150, 5, 262
W. Raisor, -, -, -, -, 35
G. W. King, 35, 45, 1000, 75, 247
J. Esrey, -, -, -, - 30
S. Tampson, -, -, -, -, 100
J.(I) Riggs, 18, 142, 350, 10, 169
P. T. Gun, 24, 14, 250, 10, 33
W. H. Gun, 15, 35, 200, 10, 99
J. T. Williams, 15, 28, 230, 5, 75
D. Hanson, 20, 20, 230, 10, 65
E. Foster, 12, 28, 150, 5, 88
Z. Hanson, 25, 15, 500, 40, 453
T. Hanson, 15, 65, 300, 70, 200
C. Galaway, 25, 55, 500, 50, 118
E. Hanson, 35, 43, 350, 10, 165
J. H. Stone, 18, 35, 400, 150, 288
W. Dye, 40, 40, 300, 15, 156
W. Wooley, 25, 35, 500, 15, 188
E. Stone, 30, 169, 800, 20, 467
M. Garrison, 25, 35, 350, 15, 167
J. Dennis, 35, 10, 400, 100, 500
A. Gunn, -, -, -, -, 124
S.W. Packwood, 25, 15, 400, 15, 229
L. Asher, 15, 25, 150, 5, 100
A. Hendix, 24, 56, 400, 25, 140
L. Vermilion, 18, 22, 300, 10, 92
H. Dennis, 30, 50, 400, 70, 183
J. Dennis, 21, 59, 400, 15, 238
P. Dennis, 16, 64, 300, 5, 100
C. Dennis, 13, 27, 200, 45, 82
A. Garrison, -, -, -, -, 116
A. Melton, 23, 57, 230, 50, 239
M. Stone, 30, 50, 600, 15, 320
M. Gentry, 20, 60, 350, 5, 179
I. Bledsow, 25, 55, 300, 8, 154
B. Duemasker, 19, 61, 300, 80, 100
S. Anderson, 15, 25, 250, 10, 239
F. M. Anderson, 30, 10, 200, 10, 239
W. Wheler, -, -, -, -, 30
J. C. Dickenson, 18, 58, 250, 15, 134
J. Gunter, 15, 25, 200, -, 259
G. W. Moore, 22, 58, 400, 20, 277

J. Benham, 30, 50, 400, 40, 832
G. Tabor (Talor), 15, 25, 150, 75, 73
J. Talor, -, -, -, -, 68
P. Smith, -, -, -, -, 80
A. Collins, 16, 24, 200, 45, 203
E. Hawk, -, -, -, -, 58
J. Philips, 30, 10, 400, 35, 138
J. Wooley, 20, 60, 230, 5, 112
H. Baker, 28, 12, 200, 10, 172
C. Wooley, -, -, -, -, 20
A. Wade, 16, 75, 250, 17, 219
J. C. Clark, 32, 48, 500, 10, 174
J. Smith, -, -, -, 10, 119
S. Patterson, 35, 85, 500, 55, 442
T. Patterson, 25, 15, 300, 60, 772
A. Patterson, -, -, -, -, 119
A. C. Wooley, -, -, -, -, 79
R. H. Griffith, 40, 40, 500, 30, 288
J. Kelley, -, -, -, 100, 14
W. McDowel, 28, 12, 200, 15, 111
E. Stone, 20, 30, 400, 70, 476
J. McDowel, -, -, -, -, 150
R. H. Fowler, 20, 12, 1160, 10, 129
J. B. Williams, 48, 121, 2600, 195, 925
E. M. Wooley, 20, 60, 400, 15, 193
L. Williams, -, -, 200, 50, 76
C. Cammons, 25, 15, 300, 10, 285
J. J. Bird, 30, 10, 300, 45, 210
A. McLain, 25, 15, 400, 10, 138
W. G. Goff, 100, 20, 1000, 400, 1759
W. Grissom, 70, 10, 600, 15, 100
A. T. Logan, -, -, -, 50, 370
J. McDowel, 10, 30, 100, 5, 70
P. Hill, -, -, -, -, 45
C. Cloud, 55, 65, 500, 75, 295
G. Clorid, -, -, -, -, 19
M. Hines, -, -, -, 60, 78
J. Hail, -, -, -, -, 20
J. C. Majors, 25, 15, 400, 60, 280
R. Grissom, 35, 15, 400, 60, 233
W. Carpenter, -, -, -, -, 68
A. Berry, 60, 20, 500, 100, 222
N. Cumberlane, 20, 20, 500, 100, 215
P. Berry, 30, 19, 800, 200, 448
H. Coffer, -, -, -, -, 120
J. Allen, -, -, -, -, 200

T. H. Cox, -, -, -, -, 60

H. Tunnel, -, -, -, -, 57

J. McGinnis, 20, 60, 350, 60, 100

W. Yoachum, -, -, -, -, 183

P. Bownet, -, -, -, -, 183

J. Langly, 14, 66, 430, 5, 40

D. Kumberlain, -, -, -, 40, 80

S. Yoachum, 17, 160, 400, 150, 790

A. Yoachum, 60, 140, 800, -, -

J. C. Chastine, -, -, -, -, 86

E. Abner, 24, 16, 300, 150, 183

E. Yoachum, 30, 30, 3800, 150, 420

A. Galaway, 25, 135, 500, 40, 307

H. Bledsow, -, -, -, -, 20

J. Wailes, -, -, -, -, 71

J. M. Walker, -, -, -, -, 80

J. Yoachum, 35, 100, 800, 15, 179

G. Yong, 35, 125, 800, 45, 190

E. Shades, 30, 10, 300, 50, 240

C. Craig, -, -, -, -, 100

T. Jackson, 10, 30, 131, 5, 80

W. Jackson, 20, 20, 250, 10, 109

N. Jackson, 15, 200, 450, 100, 280

G. Jackson, 75, 85, 450, 100, 708

C. C. Roberts, 30, 50, 300, 100, 325

J. A. Jackson, 20, 20, 200, 150, 325

P. Garner, 30, 50, 300, 100, 325

D. Morrow, -, -, -, -, 110

J. Kirk, 40, 40, 800, 125, 500

E. Linn, -, -, -, -, 42

C. C. McLain, 40, 40, 600, 15, 87

C. Estes, 16, 25, 200, 110, 438

M. Mitchell, 22, 18, 400, 15, 200

H. Mills, 16, 64, 300, 15, 72

W. Robinson, 20, 20, 230, 150, 293

J. Robison, 20, 20, 230, 150, 293

W. Long, 20, 60, 300, 100, 275

P. S. Ganard, 25, 135, 800, 15, 66

W. P. Birchfield, 60, 100, 1500, 30, 177

J. More, 30, 130, 1000, 175, 221

J. Cox, 30, 130, 1000, 175, 380

J. Anderson, 10, 30, 150, 5,182

W. Anderson, 25, 55, 500, 35, 368

H. Dunn, 18, 22, 300, 5, 173

A. Friend, 25, 15, 450, 22, 315

J. Bird, 14, 26, 200, 5, 150

D. Griffith, 10, 30, 150, 5, 64

W. Allen, 16, 24, 150, 80, 231

W. McCarty, 16, 24, 150, 5, 100

H. Coach, -, -, -, -, 94

C. Bird, 50, 10, 400, 50, 290

B. Raley, 16, 24, 250, 10, 128

J. Smith, 30, 10, 350, 50, 219

M. Jones, 60, 20, 400, 20, 200

T. S. Brown, 14, 26, 200, 5, 67

H. A. Brown, 10, 30, 150, 5, 83

A. J. Parr, 15, 25, 200, 10, 147

J. Roads, 35, 45, 700, 50, 343

A. Benton, 65, 15, 550, 50, 344

W. Foolbright, 36, 125, 600, 114, 687

M. Pea, 18, 22, 250, 5, 125

W. Owens, 90, 28, 1500, 75, 351

L. Igo, 40, 40, 400, 20, 193

J. Nichels, 20, 20, 250, 10, 191

J. D. Ragon, -, -, -, -, 90

J. Allen, 80, 80, 1000, 100, 723

J. Mathies, 20, 20, 300, 8, 169

A. McCulough, 60, 20, 1000, 285, 334

S. Stone, -, -, -, 40, 136

J. Kenady, -, -, -, -, 60

N. Wright, 20, 20, 230, 40, 300

K. Caldwell, 25, 15, 250, 40, 75

L. Pritchet, -, -, -, -, 90

P. Bird, 20, 20, 250, 10, 175

A. J. Smith, 15, 25, 150, 5, 161

J. Ferrey, 20, 20, 200, 10, 159

W. Forbus, 28, 22, 500, 30, 281

T. Day, 15, 25, 150, 100, 616

W. Guthery, -, -, -, -, 55

J. Boatman, 50, 30, 400, 10, 467

E. Jones, 18, 22, 150, 75, 168

R. Jones, 20, 60, 300, 80, 168

S. Jones, 15, 25, 500, 120, 275

P. Cox, 15, 25, 150, 10, 215

J. Elkins, 20, 20, 200, 10, 275

D. Clord, 16, 30, 150, 5, 100

F. Dobbs, 14, 26, 200, 5, 60

J. Shellingbarker, 26, 50, 250, 8, 198

W. Dye, 13, 27, 150, 10, 112

J. Dye, 15, 25, 150, 5, 74

W. Jinkins, 17, 23, 200, 25, 295

W. Brooks, 30, 10, 150, 10, 136

J. Bright, -, -, -, -, 55
J. Hayes, 24, 53, 200, 10, 78
G. Gideon, -, -, -, -, 175
S. A. Meadows, 10, 30, 250, 75, 111
M. Dyke, 10, 30, 200, 75, 250
J. Dyke, 15, 25, 150, 35, 15
J. Clevinger, 15, 25, 150, 5, 50
P. Layer, 20, 60, 300, 25, 167
B. Clevinger, 15, 25, 150, 5, 75
J. Warren, 40, 120, 400, 20, 367
E. Crawford, -, -, -, -, 118
J. Crawford, -, -, -, -, 50
N. Clevinger, 26, 15, 250, 15, 219
C. Johnson, 22, 58, 325, 75, 147
A. McIntire, 30, 50, 400, 10, 110
C. D. Edwards, 15, 25, 200, 10, 172
J. Edwards, 15, 25, 150, 5, 50
J. Magne Jr., 16, 256, 250, 5, 165
S. Berry, 20, 20 250, 15, 184
J. Jinkins, 26, 20, 250, 100, 293
J. Haton, 16, 64, 300, 200, 400
J. Hodges, 10, 30, 150, 16, 77
B. Chenowith, 15, 25, 200, 45, 119
J. Morris, 40, 40, 600, 10, 840
J. Taber, 15, 24, 200, 10, 200
J. Jinkins, 30, 50, 400, 10, 110
P(T). King, -, -, -, -, 1240
J. Atterberry, 15, 25, 150, 10, 125
J. Dennis, 15, 25, 150, 10, 100
P. Hays, 25, 15, 200, 35, 88
J. A. Gideon, 22, 68, 200, 15, 317
L. Emery, 20, 20, 100, 50, 55
S. Panner(Tanner), -, -, -, -, 88
J. Keithley, -, -, -, -, 66
J. Hubanks, 20, 20, 300, 75, 185
A. Stackstell, 15, 25, 200, 10, 224
J. Stackstell, -, -, -, -, 128
M. May, 21, 19, 200, 30, 382
R. C. Crow, -, -, -, -, 123
B. Baker, 32, 8, 200, 125, 437
F. Wooley, 15, 25, 200, 15, 88
J. S. C. Huddleston, 80, 80, 1000, 150, 676
W. P. Lewis, -, -, -, -, 75
J. O. May, 13, 27, 150, 5, 125
M. Clevinger, 20, 20, 200, 10, 97

M. Maberry, 40, 13, 400, 15, 200
H. Luallen, 60, 60, 600, 15, 256
J. Wetherman, 20, 20, 200, 15, 440
R. M. Warren(Neanew), 15, 25, 150, 5, 110
J. Duncan, 30, 65, 600, 15, 221
C. Clayton, 16, 24, 200, 10, 267
R. Huff, 25, 55, 200, 10, 225
W. Kessee, 15, 25, 150, 10, 110
J. Southson, -, -, -, -, 245
P. Felton, 30, 90, 500, 50, 420
J. McCoy, 13, 106, l500, 30, 211
J. Bird, 25, 15, 500, 75, 261
J. M. Hays, -, -, -, -, 30
J. Vaughn, 100, 300, 1000, 100, 1810
J. Wilson, -, 280, 500, 10, 46
W. Gideon, 40, 60, 1000, 100, 365
W. Gideon, 15, 25, 100, 5, 62
R. Mitchell, 15, 65, 300, 35, 200
J. Nash, 33, 247, 1000, 100, 530
E. Ray, 20, 100, 500, 75, 460
H. C. Nash, 33, 47, 400, 20, 250
J. M. Rapp, 15, 25, 200, 10, 75
N. Bozarth, 15, 25, 150, 5, 70
W. Burton, 18, 25, 150, 5, 79
J. King, 22, 18, 250, 5, 140
R. Davis, 17, 23, 150, 5, 239
W. Lorance, 16, 25, 500, 10, 240
R. Lorance, 30, 10, 400, 15, 200
J. Barns, 35, 125, 500, 100, 417
J. Right, 20, 60, 350, 30, 178
J. Cox, 30, 10, 200, 10, 189
N. Carther, 16, 24, 150, 5, 130
J. Cox, 14, 26, 130, 80, 2 ¼
J. Howard, 15, 25, 200, 10, 150
J. Hodges, 16, 25, 150, 5, 186
R. Ritter, 30, 10, 250, 10, 200
J. Herron, 20, 20, 300, 10, 317
J. Simson, 25, 15, 250, 15, 335
E. Hodges, 15, 25, 150, 5, 307
S. Lorance, 35, 45, 300, 60, 265
E. Brown, 13, 27, 150, 5, 109
J. Cox, 25, 135, 300, 5, 70
H. Day, 15, 25, 300, 50, 194
J. Prater, 25, 15, 250, 30, 226
G. W. Elam, 20, 20, 200, 10, 125

S. Elam, 40, 40, 300, 50, 416
E. Elam, 15, 25, 150, 10, 169
C. Noice, -, -, -, -, 145
J. Angel, 16, 24, 150, 10, 275
W. King, 16, 24, 150, 10, 98
C. Elliott, -, 80, 400, 5, 130
A. Pierce, 40, 40, 400, 125, 173
H. Lorance, 40, 40, 300, 20, 303
D. T. Tayton, 30, 10, 300, 30, 192
H. Johnson, -, -, -, -, 147
W. Johnson, -, -, -, -, 90
J. Turner, -, -, -, -, 79
J. Cook, 20, 20, 250, 10, 242
J. Jones, 25, 15, 300, 15, 132
J. May, 30, 10, 250, 15, 207
M. Stallcup, 60, 60, 700, 10, 280
M. Thurman, 20, 20, 400, 10, 100
W. Walker, 40, 80, 500, 125, 227
P. C. Duncan, 30, 90, 500, 10, 79
W. Chestnut, 50, 70, 1800, 500, 1566
C. Buckner, 30, 100, 500, 5, 472
E. M. Marley, 27, 133, 500, 35, 116
R. Vaughn, -, 40, 150, 45, 161
J. Byerly, 30, 10, 200, 50, 241
M. Gann, 30, 50, 400, 100, 307
J. St.Clair, 15, 25, 200, 10, 52
J. Nix, 15, 25, 150, 10, 139
W. W. Scott, 30, 75, 800, 100, 297
J. W. Martin, -, -, -, 80, 80
R. Workman, 20, 60, 250, 75, 354
J. Workman, 20, 60, 150, 15, 142
J. A. Mathies, 14, 26, 150, 30, 139
A. J. French, 18, 22, 150, 5, 60
C. Huff, 15, 25, 150, 10, 132
J. H. Larken, 25, 15, 200, 10, 250
W. Wetherman, 40, 120, 400, 100, 321
J. Wetherman, 25, 15, 200, 5, 157
S. Wetherman, 20, 20, 200, 8, 134
A. McCoy, 20, 60, 800, 100, 242
T. Murrel, -, -, -, -, 95
A. Stewart, -, -, -, -, 40
T. Barker, 35, 45, 500, 250, 667
N. Williams, 16, 24, 200, 45, 241
C. Scribner, 20, 60, 200, 10, 105
W. Turner, 30, 130, 300, 80, 371
E. Mosely, 20, 20, 300, 10, 180

E. Mosely, 10, 30, 150, 5, 70
W. A. J. Proctor, 35, 45, 300, 200, 445
S. Gimlin, 70, 170, 1500, 80, 1150
D. Ginden, 14, 26, 200, 10, 277
J. Gunlin, 30, 50, 470, 10, 362
W. Pierce, 13, 27, 150, 5, 115
H. Bradly, 30, 50, 300, 150, 527
E. Bradly, 15, 25, 300, 10, 250
H. Bradly, -, -, -, -, 141
R. Pierce, 35, 45, 400, 150, 624
L. Right, -, -, -, -, 70
B. Bozarth, 30, 10, 200, 10, 182
J. Greer, 20, 20, 300, 10, 150
J. Herron, 15, 25, 150, 100, 321
A. Taber, 30, 10, 250, 15, 122
H. Taber, 15, 25, 150, 10, 190
J. Taber, 16, 24, 150, 10, 232
T. Taber, 17, 23, 150, 15, 207
R. Morris, 25, 55, 300, 10, 169
P. Morris, 25, 15, 150, 5, 558
T. Morris, 16, 24, 150, 10, 265
Wm. Adair, -, -, -, -, 127
J. McDaniel, 30, 50, 500, 50, 431
J. P. Stacy, 32, 15, 300, 15, 65
L. Herrin, 25, 15, 300, 15, 191
S. Herrin, -, -, -, -, 57
J. Smith, -, -, -, -, 220
B. H. Smith, -, -, -, -, 42
J. W. Lemineg(Lemmeg), -, -, -, -, 20
W. Teague, 40, 40, 300, 40, 294
A. Estic, 19, 18, 300, 10, 326
J. Campbell, 17, 62, 400, 75, 220
J. Hamlet, 16, 24, 400, 15, 185
B. Majors, 40, 100, 2000, 80, 575
E. Majors, 15, 38, 400, 135, 700
C. May, -, -, -, -, 152
H. G. Snapp, 75, 85, 1500, 25, 525
H. Smith, -, -, -, -, 150
S. Speaman 15, 25, 150, 10, 175
A. McQunce, 18, 22, 200, 40, 206
B. Pheps, 20, 60, 500, 20, 60
W. Nade, 40, 40, 800, 50, 771
J. Simons, -, -, -, -, 135
H. Adams, 30, 90, 500, 15, 282
M. Yandie, 30, 18, 300, 75, 150
L. Casey, 170, 427, 5000, 300, 805

R. Rains, 30, 10, 200, 10, 167
J. Rains, 17, 23, 300, 10, 209
M. Kary, 16, 24, 150, 10, 115
E. Forgy, 30, 50, 400, 60, 325

J. Huffman, 25, 15, 250, 300, 460
D. Thurman, 20, 22, 300, 15, 150
N. Oliver, -, -, -, -, 130
H. H. Halcum, 20, 20, 300, 15, 257

Texas County 1850 Agricultural Census was filmed by the Central Microfilm Service Corp of St. Louis, Missouri, for the Missouri State Historical Society. There are 46 columns of information on the 1850 agricultural census. I have chosen to transcribe six of those columns. The columns are:

1. Name
2. Acres of Land Improved
3. Acres of Land Unimproved
4. Cash Value of the Farm
5. Value of Farm Implements and Machinery
13. Value of Livestock

James R. Gardner, 52, 148, 2000, 7, 170
John K. Hubbard, 50, -, 250, 8, 200
Peter Miller, 20, -, 150, 170, 300
Robert Davis, -, -, -, 70, 40
H. G. Davis, -, -, -, -, 50
V. Sutton, 9, 80, 200, 20, 400
Daniel Morgan, -, -, -, -, 200
James H. Davis, -, -, -, -, 300
R. Y. Smiley, 15, -, 150, 15, 400
James D. Smith, -, -, -, 5, 150
John Riley, 15, -, 150, 5, 752
Isaac N. Hughes, -, -, -, -, 150
Thomas J. Wade, -, -, -, -, 28
Joseph Allen, -, -, -, -, 10
Franklin Ellis, 6, -, 200, 5, 100
James J. Johnson, 22, -, 200, 20, 270
Asa Ellis, 45, 35, 1500, 30, 1000
Asa Ellis, 213, 733, 3450, -, -
C. H. Lattimore, 40, 120, 800, 10, 300
Richard Childers, -, -, -, -, 50
C. H. Millican, -, -, -, -, 300
Calvin McKinney, 15, -, 150, 6, 210
John Stephens, 12, 68, 1000, 20, 600
Wesley Wadley, -, - ,-, -, 146
James Davidson, -, -, -, -, 10
William Chambers, -, -, -, -, 65
David Wilson, 3, 37, 75, 2, 100
Jane Hays, -, -, -, -, 25
David Lynch, 70, 90, 3000, 30, 670
Anson McGorden, 8, 72, 100, 10, 200

Wilbern Gillmore, 50, 110, 1000, 25, 600
William Martin, 22, 58, 400, 5, 125
James M. Daugherty, 30, -, 500, 15, 700
John Johns, 29, 11, 250, 10, 225
Lewis M. Trusty, 4, 36, 200, 10, 325
Jessee Clark, 43, 293, 500, 115, 375
Stephen B. W. A. Williams, 60, 180, 100, 15, 602
Berissa Ellis, -, -, -, -, 100
William Lyed(Lepd), -, -, -, -, 280
R. S. More, -, -, -, -, 180
John Horn, -, -, -, -, 32
B. L. Eversole, -, -, -, -, 65
Terney & Sanders, 654, 200, 800, 20, 1263
William Blalock, -, 40, 50, -, 20
Elisha Boman, 10, -, 100, -, 135
Rebecca King, -, -, -, -, 125
Joseph Wolfe, -, -, -, -, 45
John C. Wickam, -, -, -, -, 205
G. W. Sullins, -, -, -, -, 130
Thomas Harvey, 30, 50, 300, 50, 256
H. F. Anasly, 82, 450, 900, 40, 1275
Washington Taylor, 50, 154, 1000, -, 85
Ezekiel Williams, 6, -, 80, -, 68
Jesse Brock, -, -, -, -, -
Joseph Riden(Biden), 60, 60, 500, 20, 72
J. J. Hardison, -, -, -, -, 50
Thomas Morrison, -, -, -, -, 140

Richard Ballew, -, -, -, -, 8
Bird Waters, -, -, -, -, 70
Matilda Julian, 9, 32, 400, -, 100
Samuel G. Poteet, 70, 30, 800, 30, 428
P. H. Taussdell, 48, 250, 1200, 125, 302
Thomas Quick, -, -, -, -, 40
Jacob Leach, -, -, -, -, 17
Wm. D. Fore, -, -, -, 60, 225
James Mooney, 10, 120, 800, 130, 855
Spencer Mitchell 75, 85, 1000, 150, 637
J. H. Brown, 33, 57, 500, 85, 100
Thomas P. Chitton, 82, 38, 200, 10, 230
John B. Bradford, 115, -, 2000, 25, 1270
Elizabeth King, -, -, -, -, 115
Robert Bradford, -, -, -, -, 135
Samuel Ducan, -, -, -, -, 85
Anna Craddock, -, -, -, -, 140
G. W. Quick, -, -, -, -, 234
Daniel McDaniel, 40, 37, 400, 25, 97
David Massey, 18, 25, 300, -, 35
Jefferson Sullins, 20, 25, 500, 120, 252
James A. Bates, 75, 400, 5000, 100, 1620
John Brewer, 12, 40, 275, 50, 211
Willis G. Jones, 10, -, 50, 10, 297
Josua T. Jones, 12, -, 100, -, 50
James Buckner, -, -, -, 150, 400
Cal. Blankenship, 18, -, 150, 80, 325
John Burnett, 125, 191, 5000, 150, 445
John E. N. Williams, -, -, -, -, -
John Lock, 10, -, 100, 10, 110
Elias Martin, -, -, -, -, 48
Dabney Lynch, 30, 10, 300, 100, 445
N. Snider, 20, 120, 150, -, 1295
James Thomas, 10, -, -, -, 175
James C. Baker, -, -, -, -, 205
William Ragan, -, -, -, -, 25
Joseph Walton, -, 40, 100,-, 83
Joseph Buckner, -, -, -, -, 88
Pleasant Parker, -, 40, 50, -, 260
James Bradford, 90, 30, 1000, 140, 415
G. Hazlewood, 3,-, 100, 10, 270
John Jones, -, -, -, -, 195
John C. Nickolds, 20, -, 40, 50, 331
John Redick, -, -, -, -, 120
Lee H. Miller, 45, 25, 1500, 100, 185

H. H. Jones, -, -, -, -, 157
Sanford Musgrove, -, -, -, -, 90
Staret P. McCain, -, -, -, -, 5
Andrew Norton, -, -, -, -, 241
Morris Stogsdell, 10, -, 100, 65, 150
C. H. Frost, -, -, -, -, 110
Joshua Gougs, 12,-, 100, 5, 105
Alfred Gates, -, -, -, -, 65
Jonathan Wells, 7, -, 75, -, 155
Sterling Ship, 10, -, 100, -, 125
James B. Childers, 10, -, 100, -, 10
Jonathan Byers, 18, -, 100, 10, 200
G. W. Thornton, 25, -, 300, 15, 155
Michjah Morris, 30, -, 200, 10, 250
James McKinney, 25, -, 200, 10, 565
John White, 27, -, 200, 10, 270
Elcaney Hughs, 14, -, 100, 10, 230
Samuel Hughs, 15, 25, 300, 16, 435
Thomas J. Wade, -, -, -, -, -
Isaac Moody, 14, -, 150, 15, 157
Henry Moody, 30, 10, 400, 15, 300
William McClelland, 50, -, 300, 10, 275
Samuel T. Rice, 3, -, 50, 5, 140
Henry Killian, 18, -, 250, 10, 160
Michael Killian, 13, -, 200, 15, 190
Johnathan Yates, -, -, -, -, 115
Daniel Killian, 17, -, 200, 10, 280
G. B. Stogsdell, 5, -, 25, 4, 32
Moses Williams, 80, 80, 700, 20, 740
John Williams, 20, -, 200, 10, 300
John Walls, 30, -, 400, 20, 575
Joseph House, 25, -, 120, 5, 375
Wesley Walls, 5, -, 100, 5, 106
Abraham Enloe, 10, -, 100, 10, 320
William Hughes, 7, -, 100, 10, 60
Nimrod Standerford, 18, -, 100, 10, 100
George F. Hamilton, 8, -, 100, 10, 100
Samuel Selfe, 65, 55, 800, 5, 250
Jason Selfe, 30, 50, 500, 5, 100
William Roberts, 30, 90, 500, 10, 241
John Skiles, 25, 55, 500, 20, 400
Thomas Hamilton, 25, -, 200, 10, 420
D. P. Hamilton, 15, -, 100, -, 390
Henry Elliott, 35, -, 300, 20, 165
Thomas Elliott, 35, -, 300, 20, 160
Jacob Ard, -, -, -, -, 10

William Vaughn, 4, -, 50, 5, 75
L. Mood, 20, -, 200, 10, 165
James & J. Farris, 20, 60, 400, 25, 430
Richard Burdine, -, -, -, -, 80
Lewis Shipley, 4, -, 50, -, 10
Levi McWhorter, -, -, -, -, 90
John Turnbull, 50, -, 400, 25, 450
David Marsh, -, -, -, -, 150
Louisa Reynolds, 14, -, 60, 5, 25
Jonathan Knight, 6, -, 50, 5, 280
Nathan V. Green, 1, -, 25, -, 20
Alfred Nicholds, 60, -, 300, 10, 130
William B. Rafily, 20, -, 125, 5, 65
Samuel C. Jones, 16, -, 150, 8, 50
John Hancock, -, -, -, 5, 85
G. W. Cole, 15, -, 100, 15, 130
Benja. C. Stephens, 40, -, 500, 20, 210
Sliphon Holt, 30, -, 300, 15, 380
A. & W. Deny, 20, -, 200, 10, 210
David Hancock, 3,-, 50, 5, 50
George Green, 10, -, 100, 10, 65
E. J. H. Green 8, -, 100, 10, 60
Philip Green, 4, -, 50, 5, 80
John Hott(Holt), 40, -, 401, 25, 550
Eli Woods, 35, -, 300, 20, 425
Elevin Green, 2, -, 50, 5, 130
Henry James, 25, 15, 300, 15, 400
Aaron James, 12, -, 100, 10, 250
James Leek, 7, -, 50, 5, 30
G. W. Daugherty, 7, -, 50, 5, 135
Fountain Self, 5, -, 50, 10, 290
Andrew McKinney, 15, -, 200, 25, 200
John Childers, 30, -, 300, 20, 265
Harvey Green, 5, -, 50, 5, 220
William Williams, 13, -, 200, 15, 170
James Prickit, 47, -, 400, 20, 340
Clabourn Gallian, 15, -, 100, 10, 85
Ezekiel Chambers, 15, -, 150, 20, 95
Jesse Williams, 18, -, 150, 10, 110
James McKinney, 15, -, 150, 10, 150
Caswell Gillmore, 10, -, 100, -, 85
Jonathan Gross, 18, -, 200, 10, 230
John P. Johnson, 20, -, 100, 10, 90
Noah Ruston, 10, -, 50, 5, 40
William McCubbins, 15, -, 150, 10, 210
Jackson Juvell, -, -, -, -, 15

William Juvell, 30, -, 200, 10, 215
Thomas Juvell, 15, -, 150, 5, 100
Sarah Tharp, 22, -, 200, 5, 130
Samuel Rose, 25, -, 100, 10, 100
Ruben Harloe, 18, -, 150, 10, 235
Barton Daniels, 8, -, 50, 10, 230
James George, 12, -, 200, 10, 130
B. Brosk, 50, 30, 500, 25, 265
Jessee Summers, 28, 12, 400, 10, 225
William Acres, 12, -, 100, 15, 340
George Hamilton, 4, -, 25, 5, 175
Peter Barton, 30, 90, 300, 10, 275
Sofiah Hamilton, 4, -, 25, 5, 175
Jane McCain, -, 40, 100, 5, 160
John S. Davis, 8, -, 75, 10, 110
Wiley Parsell, 35, 85, 600, 20, 185
Buckner Garrison, 40, 120, 100, 20, 600
Scovil Hoffman, 12, -, 200, 10, 200
Sampson Martin, 21, -, 300, 25, 360
Lewis Tash, 15, -, 100, 10, 160
Silas Gillmore, 9, -, 75, 5, 60
Roda Gillmore, 10, -, 100, 5, 50
Hiram King, 30, -, 250, 20, 350
R. L. Williams, 18, 35, 150, 10, 300
C. B. Lynch, 15, 12, 600, 10, 500
Joshua Morris, 12, -, 100, 15, 60
William Thornton, 70, 10, 1000, 25, 650
Edwin H. Thornton, 10, 40, 100, 10, 140
T & G. Leonard, 15, -, 200, 75, 215
Spencer Mitchell Jr., 4, -, 50, 10, 100
Mary Williams, 80, 10, 200, 15, 175
King D. Williams, 10, -, 100, 10, 75
John Sherrill & Ewell Sherrill, 75, 325, 1200, 25, 500
Rhoda Carter, 55, 75, 500, 25, 370
Dickerson Crow, 40, -, 350, 20, 575
Henry Ware, 37, 163, 800, -, 100
Wm. M. Brown, 12, -, 75, 5, 70
Jackson Bronson, -, -, -, -, 50
E. C. Ware, 13, 27, 200, 20, 340
James E. Tate, 15, 25, 200, 15, 175
Jessee B. Ragland, 25, 15, 300, 10, 215
Eli G. Halbert, 40, 40, 500, 20, 170
Wesley Riden, 25, 17, 250, 20, 250
Wm. C. Riden, 18, -, 150, 10, 130
Wm. Johnson, 20, 100, 300, 20, 310

Hester McKnight, 25, -, 300, 15, 130
Joel Sherrill, 60, 140, 1000, 25, 425
Elijah Pharis, 6, -, 100, 10, 45
Zachariah Emireson, 16, -, 150, 10, 120
Leroy Matkins (Watkins), 6, -, 100, 10, 190
E. H. Brigman, 13, 27, 100, 20, 225
Har___ Agee, 60, 55, 800, 25, 300
Silus K. Hamby, 50, 50, 500, 15, 220
Prior L. Thomason, 14, 66, 300, 10, 15
Benjamin Higgins(Wiggins), 25, 50, 400, 5, 250
Benjamin S. Higgins(Wiggins), -, -, -, 5, 210
R. W. Lane, 16, -, 100, 5, 55
M. D. Jones, 30, 50, 300, 10, 250
Berry (Jones), 4, -, 25, -, 10
John Berry, 25, 55, 500, 20, 450
G. W. Merrill, 25, 55, 500, 10, 100
A. Fudge, 10, -, 100, 5, 35
Louis Campbell, 15,-, 200, 15, 280
Susan Fox, 10, -, 100, 5, 100
James Gardiner, -, -, 50, 5, 85
James B. Campbell, 60, -, 500, 20, 560
John B. Campbell, 25, 15, 250, 15, 325
Boyd Campbell, 40, -, 200, 15 130
James Chambers, 15, -, 150, 15, 145
Trifina McFarland, 20, -, 400, 15, 170
James Patterson, 40, -, 300, 15, 515
David Cole, 15, -, 100, 5, 100
John Springer, 20, -, 200, 10, 130
Jeremiah Williams, 15, -, 200, 5, 130
John Gardiner, -, -, -, -, 300
William Yorke, 50, -, 300, 10, 70
James E. Yorke, 20, -, 150, 10, 75
Hiram Hodge, -, -, -, -, 250
John McDonald, 30, -, 300, 15, 140
Ephraim Stout, 25, -, 300, 20, 115
A. J. Inman, -, -, -, -, 55
M. McPrewitt, 35, -, 300, 20, 220
W. B. Walker, 30, -, 250, 20, 200
H. C. Dukes, 20, -, 150, 20, 160
Rosona Hodges, 20, 20, 205, 10, 50
Presly Hume, -, -, -, -, 60
James Cooper, 50, -, 500, 20, 275
Solomon Huffman, 12, -, 150, 5, 80

John B. Williams, 12, -, 150, 10, 25
Amos Mooney, 14, -, 100, 5, 45
Joseph Jadwin & Sons, 60, -, 1000, 25, 375
Robert Jones, -, -, -, -, 80
Nathan Martin, 30, 10, 200, 15, 214
James Brice, 7, -, 50, 5, 85
Thomas Phillips, 18, -, 150, 10, 135
H. J. Robards, 2,-, 50, 5, 130
David McKinney, 30, 130, 500, 15, 420
Cinthia Manley, 8, -, 150, 5, 150
M. Keith, 45, 35, 500, 30, 125
Jackson Trusty, -, -, -, -, 150
William Hargrave, 111, -, 150, -, 54
Peter Sanders, 10, -, 200, 60, 534
Joseph Harrison, 40, -, 300, 100, 183
Daniel Heltabrant, 8, -, 50, -, 107
Abram Heltabrant, 20,-, 100, -, 75
James Randolph, 10, -, 200, 20, 320
Mathew Douglass, 15, -, 300, 10, 300
James Coats, 20, -, 300, 15, 155
Lewis Demoss, 15, -, 300, 10, -
Thomas Johnson, 30, -, 200, 75, 100
Thomas Randolph, 5, -, 200, 20, 225
Evan Shelby, 27, -, 400, 50, 185
William Sanders, 12, -, 200, 10, 100
John Sanders, -, -, -, -, 100
Robert Reeves, 5, -, 100, 10, 155
Elijah D. Newkirk, -, -, -, -, 110
Jesse D. Baker, 20, -, 200, 20, 160
William W. Hickey, 16, -, 200, 20, 100
Benjamin W. Upton, 12, -, 150, 10, 125
Joseph Sexton, 9, -, 100, 5, 60
Lewis B. Upton, 25, -, 200, 50, 300
Ozias Upton, 75, -, 600,75, 420
Burton Sexton, -, -, -, -, 50
James Burkhartt, 22, -, 300, 10, 365
Micajah McLaughlin, 4, -, 100, 10, 80
Jemima McLaughlin, 25, 25, 400, -, 260
Joshua H. Burkhartt, 25, 40, 300, 30, 265
John J. Hawkins, 10, -, 100, 10, 160
D. H. Walton(Wallon), -, -, -, -, 100
Selman H. Burkhart, -, -, -, -, 75
John F. Wood, 18, 120, 200, 10, 50
Nathan Sullins, 15, -, 50, 75, 210

John W. Ormsby, 36, 85, 300, 25, 200
John McDonold, 25, 15, 300, 20, 340
Joshua H. McDonold, 40, -, 150, -, 185
John M. Ormsby, 5, -, 100, -, 60
Wm. T. Ormsby, 15, -, 150, -, 265
Samuel McElroy, -, -, -, -, 10
Richard Scaggs, 30, -, 300, 5, 180
John Watson, 2, -, 50, -, 135
Carlock Sow(Low), 40, -, 400, 100, 500
G. U. McElroy, -, -, -, -, 55
Wm. Norris, 20, -, 250, 15, 250
James Carroll, -, -, -, -, 80
Wilson Carroll, 15, -, 150, 10, 100
John Admire, 10, -, 100, -, 25
John Vincent, 16, -, 100, 6, 120
John R. Sullins, 20, -, 200, 20, 230
Mermanen Moore, 30 70, 200, 20, 135
Wm. Faxton, -, -, -, -, 12
Burrel Strickland, 16, -, 150, -, 50
Jonas Musgrave, 15, -, 200, 25, 161

A. S. Harrison, 10, 30, 200, 10, 215
Benjamin Ellis, -, -, -, -, 20
R. U. Rodgers, 75, 165, 1000, 50, 1243
John Collins, -, -, -, -, 10
Thomas Norris, 6, -, 50, -, 40
Wesley Butcher, -, -, -, -, 50
Jas. M. Truesdell, -, -, -, -, 140
Edward Sullins, -, -, -, -, 100
Abner Slate, -, -, -, -, 200
Byars Mooney, -, -, -, -, 300
James Thomas, 20, -, 150, -, 150
Jacob C. Harman, -, -, -, -, 50
Robert Twedy, 16,-, 150, 10, 170
John T. Foust, 45, 255, 500, 50, 340
Wm. Montgomery, -, -, -, -, 15
Russel Jones, 7, -, -, -, 160
John Brown, 20, -, 200, -, 170
James Anderson, 10, -, 150, -, 100
D. B. Commons, 45, 85, 1000, 25, 670

Warren County, Missouri
1850 Agricultural Census

Warren County 1850 Agricultural Census was filmed by the Central Microfilm Service Corp of St. Louis, Missouri, for the Missouri State Historical Society. There are 46 columns of information on the 1850 agricultural census. I have chosen to transcribe six of those columns. The columns are:

1. Name
2. Acres of Land Improved
3. Acres of Land Unimproved
4. Cash Value of the Farm
5. Value of Farm Implements and Machinery
13. Value of Livestock

Leonard Rothermick, 50, 30, 500, 50, 128
Anthoney Wyatt, 160, 220, 3600, 50, 300
James B. Davis, 70, 250, 500, 40, 650
Samuel Taggart, 30, -, 150, 12, 108
Henry Drnall, -, -, -, -, 50
William Ludiwig, 12, 28, 800, 25, 140
James Calloway, 97, 83, 1800, 120, 1458
Bennard Westmire, 25, 25, 300, 68, 285
Henry Stalkman, 14, 26, 230, 75, 127
Jarred Tipher, 30, 90, 150, 30, 179
William Dremire, 20, 100, 150, 60, 100
Undrews Neighmire, 20, 20, 150, 10, 25
Henry Schaff, 20, 62, 2000, 40, 252
Henry Schuester, 30, 90, 200, 70, 178
Simon Bomire, 27, 50, 250, 7, 85
Henry Neighenreuf, 30, 73, 300, 10, 123
Wolter Bryan, 60, 144, 2500, 40, 320
Benjamin Johnson, 45, 90, 1100, 8, 110
Fredrick Johnson, 50, 50, 1200, 15, 276
Gotlip Berg, 20, 20, 150, 10, 116
George Berg, 10, 70, 150, 10, 32
Jarred Toat, 25, 48, 75, -, 138
Jarred Schoaman, 40, 277, 600, 120, 159
Herman Dhemire, 60, 100, 700, 150, 210
Fredrick Oberhellman, 35, 168, 800, 63, 286
Dendrick Denbrock, 10, 70, 150, -, 38

Chares Sinss, 45, 100, 1000, 10, 75
George Sinss, 80, 80, 1200, 80, 228
Morgan Bryan, 50, 500, 1000, 50, 287
Melcena Lynn, -, -, -, -, 8
Conrod Bonkrus, 12, 28, 300, 4, 37
Fredrick Schester, 25, 95, 350, 10, 148
Elizabeth Gosijacod, 25, 45, 350, 10, 124
Mary Fallancone, 30, 231, 1200, 10, 160
Dedrick Bohwover, 20, 55, 350, 10, 89
Henry Gorijacob , 25, 53, 275, 8, 110
John Mether, 30, 50, 200, 60, 130
Augustus F. Grabbs, 2, -, 300, -, 60
Henry Griswold, 300, 1700, 10000, 300, 910
William Cullom, 35, 265, 2000, 20, 390
William H. Harison, 10, -, 150, 20, 160
Oliver Woodhouse, 6, 22, 130, 10, 69
Lewis A. Wabber, 30, 120, 400, 50, 143
Richard Owings, 35, 130, 300, 50, 394
Simon Stratte, 16, -, 80, 5, 60
John Wathouse, 5, -, 25, -, 50
John H. Shilling, 25, -, 250, 20, 138
Edward Harrier, 80, 120, 500, 100, 166
William James, 40, 97, 400, 80, 408
Henry Schlapper, 40, 120, 400, 50, 195
Richard Canada, 30, -, 155, 35, 205
William Crager, 20, 40, 140, -, 30
James G. Smith, 40, 50, 280, 100, 235
Henry Smith, 3, -, 100, -, 53

William Logan, 100, 240, 1500, 100, 832

William Shovengard, 40, 73, 800, 35, 94

D. Wyatt, 65, 115, 1000, 20, 367

E. Wyatt, 95, 238, 1000, 30, 408

H. Wyatt, 12, 58, 200, 7, 161

H. Buttermiler, 25, 50, 150, 15, 252

B. Ruenber, 90, 30, 680, 15, 40

G. Oberlagas(Oberlagaf), 30, 10, 150, 50, 100

Simeon Walden, 10, 30, 70, 15, 80

J. Liddmire, 16, 24, 350, 5, 190

E. Suhoe, 38, 2, 375, 75, 172

H. Headbrink, 30, -, 90, 20, 116

Fredrick Showjacob, 25, 15, 150, 65, 127

Henry Hitchman, 35, 135, 410, 60, 148

J. H. Middlehemp, 25, 95, 500, 60, 200

J. Middlehemp, 30, 40, 600, 25, 300

Fredrick Engleber, 24, 56, 400, -, 108

F. Dinasoger, 20, 60, 400, 10, 50

Wm. T. Roundtree, 30, 50, 600, 30, 180

A. Dandridge, 8, 32, 450, 40, 108

James Hill, 2, 38, 150, 70, 122

Charles Hill, 2, 35, 35, -, 122

James Hill, 12, 28, 150, 15, 168

Thomas Oden, 12, 28,150, 15, 114

Martin Barr, 35, 165, 800, 65, 139

Alex. Mire, 34, 6, 350, 100, 160

Vincent Taylor, -, -, -, 35, 170

William Painter, 20, -, 80, 30, 175

Matilda Schaw, 60, 60, 500, 50, 250

Jane Hutcherson, 30, 10, 100, 10, 350

John J. Smith, 75, 215, 1500, 250, 808

Joseph Kemp, 170, 330, 2000, 40, 835

Day Muse, -, -, 200, 12, 200

James M. Owings, 15, 361, 1500, 20, 366

Israel Earls, 10, 70, 250, 35, 198

Levi Fines, 2, 48, 60, 15, 112

W. P. Oden, 15, 35, 100, 200, 65

Miles Johnson, 20, 140, 400, 100, 133

Warren V. Stewart, 400, 1185, 25000, 260, 4236

Thomas E. Wray, 15, 65, 350, -, 50

John Strinbarger, 40, 132, 500, 100, 320

J. C. Howell, 40, 80, 500, 75, 194

Petter Haroman, 60, 100, 800, 125, 579

Hirem H. Kampen, 55, 145, 1000, 12, 257

E. Wray, -, -, 100, 100, 150

L. Kennedy (owner), 1, -, 800, 40, 100

Thomas Corder (owner), 100, 155, 3000, 150, 571

D. J. Weeber, 25, 15, 250, 58, 366

Joseph B. Hart, 60, 270, 2500, 90, 230

James Coope, 30, -, 150, 50, 270

J. S. Wyatt (owner), 200, 300, 3000, 150, 767

Mary Justin (owner), 60, 80, 250, 100, 436

John Oastrack (owner), 29, 35, 500, 20, 70

John Preston (owner), 4, 20, 50, 60, 153

Jesse Mehan (tenant), 40, -, 300, 25, 152

James Thurmon, 25, 108, 700, 100, 208

James Thurmon agt., 65, 15, 500, -, -

Leonard Kiliger, 160, 40, 700, 75, 180

Cornelius Howard, 60, 130, 600, 100, 300

Lemuel Price, 1, 130, 600, -, -

James Walls, 22, 40, 250, 75, 350

William H. Ginnings, 5, 235, 400, 30, 280

Georg Charles, 75, 205, 700, 10, 168

D. S. Crage, 2, -, 1000, -, 30

A. C. Smith, 3, -, 400, -, 30

W. M. Patten 20, 20, 150, -, 90

James Nichols, 1, -, 8, 240, -, 168

William Harper, 15, 225, 2500, -, 490

John A. Pulliam, 70, 520, 2500, 100, 308

L. S. Pennington, -, -, -, 65, 223

James Harnet, 250, 526, 5000, 182, 420

Thomas Kelley, 70, 250, 1500, -, 372

Francis Stewartkamp, 25, 15, 300, 50, 250

Thomas J. Marshall, 1, -, 500, 62, 225

John Hoseyager, 15, 25, 200, 50, 129

Casper Dolman, 50, 350, 1000, 50, 150

Walham Poolman, 30, 52, 2000, 60, 148

Jacob Harper, 30, 10, 400, 10, 50

James Patten, 65, 25, 1000, 100, 568

Henry Tripie, 25, 75, 500, 8, 268
Rudolph Boember, 20, 80, 400, 11, 150
Herman Subermire, 50, 70, 500, 10, 189
Bernard Gigber, 10, 70, 200, 10, 20
Thomas Means, 40, 116, 1000, 75, 440
Harrod Bobermire, 50, 60, 150, 70, 148
L. C. Thomas, 1, -, 200, -, 270
Alfred McClure, 30, 130, 1000, 40, 115
Martha Williams, 75, 45, 1000, 75, 215
Mary Williams, 30, 50, 500, 25, 115
F. Wyatt, 40, 60, 1000, 75, 405
Fredric Mire, 10, 150, 250, 10, 50
Herman Sevet, 10, 30, 150, 10, 100
Henry Sevet, 12, 68, 200, -, 50
J. A. Fergerson, 20, 180, 800, 25, 200
Henry Suterman, 10, 30, 150, -, 60
C___ Fomire, 10, 30, 200, 50, 160
E. Winter, 10, 30, 150, 15, 35
Fredrick Pope, 10, 30, 200, 50, 100
F. H. Fisher, 35, 97, 700, 100, 245
Christian Snider, 25, 95, 300,-, 62
Henry Bergamy, 12, 28, 150, 10, 360
Catharine Water, 15, 65, 300, 25, 47
Fredrick Stuck, 30, 50 300, 110, 90
Albert Johnson, 20, 20, 300, 75, 525
Wilford Lee, 40, 40, 600,150, 200
Elinder Buxton, 60, 160, 1000, 53, 175
Charles Slanker, 20, 60, 400, 15, 190
H. Gerding, 25, 35, 400, 68, 200
John Gerding, 10, 30, 200, 15, 98
G. W. Blair, 35, 5, 1500, 40, 345
G. Willingham, 20, 20, 150, 20, 100
S. Wray, 30, 10, 300, 130, 500
W. C. Patton, 30, 130, 500, 10, 143
G. W. Wheeler, 50, 110, 700, 85, 150
Peter Shide, 30, 120, 800, 60, 140
G. E. Shackelford, 100, 60, 800, 60, 450
Joshua Owsley, 15, 35, 120, 15, 40
C. Bates, 7, 5, 50, 10, 85
Thomas Gardner, 18, -, 40, 40, 282
Tilman Cullom, 100, 1539, 5000, 250, 1075
Sophia Foster, 24, 336, 300, 10, 100
A. Buckston, 15, 145, 350, 15, 158
D. Burgess, 65, 95, 1400, 80, 574
Earnest Cough, 15, 75, 700, 10 106

Conrod Roter, 35, 65, 600, 15, 83
Henry Roter, 10, 30, 100, 10, 85
Simon Shilling, 14, 66, 260, 10, 158
C. O'Badermire, 30, 75, 400, 10, 60
Fredrick Deaker, 10, 70, 250, 10, 55
Day Suatzy, 20, 50, 300, 10, 55
William Jeax, 7, 40, 50, -, 55
Christopher Leether, 15, 18, 200, 20, 50
Charles Hix, 20, 59, 300, 15, 116
Henry Seifelman, 9, 31, 400, -, 50
Fredrick Mifler, 15, 25, 300, 10, 80
Henry Fredermae, 15, 25, 300, 11, 68
Dultone Hankermire, 11, 30, 150, 10, 50
C. Hankermire, 10, 30, 150, 10, 40
C. Sichamire(Lichamire), 20, 26, 150, 10, 50
C. Mire, 45, 96, 350, 10, 140
Christian Tea, 45, 96, 350, 10, 140
Christian Mire, 20, 24, 300, 10, 75
Fredrick Swatsey, 40, 40, 350, 60, 160
J. B. Carter, 10 171, 1400, 60, 262
Christian Wilbensmire, 10, 30, 150, 10, 60
Earnast Kenanamire, 10, 30, 100, 10, 75
Henry Dillsmire, 20, 20, 200, 10, 85
Fredrick Waggoner, 35, 125, 500, 60, 148
Conrod Hilderdick, 30, 45, 400, 10, 80
D. Flourt, 50, 120, 350, -, 90
R. Z. Writter, 2, -, 400, -, 40
Frederick Roush, 156, 48, -, -, 40
Bernard Namber, 50, 110, 1500, 25, 260
Frederick Dothage, 25, 113, 700, 10, 25
Harman J. Dothage, 10, 70, 150, 10, 40
H. Ritter, 10, 70, 200, -, -
Earnest Dothage, 10, 100, 3000, 10, 50
Henry Bolman, 20, 60, 300, 10, 38
John D. Snicks, 40, 80, 300, 30, 230
Rinard Hersher, 55, 105, 400, 10, 81
William Whithous, 30, 50, 300, 20, 142
Fredrick Nottenmire, 20, 10, 200, 20, 100
William Hennelberger, 14, 58, 200, 10, 78
Mary Bola, 20, 20, 120, 15, 135
Phillip Habermire, 16, 18, 70, 10, 68

Henry Schoppenhast, 30, 50, 240, 50, 180

Henry Simbemburg, 15, 20, 200, 5, 80

Joseph E. Withouse, 90, 80, 800, 40, 190

Henry Frigenburn, 40, 70, 342, 70, 170

William Henfield, 30, 40, 200, 10, 125

D. M. Bricks, 20, 20, 120, 10, 120

William Schoppenhart, 40, 32, 400, 60, 218

James Hughes, 40, 50, 1000, 15, 253

Joseph Rice, 53, 153, 1500, 50, 307

Earnast Dglecamp, 12, -, 140, 59, 80

Earnest Loggerman, 12, 85, 150, 8, 75

Elizabeth Ketler, 20, -, 100, -, 140

William Katten, 18, 42, 180, 5, 90

John D. Lock, 160, 904, 8880, 200, 854

Frederick Hosmare, 20, -, 200, -, 47

Pater Wynant, 8, -, 70, 5, 94

Casper Blebesant, 30, -, 248, 5, 69

H. Ulffers, 40, 137, 1100, 65, 534

Earnest H. Shnera, 14, 66, 250, 10, 125

William Fahrenhosst, 15, 1219, 806, 10, 140

Martin Kite, 85, 153, 2500, 80, 340

Joseph G. Walber(Walker, Wabber), 175, 295, 2300, 90, 565

Conrad Eibemire, 20, 20, 300, 8, 30

Henry Bever, 16, 64, 300, 10, 94

David Bridgmon, 20, 60, 300, 10, 114

Mary E. Obymar, 8, 32, 60, 10, 67

Lawson Thoroughman, 16, 104, 300, 10, 257

Harry Borgman, 18, 62, 300, 40, 150

William Thoroughman, 7, -, 70, 10, 100

Elizabeth Johston, -, -, -, -, 95

John Mammeon, 113, 72, 1000, 100, 470

John D. Howard, 20, 60, 400, 10, 100

Nancy Hines, 23, 32, 200, 10, 138

Anne Liles, 25, 40, 200, 6, 180

Levi Hines, 16, -, 75, 12, 180

W. H. Burgess, 12, 53, 700, 65, 271

Robert J. Hueston, 40, 112, 1700, 75, 280

J. D. Gorden, 60, 130, 1000, 150, 555

J. L. Simmes, 60, 60, 1500, 80, 720

R. J. Kenaidy, 100, 600, 2600, 125, 746

E. O. Rowntree, 100, 540, 1000, 80, 350

Harman Minges, 15, 65, 156, 5, 120

Henry Coley, 20, 20, 100, 20, 110

Henry Weincishagson, 60, 60, 480, 150, 394

John Reinbas, 10, 150, 800, 25, 160

William Rainhol, -, -, -, -, 48

Henry Baragess, 25, 35, 300, 10, 229

W. S. Hodges, 75, 200, 750, 100, 333

D. Powell, 80, 186, 1500, 75, 316

Solomon Vanbiber, 14, 66, 500, 75, 226

Joseph Moore, 50, 80, 800, 140, 539

Joseph Cochran, 100, 148, 2000, 100, 162

Dnaria Logan, 70, 50, 700, 100, 634

Christophe Bogel, 15, 65, 250, 10, 61

Henry Powell, 95, 227, 1300, 100, 157

Dilbert Mason, 70, 90, 800, 100, 320

Moses Edwards, 80, 80, 1000, 95, 275

Thomas Leifer, 80, 80, 600, 75, 382

Schuyler Rice, 12, 40, 300, 75, 580

Warren Welch, 10 70, 400, 790, 256

James Welch, 80, 400, 1400, 50, 303

Sherman Welch, -, -, -, -, 67

James Spires, 25, 15, 250, 12, 167

Greenbury Spires, 40, 40, 400, 70, 185

Henry Prittchet, 100, 355, 3000, 150, 524

Adam Painter, 45, 215, 1500, 20, 367

William Welch, 9, 71, 500, 100, 138

Foster B. Simpson, 30, 50, 500, 50, 772

John S. Moore, 80, 40, 1000, 75, 583

Harrison King, 130, 220, 2000, 100, 330

W. H. Grey, 30, 50, 400, 75, 164

Joshua Prittchet, 31, 80, 600, 15, 290

Chares Sherman, 7, 73, 250, 5, 49

Jerry Harrison, -, -, -, 50, 147

P. E. Williams, 30, 120, 400, 10, 141

Mark Pringle, 125, 335, 2000, 60, 1525

Winthrop Norton, -, -, -, -, 89

Francis Sherman, 30, 50, 600, 50, 209

John D. Smith, 100, 220, 1500, 100, 250

David Sherman, 90, 470, 3000, 40, 541

Peter Randolph, 39, 50, 400, 5, 88

P. M. Bergess, 50, 310, 1210, 140, 1099

John Ruwans, 50, 110, 1000, 50, 273

Jarred Davis, 4, 56, 600, 60, 86
Henry E. Welch, 20, 60, 500, 40, 199
John Welch, 90, 150, 3000, 25, 550
August Manning, 50 70, 400, 50, 169
Larthan Welch, 30, -, 150, 10, 183
Jarred H. Bohmer, 50, 79, 800, 20, 243
John D. Runels, 30, 50, 300, 150, 235
Elexander Northcutt, 17, -, 78, 15, 127
Herman Buckhostt, 60, 140, 1400, 20, 142
Fredrick Gnauman, 20, 40, 120, 10, 83
Mattice Lohansan, 10, 50, 200, 10, 88
Asbery Thurman, 15, 40, 100, 5, 135
Henry Ingerman, 40, 120, 250, 10, 115
William Cook, 20, 28, 50, 15, 100
Jarred Schoester, 20, 18, 60, 10, 75
Samuel Moore, 25, 300, 800, 100, 165
Herman Copperman, 15, 80, 300, 10, 118
Herman Fennewald, 20, 100, 250, 200, 133
Wilham Sherman, 19, 81, 150, 60, 200
George Sherman, -, 40, 50, 40, 120
George Wilbrink, 30, 50, 300, 35, 113
Henry Gerbing, 15, 22, 200, 50, 153
Henry A. Schowberg, 16, 65, 260, 40, 80
Henry F. Brant, 80, 240, 1000, 200, 825
Herman Brant, 10, 30, 80, 5, 55
John Middlekinny, 35, 85, 300, 40, 91
Henry Ostello, 28, -, 60, 50, 80
John D. Sherman, 50, 30, 800, 50, 258
Richard Spear, 5, -, 50, -, 20
Frederich Beamecher, 25, 55, 250, 60, 120
Charls Strack, 20, 60, 300, 60, 117
Thomas Kelley, 25, 135, 250, 15, 159
Henry Schermise, 10, 70, 250, 10, 101
Jonah Hubbard, 100, 500, 2000, 100, 713
Robert C. Hill, -, 125, 400, 15, 200
William Hunter, 4, -, 20, -, 81
Christian Winter, 25, 15, 300, 25, 82
Wells E. Marvin, 35, 45, 500, 10, 195
E. N. Marvin, 10, 70, 300, 5, 120
Moses Shappard, 60, 61, 1000, 15, 155
Creed Droher, 150, 500, 400, 150, 422

Petter Stewart, 50, 190, 1000, 10, 136
Dunbar J. Long, 40, 60, 1560, 75, 229
Climpson Bryan, 1 ½, -, 150, -, 10
Grief Stewart, 100, 800, 5000, 150, 1035
David Gilbey, 50, 30, 400, 10, 289
James Bowen, 30, 50, 400, 10, 148
Wilson Hutcherson, 50, 200, 1500, 20, 210
Cyrus Carter, 25, 105, 600, 30, 140
Thomas W. Carter, 60, 60, 600, 20, 206
William Powell, 12, 68, 102, 5, 150
William Horstman, 40, 175, 700, 75, 359
Lessly Lowe, -, -, -, 10, 105
Jonathan Batt, 80, 106, 1000, 30, 209
D____ Hudson, 40, 40, 500, 50, 363
John McClure, -, -, -, 10, 108
Frederick Blackmier, 20, 100, 200, 75, 150
James Hudson, 5, 75, 300, 10, 212
Henry Wafle, 20, 60, 300, 8, 111
Henry Redhorse, 25, 95, 400, 12, 103
Fred Hansmire, 35, 17, 500, 10, 114
Sophia Lahmberg, 10, 60, 600, 10, 20
Rudolph Beniker, 160, 24, 400, 10, 50
Allen Magers, 13, 9, 30, -, 30
Granade Harrison, 8, 1, 80, -, 50
Casper Hatemer, 20, 20, 510, 8, 108
Everbeat Albus, 20, 109, 750, 30, 110
Rudolph Schowe, 14, 16, 240, 10, 50
W. K. Bryan, 6, 6, 60, -, 30
F. J. Nanber, 7, 3, 100, 5, 50
Fredrick Oberdolf, 40, 35, 700, 50, 100
Elijah Bryan, 20, 77, 300, 50, 358
Frances Lamme, 40, 172, 1000, 100, 300
Jesse Caton, 130, 312, 2650, 200, 3850
Fredrick Butler, 17, 63, 250, 10, 100
Elijah Thoroughman, 15, 25, 150, 20, 355
Arnold Brinemire, 14, 30, 150, 20, 23
Ferdinand Minor, 40, 40, 800, 75, 175
Samuel Pearl, 30, 50, 300, 7, 197
John Abshire, 20, 15, 200, 10, 177
Fredrick Shela, 20, 20, 200, 10, 180
Isaac Senbarger, 85, 155, 2500, 80, 340
William Menife, 55, 65, 500, 15, 290
J. M. Paulding, 35, 72, 500, -, 20

William Otterman, 28, 32, 200, 10, 174
Jarred Erwin, 60, 99, 700, 100, 310
John C. King, 150, 117, 1720, 100, 500
Elizabeth King, 20, 88, 265, 7, -
Henry Wyatt, 75, 101, 1500, 25, 327
Christopher Linsmith, 30, 50, 400, 20, 139
E. Surbie, 20, 22, 300, 15, 156
Fred Schuster, 20, 100, 500, 15, 185
Earnest Rottmann, 35, 45, 400, 12, 180
Rodolph Knaphead, 35, 50, 500, 10, 175
Minerva Jones, 50, 70, 600, 50, 200
William Dyer, 20, 280, 1500, 10, 110
Charles Wilson, 8, 92, 600, 70, 156
Benjamin Polber, 10, 180, 1000, -, 200
John Patton, 25, 55, 500, 80, 597
Casper Loarman, 12, -, 144, 10, 250
Isaiah Patton, -, -, -, 6, 85
Mary Stewart, 25, 40, 80, 10, 216
John Drahes, 15, 25, 150, 10, 135
Micager Merphy, 30, 50, 250, 12, 169
Rebecca Jones, 100, 60, 1500, 120, 1161
Thomas Garett, 34, 86, 500, 25, 247
John C. Dyer, 40, 150, 600, 10, 115
William Hanbine, 80, 160, 584, 125, 293
Jesse Lankford, 28, -, 300, 10, 183
Levi Garrett, 25, 160, 500, 6, 110
Henry Jones, 7, 153, 130, 10, 186
Henry D. Jones, 23, 167, 450, 35, 177
Willis Jones, 35, 165, 1000, 100, 256
Harrison Burgess, 25, 95, 400, 200, 200
William Burgess, 75, 65, 2000, 140, 320
John Bryan, 15, 25, 250, 5, 125
Francis Burgess, 10, 70, 300, 12, 55
Henry Knipmire, 25, 155, 800, 60, 175
Frederick Kings, 9, 31, 50, 5, 78
Henry Kernkamp, 20, 60, 200, 60, 84
Eaton Bobermire, 36, 125, 600, 45, 150
Henry Babermire, 20, 60, 250, 5, 99
Christian F_ader, 7, 73, 100, 5, 8
Henry Fisher, 10, 70, 400, 12, 90
Henry Rozoe, 50, 90, 640, 120, 250
Henry Boothe, 40, 120, 550, 100, 220
Frederick Busimire, 20, 20, 150, 10, 114
Carter Crouch, 12, 28, 50, 8, 140
John Crouch, 15, -, 150, 10, 53

Willis Crouch, 25, 25, 50, 8, 140
Josiah Mann, 6, 95, 500, 50, 210
Alford Laflano, 10, 90, 150, 60, 160
Edmin Robberts, 25, 15, 100, 10, 125
Milton Pratt, 100, 250, 1000, 60, 248
Jacob N. Oden, 250, 450, 1250, 50, 670
Thomas Wadkin, 60, 110, 800, 40, 252
James C. Pendleton, 65, 15, 500, 100, 333
Benjamin Hutcherson, 50, 150, 1200, 75, 288
P. B. Farrow, -, -, -, 30, 400
Frederick Bibermire, 28, 15, 200, 10, 65
Josiah Kamp, 40, 120, 450, 5, 232
Nicholis Mire, 16, -, 75, 10, 82
Strawther McGinnis, 60, 80, 1000, 35, 620
Elis Wilson, 25, 180, 400, 15, 107
Robert Allen, 100, 200, 2000, 100, 270
Isaah Baldridge, 35, 165, 1200, -, 235
Harman Kirkhoff, 15, 65, 300, 40, 37
John Hutcherson, 40, -, 1200, 15, 168
Henry Hager, 4, 36, 200, 30, 14
Josiah H. Walton, 65, 93, 4000, 120, 286
William L. Bilbey, 30, 170, 850, 25, 282
Frederick Messmaher, 20, 60, 400, 70, 162
Christian Babermire, 10, 30, 100, 3, 23
Henry Waldermire, 10, 110, 300, 50, 88
Washington Bedde, 13, 107, 600, -, 60
Silus Wadkins, 300, 250, 1700, 55, 419
William Cartwright, 6, 34, 200, -, 21
William Dever, 40, 100, 800, 12, 115
John Cahall, 14, 5, 100, 5, 63
Lewis McCann, 7, -, 40, 7, 90
Coonrad Masia, 25, 55, 200, 4, 170
George Northcutt, 35, 45, 300, 25, 232
John Arnold, 30, 46, 500, 80, 160
John Woodlan, 100, 220, 2000, 70, 410
Presley T. Oaks, 30, -, 150, 15, 180
Sandy Pratt, 50, 190, 1200, 60, 266
Charles Ellis, 65, 55, 600, 100, 338
John McConnell, 30, 90, 1000, 50, 235
William McConnell, 80, 120, 2000, 150, 320
H. F. Lions, 30, 90, 700, 75, 320

Thomas Powel, 70, 290, 1800, 10, 145
Henry Pallsgrove, 40, 40, 600, 100, 182
Abraham Kennedy, 42, 158, 1100, 75, 356
Daret Reynolds, 40, 220, 600, 10, 276
C. D. Edwards, 12, -, 100, 5, 137
Thomas Chambers, 55, 230, 1000, 75, 390
William Yearling, 37, -, 60, 60, 60
Brice Edwards, 140, 80, 2500, 130, 560
Isaac Davis, 25, 95, 700, 30, 136
Elizabeth Grey, 100, 360, 3000, 50, 270
Sidney Woods, 30, 130, 260, 700, 325
Willis Burford, 200, 100, 1000, 100, 360
Pleasant Kenedy, 15, -, 160, 30, 362
G. Watson, -, 100, 250, 6, 100
John Gibson, 42, 40, 300, 70, 465
Lewis Darnall, 120, 55, 200, 5, 27
James Calhoun, 27, 53, 300, 5, 75
W. M. Trout, 60, 220, 1000, 80, 250
Jane Collins, 200, 500, 3000, 100, 180
Joseph Ellis, 180, 220, 2000, 100, 340
Elizabeth Keber, 100, 120, 600, 100, 200
John Dyer, 60, 100, 700, 30, 188
George Dyer, 30, 120, 1000, 80, 255
John Schneider, 6, 30, 120, -, 100
W. T. Carter, 50, 150, 800, 50, 450
Edward Pleasant, 40, 380, 1500, 75, 285
J. R. Pleasant, 30, 145, 800, 40, 85
Delia Ashbern, 35, 45, 800, 100, 156
William White, 40, 200, 1000, 40, 70
James Pendleton, 60, 140, 500, 70, 300
F. W. Kingfield, 10, 30, 150, 10, 190
W. C. Rice, 20, -, 50, 10, 136
Robbert Pendleton, 50, 110, 600, 65, 223
Jane Arnold, 30, 50, 600, 5, 92
Malloy Arnold, 3, 80, 150, 20, 105
William Calwell, 30, 170, 800, 10, 85
George Messmaher, 30, 50, 225, 5, 106
Laurence Lankford, 30, 53, 400, 30, 195
John W. Adkins, 90, 45, 600, 30, 350
Frederick Althorp, 15, 35, 100, 10, 60
Phillip Rohmer, 12, -, 40, 8, 80
William Pool, 15, 25, 150, 10, 92
Thomas Colins, 40, 207, 800, 60, 155
Thomas Austin, 30, 180, 730, 100, 400

Fields Archer, 70, 270, 1500, 100, 280
Pressly Oakes, 100, 100, 2000, 100, 230
William Boid, 40, 110, 1000, 75, 310
Peter Imhof, 14, 26, 500, 75, 203
William Chrisman, 40, 80, 600, 15, 225
William Howell, 40, 120, 800, 100, 220
Thomas Archer, 100, 300, 4000, 75, 519
James Kenedy, 50, 530, 3480, 60, 554
Huldah Hubbard, 15, 51, 300, 5, 39
Richard Ross, 20, 40, 100, -, 60
Andrew Blatener, 16, 104, 700, 75, 174
Rudolph Boliger, 15, 35, 300, 20, 153
Beruch Cammison, 50, 30, 160, 60, 216
Jeramiah Troutt, 40, 80, 360, 70, 210
Joseph Pallsgrove, 35, 199, 800, 10, 138
Henry Winter, 30, 170, 400, 75, 210
Christopher Shelttering, 55, 83, 500, 30, 134
Harriet Middlekamp, 25, 55, 600, 5, 55
Henry Griece, 40, 80, 500, 70, 93
George W. Dyer, 70, 90, 2000, 120, 385
William Bryant, 25, 135, 700, 5, 95
Thomas Kent, 27, 93, 600, 6, 175
John Kent, 60, 115, 725, 45, 346
Peter Campbell, 20, 140, 480, 45, 180
Frederick Prior, 20, 100, 250, 7, 153
William Schoester, 20, 40, 100, 5, 111
John B. Shear, 45, 175, 600, 50, 146
Henry Determan, 8, 32, 100, 10, 23
Frederick Toterman, 10, -, 100, 10, 44
Frederick Devill, 12, 28, 142, 3, 30
August Kotting, 30, 90, 400, 75, 146
Newton Powell, 160, 289, 2000, 150, 979
Mary A. Kent, -, -, -, -, 215
Isaac Kent, 40, 100, 1000, 100, 330
Racem Dunham, 30, 70, 1800, 80, 290
Lewis Clinger, 30, 90, 300, 40, 113
Kittura Archer, 25, 30, 250, 10, 280
Herman Nessloger, 50, 190, 860, 50, 240
Fredrick Poleman, 30, 150, 540, 100, 173
Henry Stafford, 20, 100, 200, 50, 172
Cresser Knipmire, 25, 69, 150, 2, 80
Frederick Bunning, 18, 62, 450, 12, 133
Herman Forts, 20, 100, 480, 12, 35

Herman Knipmire, 30, 270, 300, 80, 99
Jarretfred Heneberg, 8, 85, 100, -, 21
John Heneberg, 23, 57, 320, 50, 121
John Thoroughman, 125, 500, 1200, 100, 540
Henry Pusser, 16, 23, 100, 50, 100
Harman Cranfer, 14, 26, 50, 100, 100
Jacob Leake, 20, 20, 300, 15, 113
Michael Ullmer, -, 40, 50, -, 60
Thomas Earnst, 200, 600, 3500, 10, 147
Richard Hill, 22, 58, 300, 80, 258
George Bomo (Boind), 12, -, 100, 75, 235
William Brook, 40, 80, 400, 75, 315
William Jones, 30, 130, 600, 10, 117
Robbert Black, 60, -, 210, 10, 181
Catharine Kouko, 50, 150, 1000, 20, 170
John Love, 7, -, 100, 10, 120
Walter Dix, 38, 120, 400, 100, 356
W. C. Wells, 60, 60, 500, 10, 175
Fountain Hancock, 2, 38, 100, 8, 63
Abraham Fines, 60, 160, 1500, 150, 818
Abraham Stonebarger, 30, -, 150, 10, 75
Simion Stonebarger, 16, 24, 120, 60, 89
Herod Hoss, 10, -, 25, -, 82
John Stonebarger, -, -, -, -, -
William Joiner, 20, -, 100, 10, 386
Charles Hoss, 100, 90, 1000, 40, 332
Bufferd Vincen, 35, 25, 250, 8, 214
William Mitchell, 50, -, 150, 80, 420
Henry Welch, 40, 120, 480, 10, 273
George Iton, -, 10, 50, 40, 182
William Aydlott, 35, 65, 300, 50, 222
Benjamin Joiner, 16, 84, 500, 8, 117
John Ingrum, 30, 90, 480, 70, 245
John Sherman, 45, 75, 325, 100, 441
William Oden, 30, 50, 600, 5, 272
Joseph Pennington, 20, 20, 150, 75, 182
S. _. Owings, 75, 125, 1000, 75, 540
Henry Lamore, 10, 80, 100, 8, 151
Levi Fines, 40, 160, 600, 100, 503
Christian Warman, 80, 355, 1200, 200, 398
Jane Thornhill, 30, 175, 1200, 60, 226
Frederick Bishop, 30, 90, 800, 75, 401

Benjamin Homesbey, 30, 50, 400, 10, 458
Jefferson Homesbey, 35, 55, 400, 10, 155
Sitha Baxter, 25, 55, 200, 8, 55
Samuel Ivins, 25, 157, 300, 4, 83
James Cravin, 40, 172, 1000, 30, 125
Thomas Oden, 12, 35, 100, -, 62
Richard Choate, 22, -, 200, 10, 65
Daniel Browning, 10, 110, 150, 50, 136
Jackson Young, 25, -, 350, 10, 350
Thomas Oden, 60, 180, 1000, 100, 165
Herbert Graham, 15, 80, 300, 8, 80
L. C. D. Hattchet, 70, 130, 1100, 40, 50
George Chappel, 80, 250, 700, 100, 462
Garret Baxter, 20, 100, 600, 20, 132
Robbert Shelton, 20, 60, 250, 30, 103
James Shelton, 28, 52, 300, 50, 261
Nathaniel Morris, 7, 33, 100, 7, 65
Fielding Black, 12, 40, 50, 50, 235
William Moore, 40, 57, 800, 100, 559
Able Howard, 20, 20, 200, 20, 108
Harman Wesendolf, 20, 100, 600, 20, 90
Benoni McClure, 60, 265, 1500, 100, 590
Rachel Dorithy, 12, 108, 300, 8, 75
Ephram Riddle, 110, 390, 2500, 160, 588
Thomas Schoolye, 15, 288, 500, -, 110
Christian Confus, 10, 30, 75, 8, 18
Jesse Colman, 70, 170, 800, 100, 336
Henry C. Writte, 175, 528, 8000, 200, 750
Henry Rember, 18, 102, 480, 10, 224
John Lick, 8, 37, 125, 25, 10
Thomas Nevis, 20, 30, 300, 20, 122
Windle Furber, 11, 120, 200, 40, 120
Preston Cartwright, 40, 240, 1000, 100, 147
James McFaden, 75, 525, 3000, 300, 785
Harman Gerdamon, 25, 55, 400, 50, 87
Jobe Price, 70, 210, 1000, 75, 875
Drura Mashburn, 15, 25, 100, 30, 151
James Smith, 6, -, 10, 10, 100
Charles Shermire, -, -, -, 5, 125

Andrew Wood, 100, 280, 2000, 75, 414
Write Smith, 100, 260, 2000, 200, 1535
Abraham Davison, 10, -, 15, 10, 65
Archibald Weeks, 60, -, 180, 30, 336
Allen Duckworth, 14, -, 40, 4, 94
James Duckworth, 60, 20, 600, 100, 293
Lewis Duckworth, 23, -, 60, 10, 104
Thomas Holland, 150, 1050, 6000, 60, 903
Isah Chappel, 200, 220, 3000, 130, 1280
Joshua Harden, 20, 60, 200, 40, 80
Thomas Haden, 19, 101, 650, 25, 218
William Harden, 6, 34, 100, 10, 60
Daniel Harden, 35, 30, 300, 75, 520
William Ellis, 10, -, 20, 20, 152
Thomas Potter, -, -, -, 20, 55
Abraham Smeathen, 10, 32, 125, 14, 98
John Carver, 30, 130, 600, 5, 81
Stephen Smith, 130, 110, 500, 125, 423
Sarah Ward, -, -, -, -, 206
Abraham Davison, 100, 220, 2000, 150, 495
Johnathan Davis, 25, 20, 200, 30, 198
Irvine Pitman, 150, 450, 300, 100, 459
Susan Davis, 60, 100, 600, -, 129
Clark Davis, 8, 32, 50, 100, 720
William Howard, 30, 50, 300, 15, 167
Alexander Logan, 100, 800, 2000, 175, 731
Enoch Spry, 25, 95, 500, 40, 240
Madison Jones, 40, 160, 600, 75, 453
Hugh Skinner, 40, 160, 1000, 20, 144
James Stewart, 30, 130, 600, 325, 142
Charles Carl, 12, 108, 200, 8, 61
William Cameron, 20, 20, 120, 15, 106
Mary Woodrough, 35, 90, 500, 100, 230
Jane Talbot, 70, 148, 2000, 100, 126
Thomas Talbot, 150, 300, 6000, 160, 1840
Robbert H. Patten, 11, 40, 248, 12, 195
Jacob Coil, 130, 170, 1500, 100, 460
Herman Otto, 22, 73, 700, 10, 140
Frederick Withoust, 35, 65, 1000, 40, 80
Casper H. Johnson, 20, 60, 500, 5, 150
Everheart Starkey, 40, 120, 800, 10, 134
John Brinker, 20, 100, 500, 3, 55

James F. Sharp, 70, 203, 2000, 100, 393
Henry Odelout, 50, 30, 1000, 30, 105
Charles Speckman, 10, 40, 100, 5, 55
Henry Hackman, 10, 99, 300, 15, 62
Rudolph Kenber, 40, -, 700, 48, 204
Henry Boriger, 30, 120, 400, 10, 70
Dedrick Lefholtz, 20, 8, 100, 25, 100
Henry Oberhellums, 25, 95, 450, 10, 165
Earnest Windmire, 15, 47, 300, 10, 78
Henry Koock, 15, 25, 100, 10, 74
John Z. Kent, 70, 200, 1200, 50, 270
Lewis Scelka(Sulka), 6, 10, 50, 3, 64
Earnst Closemire, 35, 45, 100, 10, 96
Earnest Loaraaison, 35, 45, 100, 10, 96
Frederick Helsker, 30, 110, 550, 15, 165
Fredrick Roge, 9, 51, 140, 10, 66
George McWilliams, 100, 530, 3000, 225, 655
John Chamberlin, 30, 120, 500, 60, 400
Stanton Brown, 170, 290, 6600, 500, 755
G. A. Anderson, 70, 380, 3000, 100, 626
Milfred Clyce, 70, 90, 1600, 75, 438
John Wyatt, 80, 296, 1200, 100, 455
John Dunham, 30, -, 300, 15, 286
William Clices, 100, 400, 1500, 100, 677
Emily Foust, 35, 95, 500, 70, 266
William Toller, 40, 75, 500, 80, 290
Luther Rides, 70, 170, 1300, 10, 295
Cinthie Floid, 25, 30, 200, 10, 195
Z. A. Carter, 25, 75, 450, 25, 216
James Shobe, 150, 150, 3500, 450, 1070
George G. Wright, 120, 680, 8000, 500, 1027
William I. Tolbot, 240, 560, 6000, 5000, 1057
John Wraber, 15, 35, 50, 10, 70
James B. Patten, -, -, -, 14, 200
Allonzo Rice, 75, 45, 500, 150, 360
Robert Peltzer, 70, -, 420, 50, 440
Heil Tolbot, 80, 40, 1000, 150, 1222
Theodook Brites, 80, 220, 2000, 200, 555
Thomas Gant, 20, 30, 200, 20, 285
Hester Owings, 160, 273, 1000, 50, 325

David Owings, 80, 20, 1000, 50, 380
Earnest Bishop, 34, 46, 550, 50, 137
Milton Friendly, 40, 105, 1100, 20, 313
Henry Brice, 70, 175, 1000, 75, 195
Father Wamire, 12, 48, 150, 15, 70
George Creger, 15, 85, 150, 10, 55
Fredrick Meyer, 20, 20, 250, 50, 186
Henry Schrader, 23, 40, 300, 40, 140
John Wyatt, 50, 340, 1500, -, -
Earnest Shovengird, 55, 45, 300, 70, 396
H. Anderson, 80, 60, 1500, 50, 315
Rebecca Howard, 75, 167, 1000, 45, 311
Henry Logamore, 24, 16, 150, 10, 107
Frederick Shovengird, 30, 50, 240, 75,
310
James Howard, 50, 70, 750, 80, 484
William Schrear, 25, 55, 120, 20, 95
Henry Doathage, 20, 60, 120, 15, 70
Abrahart Rebter, 15, 35, 80, 10, 57
Henry Jasper, 15, 35, 100, 10, 80
Fredrick Romaive, 15, 35, 100, 10, 185
Christian Beacer, 20, 40, 200, 75, 88
Frederick Graiswold, 195, 165, 2550,
200, 555
William Haze, 25, 37, 200, 30, 210
Charles F. Coonce, 70, 210, 3000, 100,
300
Charles S. Coonce, 95, 235, 4000, 200,
740
Nathaniel Heart, 50, 30, 280, 25, 318
Christopher Shellhorn, 50, -, 200, 25,
180
Berton Callahan, 80, 100, 2000, 120,
430
Samuel Fryday, -, -, -, -, -
William Steniker, 40, 60, 200, 80, 161
John Welting, 30, 50, 350, 10, 132
Herman Wamire, 20, -, 60, 5, 140
Frederick Steinkamp, 18, 32, 200, 30, 78
Henry Schowy, 24, 136, 480, 10, 107
Henry Schorman, 8, 72, 125, -, 60
Garret Hackman, 35, 85, 600, 25, 81
Charles Wamire, 20, 60, 150, 30, 120
Fredrick Sloman, 30, 70, 350, 70, 100
William Stolte, 20, 60, 150, 20, 186
Henry Sfteshar, 16, 34, 200, 15, 125

Henry Beaburm, 18, 30, 200, 12, 106
Henry Colmer, 20, 20, 150, 10, 65
John Curtermire, 14, 26, 130, 10, 59
William Backmare, 20, 20, 160, 10, 90
Herman Besker, 22, 20, 100, 25, 112
Augustis Berroth, 10, 78, 400, 20, 165
Lewis Enesman, 25, 342, 1259, 299, 616
Z. Andes L. Enesman agt, 10, 290, 850,
-, -
Fredrick Munch, 85, 248, 1000, 100, 240
George Munch, 45, 140, 800, 300, 236
Herman Berges, 20, 40, 150, -, 95
William Peatamire, 8, 30, 100, 20, 112
Henry Ishemane, 30, 50, 90, 15, 139
Herod Fowlkerdink, 20, 53, 100, 10, 100
Herman Dickhouse, 43, 80, 450, 160,
120
Elizabeth Stogsdill, 42, 125, 420, 50,
471
Andrew Marshall, 34, 170, 700, 20, 120
John Branham, 8, -, 80, -, 30
B. Rosner, 3, -, 50, -, 28
Fredrick Schlaff, 9, -, 90, -, 47
J. F. Divbert, ½, -, 60, -, 35
Georg Schontz, 30, 37, 200, 60, 96
Helman Stra, 20, 120, 350, 10, 46
Ann Simon, 50, 160, 800, 75, 230
Henry Smedker, 40, 40, 200, 52, 137
George Wigerkarth, 35, 35, 150, 60, 95
Thomas Kranser, 30, 50, 200, 60, 118
William T. Barry, 55, 500, 1800, 16, 350
Frederick Massey, -, -, -, 7, 50
Adolph Kunzel, 75, 200, 3000, 50, 275
Edward Kunzel, 50, 120, 900, 50, 297
William Williams, 40, -, 81, 10, 89
James H. James, 40, 260, 1000, 60, 115
P. L. Goler, 10, -, 100, 6, 51
Charles Smith, 32, 10, 320, 15, 124
Martin Cronk, 14, -, 140, -, 47
Jesse Louse, 14, 5, 150, 8, 116
Haden Boone, 40, 40, 150, 140, 522
Camel Marshall, 50, 150, 1000, 75, 265
Fredrick Lepp, 18, 5, 110, 40, 115
William Hancock, 100, 1500, 5720, 80,
1008
Ernst Westmire, 12, 6, 144, 5, 30

Absalom Hays, 75, 85, 1000, 50, 356   J. P. McWilliams, 15, 68, 250, 15, 194

Washington County, Missouri
1850 Agricultural Census

Washington County 1850 Agricultural Census was filmed by the Central Microfilm Service Corp of St. Louis, Missouri, for the Missouri State Historical Society. There are 46 columns of information on the 1850 agricultural census. I have chosen to transcribe six of those columns. The columns are:

1. Name
2. Acres of Land Improved
3. Acres of Land Unimproved
4. Cash Value of the Farm
5. Value of Farm Implements and Machinery
13. Value of Livestock

A. L. Boyer, 10, -, 100, 8, 150
Jno. Shone, 50, 63, 500, 5, 100
Jno. Shone, 50, 52, 500, 5, 150
William Goff, 100, 500, 5000, 20, 300
William Goff, -, -, -, -, 30
Wm. D. Christopher, 40, 300, 500, 30, 300
Thomas Boyer, 20, 80, 150, 7, 100
Theophilus Boyer, 22, 140, 600, 20, 250
Thomas Smith, 25, -, 100, 5, 150
Jno. B. Boyer, 40, 160, 400, 20, 300
Micajah Cole, 60, 100, 400, 15, 250
Thomas Bequette, 12, 97, 150, 10, 75
Peter Atchison, 8, -, -, 7, 75
Jno. Valley, 15, 100, 100, -, 20
Joseph Bequette, 60, 450, 500, 15, 300
A. D. Farron, 20, 140, 300, 6, 150
Lisbon Glone, 15, -, 1000, 15, 30
Amos Minks, 25, 55, 200, 5, 250
Charles Yates, 60, 180, 600, 25, 350
Allen Engledon, 30, 190, 800, 10, 20
Allen Engledon, -, -, -, -, 200
John B. Hague, 35, 280, 800, 25, 200
Eugene Obuchon, 80, 160, 800, 25, 400
James Owens, 100, 100, 1000, 20, 400
Ellen Hayes, 60, 100, 600, 20, 200
Samuel Cole, 75, 220, 600, -, 100
Isaac Obuchon, 8, 30, 100, 8, 200
Ferrace Degonier, -, -, -, -, -

Samuel Cummings, 50, 50, 1800, 25, 250
Richd. Matehews, 35, 45, 500, 20, 800
Peter Potelle, 45, 55, 500, 120, 200
Michael Boyer, 15, 65, 200, 8, 50
Louis Boyer, 30, 80, 400, 10, 150
Antoine C. Boyer, 14, 26, 200, 10, 260
Antoine C. Boyer, -, -, -, -, 46
Francis Polette(Potelle), 40, 40, 800, 115, 400
John B. Obuchon, 30, 50, 50, 10, 150
Wm. Smith, 15, 65, 300, 10, 180
Thos. Cummings, 18, -, 200, 20, 50
Geo. Nience, 30, -, 250, 10, 150
Jeremiah Blackwell, 100, 160, 2500, 150, 1500
William Blackwell, 40, 60, 500, 115, 200
John Whaley, 20, -, -, 10, 200
Nathan Pinson, 80, 120, 800, 20, 300
Malachi Maddin, 40, 360, 1200, -, 200
John Cork (Cook), 17, -, -, 5, 250
James Moon, 60, -, -, 5, 100
Garrett Long, -, -, -, 10, 150
Elijah Warden, 25, 115, -, 10, 60
Hersuly Boyer, 40, 40, 500, 15, 100
Elizabeth Stephens, 20, 80, 200, 115, 400
James Mason, 30, -, 300, 10, 90

Ann McClanahan, 200, 700, 4000, 50, 600
Robt. Lattimar, 50, -, 500, 60, 140
Lewis J. Boyer, 18, 22, 200, 5, 50
John B. Reando, 30, 28, 200, 10, 100
John B. Reando, -, -, -, -, 200
John Settle, 100, 228, 2000, 150, 800
Wm. M. Burris, 30, 50, 400, 25, 250
John Hinch, 18, 25, 200, 10, 260
B. Mannwaring, -, -, -, -, 45
Ferd. Kennett, 200, 1200, 10000, 1000, 700
John C. Scott, 50, 83, 500, 20, 260
Mary Scott, 70, 70, 1000, 10, 175
Mary Scott, -, -, -, -, -
Mary Scott, -, -, -, -, 150
Francis Nilhmar, 24, 66, 500, 10, 250
George Garrett, 30, -, -, 15, 100
George Garrett, -, -, -, -, -
William Derickson, -, -, -, -, 60
William Derickson, -, -, -, -, -
Nicholas Degonier, -, -, -, -, 100
Joseph Govere, 20, -, -, 5, 100
Smith Jackson, 30, 43, 300, 5, 300
Henry Rongey(Nongey), 40, 80, 700, 15, 120
R. M. Blackwell, 30, 137, 500, -, 60
D. E. Perryman, 15, 148, 500, 60, 210
Johnson Warden, 45, 130, 500, 50, 275
O. E. McIlvanne, 150, 752, 3000, 200, 800
John Gratick, 80, 1800, -, 300, 450
Phillip Cole, 150, 900, 4000, 60, 300
Alexander Polette, 30, 50, 600, 15, 250
Aaron Pinson, 80, 160, 1500, 30, 750
Peter W. Murphy, 45, 280, 1000, 40, 250
Augustus Hawkins, 50, 90, 600, 60, 300
James H. Hawkins, 40, 50, 200, 50, 180
George Cain, 60, 100, 1000, 100, 1000
James _. Wilkerson, 60, 140, 500, 20, 300
Aquilla Cole, 125, 201, 1000, 50, 650
Hyram Smith, 70, 90, 800, 120, 400
John Oluff, -, -, -, -, 80
George Marler, 12, -, 120, 3, 40

Andrew White, 40, -, 200, 25, 275
Joel Marler, -, -, -, 5, 100
Cavender Marler, 20, -, -, 20, 150
Levi Marler, 50, 45, 200, 30, 250
Thomas Cole, 40, 80, 650, 100, 250
David Bartley, 9, -, -, 20, 60
William Copelin, 10, -, -, 25, 130
John Marler, 30, -, 150, 20, 480
Isaac S. Cole, 45, 35, 200, 5, 60
John Jennings, 75, 335, 800, 10, 60
William Garrett, -, -, -, -, 100
Silas Hartsdale, 16, 64, 230, 10, 200
Ingabo Houk, 30, 50, 300, 10, 100
John Paul, 20, 70, 500, 60, 125
Charles Boyer, 40, 40, 200, 30, 200
Edmond Boyer, 16, -, -, 30, 200
Israel Boyer, 8, -, -, 30, 40
Marshall Boyer, -, -, -, 10, 100
Antoine Villemar, 15, -, -, 30, 125
E. Lamarque, 100, 115, -, 84, 500
L. W. Harris, 20, 450, 1000, 60, 300
Mary C. Reed, -, -, -, -, 10
Francis Portell, 8, 50, 100, 30, 250
John Akison, -, -, -, -, -
Joseph Coleman, -, -, -, -, -
Levi Lillson (Tillson), 12, -, -, 7, 200
Stephen Boyer, -, -, -, -, 60
Saml. C. White, 125, 400, 5000, 200, 350
Saml. C. White, -, -, -, -, -
Joseph Portell, 30, 45, 250 40, 180
John Portelle, 40, 65, 500, 30, 150
Mary Sullivan, Rented land
E. S. Clardy, -, 2 ½, -, -, 250
John Pagey, -, -, -, -, 50
Vestal Burrisaw -, 35, 100, -, 30
John Cotter, -, -, -, -, -
John Casey, 110, 294, 5000, 175, 700
Thomas C. Murphy, 30, 120, 1500, 20, 200
William Long, 85, 400, 2500, 140, 480
George Casey, 70, 120, 600, 20, 300
William Sulike, Rented, land, -, -, 20
Batist Degornia, -, -, -, -, -
Derville Boyer, -, -, -, -, 150

Sarah Rambo, 250, 400, 4000, 100, 800
James Breckinridge, 70, 300, 2000, 100, 400
Norton Glover, -, 80, 100, 10, 150
John Trimble, 40, 120, 600, 30, 175
J. H. McIlvane, 300, 500, 5000, 250, 1250
James Lancaster, 400, 75, 600, 100, 340
D. H. Scott, 12, 148, 1000, 10, 120
Mason Cultan, 35, 5, 300, 20, 150
James Catlette, 120, 90, 1000, 45, 410
Francis T. O'Buchon, 50, 100, 300, 100, 400
Marshall Rangy, 30, 100, 400, 50, 224
Joseph Miller, -, -, -, -, 75
John Dean, -, -, -, -, 60
Joshua Cole, 65, 230, 1500, 100, 365
Conrad Norewine, 43, 120, 600, 80, 350
Jackson House, -, -, -, 6, 100
Samuel Long, 80, 240, 1000, 100, 600
James Craig, 20, -, 100, 80, 200
John House, 45, 1115, 500 70, 250
Adam House Jr., 60, 100, 800, 100, 320
Willis Fight, 100, 140, 1000, 100, 1500
William Vandiver, 30, 50, 200, 10, 100
William Dinwiddy, 35, -, -, 100, 275
James Dinwiddie, -, -, -, -, 75
Alfred Long, 40, 80, 500, 15, 150
Brumnfield Long, 30, 130, 400, -, -
Robert McIvaney, -, -, -, -, -
Franklin Deguirmen, 20, 140, -, 6, 100
Addison Dearing, 30, -, -, 10, 180
Charles M. Mannwaring, 20, 20, 200, 3, 135
Paschal Duclos, 30, 12, 500, 8, 50
Louis Degornia, 20, -, -, 30, 100
Simon Roderick, -, -, -, -, 75
John Derrickson, -, -, -, -, -
John Hurd, -, -, -, -, 100
G. W. Higginbotham, 200, 470, 3000, 200, 9000
Antoine Politte, -, -, -, 10, 50
Samuel Van Reed, -, -, -, -, 10
Briggs Munsell, 18, 22, 200, 25, 350
Granville Patton, 18, 62, 500, 5, 100
Alley Roberts, 30, 80, 500, 40, 325

Archibald Cheatham, 50, 110, 800, 100, 375
William Hirst, 35, 85, 1000, 25, 300
Philip Cummings, -, -, -, -, 150
Eliza Johnson, 40, 6, 300, 40, 300
Francis Robar, -, -, -, 10, 100
Adelaide Bequette, 30, 100, 2000, 50, 310
Eli Bequette, -, -, -, -, 50
Austin Manin (Marion), -, -, -, -, 100
Edmond Bequette, -, -, -, 30, 50
Benjamin Gray, 40, 340, 1500, 200, 650
Frank Bunshaw, -, -, -, 10, 100
Raphael Music, 35, 100, 300, 40, 250
Christian Patt, -, -, -, -, 50
Isaac Moon, -, -, -, -, 50
Jonas Yates, -, -, -, -, -
William S. Murphy, 40, 240, 500, 200, 300
William Scott, -, -, -, -, 30
Celele Duclos, -, -, -, -, 100
Luke Osen, -, -, -, -, 75
Berlime Colves, -, -, -, -, 60
Jeffrey Racine, 12, 40, 200, 40, 250
Louis L. Boyer, 40, 80, 200, 75, 250
Adrian Coleman, 12, 48, 200, 30, 180
Isaac Coleman, -, -, -, 30, 160
Joseph Coleman Sr., 15, -, -, 30, 100
Joseph Coleman Jr., -, -, -, -, 20
Jeremiah Oliver, 16, 26, 250, 15, 50
Louis Boyer, 15, 25, 200, 30, 100
Paul Coleman, -, -, -, -, -
Joseph P. Boyer, 30, 370, 1000, 30, 200
Francis Burrisaw, -, -, -, -, 90
Peter Burrisaw, 10, -, -, 10, 100
John Duclos, 40, 60, 250, 10, -
Mary T. Villemar, -, -, -, -, 20
Elijah Puckett, 6, 44, 200, -, 45
Battist Coleman, -, -, -, -, 20
Robt. Puckett, 5, -, 100, -, 75
A. L. Cole, 5, 95, 250, 10, 75
Bridget Coleman, 18, 32, 200, 10, 90
Paul Robar, -, -, -, 5, 10
Francis Coleman, 30, 34, 300, 30, 150
Louis C. Boyer, 15, 315, 1500, 20, 200
M. C. Jennings, 50, 150, 800, -, 15

Michael Cann, 36, 20, 300, 150, 285
Paul Boyer, 45, 15, 200, 30, 120
Frank Duclos, 15, -, 150, 10, 225
Charles Duclos, -, -, -, -, 50
Michael Flynn, 40, -, -, -, 250
Lawrence Flynn, 40, 120, 800, 60, 200
Francis O'Farrell, 30, 50, 250, 40, 150
Daniel Goldin, 25, -, 300, 15, 75
Bryan O'Ferrill, 30, 50, 400, 40, -
George Creswell, 35, 45, 1000, 40, 225
Philip Jackson, 20, 60, 250, 75, 300
Elijah Hulsey, 21, -, 250, 15, 200
George Creswell, 130, 2000, 12000, 300, 1000
Job Day, -, -, -, -, 75
Samuel White, -, -, -, -, -
John Moyers, -, -, -, -, 40
Saml. Silvers, 30, 70, 300, 100, 250
Albert Stacey, 25, -, 150, 15, 100
Richard Wilkson, -, -, -, 10, 200
Plesant Johnson, -, -, -, 5, 50
John D. Shooly, 15, 65, 200, 10, 25
L. B. Lumpkin, -, -, -, -, -
Thomas Flynn,-, -, -, -, 100
Daniel Ranson, 12, -, -, -, 70
Benjamin Downey, -, -, -, -, 70
Thos. R. Harris, 60, 135, 500, 40, 270
Jane Peery, -, 30, 500, 75, -
Jane A. Thompson, -, -, -, -, -
David Warner, 50, -, 180, 50, 175
Solomon J. Bull, -, -, -, -, 90
Peter Shaver, 15, -, 150, 10, 75
Rhoda Hatton, -, -, -, -, 30
G. W. Williams, 10, -, -, -, 125
Milton Bell, 24, 136, 400, 10, 200
Charles Moory, 40, -, 200, 35, 260
George Cunningham, -, -, -, -, 75
John M. Martin, -, -, -, 40, 40
E. S. Ruggles, 100, 300, -, 200, 300
David Hanger, 50, 59, 700, 200, 325
George Goodyhoontz, 100, 136, 3500, 30, 225
Letitia Goodyhoontz, 35, -, 400, -, 160
Moshiville Long, -, -, -, -, 50
Robt. F. Rutledge, 200, 700, 6000, 200, 600

Alexander C. Relfe, 150, 285, 2600, 400, 1714
Smith G. Breckenridge, 40, 60, 600 100, 300
William Maxwell, 40, 65, 500, 75, 250
Josiah Mullins, 30, 140, 500, 60, 200
Timothy Phelps, 70, 1500, 1500, 10, 220
James Sloane, 90, 180, 1500, 75, 340
Joseph Lutze, -, -, -, -, 20
Geo. D. Sloan, -, -, -, 70, 175
Thomas Sloan, 70, 217, 2250, 50, 260
Jno. H. Neely, 75, 780, 1800, 80, 315
George D. Strother, 13, 43, 150, 15, 130
Emelia Bridge, 20, 135, 500, -, 40
Masters Martin, -, -, -, -, 25
Barney Richardson, -, -, -, -, 100
Malachi Eaton, 25, -, 200, 40, 215
Moses Thomas, 80, 120, 1500, 100, 400
Agnes Hudspeth, -, -, -, 10,180
Francis Strange, -, -, -, -, 50
James Strother, 55, 48, 500, 30, 190
Hannah Palmer, 20, 80, 700, 15, 115
David B. Napier, -, -, -, -, 20
Nathaniel Highley, 60, -, 600, 15, 360
George Jamison, 250, 750, 4000, 100, 400
Moses Edmunds, 16, 165, 700, 15, 160
John Thompson, -, -, -, -, 30
Edward Thomas, 100, 100, 1000, 100, 350
Reuben Thomas, 75, 325, 2000, 100, 300
Elizabeth Fitzpatrick, 65, 95, 775, 15, 200
Elisha Kirkpatrick, 15, 30, 200, 15, 85
Richard Terrie, 30, 140, 1000, 15, 145
Preston M. Robinson, 65, 28, 400, 15, 100
Samuel A. Raby_som, 100, 414, 2000, 150, 450
Hannah Kirkpatrick, 60, 49, 500, 20, 400
George N. Cook, -, -, -, -, 120
John Huff, -, -, -, -, 20
Orville McCabe, -, -, -, -, 25
Elizabeth Sweany, -, -, -, -, 110
John V. Logan, 40, 125, 1500, 100, 400

John Rice, -, -, -, -, 100
Pote Buford, 50, 300, 1500, 100, 800
Robert Sammonds, -, -, -, -, 100
William G. Wiatt, 50, 90, 750, 100, 350
Joseph L. Stephens, 30, 40, 300, 100, 150
Larkin McLany,-, -, -, -, 120
James McLany, 35, -, 350, 15, 120
James Highly, -, -, -, -, 40
William Pearce, 60, 1, 1, 100, 450
Henry Eidson, 50, 140, 1000, 100, 250
Samuel Cox, 40, 440, 1800, 100, 300
Wm. R. Moyers, 60, 150, 1000, 20, 140
Joseph C. Moyers, 66, 270, 1800, 15, 220
Jacob Moyers, -, -, -, -, 200
Alexandre Sloan, 30, -, 200, 15, 160
Haristen Russle, 150, 480, 400, 150, 550
Wm. B. Lucas, 60, 40, 1000, 120, 400
Michael Vinyard, 20, 246, 1000, 100, 130
Robert Worniack, 50, -, -, 20, 150
Margaret Hughs, 40, 123, 700, 15, 100
William Cole, 70, 90, 1800, 150, 325
Mary Hopkins, -, -, -, -, -
Samuel Imboden, 60, 180, 1200, 150, 450
Richard Helon, -, -, -, 10, 90
William Sutton, 60, 140, 800, 20, 220
John Mondy, -, -, -, -, 40
William Randall, 40, 44, 400, 100, 250
Joel _. Randall, -, -, -, -, 80
Thos. D. Alexander, 100, 100, 2000, 150, 350
Washington Howard, -, -, -, 10, 75
Evans Brewington, 40, -, 300, 15, 165
Elizabeth Singleton, -, -, -, 10, 60
John Witt, -, -, -, 160, 600
Daniel Cain, -, -, -, -, 120
Silas Merritt, -, -, -, -, 160
W. A. Moodey, 15, 25, 500, 100, 150
M. J. Howard, 100, 180, 3000, 200, 916
Jno. E. Alexander, 75, 125, 1000, 125, 420
Robt. W. Underwood, -, -, -, -, 75

Jas. Underwood, 25, 55, 400, 100, 275
David W. Proffett, -, -, -, -, 275
Ranson Carter, 10, -, -, 10, 70
Phebe Lyons, -, -, -, 50, 80
Abraham Dean, -, -, -, -, 100
Martha Trammel, -, 30, 100, -, 10
William Hughes, 30, 57, 45, 55, 275
Jno. Horton, 30, 10, 150, 50, 335
Lucy Logan, 45, 38, 400, 100, 280
Sarah W. Stephens, 40, 240, 500, 15, 200
Catherine Shelton, 60, 150, 1200, 120, 400
Jonas Henderson, 100, 190, 2000, 130, 620
A. J. Barice, -, -, -, -, 100
Tents Wells, 40, 120, 600, 10, 220
John Matthews, 100, 300, 2500, 100, 440
Elizabeth Richardson, 60, 160, 600, 100, 360
William Campbell, 30, 10, 400, 100, 200
James Satterfield, -, -, -, -, 125
John Gregg, 60, 140, 500, 15, 150
Stephen Brickstone, 25, 95, 400, 15, 140
Elisha Pool, -, -, -, -, 50
Jesse Hartgrove, 16, -, 200, 10, 120
Moses Stark, -, -, -, 10, 100
Daniel Stark, -, -, -, 5, 30
James Stark, -, -, -, 5, 100
Eli Stark, -, -, -, 5, 90
Abraham Sweaden, -, -, -, 5, 160
Josiah Wheat, 50, 30, 400, 150, 400
Mark Huges, 30, 50, 300, 10, 185
John Jamison, 60, 146, 1000, 100, 210
John Robinson, 35, 100, 350, 10, 100
James C. Johnson, 40, 200, 1000, 100, -
Maharta Gregory, 15, -, -, 10, 140
Luswick Landunsky, -, -, -, -, -
James Keith, 16, 24, 150, 10, 75
Robert Sutton, 60, 140, 1000, 100, 300
James Moor, 50, 150, 1200, 100, 300
C. F. Bonny, 40, 210, 2000, 100, 280
Emiline Roggers, 50, 146, 1000, -, 125
M. F. Williams, 60, 260, 1500, 100, 360

N. _. Buckston, 50, 110, 1000, 10, 70
Thomas C. Williams, -, -, -, -, 80
Isaac Cak(Cox), -, -, -, -, -
D. T. Green, 150, 200, 10000, 200, 700
Allen Johnson, 26, -, -, 10, 120
Frederick Woodford, -, -, -, 100, 80
William Woods, 100, 220, 2500, 100, 350
James S. Evans, 150, 500, 4000, 300, 700
James F. Davidson, 30, 610, 2000, 15, 150
Barney Brewington, -, -, -, 10, 75
James Thompson, 16, 39, 200, 10, 175
John Terril, 70, 160, 1000, 75, 275
John Imboden, 100, 75, 1000, 100, 400
William Westover, -, -, -, 10, 70
A. Trollinger, -, -, -, -, 100
John Galliher, 30, -, 200, 10, 175
Wm. Westerman, 15, -, 200, 10, 120
A. Robinson, 75, 225, 2000, 150, 325
James Aldridge, 65, -, 400, 30, 215
William Moody, 50, -, 300, 100, 230
A. Goforth, -, -, -, -, 75
John H. Black, 32, -, -, 15, 300
William Aldridge, 70, 145, 1000, 150, 450
Jackson Stewart, 9, 31, 150, 15, 60
Leer Ramsey, 30, -, 200, 20, 140
Sam W. Prior, 20, 140, 300, 15, -
Arch. Tenison, 40, -, 500, 150, 50
A. Goforth, 60, 100, 800, 50, 330
A. Goforth, -, -, -, -, -
Solomon Tenison, 45, 35, 600, 100, 340
John L. Ramsey, 10, -, -, 8, 95
A. Henderson, -, -, -, -, 40
John Tenison, 20, -, 200, 15, 215
John C. Ramsey, 30, 50, 500, 60, 340
James Tudder, -, -, -, -, 120
Alexander Ramsey, 40, 120, 400, 15, 60
Thomas Brock, 90, 420, 2200, 100, 850
James Ramsey, 20, 20, 200, 100, 150
James Robinson, 50, 150, 1500, 100, 450
Moses Morris, 60, 580, 3000, 125, 230
John McMurtry, 50, 50, 500, 150, 350

James McMurtry, 45, 55, 500, 50, 130
John Thomas, 50, 80, 800, 100, 400
William Chadwell, 15, 100, 400, 15, 200
Wilny West, 9, 71, 300, -, 60
Wilson Crawford, 22, 56, 500, 15, 20
Gabriel Pruett, 60, 20, 1000, 100, 300
Elijah Gragg, 70, 250, 3000, 15, 350
Moses Brooks, 8, 32, 100, 5, 150
C. F. Exums, 40, 40, 600, 100, 400
Peter Hughs, 10 70, 200, 15, -
Pleasant McDonald, 20, 60, 600, 15, 180
Edward F. Smith, 80, 320, 3000, 100, 450
Thomas Wright, -, -, -, 15, 90
William Vinyard, 20, 60, 400, 100, 150
Joseph Stephens, -, -, -, 15, 120
Wm. Vinyard, 80, 20, 800, 120, 400
John Bryan, 20, 80, 600, 60, 250
Elisha Tudder, 50, 590, 300, 100, 150
Wm. Carson, 300, 370, 8000, 200, 980
Nathaniel Maxwell, 40, 200, 1000, 60, 300
Hester Carson, -, -, -, -, -
Wm. J. Carson, -, -, -, -, -
Moses Berry, 20, 90, 400, 15, -
Christopher Woods, 40, 80, 600, 60, 345
Thomas Carson, 30, 55, 500, 15, 185
Isaac Berming, 70, 200, 1800, 150, 360
David M. Carson, 40, 40, 600, 15, 250
John V. Maxwell, 40, 120, 800, 100, 250
David C. Hillen, -, -, -, 10, 70
Sarah Glosup, 16, 34, 250, 20, 175
Charles Bryan, 20, 140, 800, 15, 200
John A. Humble, 60, 100, 800, 20, 130
Robert Bryan, 60, 100, 1000, 100, 275
William Gibson, 20, 60, 200, 70, 85
L. H. Davis, 110, 215, 3000, 250, 545
James Campbell, 35, 70, 400, 60, 100
William Bryan, 160, 740, 12000, 200, 1000
James Maxwell, 80, 320, 3000, -, 240
Robert Cain, 35, 500, 2500, 20, 140
John Hutchings, 45, 155, 1000, 20, 150
John A. Hunter, -, -, -, 100, 225
Allen S. Hutchings, 75, 125, 1000, 100, 250

John Highly, 50, -, 2000, 100, 700
John Farris, 100, 360, 3000, 100, 270
Wm. Ashbrooks, 90, 130, 1200, 150, 600
James Hickerson, 20, 150, 800, 20, 125
Abraham Jamison, 40, -, -, 20, 175
Harriet Byrd, 200, 440, 10000, 200, 700
E. E. Bruce, -, -, -, -, 50
Jacob Woolford, -, -, -, -, 40
George W. Stephens, 100, 200, 2000, 20, 150
John Hutchings, 75, 175, 2500, 125, 450
Harvy Hutchings, 41, 110, 1000, 75, 260
Causby Davidson, 25, 40, 300, 15, 160
William Cain, 30, 200, 600, 20, 100
Robert Maxwell, -, -, -, 10, 160
Wm. H. Myres, 15, 65, 300, 6, 65
John Shields, 32, 70, 600, 20, 350
George W. Simpson, -, -, -, -, 60
Geo. Walton, 150, 190, 200, 100, 250
Edward Smith, -, -, -, -, 300
Antwine Maul, 25, -, 200, 60, 250
Ellen Carigan, -, -, -, -, 60
Daniel O'Bryan, -, -, -, 7, 175
Daniel O'Bryan, -, -, -, -, 36
James Gillian, -, -, -, -, 100
John Pearce, 20, 60, 500, 40, 200
Hiram Smith, 35, -, 260, 30, 270
F. Manning & Co., 110, 360, 8000, 200, 1000
Jno. G. Wingo, 100, 20, 600, 60, 350
Henry Hicks, 35, 45, 400, 60, 200
Alexander Bequette, -, -, -, 10, 100
Benjamin Stephenson, 60, 170, 600, 100, 260
Joel W. Gregory, -, -, -, 10, 60
J. P. Turner, 18, -, 200, 15, 150
Joseph Key, -, -, -, 15, 120
Archibald Coniway, 20, 60, 200, 10, 40
James L. Edgar, 15, 65, 100, 10, 150
Andrew Maxwell, 25, 100, 400, -, 65
H. B. Martindale, 25, 79, 400, 10, 140
Hays Hughs, 670, 180, 1000, 20, 400
John Robinson, 50, 130, 1000, 100, 230
John Estes, -, -, -, -, 50
David Kirkpatrick, 50, -, 250, 100, 275

John Campbell, -, -, -, -, 60
Andrew J. Brent, -, -, -, -, 75
James D. Eaton, 20, 60, 300, 100, 150
Wiley Woods, 70, 210, 1500, 100, 450
John Woods,-, -, -, -, 20
Levi Wells, -, -, -, 100, 260
Lewis Wallen, -, -, -, -, 200
Wilson Wallen, -, -, -, -, 100
Reuben Edgar, 60, 30, 600, 100, 500
Jesse Eaton, 25, 55, 300, 10, 150
Rebecca Webb, 40, 160, 600, 10, 300
James Highly, 60, 100, 800, 30, 270
John Jamison, 85, 170, 1500, 200, 370
James Wiatt, 15, 25, 200, 15, 130
Charles McClain, 30, 300, 1000, 10, 50
Lewis Horton, 40, 280, 500, 100, 175
A. Gregory, 25, 55, 300, 100, 165
Absalom Eaton, 50, 50, 500, 200, 225
Joseph Kirkpatrick, 50, 150, 1000, 15, 50
Samuel McCrary, 50, 110, 1000, 100, 300
Thomas Jordon, 150, 130, 1000, 130, 500
B. W. Yeargan, 100, 40, 600, 100, 600
Nelson Wallen, 30, 50, 300, 20, 40
Zachariah Hughs, 120, 300, 2000, 150, 325
John Shaver, 40, 80, 600, 125, 350
Thomas Harden, 50, 10, 200, 15, 100
Joseph Cherry, -, -, -, 5, 80
Daniel Sutton, 30, 50, 500, 100, 278
John Wallen, 30, 180, 1000, 20, 225
Nelson Petterson, -, -, -, 5, 75
Magnes Tullock, 60, -, 500, 20, 175
Hiram Weager, 30, 10, 300, -, 75
C. Grider, 150, 750, 6000, 200, 350
Benj. Ritter, -, -, -, -, -
Ander Montgomery, 60, 100, 500, 100, 275
Hiram Montgomery, -, -, -, -, -
John Keay, 40, -, 300, 75, 175
Edward Welch, 16, -, 150, 10, 75
William Hodge, -, -, -, 150, 200
Lehew Carter, 35, 30, 300, 15, 200
Levi Reader, -, -, -, 40, 30

John Readshaw, 30, 45, 250, 15, 30
James W. McCrary, 60, 100, 700, 100, 550
James Gipson, 40, -, 250, 15, 230
Smith Proffit, 25, 15, 250, 20, 250
Felix Brand, 15, 65, 250, 60, 130
Robert Proffit, 65, 60, 1000, 150, 330
Willis McCrary, 20, 60, 300, 35, 40
John A. McCrary, 40, 40, 300, 60, 180
Zack Wilson, 30, 65, 400, 40, 190
H. W. Horton, 25, 15, 350, 75, 250
Stewart Daniel, 30, 210, 850, 75, 270
Robert Sloan, 100, 220, 2000, 150, 340
John McIntire, -, -, -, -, -
Alexander Bush, 55, 25, 300, 100, 260
Thomas J. Sloan, 90, 123, 1000, 150, 400
John Wood, 38, 165, 600, 10, 50
I. W. Ritter, -, -, -, -, -
Henry Fry, 40, 20, 200, -, -
Gideon Wood, 100, 140, 1000, 150, 265
Malen Hughs, 60, 180, 1200, 150, 350
John Hughs Sr., -, -, -, 40, 160
John Hughs Jr., 40, 220, 1200, 100, 300
John C. Sloan, 50, 190, 1200, 75, 200
William Sloan, 50, 120, 800, 75, 175
John H. Love, 100, 360, 1800, 10, 125
Patrick Proffit, 100, 300, 1800, 100, 150
John Self, -, -, -, -, 200
James Hays, 50, 150, 800, 150, 160
Tankesly Carter, 15, 105, 200, -, 1
Elizabeth McCutcheon, 11, -, -, -, -
Hiram Sauters, -, -, -, -, 65
John Fleming, 15, 25, 200, 15, 100
Joseph Neel, 50, 153, 1000, 50, 250
Henry Fry, -, -, -, -, 60
Mathew Adams, -, -, -, 10, 65
Reuben Barnes, 30, 130, 500, 15, 100
Andrew Tullock, 20, 130, 600, 60, 160
Wm. Eaton, 50, 130, 800, 30, 200
William Hunt, 150, 800, 6000, 250, 800
Lorenzo Westover, 150, 253, 2300, 150, 553
Wm. & Thos. Hunt, 150, 430, 2000, 200, 650
Adele Hagan, 40, 360, 1000, 25, 150

Charles Huffman, 15, 100, 300, 70, 175
John Hunt, 120, 120, 1500, 150, 620
A. C. Yeargan, 35, 65, 400, 30, 350
Calvin Westover, 45, 135, 1000, 30, 100
Wiley Powers, 18, -, 200, 75, 140
Ann S. Moshunn, -, -, -, 5, 75
Devro J. Yeargan, 30, 50, 400, 100, 250
Peter J. Portell, 20, -, 200, 30, 150
Joseph Bone, -, -, -, 5, 60
Washington Wilkson, 20, -, 300, 15, 160
John Owens, -, -, -, -, 100
Joseph Campbell, 30, 170, 1000, 40, 135
Thomas Brown, -, -, -, -, -
Authur Manny, -, -, -, -, 60
William White, -, -, -, -, 70
George Robinson, -, -, -, -, 100
John Shore, 10, -, -, -, 100
James Murphy, 20, 60, 250, 10, -
Edward Scott, -, -, -, -, 180
M. M. Lynch, 25, 95, 3000, 75, 1200
Z. Miller, 60, -, 600, 75, 250
George B. Coly, 100, 175, 2500, 100, 475
Solomon Gillam, -, -, -, -, 100
Charles Hutchings, 25, 135, 500, 10, -
J. W. Bridges, 50, 30, 500, 10, 175
H. McDonald, 25, 15, 300, 10, 175
Elisha Wallen, 150, -, -, -, 600
Hays Wallen, 20, -, -, -, -
Rachel Hayes, 70, 130, 800, 100, 300
James Jamison, -, -, -, -, -
James Robinson, 50, 100, 600, 15, 185
O. A. Belknap, 70, 130, 1000, 81, 380
Giles R. Belknap, 15, -, -, 10, 106
Jesse Wells, -, -, -, -, -
Joseph Bond, -, -, -, -, -
Michael Marler, -, -, -, -, 75
Robert Highley, 80, 190, 1000, 100, 380
Alpheus McCabe, -, -, -, -, 120
Francis Bond, -, -, -, 10, 200
Louis Bond, -, -, -, -, 45
Therece Loone, 12, -, -, 10, 100
Cynthia Whaley, 35, 125, 500, 20, 300
Joseph Wileman, 15, 65, 300, 15, 150
Joseph Greenea, 30, 45, 200, 100, 180
Nancy McCabe, 10, 70, 500, 100, 175

J. W. Simpson, 20, -, -, 15, 150
James Hatch, 20, 20, 300, 30, 150
Charles H. Manwaring, 25, -, -, 20, 160
W. T. Cole, -, -, -, -, 60
Geo. W. Jamison, -, -, -, -, 50
James Noland, -, -, -, -, 20
Sarah Capler, -, -, -, -, 90
Andrew Casey, 150, 150, 2500, 300, 1580
Hiel Parmley, -, -, -, -, 120
William Wood, 130, 170, 3500, 100, 175
Levi Houghstetler, 20, -, 200, 10, 225
Wm. B. Hillen, 35, 210, 500, 150, 300
John Shore, 30, 70, 300, 100, 250
William McCracken, 70, 130, 1500, 150, 350
Gilbert Shore, 100, 200, 5000, 150, 350
Thomas Shore, 150, 175, 2000, 30, 250
James Shore, 30, 50, 500, 30, 180
Margaret Springer, 150, 210, 2000, 150, 250
John Lance, -, -, -, 10, -
P. C. Duckworth, 50, 270, 1000, 100, 250
John Renfro, -, -, -, -, 40
Elias Horine, 80, 80, 800, -, 150
William Williams, 40, 40, 500, 15, 300
Josiah Johnson, 80, 80, 1000, 150, 400
Jeptha Johnson, 40, 20, 500, 100, 175
John H. Johnson, 60, 50, 500, 60, 200
Nancy Bass, 36, 46, 400, 100, 250
James M. Major, 40, 40, 400, 100, 185
James Rutlidge, -, -, -, -, 30
John B. Walzer, 20, 20, 200, 30, 200
Thos. R. Johnson, 40, 40, 500, 30, 150
Elijah Woolsey, -, -, -, -, -
Clancy & Casey, 100, 700, 1200, 200, 430
Patrick Litten, 40, 180, 700, 100, 400
John Hanson, -, -, -, -, 40
Saml. Simpson, -, -, -, -, 40
Livey Simpson, 15, -, 150, 10, 150
Joseph Evans,-, -, -, -, 75
Sliphus Cresswell, 100, 550, 200, 100,-
Benjamin Smith, -, -, -, 100, 350
Issabella Cook, 50, 110, 400, 50, 450

Sarah Parkinson, 75, 325, 3500, 100, 400
James Silvers, 30, -, 200, 10, 200
John Ford, -, -, -, 10, 75
William Hays, 20, -, 200, 10, 80
William Hays, 50, 110, 500, 40, 350
Cyrus Scott, 100, 70, 1000, 40, -
David Bays, -, -, -, -, 75
Phila Bies, -, -, -, -, 60
C. N. W. Hinkson, 25, 57, 500, 75, 220
Stephen Cumpton, 15, -, 200, 20, 180
Rachael Kelly, -, -, -, -, 50
Phillip Herline, -, -, -, 10, 100
L. H. & Wm. Silvers, 130, 570, 2000, 100, 600
John M. Duff, 40, 80, 500, 25, 75
Wm. Duff, -, -, -, -, -
Richard Simmers, 50, 50, 600, 150, 350
Isham Matlock, 25, -, 200, 15, 175
Josiah Tuffley, -, -, -, 75, 125
Samuel Simmers, 40, -, 300, 20, 150
Peter Lyons, 30, 130, 500, 40, 125
Johnathan Cumpton, 30, 10, 500, 15, 200
Margaret Cumpton, 100, 520, 1500, 150, 300
William Owens, 20, -, 200, 10, 125
Jordon Sherly, 20, -, 200, 100, 230
James Brock, 30, -, 200, 25, 250
John B. Farrow, 7, -, -, 40, 140
William C. Scott, 50, 30, 500, 400, 200
Spruce Scott, -, -, -, -, 236
Elisha Hobbs, 35, 15, 200, 150, 150
Wm. Hobbs, -, -, -, -, 100
Saml. Peashall, 40, 160, 500, 150, 250
Wm. F. Wilson, 15, -, 150, 75, 150
Gabriel Sylva, 35, 60, 350, 60, 220
Clemant Nance, -, -, -, -, 20
Edward Burgess, 20, -, 150, 40, -
Wm. H. Steward, 40, 260, 1000, 200, 150
Thomas Ames, 40, 40, 300, 40, 140
Sarah Hudson, 30, 45, 300, 10, 90
Noah Martin, 140, 100, 1500, 150, 1069
S. B. Hancock, 11, -, -, 30, 110
Thomas Scott, 80, 80, 800, 30, 100

John Moyers, 20, -, 200, 40, 150
N. B. Norville, 15, 65, 200, 10, 125
Mary Hodges, -, -, -, -, 80
Jesse Flowers, -, -, -, -, 40
John Masey, 25, -, 250, 10, 150
John Gibson, 60, -, 250, 20, 270
Winston Campbell, -, -, -, -, -
Wm. Lock, 12, -, -, 100, 60
Wm. Lafton, 40, 80, 500, 20, 170
Noah Dugan, 80, 120, 2000, 45, 500
Ant. Valley, 15, -, 200, 20, 225
Catharine Dugan, 80, 320, 300, -, -
D. Burris, 30, 50, 500, 30, 150
Samuel Twitter, 30, -, 300, 15, 200
Ephraim Twitter, 40, -, 500, 15, 120
Pleasant Manus, 15, -, 150, 30, 100
Ephraim Manus, 18, -, 200, 10, 100
H. S. Martin, 50, 130, 400, 10, 135
Antwine Teaburm, 40, 40, 250, 10, -
John Rock, 30, 50, 300, 10, 150
David Patterford, 70, 330, 1200, 10, -
Joseph Merselle, 8, 45, 150, 10, 75
Moses Merselle, -, -, -, -, -
Vetal Bouchard, 12, 28, 150, 10, 50
B. Bouchard, -, -, -, -, 150
Bat. Roussian, 30, 44, 400, 40, -
Felix Vallser, 10, 30, 400, -, -
Francis Coleman, 35, 45, 500, 40, 250
John Coleman, 10, 40, 100, 8, 70
Mary L. Roussin, 20, 60, 300, 30, 150
Thos. Levingston, 500, 200, 1500, 100,
400
Antwine Calves, 20, -, 200, 8, 100
Charles Martin, -, -, -, -, 40
Joseph Trochee, 16, -, 150, -, 65
John Hendrickson, 20, -, 200, 40, 50
David Kelly, 30, 50, 500, 30, 200
George Craig, -, -, -, -, 30
Peter McVey, 30, -, 300, 10, 100
Benj. H. Jacob, 40, 50, 500, 75, 300
L. S. Nuable, 10, -, 100, 10, 60
John Tabir, 18, -, 200, 10, 100
David Shepard, 20, -, 200, 10, 100
Nicholas Delcou(Delcow), 20, 30, 250,
30, 120

Lewis Delcou(Delcon), 20, 30, 200, 70,
250
James Rutlidge, -, -, -, -, -
Samuel Irvin, 60, 180, 1000, 100, 450
Jno. McMannes, 25, 70, 500, 20, 100
Benjamine Talbot, -, -, -, -, 50
Cornelius Obrigen, 20, 60, 300, 15, 120
Cornelius Obrigen, -, -, -, -, -
Robert Furgurson, 20, -, 200, 15, 175
Cephran Alexander, 25, 65, 300, 30, 75
Louis Mercelle, 15, -, 100, 10, 150
Louis Mercelle, 15, -, 100, 10, 50
J. C. Berkinham, 100, 400, 1500, 10, -
Denis Dace, 30, 54, 500, 100, 200
Argt. Gordon, 30, 120, 800, 30, 150
James D. Page, 30, 92, 500, 75, 150
John B. Page, -, -, -, 10, 75
Peter E. Blowe, 200, 6800, 20000, 500,
1200
P. B. Atwood, -, -, -, -, 35
Robert Lewis, 20, 23, 300, 100, 300
Alexander Palmer, -, -, -, -, 50
George Swann, -, -, -, 40, -
Battist Bouchard, -, -, -, -, 30, 100
Joseph Palmer, 25, -, 300, 100, 100
Losan Saucise, -, -, -, -, 80
Michan Polette, 15, 25, 200, 10, 200
Jefferson Rusbo(Renbo), 5, -, -, 10, -
Est. Roussan, 400, 700, 40000, 100, 400
Charles Roussin, 15, 5, 250, 10, 150
James Gesarque, 30, 50, 300, 40, 200
Alpheus Lequt, 25, 55, 300, 40, 200
Louis Teaban, 24, 53, 200, 100, 250
Louis Teaban, -, -, -, -, 100
John Rogers, 35, 22, 200, 15, -
Phillip Monday, 100, 600, 2500, 150,
500
Benj. Horine, 140, 260, 2000, 100, 500
Jas. Calvis, -, -, -, -, -
E. Hinch, -, -, -, -, -
Patrick Cavanaugh, 30, 120, 550, 30,
200
William Barnus, 20, -, 200, 20, 40
George Gregory, 70, -, 600, 100, 350
Gabriel Love, 10, -, 100, 10, 175

Gabriel Grey, -, -, -, -, -
John Tagget, 50, 120, 800, 40, 300
Mrs. Morra, -, -, -, -, 60
Sophia Cordill, -, -, -, -, 50
Manuel Arnly(Amly), 40, 163, 700, 10, 100
Lousan Shabenas, 30, 130, 300, 30, 50
Joseph Sancressee, 15, 5, 300, 30, 100
Henry Bequette, 25, 55, 350, 45, 200
Joseph Rule, 40, 40, 350, 10, 65
James Hopkins, 12, -, 200, 10, 100
Thomas Haynes, 45, 35, 400, 75, 150
Noah Nowell, 18, 25, 500, 60, 300
Thomas Flanagan, 40, 40, 300, 40, 220
Anthony Fisher, 21, 21, 200, 40, 150
Simpson Musgrove, 40, -, 150, 10, 70
George W. Fisher, 50, 70, 800, 75, 400
Samuel Birk, 65, 60, 500, 10, 50
Henry Capler, 25, -, 200, 10, 100
Thomas Patton, 25, 10, 200, 10, 60
James Rose, 12, 40, 200, 10, 50
Thos. B. Smith, 18, -, 300, 45, 200
John Petre, 30, 50, 300, 50, 100
Hester Gibson, 20, -, 200, 10, 150
Thomas Bass, -, -, -, 7, 75
Jared Farrar, 40, 40, 450, 30, 350
John Hulsey, 15, -, 200, 30, 200
Eli Hulsey, 45, -, 400, 100, 175
Daniel Prater, 100, 240, 1500, 50, 500
Abijah Sparks, 40, 40, 400, 70, 200
Andrew Shelton, 40, 40, 500, 75, 100
John Simons, -, -, -, -, 100
A. Bryan, 10, 30, 200, 10, 200
William Hulsey, 60, 120, 1300, 250, 640
David Baker, 20, -, 200, 20, 270
Wm. Jackson, 15, -, 200, 20, 150
Josiah Nichols, 35, 45, 250, 10, 120
A. C. Shook, 15, 85, 250, 10, 215
John Hough, 15, -, 300, 10, 120
Thomas G. Yarbrough, 36, -, 300, 10, 200
George Wetsithcost, 15, 150, 10, 40
Joseph Bass, 25, 55, 300, 40, 200
Thos. B. Stovall, 30, 50, 250, 10, 150
William Land, 30, 50, 300, 10, 150
John Northcut, -, -, -, -, 60

Moses Todd, 35, 125, 400, 40, 200
Benjamin C. Goforth, 18, -, 150, 10, 60
Francis Branson, 30, -, 300, 10, 140
Joseph Todd, -, -, -, 8, 75
Richard Simmons, 13, -, -, 75, 200
Lewis Morrison, 45, 175, 1000, 10, 300
Richard Kimberlin, 18, 85, 500, 10, 250
Hulet Hughs, -, -, -, -, 60
Joshua Blanton, 18, -, 200, 10, 200
Stephen Blanton, 10, -, 150, 10, 40
Martha Goforth, -, -, -, 6, 100
Alexander Blanton, 20, 60, 300, 10, 75
John Allen, -, -, -, -, 80
Abner Blanton, 40, -, 300, 40, 150
Gilbert Benson, 10, -, 100, 8, 75
James Pratt, 10, -, 200 10, 150
Jonas Anthony, 100, 180, 2000, 75, 350
M. B. Hill, 70, 130, 600, 80, 250
Isaac Harper, 10, -, 150, 8, 130
C. M. Swann, 50, 250, 1000, 75, 250
Oliver Wood, 16, 64, 250, 8, 150
Hamble Fitzwater, 20, 20, 200, 60, 120
Joseph Pinson, 30, 10, 300, 30, 350
Elijah Pinson, 20, -, 200, 10, 300
Phebe Harper, 25, -, 250, 40, 180
William Summers, 40, 50, 400, 40, 350
Robt. H. Scott, 20, 20, 300, 35, -
Martin Bruse, 30, 10, 300, 75, 250
John Isgruggs, 20, -, 300, 75, -
Arthur Metcalf, 40, 80, 1000, 75, 350
Matisan Isgreg, 30, 10, 280, 10, -
John Harmon, 40, -, 300, 75, -
Josias Harmon, 15, -, 200, 10, -
Noah Harper, 30, -, 200, 60, -
Jacob H. Rambo, 35, 100, 700, 10, -
Phillip Weager, -, -, -, -, 175
Albert Lewis, -, -, -, -, 35
Robert Peebles, -, -, -, -, -
Arthur Myres, -, -, -, -, -
Augustus Love, -, -, -, -, -
Isom Drisham, 20, 19, 200, 70, 100
Henry Batteral, -, -, -, -, 50
Charles McClain, -, -, -, 5, 100
James McClowrey, 40, -, 200, 100, 300
Charles Jolly, -, -, -, 10, 200
Wm. Christopher, -, -, -, -, 50

Milly Armstrong, -, -, -, -, 180
John Jolly, -, -, -, -, -
V. B. Misplay, 100, 120, 1500, 40, 200
Charles Boyer, -, -, -, -, 75
Mary Rongy, -, -, -, -, 80
Louis Trude, -, -, -, 10, 150
John Forshee, -, -, -, 10, 75
L. G. Burton, 17,-, 100, 15, 150
Vetal Misplay, -, -, -, 8, -
Jacob Boas, 300, 400, 600, 250, 1640
Elizabeth Waugh, -, -, -, -, 130
Henry Boas, 40, -, 500, 10, 30
A. H. Hawkins, 200, 400, 2000, 200, 500
John Moor, 80, 420, 1500, 150, 300
George Day, -, -, -, 15, 50
John Evans, 120, 520, 5000, 40, 1325
John Slee, 50, 100, 800, 75, 340
Judiah Vaugn, -, -, -, 10, 130
Jesse Elders, 40, 130, 500, 150, 350
Isaac Crump, 15, -, 200, 5, 100
Henry Harrison, -, -, -, -, 125
Abraham Ringer, 40, 200, 500, 20, 370
Henry Norwins, 40, 40, 400, 75, 150
Eli Vandiver, 29, 20, 200, 75, 75
Mary Vandiver, 28, 12, 200, 15, 75
Catharine Thornton, 30, 160, 500, 75, 200
John Thornton, -, -, -, 10, 25
John B. Pratt, 25, 55, 250, 15, 125
Paul Duclois, 25, -, 150, -, -
Joseph Eavers, 8, -, -, 1, 100
Peter Sronce, 30, 90, 400, 10, 20
William Parkin, -, -, -, -, 150
Catharine Huff, -, -, -, -, 50
Rebecca Stow, 30, 10, 2500, 10, 225
Elbert Thompson, -, -, -, -, 65
James Thompson, 35, 205, 500, 100, 160
Sloman Brown, 18, -, 200, 15, 225
William Jinkerson, -, -, -, 5, 100
Robert Mitchel, -, -, -, -, 140
William Hull, 30, 100, 500, 150, 180
Louis Rame, -, -, -, -, 30
Joseph Jolly, -, -, -, -, 40
George Sauters, -, -, -, -, 200
John Richardson, -, -, -, -, 50

Elizabeth Laclese, 40, 600, 1500, 60, 130
Milton Long, 12, 120, 500, 20, 150
George Jinkerson, 20, 20, 150, 20, 250
Joseph Barrow, -, -, -, -, 60
John Moor, -, -, 150, 10, 150
Thomas B. Mefield, 12, 30, 150, 10, 100
A. J. Wisdom, 16, -, 100, 15, 120
Rice Harris, -, -, -, -, 60
Gabriel Barrow, -, -, -, 30, 140
Peter Deselle, -, -, -, 5, 50
Joseph Yakely(Yokely), -, -, -, 15, 100
Henry Pinkly, 15, -, -, -, 100
Issabella McGready, 70, 70, 1200, 150, 475
Garnold Nuckles, 75, 170, 3500, 150, 250
Charles Bone, 21, 59, 300, 15, 120
George Reynolds, 55, 165, 400, 40, 75
W. W. Summers, -, -, -, -, 100
Wm. Martin, -, -, -, -, -
John Bouchard, -, -, -, -, 140
Akan Seabo, -, -, -, -, 100
Francis Sancesse, -, -, -, -, -
Elizabeth Craig, -, -, -, -, 175
Charles Coleman, -, -, -, -, -
Felix Villemar, -, -, -, -, -
Louis Villemar, -, -, -, 25, 150
Antwine Duclos, 20, 20, 150, 25, 150
Celeste Boyer, 30, 50, 300, 40, 250
Sylvanus Ellison, 40, 100, 1000, 75, 400
Ann Castleman, -, -, -, -, 150
Wm. H. Matthews, -, -, -, -, 600
A. Jones, -, -, -, -, 100
L. W. Burris, 12, 117, 1200, 5, 130
A. M. Anderson, -, -, -, 10, 300
John Casey, 50, 700, 8000, 150, 500
Furman Desloge, -, -, -, -, 175
M. A. Todd,-, -, -, -, 100
Mason Frizzell, 40, -, 1000, 75, 300
John Deane, 100, 3400, 15000, 400, 1200
Samuel Harrison, -, -, -, -, 100
Michael Rerpoint, -, -, -, -, 70
Israel McGready, 100, 150, 4000, 90, 350

Benjamine Davidson, -, -, -, -, 60
John F. Cowan, -, -, -, -, -
Mary Jamison, -, -, -, -, 60
Volney Downard, -, -, -, -, 35
Jno. S. Brickey, 25, -, 400, 30, 175
James Griffin, -, -, -, -, 30
Matehew Webber, -, -, -, 175, 600
A. Blaine, -, -, -, -, 150
John Casey, -, -, -, -, 100
Joseph Ketchum, -, -, -, -, 60
Sarah Perry, -, -, -, -, 20
James E. Sloan, -, -, -, -, 20
G. W. Wallace, -, -, -, -, 50
P. P. Bricky, 60, 240, 7000, 200, 250
Thomas Johnson, 30, 90, 500, 75, 200
Wm. E. McGready, 60, 240, 1000, 75, 200
Stephen Dunklin, -, -, -, -, 75
James Creswell, 16, 24, 150, 10, 75
Robert Hornsey, -, -, -, 75, 200
George Edgat, -, -, -, 90, 175
Wm. Nicholdson, 230, 670, 2500, 100, 700
Epraim Turley, 40, 80, 600, 45, 250
Peter Hughes, 45, 115, 600, 100, 250
John Teadill, 40, 60, 800, 65, -
Daniel Turner, 36, -, 300, 60, 300
James Laremore, 40, -, 300, 10, 200
Joseph Coffman, 20, -, 200, 10, 125
Augustus Wood, 25, -, 220, 10, 180
A. H. Larimer, 23, -, 200, 10, 150
Samuel Fenison, 65, 25, 1000, 75, 500
John Falker, 50, -, 300, 60, 220
Jesse Sanders, -, -, -, -, 80
William Love, 40, -, 350, 60, 300
John Love, -, -, -, -, 120
John Chumnet, 22, -, 208, 300, 200
Henry Sanukton, -, -, -, -, 20
Volentine Neel, 25, -, 200, 10, 200
William Davis, 20, -, 200, 25, 275
George Sumpter, 25, -, 200, 10, 140
Alex. Sumpter, 40, -, 300, 10, 200
William J. Goggin, 25, -, 250, 10, 180
George Hawk, 25, -, 250, 40, 250
George Vandergrift, 25, -, 200, 10, 150
John Counts, 35, -, 300, 10, 600

William Counts, 20, -, 200, 40, 400
Canall Counts, 15, -, 200, -, 130
Jno. Yount, 40, -, 400, 65, 300
A. Yount, 20, -, 200, 10, -
Watson Cole, 40, 40, 800, 15, 200
James Moody, 10, -, 150, 8, -
Jane Moody, 10, -, 150, 8, 25
Benjamine Gillam, 35, 25, 400, 10, 300
Geo. Gilliam, 15, -, 200, 10, 150
William Hunt, 30, 10, 350, 30, 175
Daniel Birks, 12, -, 150, 5, 120
William Cash, 30, -, 250, 10, 60
Jeremiah Wilkerson, 30, -, 300, 10, 175
David Yount, 70, -, 450, 200, 250
Fuster Jarvis, 12, -, 200, 16, 80
John Whight, 15, -, 200, -, 100
Samuel Dunken, 25, -, 200, 10, 100
William Hill, 15, -, 200, 10, 65
A. S. Dickey, 30, -, 300, 15, 300
James Robinson, 20, -, 300, 60, 250
Harvy Settem, 40, 120, 600, 40, 200
William Hall, -, -, -, 30, 60
Daniel Smith, 18, -, 250, 10, 60
Alice Gibson, -, -, -, -, 60
Robert Gibson, 30, 10, 300, 60, 150
James Bayes, 20, -, 210, 60, 200
Harrison Hall, 6, -, -, -, 60
Obediah Hensley, 12, -, -, -, -
James Montgomery, -, -, -, -, 65
J. W. Thomas, -, -, -, -, 100
Peter L. Blount, 25, 55, 301, 30, 250
Thomas Maxwell, 40, 40, 250, 20, 200
John Cole, 40, -, 300, 10, 120
Lawrence Smith, 30, 50, 300, 40, 175
Jno. Varner, 20, 60, 400, 10, 130
Charles League, 20, 60, 400, 60, 175
Elijah Matthews, 100, 900, 300, 75, 300
Jane Scott, 25, 55, 300, 10, 90
Solomon Gillam, -, -, -, -, 100
Allen Davis, 30, 50, 400, -, -
Thomas Matthews, 60, 100, 2000, 60, 150
Peter Crites, 40, 40, 300, 20, 160
Mary Staples, 50, 150, 800, 30, 150
Sarah Booth, 40, 120, 500, 10, 165
Phillip Rickhart, 30, 10, 200, -, 200

James Whitney, 50, 120, 600, 10, 200
William N. Fall, -, -, -, -, -
T. Johnson, 30, 50, 500, 12, 200
Booker Goard, 65, 100, 600, 30, 300
R. Batterton, 100, 260, 2000, 100, 350
Henry D. Long, 20, 100, 250, 20, 120
Samuel Stringer, 30, -, -, -, 100
William Brown, 40, 230, 600, 10, 200

Deacy Goard, -, -, -, -, 40
Jesse Mason, 25, 55, 250, 50, 175
Jas. H. Medgit, 20, -, 200, 15, 75
Robt. Mason, 25, -, 200, 60, 150
Thomas Goard, 25, -, 200, 10, 35
Andrew Cliff, 30, -, 200, 60, 200
Nathan Turner, 30, 20, 200, 10, 90

Wayne County 1850 Agricultural Census was filmed by the Central Microfilm Service Corp of St. Louis, Missouri, for the Missouri State Historical Society. There are 46 columns of information on the 1850 agricultural census. I have chosen to transcribe six of those columns. The columns are:

1. Name
2. Acres of Land Improved
3. Acres of Land Unimproved
4. Cash Value of the Farm
5. Value of Farm Implements and Machinery
13. Value of Livestock

Nathan Davis, 80, -, 500, 100, 400
Joseph S. White, -, -, -, -, 125
Thomas C. Cattron, 40, 30, 300, 10, 125
William E. Flinn, -, -, -, 25, 125
Zenas Smith, 150, 350, 3000, 250, 1725
David V. Parrish, 80, 1275, 1200, 75, 350
John W. Selivent, 80, 40, 750, 100, 570
Allen C. Wallis, 25, 20, 250, 50, 125
Levi Rowden, 14, 26, 200, -, 104
John Bounds, 40, 600, 800, 40, 175
Wiley Wallis, 32, 48, 150, 60, 390
C. C. Montgomery, 18, 22, 75, 60, 200
Hiram Ward, 8, 32, 250, 25, 100
Joseph Smith, 60, 80, 300, 50, 200
James Montgomery, 70, 470, 350, 15, 60
Charles Kelly, 11, 29, 100, 50, 200
David W. Shaver, 100, 100, 1000, 10, 128
Joseph D. Hughs, 40, -, 100, 10, 150
William E. Hughs, 25, 15, 150, 60, 200
Joaner Kuhn, 50, 150, 1000, -, 85
Holmes Hughs, 50, 190, 1000, 20, 180
Anderson Hughs, 20, 60, 260, 6, 118
Steven Johnson, 12, 68, 200, 4, 110
Elijah Jett, 100, 125, 700, 100, 300
Peter Tittle, 45, 140, 500, -, 80
Henry Scaggs, 20, 60, 500, 50, 160
Washington Short, 10, 190, 500, 100, 100

Alexander A. Short, 150, 250, 2000, 65, 525
Cyntha Miller, 10, 150, 200, 4, 70
Samuel T. Coker, 10, 30, 150, -, 103
Warren P. Coke, 80, 180, 1800, 200, 300
Hiram C. Ford, 12, 68, 225, 80, 120
Robert L. Taylor, 30, 143, 4000, 50, 82
William B. Wakefield, 14, 66, 180, 8, 63
Brice M. Hammack, 5, 35, 100, -, 17
John Fuller, 35, 55, 295, -, 93
Robert Collier, 11, 29, 150, 5, 40
John Ellis, 35, 165, 500, 60, 337
Daniel K. Wakefield, 12, 68, 200, 4, 45
John D. Rees, 9, 31, 115, -, 75
Joseph Icenogles, 14, 26, 150, -, 80
Rhoda Short, 14, 46, 200, 7, 35
Jacob Collins, 30, 90, 800, 70, 515
Charles Belmire, 45, 75, 800, 15, 250
William Harris, 25, 15, 150, 5, 131
Anderson Ward, 12, 28, 150, 50, 225
William Cline, 22, 18, 150, 15, 122
Phillip Bollinger Sr., 25, 95, 500, 115, 300
Phillip Bollinger Jr., 20, 40, 400, 6, 203
Robt. E. Montgomery, 15, 25, 150, 50, 55
Elijah Bennett, 20, 20, 100, 30, 200
Conrod Kinder, 70, 210, 1500, 45, 325
Joel Medder, 35, 25, 400, 48, 150

Ruben Burnett, 10, 30, 150, 5, 67
John Cline, 30, 10, 400, 25, 200
William Cosby, 80, 20, 600, 190, 150
Tillman Blades, 20, 20, 150, 5, 53
Samuel Black, 75, 545, 1000, 200, 610
Levi Gipson, 100, 540, 1000, -, 100
John T. Davis, 10, 160, 600, 100, 350
Isaac Davison, 40, 40, 400, 50, 300
John Hamson, 15, 35, 150, 5, 135
Houston Loyd, 16, 34, 150, 5, 103
Solomon Aley, 40, 75, 500, 5, 85
William Linville, 30, 50, 200, -, 37
Rufus Sitford, -, -, -, 7, 71
William Anderson, -, -, -, -, 75
James Harison, 35, 5, 300, 15, 122
William Crager, 5, 35, 80, 2, 75
Elihu Thompson, 23, 57, 250, 5, 175
John A. Head, 80, 200, 1000, 120, 654
Girard B. Berryman, 12, 111, 250, 25, 266
Wesley M. Eldrige, -, -, -, -, 20
William Potts, 14, 26, 150, 19, 70
Jacob W. Miller, 25, 23, 300, 50, 100
Nathan Montgomery, 3, 102, 500, 40, 60
Isaac Nichols, 31, 9, 250, 10, 64
Joseph Crawley, 15, 25, 100, -, 75
William C. Byrd, 10, 30, 120, 3, 31
John Chiller, 20, 50, 200, 35, 150
Robert S. Ross, 15, 25, 150, -, 90
William Harris, 40, 60, 400, -, -
John Sharp, 20, 60, 150, -, 75
Charles M. Roberts, 20, 60, 325, 8, 100
Jepptha Wells, 15, 65, 300, 10, 13
Samuel Dunagan, 70, 30, 125, 50, 150
James Reed, 12, 28, 200, 20, 60
Lydia Chilton, 50, 30, 200, 30, 242
James Chilton, 12, 28, 150, 5, 127
Petter Woodward, 50, 110, 600, 65, 622
Thompson Hubble, 9, 31, 100, -, 46
Isom Chilton, 10, 30, 100, -, 51
John Vance, 25, 15, 150, -, 40
Andrew Wallis, 25, 55, 350, -, 103
Thompson Winn, 8, 32, 150, 4, 50
James McFaddin, 50, 40, 500, 15, 201
Henry Ruble, 15, 25, 150, 8, 97
Thomas D. Lashley, 11, 29, 125, -, 108

Peter Ruble, 20, 60, 350, -, 50
Massa Ruble, 25, 15, 100, -, 50
Rock M. Wallis, 45, 35, 600, 60, 195
James H. Selivent, 40, 40, 300, 70, 389
Samuel McFaddin, 100, 60, 500, 20, 576
Henderson C. Stevenson, 14, 26, 250, 5, 175
Samuel Andrews, 35, 75, 500, 60, 150
Andrew Wight, 50, 150, 1000, 60, 442
Robert J. Yancy, 20, 60, 400, 5, 115
John Coats, 5, 500, 1000, 100, 300
James A. Atkins, 100, 200, 1500, -, 160
William Gill, 100, 800, 3000, 200, 700
Thomas Gill, 50, 75, 800, 125, 367
Hugh Fulton, 45, 155, 800, 100, 350
James Reid, 50, 150, 800, -, -
Andrew K. McFaddin, 15, 65, 600, 100, 212
Moses J. Bonner, 6, 34, 100, -, 25
William E. L. Charlton, 15, 25, 150, 125, 231
Joseph Isbell, 8, 120, 700, 60, 103
John Firtle, 15, 25, 100, -, 98
Robert Fulton, 90 110, 1600, 80, 522
David Rimes, 16, 4, 400, -, 135
Isom Mallory, 5, 35, 75, -, 40
James M. Bollinger, 10, 51, 500, -, 146
Pleasant Wiley, 60, 60, 400, 20, 250
James Fulton, 70, 208, 1350, 150, 432
Edward Maxwell, 20, 60, 300, 20, 150
James S. Wilson, 10, 30, 150, 6, 150
William M. Johnson, 13, 27, 200, -, 93
Sarah Bush, 14, 20, 125, -, 45
Elijah Howard, 25, 15, 200, 8, 150
James J. Howard, 3, 26, 100, -, 70
James B. Crow, 25, 25, 600, 75, 90
Robert P. Paremore, 96, 104, 1000, 10, 135
John G. Risenhover, 12, 28, 150, 10, 160
William Steel, 40, 40, 250, -, 79
Steven Mayfield, 50, 120, 500, -, 85
William Patterson, 60, 180, 1000, 35, 246
John Rutledge, 80, 320, 2000, 50, 214
William Clark, 16, 184, 500, 3, 65
Mary Clark, 75, 245, 600, 25, 414

Valentine Kimes, 21, 59, 290, 10, 167
John Clark, 50, 30, 600, 10, 319
Leftwich Montgomery, 20, 20, 250, 6, 77
Steven McCallister, 5, 35, 125, -, 115
Jesse McCallister, 45, 35, 500, -, 84
Alfred Grayham, 6, 34, 100, -, 75
Cornelious Hickey, 17, 23, 250, 5, 80
John H. Montgomery, 15, 25, 300, 5, 125
William Street, 27, 13, 350, 10, 50
Frances Street, 8, 31, 150, 5, 72
Samuel Street, -, -, -, -, 51
Mary Gilbreath, 20, 60, 300, 5, 332
Hiram Kimes, 25, 15, 300, 60, 263
John Hackworth, 20, 60, 350, 10, 107
Thomas Hackworth, 10, 30, 125, -, 42
James Hammel, 35, 85, 400, 150, 217
Benjamin Marbury, 15, 25, 150, 5, 140
John Marbury, 40, 40, 500, 50, 197
James F. Edington, 20, 20, 200, 10, 153
Daniel Null, 30, 50, 350, 5, 180
Moses Collins, 30, 130, 400, 10, 150
Preston Hackworth, 26, 14, 300, 75, 135
Isaac Cox, 25, 15, 250, 90, 132
Archy McCallister, 22, 58, 250, 3, 40
James Daniels, 23, 17, 250, 5, 105
Catherine Kizer, 15, 25, 200, 5, 85
Ruel W. Williams, 40, 40, 350, 75, 323
William Wilson, 20, 60, 400, 50, 119
John L. Pettit, 80, 87, 1000, 125, 1193
George Parker, 15, 25, 200, 35, 270
Richard Warmack, 35, 5, 450, 15, 195
Delila Logan, 35, 5, 300, 10, 130
John A. Gofrett, 22, 33, 300, -, 60
James Warmack, 20, 20, 250, 50, 130
John B. Carter, 45, 35, 400, 150, 614
Thomas J. Sweazea, 180, 200, 2000, 100, 895
William C. Farris, 12, 28, 150, 10, 189
Enoch Walten, 20, 20, 150, 65, 103
Ezekiel Rubotton, 50, 30, 500, 100, 473
Ann Bennett, 50, 30, 400, 20, 450
Lebas Bennett, 20, 20, 200, 5, 75
Levi Gentry, 50, 110, 500, 100, 400
David Joiner, 8, 32, 150, -, 85

John L. Miller, 11, 29, 100, -, 96
Elias Howard, 16, 24, 200, -, 200
Joseph Risenhoover, 4, 36, 125, 35, 135
Jacob Atnip, 7, 33, 125, 50, 175
James M. Smith, 15, 25, 150, 5, 63
George Graham, 32, 8, 500, 75, 200
George Null, 30, 10, 400, -, 208
Ephraim Null, 16, 24, 200, 60, 142
George W. Brooks, 10, 30, 150, -, 150
Steven Pigg, 23, 17, 250, 5, 175
James Ferrel, 30, 50, 400, 40, 240
William Crealy, 50, 40, 800, 100, 257
Riley Radford, 25, 55, 400, 5, 212
John Fathmer, -, -, -, -, 70
Vincent Forkner, 35, 125, 700, 10, 288
Jesse B. Wallis, 60, 100, 1000, 60, 458
Josiah Duncan, 40, 40, 400, 60, 368
James Dees, 15, 25, 150, 5, 87
George Smith, 25, 15, 450, 150, 391
Jonathan Dees, 30, 10, 400, 50, 255
Jesse Dees, 25, 15, 400, 5, 150
David Dees Sr., 25, 35, 500, 35, 377
David Dees Jr., 14, 26, 200, 60, 282
Henry S. Stevenson, 75, 85, 600, 200, 667
Samuel Baird, 50, 30, 400, 20, 100
Thomas Morrison, 25, 55, 500, 60, 275
Charles E. Haney, 12, 28, 300, 8, 195
Asa Estes, 30, 50, 400, 25, 225
Alexander Sloan, 90, 70, 1200, 85, 930
Isaac M. Bounds, 15, 25, 200, 25, 250
William Wilkinson, 25, 15, 200, 75, 122
David Pea, 30, 90, 500, 80, 275
Alexander Edwards, 8, 32, 125, 5, 145
James H. Wight, 30, 110, 1000, 5, 50
William V. Thompson, 40, 40, 400, 50, 256
Henry Blackburn, 15, 25, 100, 55, 320
West Owensby, 25, 15, 250, 55, 125
Robert Oliver, 14, 26, 200, 60, 138
William P. Dodson, 10, 30, 125, -, 75
Gabriel Jones, 20, 20, 300, 20, 194
John Jones, 10, 30, 150, 10, 116
Jonas I. Davidson, 20, 60, 250, 10, 138
James Carter, 25, 15, 400, 50, 112
Harvey W. Davidson, 25, 15, 150, 5, 140

Thomas J. Davidson, 50, 30, 500, 25, 340
William C. Davis, 75, 45, 600, 145, 462
John Dunn, 25, 15, 250, 10, 110
Conrod Shearheart, 20, 20, 200, 10, 100
Andrew J. Smith, 25, 15, 250, 8, 134
Steven Thornton, 10, 30, 150, 10, 141
Joel Nugent, 25, 55, 250, 60, 256
Polly McDaniel, 10, 30, 150, -, 110
Daniel Hinkle, 60, 60, 650, 75, 300
Darling Hinkle, 30, 50, 500, 5, 295
David Lawrence, 15, 25, 125, 30, -
Samuel Long, 80, -, 400, 80, 425
William Helm, 30, 10, 200, 10, 334
Mary Rea, 40, -, 250, 5, 88
Major L. Childers, -, -, -, -, 110
Alexander Helm, 5, 35, 125, -, 150
Moses Finley, 25, 15, 150, 20, 165
John Childers, 12, 28, 125, 60, 184
Robert H. Cozort, 30, 50, 300, 10, 126
Lewis Medder, 10, 30, 150, -, 66
John Medder, 15, 25, 125, 4, 96
Thomas Medder, 20, 20, 200, 10, 108
Nathan Neighbors, 13, 27, 155, 80, 65
Chesley Cozort, 16, 24, 150, 5, 85
John Oliver, 30, 10, 500, 5, 65
Philip Mallon, 5, 95, 200, 30, 114
Milton Miner, 35, 5, 250, 20, 100
Penington McFaddin, 65, 55, 800, 50, 504
Richard Johnston, 40, 40, 500, -, 432
Elizabeth McFaddin, 75, 5, 800, 15, 260
James Rodgers, 35, 45, 400, 30, 296
Arnold Moss,-, -, -, -, 150
Daniel Moss, 83, 37, 1200, 120, 430
William C. Moss, 20, 20, 150, 10, 215
Lysander Doney, 50, 70, 1000, 70, 379
Charles Sweazea, 40, 20, 800, 10, 215
Hiram Baker, 20, 20, 150, 10, 154
James M. Sweazea, 80, 40, 1250, 175, 642
James A. Collum, 20, 20, 200, 5, 26
Pharis M. Sweazea, 23, 17, 175, 10, 115
David Snodgrass, 10, 30, 150, 10, 110
John Wood, 12, 28, 150, 5, 26
Mastern Box, 10, 30, 150, 5, 80

Wiley Moss, 16, 24, 175, 8, 100
Thomas Moss, -, -, -, -, 90
Wiley Pumpfry, 20, 20, 200, 10, 30
Thomas G. Mulugin, 10, 30, 150, -, 40
John Luster, 30, 50, 300, 25, 162
John Williams, 70, 50, 1200, 100, 425
Richard Williams, 50, 75, 800, 100, 606
Daniel Luster, 18, 28, 150, 5, 114
Allen Rodes, 20, 20, 300, 10, 206
Cary Coopland, 50, 30, 600, 20, 281
Thomas Newman, 30, 10, 200, 10, 125
William McDaniel, 47, 33, 500, 100, 625
Green P. Coopland, 50, 30, 500, 50, 176
Arabia Brown, 30, 50, 500, 50, 225
John Shout, 25, 15, 400, 5, 110
William Williams, 70, 40, 1200, 150, 570
Frances Williams, 25, 15, 300, 10, 179
David Rodgers, 10, 30, 150, 5, 115
Alexander Hillis, 12, 28, 150, -, 91
Wm. F. Williams, 18, 28, 200, 5, 46
George Miller, 18, 28, 350, 10, 110
William C. Epps, 15, 25, 150, 5, 172
Frederick Miller, 70, 90, 2000, 300, 1984
Edward Burgett, 35, 45, 500, 100, 251
Daniel Burgett, 25, 55, 200, 10, 88
Samuel Stroup, 50, 30, 400, 50, 340
Robert Green, 30, 10, 250, 5, 215
John L. Carpenter, 15, 25, 150, -, 150
Elisha Landers, 60, 20, 400, 8, 275
James Kirkpatrick, 80, 50, 250, 80, 1060
Robert McCollough, 100, 140, 2500, 200, 559
James Oliver, 60, 75, 800, 75, 269
Isaah Wilson, 15, 25, 150, 50, 240
William McCollough, 12, 28, 300, 5, 120
Alfred Smith, 20, 20, 200, 50, 260
Jonathan Beaty, 35, 45, 350, 20, 188
Berry Leadbetter, 15, 130, 500, 5, 60
Henry Leonard, 22, 18, 150, 75, 257
Right Brannock, 20, 20, 200, 25, 85
John Holmes, 60, 120, 1000, 150, 616
Rufus Holmes, 25, 55, 300, 5, 194

John Dudley, 15, 25, 150, 50, 106
Daniel McGinnis, 50, 30, 400, 10, 266
James Dickson, 60, 100, 1200, 100, 1285
Lewis Waters, 20, 20, 250, 110, 334
James D. Wiggins, 40, 40, 300, 15, 250
Ira M. Rany, 16, 24, 150, 2, 100
James Nevell, 14, 26, 125, 30, 60
Fielding H. Ivy, 35, 45, 600, 30, 212
Phillip C. Ivy, 40, 40, 450, 60, 275
Johnson Ward, 30, 50, 300, 10, 131
Robt. F. Larrance, 10, 30, 200, 5, 75
Mashack Ward, 40, 40, 400, 40, 155
Jonathan Ward, 12, 28, 150, -, 70
Ramey Ward, 14, 66, 150, 45, 60
Abner Bennett, 15, 25, 200, 5, 80
Andrew J. Ward, 25, 55, 300, 10, 86
John Pedrick, 40, 40 600, 60, 320
Irvin Pedrick, 26, 14, 300, 30, 202
Charles Ward, 60, 20, 300, 60, 355
John S. Bennett, 30, 10, 200, -, 165
John Burch, 27, 35, 400, 30, 197
Alexander Bennett, 30, 50, 300, 40, 251
James Bennett, 20, 60, 250, 10, 195
Lawson Pope, 7, 33, 100, -, 50
William Bennett, 11, 29, 150, 5, 101
Abner Bennett, 20, 20, 150, 5, 80
Michael Butts, 18, 22, 150, 40, 98
Peter Butts, 100, 140, 1000, 300, 313
Samuel Pew, 40, 40, 300, 10, 162
Moses Hovas, 14, 26, 500, 15, 98
Absalom Whitener, 30, 130, 400, 5, 150
Henry M. Whitener, 15, 105, 500, 15, 265
Phillip D. Whitener, 40, 140, 1000, 150, 362
John Kinder, 100, 180, 2000, 150, 972
Solomon Whitener, 60, 160, 1000, 100, 460
Theobalt Bollinger, 60, 225, 3000, 100, 471
David Bollinger, 50, 310, 2750, 100, 436
Nehemiah Rey, 30, 50, 300, 15, 196
Susan Abernathy, 75, 5, 1000, 60, 369
Miles Sanders, 20, 20, 150, 5, 99
John D. Slaughter, 25, 15, 200, 5, 70

Rubin Young, 20, 20, 150, 5, 70
Harrison Jackson, 20, 20, 150, 5, 78
Raiford Cooper, 12, 28, 150, 5, 67
David Fowler, 12, 28, 150, 5, 75
Kinion Cooper, 10, 30, 125, 5, 100
David Silze, 30, 50, 400, 15, 232
Anthony Long, 40, 40, 500, 150, 632
Joel Bollinger, 70, 330, 2000, 40, 513
Andrew Sitze, 150, 602, 4500, 150, 990
Alexander Ward, 33, 17, 200, 5, 275
Franklin Ladd, 25, 15, 150, 5, 75
Washington Ward, 30, 10, 150, 15, 100
Andrew J. Ward, 35, 15, 200, 20, 90
Jacob Hoober(Hoover), 20, 20, 150, 5, 65
John Turner, 25, 15, 100, -, 126
Pierce Turner, 30, 10, 250, 75, 111
John Rea, 50, 30, 600, 65, 333
Samuel McMinn, 100, 140, 2000, 253, 731
Alfred McMinn, 34, 126, 1200, 20, 295
Henry B. Barnheart, 50, 310, 1000, 50, 644
Rachel Kinder, 20, 20, 175, 5, 100
Henry Myers, 60, 20, 500, 100, 398
Benjamin Myers, 25, 35, 300, 5, 108
John Myers, 12, 28, 250, 5, 182
Thomas Dunn, 60, 140, 1000, 100, 426
James M. Daner, 20, -, 200, 10, 129
Louisa Kinder, 20, 280, 1500, 20, 404
Richard D. Cowan, 75, 485, 1200, 150, 469
Avris Gibbs, 40, 120, 1000, 125, 442
Joseph S. Burk, 90, 270, 2520, 250, 931
Jonas Myers, 12, 28, 250, 5, 108
Moore Rowland, 37, 43, 400, 23, 222
Nancy Polly, 35, 125, 600, 50, 258
Steven Hail, 35, 45, 300, 115, 277
Harverson Hail, 10, 36, 100, 7, 75
Elizabeth Hail, 22, 18, 150, 18, 168
Samuel Hog, 15, 25, 100, 8, 141
Richard Whit, 50, 100, 700, 65, 397
Isom Southerland, 20, 20, 150, 20, 238
Selvanus Sutton, 20, 20, 150, 6, 115
William Haws, 20, 20, 150, 54, 337
William W. Stroud, 10, 30, 90, 5, 75

Ira Byers, 10, 30, 100, 3, 40
Latisia Edwards, 14, 20, 100, 14, 200
David Buchanan, 10, 30, 100, 3, 80
Josiah Wilson, 25, 15, 200, 4, 169
Alfred Woolard, 55, 25, 300, 10, 237
John Harley, 30, 10, 200, 7, 184
Gibson Joiner, 20, 20, 100, 3, 71
James G. Cattron, 50, 116, 700, 55, 713
Jacob Cattron, 100, 50, 600, 100, 1515
Mary A. Stevenson, 45, 35, 300, 25, 258
Joshua Joiner, 40, 40, 300, 30, 665
Simeon C. W. John, 10, 30, 100, 5, 110
William Hasting, 10, 30, 100, 6, 166
All Woolard, 10, 30, 100, 5, 41
Henry Tune, 20, 20, 150, 7, 57
John Ransey, 20, 20, 150, 5, 51
William Hix, 20, 20, 150, 5, 254
Richard Hix, 10, 30, 100, 3, 50
Lott Joiner, 40, 40, 300, 30, 500
Martin Staggs, 30, 10, 150, 6, 80
John B. Conner, 116, ½, 1600, 100, 618
Wesley Byers, 35, 125, 700, 15, 275
John O. Bettis, 20, 14, 150, 49, 220
Rowland Kimbrel, 10, 30, 100, 6, 65
William H. Punch, 10, 12, 200, 25, 166
James C. Punch, 20, 20, 150, 5, 93
Sarah Punch, 21, 105, 500, 25, 150
David R. Rubotton, 65, 115, 500 87, 507
Benjamin F. Conner, 20, 72, 300, 9, 163
H. T. Hellums, 15, 25, 150, 8, 208
Burnabus Stanley, 15, 25, 150, 5, 113
James J. Stanley, 45, 35, 500, 20, 288
Jeremiah Childers, 8, 32, 75, -, 48
James Pruet, 15, 25, 150, 6, 88
David Epley, 20, 20, 150, 7, 85
William Lee, 10, 30, 100, 5, 98
James Kile, 33, 47, 400, 41, 208
Thomas Haile, 80, 101, 700, 120, 452
Sarah Baker, 20, 20, 200, 10, 126
James Lee, 16, 24, 150, 10, 139
James Sutton, 15, 25, 100, 6, 131
Samuel Sutherlin, 14, 20, 150, 10, 114
Henry Elam, 22, 18, 125, 35, 131
Mary Evans, 15, 25, 150, 20, 210
Lankston Stanley, 35, 5, 250, 47, 359
Nancy Butler, 10, 30, 100, 6, 87

John McClain, 20, 20, 150, 10, 220
John Turlton, 30, 10, 150, 10, 152
Jesses J. Dodson, 25, 55, 300, 100, 283
John Turlton, 25, 135, 500, 25, 423
William Wills, 15, 25, 100, 8, 245
John McCollister, 25, 15, 175, 6, 147
Sturling Wells, 30, 10, 150, 7, 162
Abraham Crites, 25, 15, 150, 7, 98
George W. Jones, 6, 34, 100, 8, 114
James Brantley, 42, 38, 300, 20, 191
Thomas Lodmel, 10, 30, 100, 40, 66
Wilson McCullough, 10, 30, 100, 7, 62
James McGinnis, 30, 10, 300, 12, 261
E. H. James, 12, 28, 125, 12, 230
Thomas McGee, 100, 40, 800, 200, 977
Daniel McGee, 60, 50, 600, 10, 490
Richard Cato Sr., 50, 100, 600, 60, 431
Richard Cato Jr., 20, 140, 250, 10, 140
Henry Cato, 25, 15, 150, 5, 155
Charles Haile, 15, 25, 125, 5, 65
Nathan Cato, 6, 34, 100, 10, 81
Robert Guinn, 20, 20, 150, 10, 117
Joseph Moseley, 10, 30, 150, 10, 125
Samuel Logan, 45, 35, 300, 50, 446
Sterling Cato, 25, 15, 150, 10, 149
James Logan, 45, 35, 400, 10, 279
Jacob Brown, 5, 35, 100, 10, 86
Thomas Winchester, 20, 20, 250, 10, 221
Thomas Wilson, 55, 35, 440, 75, 392
Fredk. Abernathy, 20, 20, 150, 65, 196
John Dennis, 7, 33, 100, 10, 156
Lewis Dennis, 20, 20, 150, 7, 125
John Dennis Sr., 50, 20, 400, 10, 287
William C. Arnold, 25, 15, 150, 40, 273
Coleman Bennett, 25, 15, 150, 10, 303
Ira Abernathy, 15, 25, 150, 8, 91
William Cato, 35, 45, 300, 50, 308
Wiley Cato, 47, 33, 300, 8, 548
Sarah Cato, 50, 30, 500, 10, 475
Simeon Cato, 12, 28, 100, 10, 122
Chapman Cato, 20, 20, 150, 25, 235
Green Cato, 15, 25, 150, 15, 227
Sarah Kinder, 10, 30, 125, 5, 120
Benjamin Cato, 20, 20, 150, 8, 180
Arick Pope, 25, 65, 400, 35, 89

Henry Pope, 9, 71, 200, -, -
Mary Pope, 20, 60, 400, -, -
Daniel Bollinger, 30, 120, 700, 50, 173
Archable D. Moore, 19, 21, 150, 10, 110
Wilson Cato, 20, 20, 175, 10, 227
Isaac Hinkle, 50, 30, 500, 38, 208
Henry Cato, 10, 30, 125, 10, 109
Green B. Ellis, 25, 15, 200, 65, 544
Jesse Shell, 30, 90, 500, 45, 361
Jemima Dennis, 35, 45, 200, 7, 147
Daniel Clubb, 30, 90, 250, 10, 233
John Hinkle, 20, 100, 400, 8, 200
Peter Kinder, 24, 90, 400, 30, 171
Ephraim Myers, 50, 110, 600, 90, 323
Daniel Myers Jr., 18, 22, 150, 18, 158
Daniel Myers Sr., 18, 22, 150, 15, 204
Thomas Eaker, 25, 95, 600, 53, 243
Mary Berkins(Perkins), 20, 20, 175, 5, 130
Moses Dillinger, 22, 18, 175, 8, 129
Michael White, 7, 33, 100, 5, 120
Samuel Meridy, 26, 92, 500, 25, 175
Davalt Hahn, 30, 10, 200, 60, 321
Allen Carlton, 26, 14, 200, 35, 158
John F. Frazier, 20, 20, 150, 40, 109
Jacob Bollinger, 95, 141, 950, 52, 408
Alexander McDonald, 20, 20, 150, 5, 124
Pinkney Collins, 35, 45, 300, 10, 132
Berry Collins, 20, 20, 150, 10, 211

Joel Cargile, 30, 50, 300, 75, 145
Steven Cobb, 35, 5, 300, 40, 272
John Cato, 10, 30, 125, 5, 106
John Can (Carr), 32, 108, 1000, 65, 353
Cornelious Mabry, 40, 40, 300, 20, 212
George Midget, 15, 25, 150, 10, 115
Joseph Matthews, 30, 10, 200, 10, 270
John L. Beach, 40, 36, 700, 90, 667
John Hopkins, 30, 76, 300, 70, 369
Alexander H. Dunn, 27, 173, 350, 20, 172
Benjamin Shell, 20, 60, 400, 30, 178
William Berry, 16, 24, 150, 5, 107
Thomas Lasater, 40, 20, 500, 20, 285
William Carlton, 10, 30, 100, 10, 85
William Hinkle, 50, 70, 600, 50, 417
George Berry, 20, 60, 400, 35, 127
John Hammonds, 15, 25, 100, 5, 105
Daniel A. Jackson, 25, 75, 400, 10, 238
Elisha Ladd, 15, 25, 150, 10, 92
Michel Underwood, 40, 80, 600, 60, 257
Sterling Ladd, 20, 20, 150, 18, 90
Elizabeth Shell, 35, 85, 600, 30, 233
Thomas Hopkins, 25, 55, 1000, 150, 328
Mary Reed, 55, 65, 800, 17, 343
John R. Smith, 30, 10, 150, 20, 179
Eli W. Cowan, 25, 615, 1000, 15, 265
Wm. S. Woodward, 80, 80, 900, 110, 398
Young F. Stevens, 80, 80, 1000, 92, 246
Henry McDonnold, 16, 24, 80, 4, 93

Wright County, Missouri
1850 Agricultural Census

Wright County 1850 Agricultural Census was filmed by the Central Microfilm Service Corp of St. Louis, Missouri, for the Missouri State Historical Society. There are 46 columns of information on the 1850 agricultural census. I have chosen to transcribe six of those columns. The columns are:

1. Name
2. Acres of Land Improved
3. Acres of Land Unimproved
4. Cash Value of the Farm
5. Value of Farm Implements and Machinery
13. Value of Livestock

Thomas B. Love, 225, 275, 3509, 300, 6012
Wm. E. Young, 30, 10, 359, 100, 226
A. S. Kiley, 25, -, 150, -, -
Wm. Brisey, 73, 367, 2500, 150, 516
A. Smith, 30, 10, 309, 119, 388
S. Hancok, 45, -, 300, 130, 260
L. W. Julian, 12, 68, 250, 15, 100
H. A. Bratton, -, -, -, -, 110
E. W. Walls, -, -, -, -, 280
G. W. Wamack, 6, -, 150, 10, 58
Taverner Hailey, 50, 150, 800, 100, 511
D. G. Burrow, 50, 157, 1809, 150, 400
E. Julian, 20, 60, 400, 7, 178
Stephen Julian, 70, 130, 1000, 50, 375
John Eliot, -, -, -, -, 270
Robert Philips, 45, 105, 1000, 125, 290
John Crider, -, -, -, -, 98
Wm. Christmas, 10, -, 150, 5, 258
J. H. Casky, -, -, -, -, 75
Jeremiah Deason, 50, 190, 1500, 100, 450
J. A. Kate, -, -, -, -, 15
Samuel Dillard, 20, 140, 400, 15, 380
J. Alexander, 40, 40, 400, 20, 100
G. Alexander, -, -, -, -, 1852
J. W. McClurg, 13, 108, 800, 30, 465
B. D. Freeman, 24, 24, 300, 20, 227
Jesse Foster, 45, 115, 1000, 75, 265
John Cummins, 50, -, 507, 100, 216

Wm. Roper, 16, 24, 800, 50, 265
J. H. Roper, 26, 95, 600, 15, 86
V. Wyatt, -, -, -, -, 195
Asa Moore, 25, 15, 250, 50, 168
Thos. Moore, -, -, -, -, 185
S. Clifton, 25, 15, 500, 10, 83
John Krider, 70, 110, 800, 100, 418
Wm. Moore, 12, -, 150, 50, 54
R. C. Blankinship, 25, -, 300, 100, 164
Z. Barnard, -, -, -, -, 185
J. Nobles, -, -, -, -, 120
Mrs. E. Rhodes, 15, -, 150, 15, 123
N. Pilkington, 50, 110, 600, 50, 551
John C. Trimble, 50, 120, 600, 75, 540
J. Alcorn, 50 70, 1000, 25, 189
Joseph Alcorn, 20, 20, 250, 6, 560
N. Alaxander, 14, 66, 300, 15, 50
S. W. Johnson, 12, -, 200, 75, 322
B. F. Shields, 12, 40, 50, 7, 113
Thos. H. Hutchinson, -, -, -, -, 50
L. T. Freeman, 30, 25, 500, 125, 330
Mrs. E. Morrice, -, -, -, -, 156
Mrs. L. Foster, -, -, -, -, 36
Jno. Matney, -, -, -, -, 70
D. Goss, 42, 38, 500, 40, 250
B. Harper, -, -, -, -, 70
J. M. Juce(Ince), -, -, -, -, 70
Jno. Ince, 18, 62, 500, 100, 134
B. Gentry, 65, 135, 1000, 100, 456
Wm. Ince, 60, 40, 1500, 185, 717

136

S. A. Julian, 95, 55, 500, 10, 130
Jno. Foster, 90, 60, 500, 10, 200
J. C. Johnson, -, -, -, -, 35
B. M. Smart, 40, 40, 500, 30, 610
L. Davis, -, -, -, -, 86
A. J. Wamick, 8, -, 100, 10, 117
F. Johnson, 10, 90, 500, 50, 426
Wm. R. Roggers, -, -, -, -, 30
J. C. Johnson, 15, -, 150, 5, 15
J. McMahan, 150, 202, 2000, 125, 1160
Wm. Cunningham, 20, -, -, 100, 280
H. Ferrill, 10, -, 25, 5, 82
G. A. Wilson, 25, -, 100, 100, 180
J. F. Prock, -, -, -, -, 34
Wm. R. Prock, 20, 35, 300, 30, 220
T. Young, 25, -, 300, 40, 210
M. Davis, -, -, -, -, 75
Silas Prock, 12, -, 200, 5, 75
S. Boyer, 18, -, 500, 40, 166
C. Critcher, 75, 22, 500, 25, 505
E. Prock, 10, -, 100, 66, 110
J. A. Butler, -, -, -, -, 114
Mrs. A. Todd, 20, 14, 200, 5, 193
John Baysley, 20, -, 200, 5, 128
F. Todd, 14, 18, 300, 5, 303
James Newton, 25, -, 300, 65, 400
Simon Stacy, 9, -, 250, 5, 169
E. Stacy, 8, -, 150, 5, 113
Thos. Dolls, -, -, -, -, 83
Jacob Reece, 40, -, 300, 75, 347
Joseph Lee, 25, -, 200, 15, 150
Andrew Newton, 20, -, 100, 25, 215
_. Rippee, 24, -, 300, 15, 212
H__um Young, 21, -, 150, 80, 391
James Kelly, 20, -, 200, 40, 165
E. Luntsford, 17, -, 200, 5, 275
Josiah Nance, -, -, -, -, 77
Rite Nance, -, -, -, -, 70
George Rodgers, 25, -, 200, 10, 150
Isaac Rodgers, 10, -, 100, 5, 50
John N. Rodgers, 14, -, 100, 9, 55
John Strong, -, -, -, -, 35
John Young, -, -, -, -, 65
George Storey, 20, -, 300, 105, 220
David Young, 28, -, 250, 20, 200
Mrs. S. Benton, -, -, -, -, 85

Alford Young, 80, 15, 600, 90, 624
Wm. K. Benton, 25, 20, 300, 80, 320
M. McKenzy, 15, -, 50, 5, 110
D. A. W. Morehouse, -, -, -, -, 356
H. W. Riley, -, -, -, -, 50
J. M. Gorman, 30, 50, 500, 175, 517
N. Ford, -, -, -, -, 84
S. M. Nicholds, -, -, -, -, 140
Isaac Burkey, 30, 10, 400, 50, 270
Wm. Franklin, 100, 10, 1000, 300, 295
George Garner, 10, -, 100, 10, 100
Wm. Binkly, 45, 40, 500, 130, 220
Wm. F. Young, 40, 40, 1000, 150, 3026
William Scott, 30, -, 200, 25, 308
A. C. McDowell, -, -, -, -, 16
John Hutson, -, -, -, -, 25
Nevles Young, 40, 30, 800, 150, 178
David Crider, 20, -, 200, 100, 532
Y. B. Robinett, -, -, -, -, 70
J. N. Tucker, -, -, -, -, 170
J. H. Tyler, -, -, -, -, 225
Samuelle Cody, 30, -, 300, 25, 189
Thos. Deutz, 35, -, 400, 30, 476
J. W. Summers, -, -, -, -, 65
Henry Moody, 20, -, 100, 8, 100
John England, 4, -, 100, 5, 380
John Gorden, 15, -, 150, 50, 258
J. Lucus, -, -, -, -, 20
Mrs. E. Cody, -, -, -, -, 75
Daniell Breals, 14, -, 100, 5, 72
W. P. Garner, 15, -, 100, 10, 100
L. Meadows, -, -, -, -, 45
W. Calton, -, -, -, -, 10
J. McKey, 25, -, 100, 40, 1850
G. C. Hennessee, 30, -, 300, 15, 298
A. McFadden, -, -, -, -, 76
Thos. Hyslip, -, -, -, -, 110
James Weaver, 180, 500, 3200, 325, 1500
Login Tate, 16, -, 100, 15, 175
Wm. Young, 36, -, 400, 65, 114
Edward Garner, 23, -, 200, 60, 232
J. Sparks, -, -, -, -, 80
J. Nunn, 27, 330, 1000, 150, 375
A. B. Sparks, -, -, -, -, 39
W. H. Nunn, 12, -, 100, 5, 229

J. Hickman, 21,-, 200, 50, 228
M. Hickman, -, -, -, -, 20
David Newman, 10, -, 150, 20, 192
George Hopkins, 13, 67, 300, 10, 113
R. Palmer, -, -, -, -, 50
John McEwing, 37, 158, 1000, 125, 444
James M. Tunnell, 15, 25, 200, 15, 250
James Pearson, 35, 90, 500, 15, 175
W. F. Elidge, -, -, -, -, 10
J. P. Pool, 80, 90, 1000, 10, 95
Wm. Cody, 30, -, 300, 30, 380
James Cody, 30, -, 300, 50, 223
A. Young, 10, -, 100, 4, 160
Jonathan Moody, 20, -, 100, 5, 107
G. V. Blair, 37, -, 400, 100, 475
A. Adamson, 16, -, 200, 40, 89
G. W. Calhoun, 10, -, 100, 5, 75
J. Saunders, 35, -, 300, 50, 207
Jno. Cody, 28, -, 250, 40, 319
James Merril, 10, -, 150, 5, 150
James Garrett, -, -, -, -, 136
Mrs. M. C. Graves, -, -, -, -, 50
Dan Moody, -, -, -, -, 80
Peter Saunders, 18, -, 250, 5, 175
Wm. Sanders, -, -, -, -, 36
Zac Willson, 14, -, 150, 5, 108
Henry Moore, 12, -, 150, 8, 110
Wm. Tazbutton, -, -, -, -, 72
Jas. Moore, 15, -, 150, 30, 100
W. D. Moore, 9, -, 150, 10, 120
C. R. Wamack, 8, -, 150, 5, 100
S. Christian, 18, -, 250, 10, 195
Obed. Christian, 9, -, 150, 5, 165
J. P. Baker, 30, 30, 300, 75, 254
Jno. Baker, 27, 45, 250, 25, 283
Robt. Baker, 13, -, 150, 15, 170
J. H. Hight, 70, 40, 300, 50, 457
Jas. Hight, -, -, -, -, 60
Joshua Rippy, 20, 20, 250, 10, 123
Hiram Rippy, 50, 20, 500, 70, 270
A. Hyne, -, -, -, -, 102
E. Matney, -, -, -, -, 43
Elijah Pruit, 16, -, 200, 10, 185
F. McRoberts, 10, -, 150, 5, 70
M. Breedlove, -, -, -, -, 17
J. Stafford, -, -, -, -, 66

Jas. Wamack, 18, -, 150, 6, 100
Jas. Bippy, 30, -, 250, 125, 320
Jno. Rippy Sr., 40, 30, 300, 150, 500
Wilson Newton, 25, 15, 150, 30, 253
J. Brawley, 15, -, 150, 100, 382
E. Welch, -, -, -, -, 147
J. B. Matney, 12, -, 100, 5, 68
F. Goss, 25, 15, 300, 45, 225
W. _. Grellb, 30, 30, 200, 18, 100
Jacob Givens, -, -, -, -, 40
Mc. C. Allin, -, -, -, -, 163
Israel Julin, 55, -, 500, 70, 328
Thos. Bonner, 15, -, 100, 25, 110
Noah Malone, 15, -, 150, 6, 130
Wm. Day, 45, 20, 500, 40, 876
Edward Allin, 35, -, 150, 50, 290
Crefferes Deng(Denz), 35, -, 150, 5, 310
N. Lausetoun(Teneselour), 13, -, 150, 13, 40
D. Tenesetoun, -, -, -, -, 129
Anson Philpot, 28, 18, 400, 100, 338
Mrs. F. McGowen, 20, -, 200, 50, 223
J. P, Campbell, 30, -, 300, 100, 123
M. B. Smith, -, -, -, -, 40
Mrs. P. Mahears, 15, -, 150, 5, 173
William Mobly, 24, -, 200, 10, 230
John Brixey, 28, -, 200, 7, 240
Charles Cogz, 40, 40, 300, 65, 448
G. W. Cibry, -, -, -, -, 125
Mrs. M. Denney, 35, -, 250, 50, 331
Charles Denez, 17, 23, 200, 10, 126
John Denney, -, -, -, -, 100
J. Childers, 30, -, 400, 135, 539
M. Roley, 10, -, 100, 5, 100
Jno. H. Sweat, 12, -, 125, 5, 100
Grisham Lee, -, -, -, -, 19
A. W. Ellison, 25, -, 150, 10, 139
Jobe Hight, -, -, -, -, 17
J. James, 18, -, 150, 30, 171
James Jones, 22, -, 200, 10, 317
J. Garrett, 12, -, 100, 5, 80
John Cook, 15, -, 150, 5, 122
Wm. Smart, 50, -, 300, 10, 971
John Smart, -, -, -, -, 486
J. B. Smart, -, -, -, -, 100
P. Cox, 9, -, 75, 5, 184

Stephen Lee, 30, -, 200, 10, 125
J. Hammins, 18, -, 200, 6, 148
Thos. Ruchana, -, -, -, -, 73
Mrs. A. Denez, 30, -, 200, 30, 96
Mrs. E. Johnson, -, -, -, -, 40
Mrs. M. Griden(Grider), -, -, -, -, 1
Selm Grider, 12, -, 150, 5, 70
Dreury Lee, 20, -, 300, 10, 252
Andrew Hartly, 25, -, 50, 5, 50
C. Delozier, 17, -, 150, 50, 115
A. Davis, 10, -, 75, 5, 227
E. Davis, 25, -, 200, 5, 133
C. C. Davis, 15, -, 300, 20, 150
C. S. Johnson, 25, -, 300, 5, 75
Wm. Williams, 50, 60, 1000, 50, 380
Georg Alcorn, 24, -, 300, 10, 200
S. Ballowes, -, -, -, -, 80
Harrison Smith, -, -, -, -, 75
Wm. Goss, 8, 40, 80, 5, 65
John Rippee Sr., 30, 30, 500, 25, 440
John Macky, 11, -, 150, 50, 150
Briton Freeman, 45, 30, 300, 100, 322
A. Young, 40, 20, 350, 25, 191
A. Rippee, 25, -, 150, 10, 189
Henry Turbotton(Tarbotton), 30, 50, 400, 125, 344
Allin Cox, 60, 20, 600, 150, 430
Wyly Copley, 12, -, 150, 10, 180
Samuel Young, 10, -, 100, 10, 60
Wm. Johnson, 25, 20, 400, 20, 656
Tennard Crider , 56, 144, 2000, 50, 390
A. P. Pool, 25, 55, 1000, 40, 344
R. P. Pool, 30, 105, 1000, 35, 262
David Butchen, 80, 200, 1500, 175, 1000
John Tucker, 40, 46, 800, 75, 183
J. Ellison, -, -, -, -, 65
R. Hopkins, -, -, -, -, 100
R. Montgomery, 25, 65, 400, 100, 347
M. Hunter, 16, -, 200, 13, 180
J. M. Kendrick, -, -, -, -, 30 2/3
Caroline Miller, -, -, -, -, 153
J. R. Sprauge, 50, 150, 1000, 140, 434
John Ellis, 45, 50, 300, 75, 313
J. A. Rider, 10, -, 75, 12, 75
J. Drummons, 13, -, 100, 12, 157

W. R. Ellis, 8, -, 100, 10, 57
J. L. Sullens, 35, -, 350, 40, 225
C. P. Upton, 22, -, 250, 15, 143
Benjamin Ellis, 15, -, 250, 10, 160
Francis Holt, 25, 25, 250, 5, 374
J. T. Green, 15, -, 150, 5, 40
Eli Sharp, 30, -, 200, 50, 440
Isaac Ellis, 20, -, 150, 10, 80
B. Culburth, -, -, -, -, 169
John Holt, -, -, -, -, 106
William Anderson, -, -, -, -, 16
Wm. K. Stroud, -, -, -, -, 156
Martin Woods, 40, 30, 400, 15, 225
A. Abshire, 35, 60, 400, 80, 420
D. D. Cantrel, 8, -, 150, 5, 25
B. Williams, 25, -, 100, 50, 243
William Cankan, 30, -, 250, 100, 300
James Climer, 9, -, 150, 10, 142
William Grigsby, 10, -, 100, 50, 70
William Worthy, -, -, -, -, 55
Edmund Kendrick, 20, -, 100, 10, 80
Mrs. R. Dyke, 25, -, 150, 60, 340
Isaac Whittenburg, 20, 60, 400, 20, 212
Isaac Climer, -, -, -, -, 60
William Hyde, 33, -, 100, 75, 206
Levi Ezell, -, -, -, -, 36
John McCain, 18, -, 150, 10, 107
Joseph Kendrick, 7, -, 150, 8, 77
Solomon Weaver, -, -, -, -, 69
John Hyde, 50, 10, 500, 100, 340
Rachel Hyde, 35, -, 300, 50, 314
A. Whittenburg, 80, -, 500, 150, 315
Enoch Epps, 30, 74, 400, 20, 300
W. Weaver, 40, 15, 700, 100, 379
Thos. Spann, -, -, -, -, 34
J. Taggard, 75, 40, 1000, 130, 521
J. Gardner, -, -, -, -, 33
W. H. King, -, -, -, -, 94
Wm. Edington, 15, 14, 150, 10, 183
C. M. Stewart, -, -, -, -, 38
Wm. Stean, 58, 300, 800, 30, 570
Mrs. L. Burnell, 125, 300, 2000, 20, 147
J. M. Tate, 80, 50, 700, 125, 471
S. Hendricks, 14, -, 125, 15, 178
Alford Ellis, 14, -, 200, 30, 128
James Dryer, -, -, -, -, 69

D. C. Finley, 40, 60, 600, 50, 325
Robert Maxwell, 50, -, 500, 70, 356
Jesse Decker, 12, -, 150, 10, 168
Jessee Livley, 30, -, 250, 5, 45
Mrs. L. Ichard, 40, -, 300, 10, 224
John Ichard, 25, -, 200, 15, 360
Joseph Daugthey, 45, 175, 600, 80, 387
Daniel Ichard, 20, -, 200, 60, 166
H. Ichard, 20, -, 200, 15, 212
George Ichard, 40, 40, 500, 75, 465
N. P. Newebill, 75, 45, 1000, 25, 2148
Mrs. K. Newbill, -, -, -, -, 270
T. G. Newbill, 105, 135, 1500, 200, 802
C. Eddings, -, -, -, -, 177
J. Russell, 50, -, 500, 40, 285
Mrs. M. Taggard, -, -, -, -, 60
Marston White, 20, -, 100, 5, 120
A. Finley, 50, 40, 600, 10, 300
Jrs. I. Duglass, -, -, -, -, 50
John Davis, 9, -, 100, 5, 60
Lewis Sawton(Lawton), -, -, -, -, 30
Henry Bura_, 25, 70, 300, 75, 259
Jepthy More, 20, 37, 250, 26, 339
J. Huff, 32, 36, 300, 50, 590
S. C. Harden, -, -, -, -, 135
Duke Cantrell, 35, -, 250, 15, 230
A. Cantrell, 12, -, 150, 5, 97
_. Hyett, 25, -, 300, 75, 239
J. McCormick, 7, -, 80, 40, 65
Joseph Walkins, 10, -, 100, 8, 215
Alford Pitts, 10, -, 100, 60, 285
M. Pitts, 10, -, 100, 50, 265
Edward Durbin, 20, -, 200, 8, 270
William Mitchell, 20, 60, 400, 10, 315
Marshell Twithy, 12, 28, 250, 5, 60
James Massey, 27, -, 250, 8, 250
Henry Massey, 20, -, 300, 25, 286
Wm. Brook, 30, 20, 400, 30, 166
John Harrison, 14, -, 150, 5, 200
M. Rose, -, -, -, -, 136
H. Crisp, 30, -, 100, 5, 50
P. Kinchetto, 30, -, 200, 26, 355
Mrs. N. Montgomery, 80, 80, 2000, 35, 517
Dan Green, 15, -, -, -, 250
Wilson Hillhouse, 40, 10, 400, 20, 306

Squire Crisp, 20, 50, 400, 40, 235
Rufus Crisp, -, -, -, -, 50
J. B. Crisp, -, -, -, -, 75
Preston Brock, 30, 50, 400, 15, 355
John Forest, 30, 17, 200, 50, 204
G. W. Sparks, 10, -, 200, 10, 770
N. Binkley, 6, -, 50, 5, 75
James McConrad, 89, -, 150, 5, 85
J. B. Johnson, 9, -, 50, 3, 70
J. A. Garner, 25, -, 125, 40, 122
Johnathan Owens, 15, -, 200, 40, 232
Mrs. M. Finley, 15, 30, 200, 5, 140
W. B. Mayberry, -, -, -, -, 97
Ambrose Paul, 50, -, 500, 30, 522
Wm. Odle, 19, 21, 250, 50, 315
Samuel Boyd, -, -, -, -, 115
James Gillmore, 25, -, 200, 10, 388
Jessee Ridens, 24, 56, 400, 12, 239
W. B. Todd, 35, 33, 400, 40, 286
W. H. Ridens, 28, 40, 250, 10, 93
John Franklin, 30, -, 1000, 10, 375
Jonathan Franklin, 10, -, -, 3, 130
M. Robinson, 20, -, -, 3, 169
N. Newton, 25, -, 250, 20, 245
H. G. Nunn, 40, 120, 600, 100, 430
Rice Nunn, 30, -, 350, 75, 329
Paul Brock, 6, -, 75, 5, 50
John Jones, 56, -, -, -, 30
E. Butcher, 25, 15, 140, 10, 20
Wm Newton, 40, 3, 500, 80, 300
George Newton, -, -, -, -, 142
A. Newton, 30, 50, 500, 75, 300
Hiram Crider, 25, 65, 600, 25, 108
Mrs. S. Berry, 25, 130, 350, 15, 214
John Spence, 19, 33, 200, 85, 130
Evans Gaskill, 30, -, 150, 25, 225
Danul Crider, 42, 178, 800, 75, 235
A. J. Wilkerson, 25, 70, 250, 125, 340
Martin Welch, -, -, -, -, 40
J. Harper, 8, 32, 300, 70, 175
Miles Birdsong, -, -, -, -, 150
L. P. Hailey, 10, 30, 150, 8, 100
B. Robinett, 23, 160, 250, 125, 380
Wm. Eaton, 23, -, 150, 15, 250
Robert Johnson, -, -, -, -, 90
S. B. Tompson, 456, 150, 800, 25, 20

P. B. Bradshaw, 13, -, 150, 75, 193
S. Abshear, 35, -, 250, 50, 276
George Watson, 25, -, 200, 15, 364
A. J. Sanders, 35, -, 300, 60, 516
John Owens, 20, -, 200, 50, 100
Joshua Rippee, 50, 50, 500, 50, 250
H. S. Brazier, 12, 68, 400, 5, 46
S. Casey, 20, -, 150, 6, 367
J. Casey, 15, -, 150, 5, 200
J. Stroud, 18,-, 100, 5, 18
Squire Wilson, -, -, -, -, 95
E. Birdsong,-, -, -, -, 50
J. Hailey, 12, 35, 200, 6, 100
J. Lyons, 50, 110, 500, 150, 425
C. Stewart, -, -, -, -, 45
Mason Stewart, 14, -, 300, 10, 133
B. Shields, 40, 40, 500, 45, 186
S. Lee, 13, 30, 300, 100, 292
Zac Sawer, 6, -, 100, 4, 120
J. Goodnight, 30, -, 350, 10, 368
D. Letterman, 9, -, 100, 3, 72
M. Vaughn, -, -, -, -, 100
John Hargus, 20, -, 200, 10, 130
Thos. Hargus, 30, -, 400, 20, 200
A. Hargus, 20, -, 250, 10, 191
J. Barby, 18, -, 151, 15, 110
Wilcom Letchwerk, 40, 30, 500, 75, 210
Mrs. S. Robinson, 40, 140, 500, 10, 200
J. B. Johnson, -, -, -, -, 62
John Smith, 30, 60, 300, 50, 300
George Pendolum, 40, -, 300, 100, 350
A. J. Garner, 40, 45, 500, 25, 500
G. W. Crow, 50, 30, 600, 200, 670
James Eddington, 20, 20, 300, 125, 310
John Eddington, 15, 40, 200, 6, 105
Mrs. M. Curtin, -, -, -, -, 56
Wm. D. Miller, 55, 165, 7700, 100, 240
M. Cunningham, -, -, -, -, 63
Mrs. S. Worthy, -, -, -, -, 25
J. Gardner, -, -, -, -, 35
C. Decker, -, -, -, -, 43
Thomas Roe, 25, -, 250, 150, 270
Wm. Decker, 20, -, 200, 35, 200
Thos. J. Alexander, 16, -, 150, 50, 280
Wm. Mathews, 15, -, 150, 60, 220
M. Cofer, 12, -, 100, 15, 80

David Tery, -, -, -, -, 85
Samuell Dozier 25, -, 200, 55, 86
B. Rimmer, 10, -, 200, 10, 150
James Morrow, 30, -, 200, 100, 563
J. W. Morgin, 60, -, 200, 35, 165
David Scott, -, -, -, -, 50
Rice Williams, -, -, -, -, 100
S. H. Hyde, -, -, -, -, 70
Saml. Cotton, 6, -, 50, 5, 150
M. Dunn, 22, -, 200, 10, 115
F. Davis, 10, -, 150, 6, 86
Samuell Gess, 12, -, -, 60, 200
George Pearson, 25, -, 300, 10, 125
J. Smittee, 30, -, 300, 100, 363
G. W. Long, 12, -, 200, 12, 66
John Smithee, -, -, -, -, 25
Sampson More, 16, -, 150, 100, 400
E. Bohannan, 35, 125, 400, 100, 510
William Williams, 15, -, 150, 50, 113
John Smith, 30, -, l200, 50, 261
A. Smith, 10, 30, 200, 7, 193
David Johnson, -, -, -, -, 100
Enoch Odel, -, -, -, -, 196
Mrs. S. Henson, 20, -, 150, 10, 120
John Ridens, -, -, -, -, 40
Johnson Corbin, 30, -, 200, 100, 265
William Mise, 12, -, 100, 8, 200
J. D. Smith, 7, -, 100, 55, 100
J. W. Smith, 6, -, 100, 5, 75
John Canady, 38, 90, 600, 25, 172
B. Ellis, 20, -, 250, 10, 116
John Wimberley, 18, -, 150, 35, 250
E. Guschin(Geeschin), 8, -, 75, 25, 60
Andrew Dougless, 50, 30, 800, 16, 300
J. Montgomery, 30, 50, 300, 10, 150
Thos. Spraggins, -, -, -, -, 33
E. H. Miller, 10, -, 100, 5, 245
James Moore Sr., 20, 20, 250, 10, 300
John Moore, 20, -, 200, 10, 130
James Moore, -, -, -, -, 76
J. Yates, 8, - 100, 5, 200
Oliver Wilson, 10, -, 100, 5, 80
James Harrison, 16, -, 200, 5, 150
B. Harrison, 23, -, 300, 25, 230
Mrs. R. Evans, 14, 36, 150, 6, 75
Robert Moore, 110, 160, 1000, 125, 640

Mrs. S. Henson, -, -, -, -, 65
J. Crider, 10, -, 150, 5, 46
Thos. Read, 9, -, 160, 5, 60
Mrs. M. Moore, 16, -, 150, 5, 120
Mrs. F. Robinett, -, -, -, -, 75
Mrs. R. Bowers, -, -, -, -, 50
Jesse Robinett, 20, 100, 2000, 30, 370

James Robinett, 30, -, -, 50, 236
Rufus Robinett, 20, -, -, 5, 350
H. H. Lea, -, -, -, -, 180
Thos. Randel, 6, -, 100, 5, 170
Sam. McKinly, 6, -, 100, 25, 150
William Barnett, -, -, -, -, 100

Index

Baskett, 86
Baskitt, 70
Bass, 4, 29, 123, 125
Baston, 30
Basye, 12
Bateman, 10
Bates, 28, 35-36, 100, 106
Batt, 108
Batte, 2
Batteral, 125
Batterton, 128
Battoe, 83
Batton, 53, 56
Bauer, 38
Baugh, 20
Bauldridge, 1
Bauman, 19
Baumgertner, 41
Bautilit, 18
Baxter, 29, 111
Bay, 68
Bayes, 127
Bayless, 12
Bays, 123
Baysley, 137
Beaburm, 113
Beacer, 113
Beach, 135
Beacham, 89
Beal, 9
Bealer, 61
Bealeys, 27
Beamecher, 108
Bean, 12
Bear, 61
Beard, 16, 21
Bearland, 20
Bearley, 2
Beasley, 48, 51, 83, 93
Beason, 81
Beat, 37
Beatty, 49
Beaty, 47-48, 132
Beaupried, 24
Becherer, 35
Beck, 16

Becker, 36, 38-41
Beckett, 5
Beckler, 40
Beckley, 6
Beckman, 5
Beckwith, 62
Bedell, 7
Beeding, 42
Beeler, 52-54
Behnar, 25
Behorst, 80
Behr, 41
Behring, 71
Belknap, 122
Bell, 6, 8, 14, 37, 72, 76-77, 118
Bellas, 30
Beller, 25
Bellew, 93
Belmire, 129
Benham, 89, 94
Beniker, 108
Benion, 66
Bennefield, 66
Bennet, 12, 16, 54, 56, 85, 87-88, 129, 131, 133-134
Benoist, 35
Benson, 125
Bentley, 14
Benton, 95, 137
Bequetre, 20
Bequette, 13, 115, 117, 121, 125
Berg, 104
Bergamy, 106
Berger, 65
Berges, 113
Bergess, 107
Berghorn, 36
Berglar, 33
Berkelow, 4
Berkemeyer, 32
Berkinham, 124
Berkins, 135
Berkley, 14
Berming, 120
Bernard, 41
Bernes, 38

Berroth, 113
Berry, 21, 23, 30-32, 69, 76, 91-92, 94, 96, 102, 120, 135, 140
Berryman, 130
Berthole, 33
Bertholomey, 64
Bertram, 36, 40
Besker, 113
Bess, 12, 82
Bessell, 26
Bethards, 71
Bethel Company Farm, 78
Bettis, 134
Betz, 35
Bever, 107
Bevins, 10
Beyer, 36
Bibb, 62
Bibby, 138
Bibermire, 109
Bice, 18-19
Biden, 99
Bier, 71
Bies, 123
Biggs, 76
Bilbey, 109
Bilups, 58, 63
Bingham, 34, 48, 50, 86-87
Binkley, 140
Binkly, 137
Birchfield, 95
Bird, 2, 46, 75, 94-96
Birdsong, 140-141
Birel, 86
Birk, 125
Birks, 127
Birrus, 10
Bisch, 14
Biser, 19
Bish, 58-59
Bishop, 74, 111, 113
Bissell, 24
Biswell, 55
Black, 4, 35, 65, 79, 87, 111, 120
Blackburn, 26, 76-77, 131
Blackford, 76

Blackmier, 108
Blackwell, 12, 19, 115-116
Blades, 130
Blaine, 60, 127
Blair, 26, 34, 106, 138
Blakely, 43
Blalock, 89, 99
Blancett, 56
Blane, 59
Blankenship, 100, 136
Blanks, 11
Blanton, 125
Blatener, 110
Blebesant, 107
Bledsoe, 52
Bledsow, 92, 94
Blevins, 93
Blizzard, 74
Blockledge, 21
Bloid, 51
Blom, 35
Blomett, 54
Bloom, 21
Blount, 127
Blowe, 124
Blue, 22
Bly, 36
Boardwine, 15
Boarman, 20-21
Boas, 126
Boatman, 95
Boatright, 45
Bobb, 33
Bobermire, 106, 109
Boche, 40
Boember, 106
Boeme, 36
Boenning, 35
Bogart, 25
Bogel, 107
Bogy, 20
Bohannan, 141
Bohart, 64, 66
Bohmer, 108
Bohn, 35
Bohrer, 33

Brees, 34
Brennan, 39
Brent, 121
Bressie, 16
Brewen, 12
Brewer, 51, 63, 100
Brewington, 119-120
Brian, 38
Brice, 45, 102, 113
Brickey, 127
Bricks, 107
Brickstone, 119
Bricky, 127
Brideshaw, 80
Bridge, 118
Bridgerand, 19
Bridgers, 12
Bridges, 8, 54, 122
Bridgmon, 107
Bridshaw, 80
Bridwell, 55
Briggs, 61, 63
Bright, 49, 79, 96
Brightwell, 43
Brigman, 102
Brim, 15
Brinchley, 76
Brinemire, 108
Brinker, 112
Brisey, 136
Bristoe, 8
Brites, 112
Brixey, 138
Brock, 99, 120, 123, 140
Broden, 88
Bronson, 101
Brook, 111, 140
Brookhart, 62
Brooks, 30, 69, 95, 120, 131
Brookshire, 87
Brosk, 101
Brotherton, 26
Broughton, 76
Brower, 53-54
Brown, 5, 7, 9, 16, 20, 25-28, 37, 41, 45, 47, 50-51, 55, 58, 72, 75, 80, 90-91, 93,

95-96, 100-101, 103, 112. 122, 126, 128, 132, 134
Brownfield, 11
Browning, 6, 8, 10, 49, 75, 88, 111
Brownlee, 48
Bruce, 9, 50, 121
Bruger, 20
Brune, 4
Bruse, 125
Bruster, 28
Bryan, 1, 15, 21, 24, 82, 104, 108-109, 120, 125
Bryant, 53, 55, 59, 61-62, 110
Bryer, 13
Bucey, 53
Buchanan, 58, 134
Buchshort, 40
Buciner, 100
Buck, 7, 28, 48-49
Buckhostt, 108
Bucklin, 58
Buckner, 93, 97, 100
Buckston, 106, 120
Buford, 48, 52-53, 56, 74, 119
Bull, 118
Bullard, 27
Bullenbacher, 31
Bullmaner, 40
Bunch, 6, 9, 88
Bunchley, 76
Bundridge, 89
Bundurant, 89
Bunning, 110
Bunshaw, 117
Bura__, 140
Burbanks, 5
Burch, 133
Burchett, 8
Burdine, 101
Burdis, 87
Burdlong, 37
Burele, 40
Burford, 8, 30, 110
Burg, 40
Burgel, 39
Burgemaster, 1

Burger, 9, 19
Burgess, 106-107, 109, 123
Burget, 40
Burgett, 132
Burgin, 52
Burk, 20, 133
Burke, 10, 48, 91
Burkes, 22
Burkey, 137
Burkhardt, 40
Burkhart, 92, 102
Burkhartt, 102
Burks, 22, 52-53, 55
Burkte, 34
Burnell, 139
Burner, 63
Burnett, 50, 100, 130
Burnham, 16
Burns, 9, 16, 35, 51
Burnsides, 45
Burris, 116, 124, 126
Burrisaw, 116-117
Burrow, 136
Burrrows, 7
Burrus, 59
Burton, 96, 126
Bush, 20, 77, 122, 130
Busick, 85
Busimire, 109
Buskirk, 61
Busler, 20
Butchen, 139
Butcher, 83, 103, 140
Butler, 57, 62, 108, 134, 137
Butt, 43
Buttermiler, 105
Butterton, 92
Button, 55
Butts, 51, 133
Buxton, 106
Byan, 1
Byerly, 97
Byes, 100, 134
Byington, 22
Bynum, 78
Byrd, 121, 130

Byrne, 20, 74
Byrnes, 65
Cabiness, 13
Cadle, 75
Caffey, 45
Cahall, 109
Caher, 31
Cain, 116, 119-121
Cak, 120
Calbert, 33, 38
Caldwell, 79, 91, 95
Calhouin, 65
Calhoun, 110, 138
Calihan, 86
Callahan, 34, 113
Callaway, 14
Calliot, 22-23
Calloway, 57, 104
Calmes, 47
Calton, 137
Calves, 124
Calvin, 39
Calvis, 124
Calwell, 110
Cam, 93
Camden, 11
Cameron, 44, 112
Cammison, 110
Cammons, 94
Campbell, 1, 43, 49, 68, 80, 91, 97, 102, 110, 119-122, 124, 138
Can, 135
Canada, 104
Canady, 141
Candif, 22
Cankan, 139
Cann, 118
Cannada, 7
Cannefax, 93
Cannon, 3, 22
Cantrel, 139
Cantrell, 11, 14, 140
Capler, 123, 125
Capps, 53-55, 69
Carberry, 63
Carder, 13

Crider, 19, 136-137, 139-140, 142
Crisace, 18
Crisman, 47
Crisnce, 18
Crisp, 140
Crist, 88
Critcher, 137
Crites, 127, 134
Crocker, 61
Crockett, 9, 49
Crofoot, 89
Cronk, 113
Croslin, 42
Croson, 52
Cross, 29, 41, 81, 83
Crouch, 109
Crouse, 71
Crow, 3, 12, 26, 58, 64, 96, 201, 130, 141
Crowder, 54, 69
Crowford, 92
Crowley, 59
Crump, 15, 54, 126
Crumpacker, 89
Cruncleton, 13
Cruse, 83
Crutcher, 58
Crytes, 83
Culberson, 81-82
Culbertson, 6-8
Culburth, 139
Culciah, 18
Culler, 73
Cullom, 104, 106
Cultan, 117
Cumberlane, 94
Cummings, 115, 117
Cummins, 6, 80, 136
Cumpton, 123
Cuningham, 22, 91
Cunnifer, 20
Cunningham, 4, 13, 15-16, 82, 92, 118, 137, 141
Cunniperd, 20
Cunsen, 44
Cuol, 85

Curlin, 39
Curling, 31
Curtemire, 113
Curtin, 141
Curtis, 87
Custer, 1, 3
Cutberth, 92
Cutbertson, 75
Dace, 124
Dachroden, 37
Dade, 10
Daggs, 62-63
Daily, 85
Dale, 9, 19
Dallas, 9
Dalton, 12
Daly, 41
Dandridge, 105
Daner, 133
Danforth, 91
Daniel, 122
Daniels, 21, 58, 101, 131
Darby, 32, 40, 58, 62
Darnall, 110
Darniel, 57-56
Darrow, 13
Darst, 41
Daton, 85
Daugherty, 64, 99, 101
Daughtey, 140
Dauphin, 31
Davenport, 28
David, 23
Davidson, 4, 16, 26, 32, 50, 53, 58, 99, 120-121, 127, 131-132
Davis, 15-16, 18, 22, 24-26, 41, 44, 46-48, 52, 54-55, 58, 76-77, 81, 83, 91, 96, 99, 101, 104, 108, 110. 112, 120, 127, 130, 132, 137, 139-141
Davison, 77, 112, 130
Dawning, 28
Dawset, 28
Dawson, 8, 14, 25, 61, 68, 74
Day, 15, 93, 95-96, 118, 126, 138
Dayley, 36
Deaker, 106

Dyson, 26
Eads, 6-7, 24
Eaker, 82, 135
Eakle, 76
Eans, 4
Earles, 88
Earley, 2
Earls, 105
Early, 39
Earnco, 25
Earnest, 71-72
Earnst, 111
Earnst, 4
Eascasinian, 19
Easles, 88
Eason, 54
Eaten, 85
Eaton, 72, 76, 118, 121-122, 140
Eavans, 25
Eavers, 126
Eaves, 16
Ebenvien, 29
Eckunflg, 19
Eclbeck, 50
Edbeck, 50
Eddings, 140
Eddington, 141
Eddy, 32, 38
Edecker, 38
Ederrton, 34
Edes, 32
Edgar, 121
Edgat, 127
Edhart, 41
Edington, 131, 139
Edmonds, 73
Edmunds, 14, 118
Edward, 93
Edwards, 2, 22, 25, 46, 59, 83, 90, 96,
107, 110, 131, 134
Egbert, 16
Egger, 33
Eggert, 35
Ehleu, 71
Eibemire, 107
Eidson, 77, 119

Eile, 39
Elam, 96-97, 134
Elders, 22, 126
Eldrige, 130
Elgin, 75
Elidge, 138
Eliot, 136
Elison, 92
Elkin, 7
Elkins, 95
Elliott, 52, 97, 100
Ellis, 58, 62, 65-66, 99, 103, 109-110,
112, 129, 135, 139, 141
Ellison, 126, 138-139
Ellmuceller, 35
Elmore, 87
Elsey, 73
Elsworth, 83
Elvins, 15
Emelong, 28
Emerson, 43
Emery, 96
Emireson, 102
Emmerson, 5
Emmurman, 55
Enesman, 113
Engel, 33
Engels, 32
England, 90, 137
Engleber, 105
Engledon, 115
Englehardt, 34
English, 38, 74
Enloe, 100
Enman, 38
Ennis, 30
Eoff, 29
Epley, 134
Epperson, 42-43
Epps, 132, 139
Eppstein, 38
Epstein, 34
Erb, 41
Erbe, 40
Erne, 31, 38
Ernest, 9, 35

Finneman, 31
Finney, 59, 61, 76-77
Fins, 40
Firinch, 51
Firtle, 130
Fischer, 19
Fise, 86
Fish, 52
Fisher, 37, 73, 106, 109, 125
Fisk, 67
Fitzcom, 19
Fitzgerald, 30
Fitzpatrick, 118
Fitzwater, 125
Fizer, 50
Flanagan, 125
Flanary, 12
Flare, 5
Fleming, 10, 13, 56, 122
Fletchall, 43
Fletcher, 44, 51, 54
Flewrer, 75
Flinn, 129
Floid, 112
Flourit, 106
Flowers, 124
Floyd, 5, 55
Flynn, 118
Foeke, 35
Foglesong, 55-56
Fomire, 106
Fonpelt, 64
Foolbright, 95
Forbes, 38, 52
Forbus, 95
Ford, 43, 72, 80, 89, 123, 129, 137
Forder, 40
Fordney, 60
Fore, 100
Foreman, 57-58, 60
Forest, 140
Forester, 60
Forgy, 98
Forkner, 131
Forman, 39, 73-74, 76
Fornich, 51

Forsha, 61
Forshee, 126
Forstner, 71
Forsythe, 74-75
Fortin, 25
Forts, 110
Foster, 7-9, 51-52, 59, 64, 80, 90, 92, 94,
, 106, 136-137
Foulk, 58
Foulks, 66
Foust, 103, 112
Fowler, 60, 64, 77, 94, 133
Fowlkerdink, 113
Fox, 33, 102
Fraley, 86
France, 3, 48
Francis, 8, 37
Francisco, 47-49
Franklin, 26, 75, 77, 86, 89, 91, 137, 140
Frantz, 26
Fraring, 18
Fray, 37
Frazier, 135
Frazser, 1
Frazure, 88-89
Frederick, 81
Fredermae, 106
Frednand, 19
Freeman, 22, 92, 136, 139
Freet, 42
French, 97
Frezes, 2
Friechle, 39
Friend, 55, 65-66, 95
Friendly, 113
Frigenburn, 107
Frish, 67
Frizzell, 46
Frost, 93, 100
Fruechle, 39
Fry, 15, 26, 62, 122
Fryday, 113
Fryrean, 58
Frysean, 58
Fucen, 19
Fuchs, 38-39

Gill, 1, 130
Gillam, 122, 127
Gillan, 32
Gillaspie, 86
Gillaspy, 76
Gilliam, 7-8, 42-43, 127
Gillian, 121
Gillmore, 99, 101, 140
Gilly, 79
Gilmer, 47
Gilmore, 4, 86
Gilstrap, 86
Gimlin, 97
Ginden, 97
Ginger, 73
Ginlen, 92
Ginnings, 105
Gipson, 83, 122, 124, 130
Girkin, 71
Girshater, 19
Gist, 66
Givans, 76-77
Given, 40
Givens, 3, 83, 138
Givins, 61
Glanville, 29
Glascock, 66, 75
Glaze, 86-87
Glendening, 53
Glendy, 15
Glenn, 74
Glone, 115
Glossner, 73
Glosup, 120
Glouce, 65
Glover, 117
Gnauman, 108
Goard, 128
Goden, 33
Godin, 20
Goen, 15
Goff, 94, 115
Goforth, 68, 120, 125
Gofrett, 131
Goggin, 127
Goldin, 118

Goldsberry, 53
Goler, 113
Gooch, 72, 76-77
Good, 8
Goode, 43
Gooden, 93
Goodin, 79
Goodman, 42, 53
Goodnight, 141
Goodwin, 77, 86
Goodyhoontz, 118
Goore, 21
Goosey, 56
Goran, 4
Gorden, 89, 107, 137
Gordon, 12, 36, 124
Gore, 74, 78
Gorman, 137
Gose, 78, 85, 88-89
Gosey, 81
Gosh, 77
Gosijacod, 104
Gosney, 4
Goss, 136, 138-139
Gougs, 100
Gover, 7
Goverd, 19
Govere, 116
Govne, 20
Govrro, 18
Grab, 33
Grabbs, 104
Grabe, 40
Gracey, 64
Grady, 22
Grage, 93
Gragg, 120
Graham, 7, 25, 27, 72, 111, 131
Graiswold, 113
Gran, 37
Grass, 20
Grate, 39
Gratick, 116
Grauman, 5
Grave, 5
Graves, 44, 62, 74, 138

Haislip, 3-4
Halbert, 89, 101
Halcum, 98
Haldwin, 38
Hale, 31, 36-37, 65, 67, 72-73, 81
Haley, 42, 90
Hall, 7, 13, 24, 26, 31, 42, 48-49, 51, 54, 56, 59, 65, 71, 73-74, 81, 91-92, 127
Haller, 85
Halloway, 36
Halstead, 12
Ham, 12, 42-43
Hambrick, 82
Hamby, 102
Hame, 39
Hamilton, 12, 34, 37, 49, 54, 66, 92, 100-101
Hamlet, 97
Hamm, 87
Hammack, 129
Hammel, 131
Hammers, 21
Hammins, 139
Hammonds, 92, 135
Hampton, 14-15, 42
Hamrick, 89
Hamson, 130
Hanbine, 109
Hancock, 14, 21, 50, 101, 111, 113, 123
Hancok, 136
Hand, 21
Hanebruck, 39
Hanes, 21
Haney, 8, 21, 131
Hanger, 118
Hankermire, 106
Hanks, 42
Hanley, 25
Hannon, 88
Hanreth, 33
Hansbrough, 6, 47-48
Hansel, 4
Hansels, 32
Hansmire, 108
Hanson, 94, 123
Happel, 40

Harben, 57
Harberson, 36, 65
Harbert, 93
Harbison, 14
Hardeman, 50
Hardin, 72, 81, 112, 121, 140
Harding, 30, 71
Hardison, 99
Hardman, 27
Hardspeer, 30
Hardwick, 89
Hardy, 29, 76-77
Hargrave, 102
Hargus, 88, 141
Harien, 35
Harison, 85, 104, 130
Harlan, 52
Harley, 134
Harloe, 101
Harman, 103
Harmon, 64, 89, 125
Harnet, 105
Haroman, 105
Harper, 25, 38, 81-82, 105, 125, 136, 140
Harrelson, 50
Harrier, 104
Harring, 43
Harrington, 76
Harris, 3, 6, 11-13, 15, 22, 28, 34, 37, 43-44, 48-49, 58, 81, 83, 86, 88-89, 116, 118, 126, 129-130
Harrison, 2, 29, 37-38, 48, 55, 65, 68, 69, 89, 102-103, 107-108, 126, 140-141
Hart, 13, 21, 105
Harter, 21
Hartgrove, 119
Hartison, 44
Hartly, 139
Hartman, 54
Hartsdale, 116
Hartz, 79, 83
Harvey, 45, 99
Harvy, 79, 82
Harwood, 50
Haryman, 62

Herline, 123
Herman, 19, 60
Hernden, 20
Herndon, 3, 6, 8-9
Herod, 58
Herrald, 2
Herrin, 97
Herrod, 22
Herrold, 3
Herron, 96-97
Herschbach, 32
Hersher, 106
Herst, 92
Herz, 35
Hester, 7-8, 76
Heters, 31
Hewitt, 75
Hewlett, 54, 56
Hibbits, 1
Hibbs, 82
Hibler, 28, 30
Hickenson, 44
Hickerson, 121
Hickey, 102, 131
Hickman, 43-44, 60, 77, 138
Hicks, 10, 56, 59-61, 80, 121
Hickson, 63
Hienlon, 26
Higenbottom, 2
Higgens, 32
Higginbotham, 117
Higgins, 31-32, 48, 102
Highbarger, 60
Highley, 118, 122
Highly, 119, 121
Hight, 138
Hightower, 77
Hilbert, 5
Hilbrecht, 40
Hildebrand, 28
Hilderbrand, 14
Hilderdick, 196
Hile, 8
Hiley, 14, 48
Hill, 3, 9, 12, 15, 31, 42, 44, 52, 70, 73, 81, 88, 90, 94, 105, 111, 125, 127

Hillbrant, 60
Hillen, 120, 123
Hillhouse, 140
Hillis, 132
Hillman, 64
Hillsman, 10
Hilton, 14, 51, 72
Hinch, 116, 124
Hiner, 2
Hines, 74, 89, 94, 107
Hinkle, 22, 66, 132, 135
Hinkson, 123
Hinsey, 554
Hinsh, 19
Hireing, 66
Hirst, 117
Hisey, 45
Hitch, 3
Hitchman, 105
Hite, 8, 53
Hitt, 80
Hix, 106, 134
Hizer, 43
Hoag, 19
Hobbs, 82, 123
Hobfer, 88
Hobson, 69
Hock, 30, 83
Hocker, 53
Hockurn, 31
Hodge, 15, 102, 121
Hodges, 10, 25, 69, 83, 96, 107
Hodsamont, 27
Hoeckor, 41
Hoffman, 1, 33, 35, 101
Hoffmann, 34-35, 38-40
Hofmeister, 32, 40
Hofner, 34
Hog, 133
Hoganison, 19
Hogens, 9
Hogg, 29-30
Hogshead, 43
Hohns, 33
Hoke, 26, 46
Holaday, 21

Kenady, 95
Kenaidy, 107
Kenanamire, 106
Kenber, 112
Kendrick, 139
Kenedy, 110
Kenley, 89
Kennedy, 16, 27, 34, 105, 110
Kenner, 16, 21
Kennerly, 38-39
Kennett, 116
Kent, 90, 110, 112
Keolegan, 20
Kerbow, 93
Kerby, 54
Kerkelow, 5
Kerker, 24
Kerkwood, 93
Kermikle, 93
Kernitte, 55
Kernkamp, 109
Kerns, 87
Kert, 40
Kesler, 32
Kessee, 96
Kester, 47, 49
Ketchum, 127
Ketler, 40, 107
Kettinger, 20
Keviner, 2
Kew, 66
Key, 121
Kezle, 3
Kidd, 88
Kidwell, 12, 74
Kiff, 52
Kihre, 37
Kilburn, 90
Kilderbrandt, 38
Kile, 44, 134
Kiley, 136
Kiliger, 105
Killgore, 29
Killian, 100
Kimberlin, 125
Kimble, 58

Kimbough, 3
Kimbrel, 134
Kimes, 131
Kincaid, 53, 60
Kincheloe, 59
Kinchetto, 140
Kinchloe, 76
Kindall, 38
Kinder, 81, 129, 133-135
King, 8, 13, 16, 32, 46, 49, 71-72, 93-94, 96-97, 99-101, 107, 109, 139
Kingfield, 110
Kings, 109
Kinkead, 11, 28, 50
Kinnerson, 65, 67
Kinnion, 80
Kinny, 88
Kiper, 94
Kirbey, 43
Kirchhoff, 5
Kirk, 39, 95
Kirkhoff, 109
Kirkpatrick, 7, 62, 66, 81, 90, 118, 121, 132
Kiser, 47
Kist, 20
Kitchen, 81-82
Kite, 59, 107
Kizer, 131
Kleibecher, 35
Klein, 27, 30
Kleinschmidt, 40
Kleinsorge, 32
Klincke, 35
Kline, 53
Kluie, 19
Klump, 34
Klund, 33
Knaphead, 109
Knee, 80
Knifong, 87
Knight, 101
Knight, 49, 52, 71, 83
Knipmire, 109-111
Knipper, 73
Knisely, 58

Knoust, 4
Koch, 33, 38, 50, 53
Kochnemann, 32
Kockeritz, 35
Koeck, 34
Koehn, 41
Koen, 16
Kofer, 31
Koff, 32
Koock, 112
Kotting, 110
Kouko, 111
Kraemer, 40
Kraft, 41
Krail, 71
Kramer, 4
Kranser, 113
Kraugh, 38
Kraus, 33
Kretzberger, 5
Krichbaum, 1
Krider, 136
Kroening, 36
Kroeninger, 39
Kroenung, 35
Kroner, 35
Kruechter, 35
Kruse, 4
Krutsinger, 46
Kuchen, 20
Kudir, 28
Kueper, 41
Kuhn, 129
Kumberlain, 95
Kunz, 41
Kunzel, 113
Kurlhaus, 73
Kuster, 30
Kutlaf, 19
Kyle, 45, 74
Labruegue, 19
Lacewell, 79-80
Lacey, 3, 50
Lachance, 22
Lackland, 24, 28
Laclese, 126

Lacy, 29
Ladd, 83, 133, 135
Lafevers, 88
Laflano, 109
Lafton, 124
Laggs, 92
Lahaie, 23
Lahe, 35
Lahman, 35
Lahmberg, 108
Lair, 74-75
Lake, 53, 73
Lakelumdin, 19
Lakeman, 25
Lalamendiex, 23
Lalemundin, 18
Lalemundin, 19
Lalumindine, 20
Lambac, 32
Lambeth, 14
Lamme, 108
Lamore, 111
Lancaster, 31, 117
Lance, 123
Land, 43, 125
Landers, 132
Landrum, 12
Landunsky, 119
Landware, 1
Lane, 15, 53, 60, 66, 80, 102
Lang, 41
Langan, 47-48
Langelier, 21
Langenhider, 34
Langford, 50
Langhebel, 31
Langly, 95
Langueven, 27
Lankford, 109-110
Laraso, 18-20
Larass, 18
Laremore, 127
Larimer, 127
Larimore, 27
Larken, 97
Larlett, 25

Miller, 1, 7, 11, 16, 21, 25, 30, 33-38, 47-48, 51, 59, 62, 64, 71, 73-74, 78, 80-81, 83, 88, 99-100, 117, 122, 129-131, 139, 141

Millican, 99

Milligan, 17

Millikin, 91

Million, 77-78

Millon, 90

Mills, 52, 64, 73, 95

Millsaps, 43

Milton, 80

Mincke, 35

Mineas, 51

Miner, 25, 132

Minges, 107

Minick, 52, 54

Minis, 86

Minks, 115

Minor, 72, 108

Minos, 45

Minter, 15, 74

Mire, 86-87, 105-106, 109

Mise, 141

Mismeyer, 34

Misplay, 126

Misser, 11

Missic, 19

Mitchel, 126

Mitchell, 15-16, 47, 52-53, 69, 77, 95-96, 100-101, 111, 140

Mitelberg, 35

Mize, 85

Mobly, 138

Mock, 55

Mockabee, 5

Modmel, 134

Moehlenhamp, 40

Moehlenhoff, 39

Moffett, 74

Mohler, 71

Moke, 24

Molitor, 5

Moll, 55

Monday, 124

Monder, 27

Mondy, 119

Monnay, 8

Monnier, 38

Monroe, 9

Montgomery, 2, 9-10, 55, 19, 55, 58, 64-65, 76, 85, 89, 103, 121, 127, 129-131, 139, 140-141

Mood, 101

Moodey, 119

Moody, 120, 127, 137-138

Moon, 15, 115, 117

Mooney, 69, 100, 102-103

Moor, 119, 126

Moore, 1-2, 7-8, 11, 24, 47-48, 59, 63-68, 74-77, 81, 83, 91, 93-94, 103, 107-108, 111, 135-136, 138, 141-142

Moory, 118

Moran, 18

Mordock, 23

More, 88, 90, 95, 99, 140-141

Morehead, 55

Morehouse, 137

Moreland, 55

Morelock, 86, 88, 90

Morgan, 9, 62, 75, 81, 86, 91-92, 99

Morgin, 141

Morice, 20

Moro, 18

Morra, 125

Morrice, 136

Morris, 9, 23, 29, 34, 36, 55-56, 60, 62, 70, 76, 83, 87, 89, 92, 96-97, 100-101, 111, 120

Morrison, 2, 88, 99, 125, 131

Morton, 38, 53-54

Mosbucker, 36

Mose, 90

Moseley, 29, 134

Mosely, 97

Moshunn, 122

Mosley, 91

Moss, 25, 74, 77, 132-133

Mostiller, 13

Mott, 55

Moulton, 34

Mount, 30

Ow, 51
Owen, 82-83, 92
Owens, 2, 14, 49, 57, 61, 65, 95, 115, 122-123, 141
Owensby, 131
Owings, 104-105, 111-113
Owins, 87
Owsley, 106
Owsly, 20
Oxford, 83
Pace, 7-8
Packwood, 94
Padget, 62
Paffroth, 34
Page, 34, 43, 124
Pagen, 26
Pagey, 116
Pagr, 52
Paige, 88-89
Pain, 92
Paine, 86
Painter, 105, 107
Palladee, 5
Pallardee, 5
Pallsgrove, 110
Palmer, 14, 24, 51, 57, 61, 81, 118, 124, 138
Palmern, 20
Panner, 96
Panter, 76
Paremore, 130
Paris, 58
Parish, 62, 73, 76, 82
Park, 63
Parke, 32
Parker, 48, 54, 69, 74, 76-77, 85, 100, 131
Parkes, 22
Parkin, 126
Parkinson, 123
Parks, 5, 14, 54, 92
Parman, 92
Parmley, 123
Parr, 95
Parrias, 56
Parrish, 129

Parrott, 66
Parsell, 101
Parsley, 81
Parsons, 45-46, 49, 74-75
Parton, 51
Paterson, 21
Patt, 24, 117
Patten, 105, 112
Patterford, 124
Patterson, 10, 13, 22, 25-27, 31, 58, 65, 68, 94, 102, 130
Patton, 23, 37, 70, 72, 106, 109, 117, 125
Paul, 116, 140
Paulding, 69, 108
Paxton, 45
Payne, 26, 44, 65, 74
Payter, 25
Payton, 52, 56
Pea, 42, 95, 131
Pearce, 2-3, 58, 89, 119, 121
Pearciful, 83
Pearl, 108
Peashull, 123
Pearson, 47, 138, 141
Peatamire, 113
Peck, 66
Pedrick, 133
Peebles, 125
Peebly, 6
Peers, 12
Peery, 118
Peipenbriar, 1
Peiper, 5
Pell, 56
Peltzer, 112
Pemberton, 47
Pendleton, 109-110
Penel, 19
Pendolum, 141
Penn, 27, 62, 66
Pennington, 48-49, 105, 111
Penwell, 63
Peoples, 73
Pepper, 76-77
Peppercorn, 66

Perkins, 13, 15, 69, 80, 89, 135
Perod, 25
Perry, 14, 24, 44, 72, 75, 127
Perryman, 116
Pervis, 60
Peters, 90
Petitt, 50
Petre, 125
Petteson, 121
Pettigrew, 86
Pettit, 89, 131
Pettitt, 60
Petty, 60
Pew, 133
Peyton, 13
Pfeiffer, 29
Pflager, 21
Pfumny, 91
Pharis, 82, 102
Phelps, 118
Pheps, 97
Phiffs, 91
Philabert, 93
Philips, 1, 53, 59, 94, 136
Phillips, 2, 7-9, 29, 73, 102
Philpot, 138
Pickering, 56
Picket, 73
Pickett, 73
Pierce, 54, 85, 87, 93, 97
Piercy, 55
Pigg, 13, 89, 131
Pignaud, 41
Pilcher, 89
Pilkington, 136
Pinkley, 21, 93
Pinkly, 126
Pinkney, 93
Pinkston, 22
Pinson, 88, 115-116, 125
Piot, 37
Piper, 7, 43, 48, 50, 55
Pipes, 53, 89
Pipkin, 32
Pipkins, 33
Pirot, 37

Pitman, 112
Pitt, 24
Pittman, 5
Pitts, 1, 8, 93, 140
Pitty, 52
Placet, 23
Pleasant, 110
Plumly, 93
Poe, 22, 79
Poellmann, 35
Pohlmann, 33
Poinselott, 4
Polber, 109
Poleman, 110
Polette, 115-116, 124
Politte, 117
Pollard, 73
Pollock, 29
Polly, 133
Pool, 110, 119, 138-139
Poolman, 105
Poor, 53
Poore, 75
Pope, 60, 106, 133-135
Poplin, 81
Porice, 18
Portell, 116, 122
Portelle, 116
Porter, 11, 13, 85
Posey, 87
Post, 24
Postin, 6
Poston, 13-15, 23
Poteet, 100
Potelle, 115
Potter, 10, 91, 112
Potterfield, 37
Potts, 11, 130
Poupeney, 40
Pouson, 4
Powel, 110
Powell, 1-7, 15, 43, 51-53, 63, 73, 107-108
Power, 30
Powers, 62-63, 122
Prater, 96, 125

Rast, 75
Ratcliffe, 91
Rath, 19-20
Rauchen, 33
Raussin, 19
Rawlings, 75
Ray, 5, 75, 96
Rayburn, 26
Rea, 82, 132-133
Read, 87, 89, 142
Reader, 121
Readshaw, 122
Reando, 116
Rebter, 113
Records, 61
Redford, 92
Redger, 4
Redhorse, 108
Redick, 100
Redman, 26
Redmond, 8
Reece, 137
Reed, 9, 12, 16, 51, 68, 116, 130, 135
Rees, 129
Reese, 6, 9
Reeves, 46, 102
Reevis, 52
Reheis, 39
Reicus, 16
Reid, 27, 42-43, 130
Reifer, 4
Reigley, 3
Reiker, 40
Reiley, 35
Reinbas, 107
Relfe, 118
Rember, 111
Renard, 28
Renbo, 124
Renecke, 32
Renfro, 123
Renick, 16, 46
Renkel, 26-27
Rerpoint, 126
Reser, 57
Resinger, 22

Retherford, 66
Rett, 35, 48
Retter, 66
Reubee, 24
Reutz, 73
Revau, 41
Revell, 80-81
Revis, 10
Rewey, 31
Rey, 133
Reynolds, 12, 29, 45, 77, 82, 88, 101, 110, 126
Reysinger, 15
Rheino, 19
Rhine, 31
Rhinehart, 30
Rhoades, 42
Rhodes, 54, 56, 60-61, 80-81, 136
Ribauh, 18
Rice, 5, 9, 45, 53, 55, 61, 83, 100, 107, 110, 112, 119
Richards, 3
Richardson, 13, 34, 47, 52, 57, 60, 89, 118-119, 126
Richend, 19
Richeson, 92
Richmond, 91
Rickard, 22
Ricketts, 8
Rickey, 10
Rickhart, 127
Rickman, 7
Ridamann, 34
Riddle, 83, 111
Ridel, 37
Riden, 99, 101
Ridens, 140-141
Rider, 139
Ridgely, 62
Ridgley, 35
Ridgway, 10
Riecke, 41
Riegler, 35
Riehl, 39
Riff, 52
Rigert, 36

Schlaff, 113
Schlapper, 104
Schlessen, 33
Schmacks, 27
Schmidt, 32, 40
Schnauffer, 71
Schneider, 32, 34, 38, 50-41, 71, 110
Schneith, 33
Schnerwind, 4
Schniedemeyer, 32
Schnuhr, 41
Schoaman, 104
Schoenthaler, 40
Schoester, 108, 110
Schontz, 113
Schoolye, 111
Schoppenhart, 107
Schoppenhast, 107
Schorman, 113
Schowberg, 108
Schowe, 108
Schowy, 113
Schrader, 113
Schrear, 113
Schreor, 3
Schrolder, 36
Schuehrmann, 40
Schueler, 34
Schuester, 104
Schuetz, 39
Schulenburg, 40
Schuler, 41
Schultz, 28, 39
Schuste, 32
Schuster, 109
Schwuab, 41
Scism, 83
Scoby, 6
Scofield, 66
Scott, 2, 4, 9, 18, 20, 44-45, 50, 79, 90, 92, 97, 116-117, 122-123, 125, 127, 137, 141
Scribern, 97
Scribner, 91
Scruggs, 2
Seabo, 126

Seal, 35
Seamster, 53-54
Searcy, 54
Sears, 52, 90
Seate, 18
Sebastian, 11-12, 17, 22
See, 77
Seebich, 18
Seebul, 20
Seibuch, 20
Seibush, 19
Seifelman, 106
Self, 101, 122
Selfe, 100
Selivent, 129
Sellers, 11
Selsor, 72
Semple, 26
Senbarger, 108
Senno, 18
Sepp, 31
Settem, 127
Settle, 75, 116
Seveis, 20
Sevet, 106
Sewing, 34
Sexton, 102
Sfteshar, 113
Shabenas, 125
Shackelford, 43, 106
Shades, 95
Shafer, 71
Shanks, 59
Shannon, 13
Shappard, 108
Sharp, 3, 46, 73, 86, 112, 130, 139
Shaver, 118, 121, 129
Shaw, 11, 62, 64, 72-73, 88
Shaylor, 9
Shear, 110
Shearer, 28
Shearheart, 132
Shedd, 69
Sheet, 78
Sheets, 75
Shehan, 24

Torbes, 52
Toterman, 110
Totson, 85
Totten, 15, 77
Toule, 64
Towles, 45, 52-53, 66
Townsand, 21
Townsend, 11, 48-49, 57
Townsley, 20-21
Tramell, 53
Trammel, 119
Travis, 3
Tremmeier, 41
Trenaux, 41
Trible, 55
Trigg, 48
Trimble, 59, 117, 136
Tripie, 106
Triplet, 85
Triplett, 29, 32
Tritsch, 38
Trochee, 124
Trojast, 85
Trollinger, 120
Tronstrum, 19
Trotter, 64-65
Trout, 110
Trouth, 62
Troutt, 110
Trude, 126
Truesdell, 103
Trumbull, 14
Trusty, 99, 102
Tucker, 11-12, 20, 48-49, 53, 75, 93, 137, 139
Tudder, 120
Tuffley, 123
Tuggle, 72
Tullock, 16, 121-122
Tune, 134
Tunnel, 95
Tunnell, 86, 90, 138
Tunstall, 26
Turbotton, 139
Turley, 14, 22, 127
Turlton, 134

Turnbaugh, 3
Turnbough, 91
Turnbull, 101
Turner, 30, 39, 62, 67, 72, 75-76, 78, 97, 121, 127-128, 133
Turpin, 69
Turtle, 62
Tusk, 51
Twedy, 103
Twen, 46
Twillman, 27
Twine, 45
Twithy, 140
Twitter, 124
Tyler, 35, 137
Tylor, 36
Tymony, 44
Tyre, 86
Uhl, 35
Ulffers, 107
Ullmer, 111
Ulmiston, 20
Umphries, 89
Underwood, 20, 119, 135
Upton, 102, 139
Urion, 37
Usey, 31
Usinger, 32-33
Usky, 22
Utz, 25, 77
Vacci, 19
Vacher, 73
Vaith, 19
Valis, 18
Valle, 20
Valley, 115, 124
Valli, 18
Vallser, 124
Van Talge, 38
Vanarsdel, 59
Vanbiber, 107
Vance, 12, 16, 130
Vanderen, 71
Vandergrif, 83
Vandergrift, 127
Vandiver, 72-73, 76, 117, 126

Warncer, 37
Warner, 54, 118
Warnum, 88
Warren, 79, 81, 83, 87-88, 96
Warrenburg, 34
Warriner, 55
Warson, 43
Wash, 26
Wash, 38
Watembarger, 90
Water, 106
Waters, 75, 87, 100, 133
Wathouse, 104
Watkens, 26
Watkins, 39, 53, 62, 72, 86, 102
Watson, 1-2, 27, 37-38, 44, 53, 58, 72, 87, 103, 110, 141
Watts, 1, 22, 28, 65
Waugh, 51, 64
Wayland, 59-60
Weager, 125
Wease, 49
Weatherford, 55
Weaver, 71, 87, 89, 121, 137, 139
Webb, 2, 9, 26, 46, 63, 74, 77, 81, 89, 121
Webber, 127
Weber, 35, 39, 58
Webster, 51, 55, 90
Weeber, 105
Weeden, 47, 49
Weedon, 48
Weeks, 112
Wehterman, 97
Weichens, 4
Weichishagson, 107
Weidener, 32
Weigers, 41
Weihammer, 37
Weihard, 33
Weiler, 20
Weiley, 2
Weir, 7-8
Weitzonecker, 35
Welborn, 16
Welbourn, 55

Welch, 80, 107-108, 111, 121, 138, 140
Weldprecht, 34
Welker, 11
Wellborn, 16
Weller, 47
Wellis, 32
Wells, 1, 32, 39, 51, 55, 69, 100, 111, 119, 121-122, 130, 134
Welsh, 46
Welting, 113
Wendel, 35
Wenting, 29
Werlher, 33
Wermeier, 41
Werner, 39
Wesendolf, 111
Wesfall, 34
Wessel, 34
Wessithcost, 125
West, 28-29, 59, 68, 120
Westerman, 120
Westell, 21
Westmire, 104, 113
Westoph, 56
Westover, 16, 120, 122
Wetherman, 92, 96
Weyer, 58
Whaley, 115, 122
Wheat, 119
Wheeler, 33, 43-45, 48, 91, 106
Wheler, 91-92, 94
Wherry, 28
Whight, 127
Whiles, 77
Whit, 133
Whitaker, 51
White, 12, 14, 28, 46, 51-52, 75, 83, 92-93, 100, 116, 118, 122, 129, 135, 140
Whitehan, 15
Whitehead, 81-82
Whitelock, 75
Whiteman, 31
Whitener, 133
Whiteside, 34
Whitesides, 53
Whitford, 81

www.ingramcontent.com/pod-product-compliance
Lightning Source LLC
Chambersburg PA
CBHW080611270326
41928CB00016B/3010